D0586013

A NEW
COMPANION TO
SHAKESPEARE
STUDIES

EDITED BY
KENNETH MUIR
AND
S. SCHOENBAUM

CAMBRIDGE
AT THE UNIVERSITY PRESS
1971

Published by the Syndics of the Cambridge University Press
Bentley House, 200 Euston Road, London NW1 2DB
American Branch: 32 East 57th Street, New York, N.Y.10022

Library of Congress Catalogue Card Number: 78-118066

ISBNS:

0 521 07941 1 hard covers
0 521 09645 4 paperback

First published 1971
Reprinted 1972

Printed in Great Britain
at the University Printing House, Cambridge
(Brooke Crutchley, University Printer)

CONTENTS

ILLUSTRATIONS

PREFACE

The first *Companion to Shakespeare Studies*, edited by Harley Granville-Barker and G. B. Harrison, was published in 1934. It has been in constant demand ever since; and the present volume attempts, with some difference of emphasis, to fulfil a similar need. Shakespeare criticism has so proliferated during the last thirty-five years that both the student and the general reader need a guide to the most important developments. We had to select from a much larger series of topics, and some of those we had to omit are discussed in *Shakespeare Survey 17* ('Shakespeare in his Own Age'). All the contributors to the former companion were British, with the possible exception of T. S. Eliot. We have obtained contributions from both sides of the Atlantic.

K.M.
S.S.

1

THE LIFE OF SHAKESPEARE

S. SCHOENBAUM

'All that is known with any degree of certainty concerning Shake-speare, is – that he was born at Stratford upon Avon, – married and had children there, – went to London, where he commenced actor, and wrote poems and plays, returned to Stratford, made his will, died, and was buried.' Thus wrote a great Shakespearian scholar of the eighteenth century, George Steevens. His remark has been often quoted, and others have made essentially the same comment in less memorable words. But Steevens exaggerated, and since his time much has been learned about the poet, his ancestors and family, and his Stratford and London associations. These facts, it is true, are of a public character, and are recorded in official, mainly legal, documents – con-veyances of property, tax assessments and the like; as such, they afford no insight into the interior life of the artist, wherein resides the chief fascination of literary biography. Yet we know more about Shake-speare than about most of his fellow playwrights. John Webster, for example, the author of two great tragedies, remains little more than an elusive ghost. And, however impersonal, what we know about Shakespeare is not without interest or meaning.

The parish register of Holy Trinity Church records his baptism on 26 April 1564. Tradition assigns his birthdate to the twenty-third. An interval of three days between birth and christening is not unlikely, and supporting evidence is provided by the inscription on the drama-tist's tomb, which states that he died on 23 April 1616, in his fifty-third year. But the date of Shakespeare's birth is not precisely known, and behind the conventional assignment lurks the urge to have the National Poet born on the day of St George, patron saint of England; the wish is father of many a tradition. The register of Stratford Church records also the baptism of seven brothers and sisters. Of these, three – Margaret, Anne, and the first Joan (another Joan was christened later) – died in childhood. The infant William may himself have narrowly escaped mortality, for the plague gripped Stratford in 1564, carrying off over 200 souls in six months. Of the surviving siblings, most interest attaches to the playwright's youngest brother Edmund, christened on 3 May 1580; he became an actor in London, where he

I

died young. He was buried in December 1607 in St Saviour's Church in Southwark.

The name of Shakespeare is of great antiquity in Warwickshire: as far back as 1248 a William Sakspere of Clopton was hanged for robbery. John Shakespeare, the dramatist's father, was probably the eldest son of Richard, a husbandman of Snitterfield, a village some three miles north of Stratford. This Richard Shakespeare held lands as a tenant on a manor belonging to Robert Arden, a gentleman of worship in the hamlet of Wilmcote, north-west of Stratford. Arden's youngest daughter Mary inherited from him the Asbies estate of fifty acres when he died in 1556. Shortly thereafter she married John Shakespeare.

He had by 1552 migrated to Stratford, and there set himself up as a glover and whittawer (curer and whitener of skins), an occupation requiring a seven-year apprenticeship. He prospered. In addition to his glove business, he is known to have sold barley, timber, and wool. In 1556 he bought a house, with garden and croft, in Greenhill Street, and a house adjoining the one he already occupied in Henley Street. Tradition identifies the double house in Henley Street as the poet's birthplace. Civic recognition came to John Shakespeare: first appointed to minor offices – inspector of ale and bread, constable, affeeror (assessor of fines not determined by the statutes) – he became, in turn, chamberlain, member of the town council, one of the fourteen aldermen privileged to wear a black cloth gown trimmed with fur, and finally, in 1568, high bailiff (the equivalent today of mayor). Yet he was probably illiterate, for no signature exists for him. He signed documents with his mark, a pair of glover's compasses, or with a cross.

Some time in the mid-seventies John Shakespeare considered applying for a grant of arms, but nothing came of it, apparently because he had fallen on hard times. After 1575 he purchased no more property. The aldermen excused him, in 1578, from paying his 4d. weekly tax for poor relief. He stopped attending council meetings, and in 1586 was deprived of his alderman's gown. He contracted debts, and had to mortgage part of his wife's inheritance. In 1592 he appears in a list of persons 'heretofore presented for not coming monthly to the church according to Her Majesty's laws'; the document has been interpreted as offering evidence of John Shakespeare's recusancy, but a note appended to it indicates that he avoided services 'for fear of process for debt', arrests by sheriff's officers being then permitted on Sunday. (That he subscribed to the old faith is, however, possible, and is supported by a Spiritual Last Will and Testament, a Catholic profession attributed to 'John Shakspear' and purportedly found in the roof of the Henley Street homestead in the eighteenth century; however, this document, since lost, is of doubtful authenticity.) John's straitened circumstances forced him, before 1590, to part with his house on Greenhill Street, but he never became so desperate that he had to sell his Henley Street dwelling. The grant of arms that in 1596 conferred the status of gentleman on John Shakespeare was probably instigated by his son, who had by then succeeded handsomely in the London theatrical world.

Fortunately the education of his children cost him nothing. According to Nicholas Rowe, who published the first connected life of Shakespeare in 1709, the dramatist's father bred him 'for some time at a free school'. Although records for pupils at the King's New School of Stratford-upon-Avon in the sixteenth century have not come down, there is no reason to doubt Rowe. It was a superior institution of its kind: the masters during Shakespeare's boyhood held bachelor's and master's degrees from Oxford University, and received good remuneration – £20 a year plus a dwelling – by the standards of the day. A child entering at about the age of five probably passed his first two or three years at an attached petty school where, under the tuition of the usher, he mastered the alphabet and learned the rudiments of reading and writing. Then, at the grammar school proper, he spent long hours – from seven until eleven in the morning, and one to five in the afternoon – memorizing by rote his Latin grammar, an experience perhaps ruefully recalled in *The Merry Wives of Windsor* when the Welsh pedagogue Sir Hugh Evans puts little William through a model interrogation for the benefit of his disgruntled mother:

EVANS   Show me now, William, some declensions of your pronouns.
WILLIAM   Forsooth, I have forgot.
EVANS   It is *qui, quae, quod*; if you forget your *qui's*, your *quae's*, and your *quod's*, you must be preeches [i.e., flogged].

Having survived Lilly's *Grammatica Latina*, the scholars moved on to their Latin axioms and phrases, then to *Aesop's Fables* and the *Eclogues* of Baptista Spagnuoli Mantuanus ('Old Mantuan, old Mantuan!' ecstatically declares Holofernes the schoolmaster in *Love's Labour's Lost*, 'Who understandeth thee not, loves thee not'). There followed literary classics – Vergil, perhaps Horace, Plautus or Terence (sometimes acted by the children), and especially Ovid, who would remain the dramatist's favourite – as well as training in rhetoric (Cicero) and history: Caesar or Sallust. Thus Shakespeare acquired the small Latin with which Jonson credits him; possibly in the upper forms he obtained his 'less Greek'. How long Shakespeare attended the free school we can only guess. Rowe, whose information derives from Stratford traditions, reports that the father was forced, because of 'the narrowness of his circumstances, and the want of his assistance at home . . . to withdraw him from thence'.

For the next episode in Shakespeare's life better documentation is available. On 28 November 1582 the Bishop of Worcester, in whose diocese Stratford lay, issued a bond authorizing the marriage of 'William Shagspere' and 'Anne Hathwey of Stratford' after one asking of the banns, rather than the customary three. (Pronouncement of the banns in church allowed members of the congregation to come forward if they knew of any hindrance to the match.) Fulke Sandells and John Richardson, the friends of the bride's family who signed the bond, obligated themselves to pay the Bishop or his officials £40 should any action be brought against them for issuance of the licence. The licence itself is not preserved, nor is any record of the ceremony.[1] Of Anne Hathaway we know little, except that she was probably the eldest daughter of Richard, a husbandman living at Hewlands Farm in Shottery, a hamlet a mile west of Stratford; on this property stands the thatched farmhouse today known as Anne Hathaway's Cottage. In his will, dated 1 September 1581 and drawn up shortly before his death, Hathaway mentions no daughter Anne, but the names Anne and Agnes were used interchangeably, and the latter is bequeathed ten marks (£6 13s. 4d.) to be paid to her on her wedding day. At the time of the marriage she was twenty-six, and the groom eighteen. An entry in the Stratford register recording the baptism on 26 May 1583 of Susanna daughter to William Shakespeare may help to explain why he married so early. On 2 February 1585 his twins, Hamnet and Judith, were christened at Holy Trinity. They were named after lifelong family friends, Hamnet and Judith Sadler; years later Hamnet, a baker of Stratford, witnessed the poet's will and was remembered in it.

Between the birth of the twins in 1585 and the first reference to Shakespeare in London in 1592 no records exist, and the so-called Lost Years have occasioned much speculation. The seventeenth-century gossip Aubrey reported, on the authority of the actor William Beeston (whose father knew Shakespeare) that 'he had been in his younger years a schoolmaster in the country' – a suggestion that has met with unsurprising favour on the part of academic biographers. The circumstances of the poet's departure from Stratford are the subject of a celebrated legend which Rowe included in his Life:

He had, by a misfortune common enough to young fellows, fallen into ill company; and, amongst them, some that made a frequent practice of deer-stealing engaged him with them more than once in robbing a park that belonged to Sir Thomas Lucy of Cherlecot, near Stratford. For this he was prosecuted by that gentleman, as he thought, somewhat too severely; and

4

in order to revenge that ill usage, he made a ballad upon him. And though this, probably the first essay of his poetry, be lost, yet it is said to have been so very bitter, that it redoubled the prosecution against him to that degree that he was obliged to leave his business and family in Warwickshire for some time, and shelter himself in London.

A somewhat earlier version of the same story recorded by Richard Davies, rector of Sapperton, has Shakespeare 'much given to all unluckiness in stealing venison and rabbits, particularly from Sir —— Lucy, who had him oft whipped and sometimes imprisoned and at last made him fly his native country, to his great advancement'. For centuries accepted unhesitantly by most biographers, the deer-poaching tradition has certain inherent improbabilities (Lucy, for example, did not then have a park at Charlecote) and is now consigned to the Shakespeare mythos, although a few responsible scholars – notably Sir Edmund Chambers and G. E. Bentley – are willing to allow it a possible grain of truth.

Shakespeare may have joined one of the touring companies – Leicester's, Warwick's, the Queen's – that played at Stratford in the eighties; the Queen's men, we know, lacked a player in the summer of 1587. By 1592 Shakespeare had established himself in the London theatrical world as actor and playwright, for in that year he was subjected to a venomous attack by another dramatist, Robert Greene. In his *Groatsworth of Wit, Bought with a Million of Repentance*, written as he lay dying, Greene warns his friends – fellow playwrights trained up (unlike Shakespeare) in the university – against 'those puppets. . . that spake from our mouths, those antics garnished in our colours', and particularly against one:

an upstart crow, beautified with our feathers, that with his *Tiger's heart wrapped in a player's hide*, supposes he is as well able to bombast out a blank verse as the best of you: and being an absolute *Johannes fac totum*, is in his own conceit the only Shake-scene in a country.

The punning reference to a Shake-scene and the parody of a line from *3 Henry VI* ('O tiger's heart wrapp'd in a woman's hide!') identify the victim unmistakably. Less clear is the purport of the attack, couched as it is in obscurely allusive language; but Greene seems to be sneering at a mere player, one of the 'antics garnished in our colours', who deigns to set himself up as a universal genius (*Johannes fac totum*) and to rival his betters by turning out plays in stilted blank verse. The notice, however hostile, pays tribute to a successful competitor.

The *Groatsworth of Wit* stirred protest which, Greene being dead, fell on the head of the man who had prepared the manuscript for the printers. Before the year was out Henry Chettle had included, in the prefatory address to his *Kind Heart's Dream*, a handsome apology to the actor-playwright: 'I am as sorry as if the original fault had been my fault, because myself have seen his demeanour no less civil than he excellent in the quality [i.e. acting] he professes. Besides, divers of worship have reported his uprightness of dealing, which argues his honesty, and his facetious grace in writing, that approves his art.'

Who the divers of worship were that vouched for Shakespeare's good character is not recorded. We do know, however, that in the next year, 1593, he published *Venus and Adonis* with a dedication to Henry Wriothesley, third Earl of Southampton and Baron Titchfield. The respectfully formal terms with which the patron, then nineteen, is addressed do not argue close personal acquaintance on the poet's part, but a warmer note enters into the dedication, the next year, of *The Rape of Lucrece* to the same nobleman:

The love I dedicate to your Lordship is without end; whereof this pamphlet, without beginning, is but a superfluous moiety. The warrant I have of your honourable disposition, not the worth of my untutored lines, makes it assured of acceptance. What I have done is yours; what I have to do is yours; being part in all I have, devoted yours.

Both poems issued from the press of a former Stratford neighbour, Richard Field, whose father's goods John Shakespeare had appraised in 1592; Field, three years William's senior, had migrated to London in 1579. What dealings, if any, Shakespeare had with Southampton after the appearance of the two poems can only be conjectured, and of speculation there has been a sufficiency. No further document links the two men; the Earl is not one of the patrons to whom Shakespeare's old friends and colleagues, Heminges and Condell, dedicated the First Folio of his works in 1623. Many believe that Southampton is the Fair Youth celebrated in the Sonnets, and although this is possible, it cannot, in the nature of things, be demonstrated.

Shakespeare wrote *Venus and Adonis* and *The Rape of Lucrece* during the catastrophic plague season that halted London theatrical activity from the summer of 1592 until the spring of 1594. Non-dramatic writing cannot have diverted Shakespeare more than temporarily from his principal occupation. During the Christmas festivities of 1594 the Lord Chamberlain's men acted two plays before Queen Elizabeth at court, and the following March, Shakespeare along with William Kempe and Richard Burbage signed a receipt for the company's honorarium of £20. Kempe was then the outstanding comedian of the age; Burbage would soon gain equal pre-eminence as a tragedian. This first extant reference to Shakespeare as a member of a troupe thus shows him already fully established and representing his company in an official capacity. Burbage is again associated with the dramatist in a scurrilous anecdote that John Manningham, a young law student, jotted down in his commonplace book in 1602:

Upon a time when Burbage played Richard the Third there was a citizen grew so far in liking with him that before she went from the play she appointed him to come that night unto her by the name of Richard the Third. Shakespeare, overhearing their conclusion, went before, was entertained and at his game ere Burbage came. Then message being brought that Richard the Third was at the door, Shakespeare caused return to be made that William the Conqueror was before Richard the Third.

The story may or may not be true.

About another aspect of Shakespeare's career we have surer information: he acted in 1598 in Jonson's *Every Man in His Humour* and, in 1603, in the same author's *Sejanus*. From traditions of uncertain reliability we learn that Shakespeare played 'kingly parts', and that he took the roles of the faithful old servant Adam in *As You Like It* and the Ghost in *Hamlet*. He was not one of the celebrated actors of the period, although Aubrey reports that he 'did act exceedingly well'.

When in 1598 the Lord Chamberlain's men tore down their regular playhouse, the Theatre, and used the timber to build the Globe, they set up a species of proprietorship in which (as a later document shows) Shakespeare was entitled to 10 per cent of the profits. These were considerable, although over the years the value of Shakespeare's share fluctuated, depending upon the number of shareholders. As part-owner he of course helped to direct company policy. Thus he served his troupe in a triple capacity: as playwright, actor, and business director.

In the royal patent by which the Lord Chamberlain's men became, in 1603, the King's men, Shakespeare's name appears near the head of the list. The next year he is the first mentioned of the nine players allowed cloth for new liveries in order to participate, as grooms of the King's chamber, in the coronation procession.

Shakespeare lived near where he worked. From tax assessments we know that before October 1596 he dwelt in St Helen's, Bishopsgate, a short distance from the Theatre, and that later (by October 1599) he had moved across the river to the Liberty of the Clink on the Bankside, where, in Southwark, the Globe stood. He may have been living on the Bankside as early as Michaelmas Term, 1596, when one William Wayte swore the peace against William Shakspere, Francis Langley, and two unknown women. This Langley owned the new Swan playhouse; Wayte was the stepson and instrument of William Gardiner, a litigious Surrey Justice of the Peace who sought to put the theatre out of business. The nature of Shakespeare's involvement in this feud remains a mystery; possibly he was a mere bystander.

Some time before 1604 he was lodging – for how long is not certain – with the family of a French Huguenot tiremaker (i.e. manufacturer of ladies' ornamental headdresses) in Silver Street, near St Olave's church in north-west London. So much we learn from a suit brought against Mountjoy in 1612 by his son-in-law and former apprentice, Stephen Bellott. The documents in the action afford a rare personal glimpse of Shakespeare. The Mountjoys were eager to marry their daughter Mary, an only child, to Belott, who by 1604 had completed his apprenticeship and was working for a fixed salary in the groundfloor shop. But he held back, and Madame Mountjoy 'did send and persuade one Master Shakespeare that lay in the house to persuade the plaintiff to the same marriage'. The dramatist conveyed to Belott the father's promises with respect to the marriage portion, and also the information that, should he refuse the match, 'she should never cost him, the defendant her father, a groat. Whereupon, and in regard Master Shakespeare had told them that they should have a sum of money for a portion from the father, they were made sure by Master Shakespeare by giving their consent, and agreed to marry...' Thus deposed Daniel Nicholas, friend and neighbour of the Mountjoys. The wedding took place at St Olave's church on 19 March 1604. Later Belott quarrelled with his father-in-law over the dowry and a promised legacy; hence the suit. In his testimony Shakespeare, described as a gentleman of Stratford-upon-Avon, remembered the plaintiff as an apprentice who 'did well and honestly behave himself', and the defendant as one who showed 'great good will and affection towards the said complainant'. But the crucial points – the amount of the portion and when it was to be paid – Shakespeare could not recall, nor could he remember what Mountjoy had promised his daughter after his decease. The court referred the case to the elders of the French church in London for arbitration.

No records exist to connect the playwright's wife and family with any of his residences in the capital; presumably they awaited his visits to Stratford. According to Aubrey, 'Master William Shakespeare was wont to go into Warwickshire once a year.' Unlike Marlowe, he did not sever himself from his provincial roots, but instead carefully nurtured over the years his connection with the town of his birth. There he bought houses and land, and engaged in other dealings with the inhabitants: loans, sales, negotiations, and suits. These transactions testify to his prominence in the life of Stratford.

In 1597 he purchased the Great House of New Place. Three storeys high and with five gables (in the sketch, recently recovered, made from memory by the eighteenth-century artist Vertue), it had a frontage of sixty feet on Chapel Street and a depth of seventy feet along Chapel Lane. The second largest dwelling in Stratford, New Place became Shakespeare's permanent residence until his death. In the seventeenth century the garden was noted for its grapevines, and there, tradition holds, Shakespeare planted with his own hands a mulberry tree; it eventually became the source of a ceaseless stream of curios and relics. The family seems to have moved into the house in 1597, for early the next year a survey of the Chapel Street Ward showed Shakespeare as owning ten quarters (or eighty bushels) of corn and malt. In January 1599 he sold the Stratford Corporation a load of stone perhaps left over from the repair of the Great House.

No sooner had he bought the property than Shakespeare was open to other real-estate investments. 'It seemeth,' wrote Abraham Sturley on 24 January 1598 to Richard Quiney in London, '...that our countryman Master Shakspere is willing to disburse some money upon some odd yardland or other at Shottri or near about us.' This same Quiney, whose father had served together with John Shakespeare on Corporation business, wrote on 25 October the only extant letter to the poet. Addressed 'To my loving good friend and countryman Master William Shackespere', it requests a loan of £30 to help Quiney with his London debts. The fact that the letter was discovered among the Quiney papers suggests that it was never delivered.

On 1 May 1602 Shakespeare bought a large tract, 107 acres of arable land plus 20 acres of pasture, in Old Stratford, a farming area about a mile and a half north of town. For this freehold estate he paid William and John Combe the substantial sum of £320 in cash. That month the poet also bought a cottage (perhaps to lodge a servant) and a quarter of an acre of land on the south side of Chapel Lane, facing the garden of New Place. Three years later, on 24 July 1605, Shakespeare invested £440 in the purchase of a half interest in the lease of tithes on 'corn, grain, blade, and hay' from Old Stratford, Welcombe, and Bishopton, and on 'wool, lambs, and other small and privy tithes' from Stratford parish; he also agreed to pay rents totalling £22 a year, and to collect – or have collected – the tithes himself. They brought him a net income of £60 per annum.

In 1608 Shakespeare sued John Addenbrooke, gentleman, for a debt of £6 in the Stratford court of record. The same bench had heard his complaint, a few years previously, against Shakespeare's neighbour, Philip Rogers, who had bought from him twenty bushels of malt and borrowed 2s. but had repaid only 6s. of the entire debt. Such litigation is commonplace in the period.

9

In the last two years of his life Shakespeare was involved (although not very deeply) in a fierce debate over enclosure in the Welcombe area, where lay some of his tithe holdings. Several landholders in the neighbourhood urged the enclosure, which would have combined the narrow strips of cultivated soil into larger units surrounded by fences. If more productive agriculture resulted, Shakespeare would have stood to gain; if, on the other hand, the scheme involved converting arable land into pasture, he would have been placed at a disadvantage. What his views on the question were, we do not know; possibly he favoured enclosure. Late in 1614 Thomas Greene, his cousin who was the town clerk of Stratford and a tithe holder opposing the plan, sounded out some of the leading citizens, among them Shakespeare, whose name appears in Greene's memoranda. On 23 December he noted: 'Letters written: one to Master Manneryng, another to Master Shakespeare, with almost all the Company's hands to either. I also writ of myself to my cousin Shakspeare the copies of all our oaths made; then also a note of the inconveniences would grow by the enclosure...'

Shakespeare's portfolio of real-estate investments included one made in London. On 10 November 1613 he sealed a deed for the purchase of the Blackfriars Gate-house from Henry Walker, 'citizen and minstrel of London', for £140. The next day Shakespeare mortgaged the property back to Walker for £60; apparently £80 was paid down in cash, with the mortgage a security for the remainder. So far as we can gather, the dramatist bought the house, which stood close by to the Blackfriars Theatre, as a speculation rather than for use as a dwelling. He had by then retired to Stratford, and made only occasional visits to London.

Thus, during the middle years of his career, while he was becoming the most popular playwright of the London stage, Shakespeare maintained his ties with Stratford and built an estate that he would pass on to his heirs. Meanwhile, the cycle of birth and marriage and death went on. The parish register of Holy Trinity records, on 11 August 1596, the burial of Hamnet Shakespeare at the age of eleven. John Shakespeare died in September 1601; his widow survived him for seven years. The poet's favourite daughter Susanna married John Hall on 5 June 1607. A Stratford physician, he won (we are told) 'great fame for his skill, far and near'. Perhaps the pair lived for a time at the handsome house in Old Town, near the church, known today as Hall's Croft; after Shakespeare's death they took up residence at New Place. They had one child, Elizabeth, christened 21 February 1608. Shakespeare's younger daughter Judith did not marry until 1616, when she was thirty-one. She took for her husband Thomas Quiney, son of the Richard who had sought to borrow money from the poet in 1598.

A vintner whose character was not exemplary, Thomas set up shop, shortly after the wedding, at The Cage, a house at the corner of High Street and Bridge Street in Stratford. They had three children, all born after Shakespeare's death.

One January, either in 1615 or 1616, when he was still 'in perfect health and memory', Shakespeare drew up his last will and testament. Later, after Judith's wedding, he called in his lawyer Francis Collins (who had previously represented him in some of his business transactions) to make revisions. This was on 25 March, and by then Shakespeare's health was failing: he signed in a quavering hand, and he could not recall the name of one of his three nephews – the solicitor had to leave a blank space.

In his will Shakespeare provided for his survivors. To the poor of Stratford he left £10. He remembered local friends: William Reynolds, Anthony Nash, and his brother John Nash. Thomas Combe, whose rich and usurious uncle had bequeathed the poet £5, received his sword; to his lifelong friend Hamnet Sadler he gave money to buy a memorial ring. Nor did Shakespeare overlook his London colleagues of the days with the King's men, but left sums for rings to Richard Burbage, John Heminges, and Henry Condell; they would not forget him. His sole remaining sister, Mrs Joan Hart, was allowed to stay for the rest of her life in the Henley Street homestead, and was given £20 in cash and the testator's wearing apparel. Her three sons received £5 each. A godson, William Walker, aged eight, was left 20s. in gold. To his daughter Judith, Shakespeare bequeathed his broad silver-gilt bowl, £100 as a dowry and another £50 for relinquishing her interest in the cottage on Chapel Lane; also an additional £150, provided 'she or any issue of her body be living at the end of three years next ensuing the day of this my will'.

The Halls, whom he designated as his executors, figure most prominently in the instrument. Their eight-year-old daughter Elizabeth received Shakespeare's plate. The bulk of the estate went to Susanna:

All that capital messuage or tenements with the appurtenances, in Stratford aforesaid, called the New Place, wherein I now dwell, and two messuages or tenements with the appurtenances situate, lying, and being in Henley Street within the borough of Stratford aforesaid; and all my barns, stables, orchards, gardens, lands, tenements, and hereditaments whatsoever, situate ...within the towns, hamlets, villages, fields, and grounds of Stratford-upon-Avon, Old Stratford, Bushopton, and Welcombe, or in any of them in the said county of Warwick. And also all that messuage or tenement with the appurtenances wherein one John Robinson dwelleth, situate...in the Blackfriars in London near the Wardrobe; and all other my lands, tenements, and hereditaments whatsoever.

After her decease the entailed estate was to go to her eldest surviving son, and then to that son's male heirs, and (in default of such issue) to the male heirs of Shakespeare's younger daughter. Thus he sought to keep from dissolution the substantial estate that with toil and shrewd investment he had over the years assembled. But his intention was frustrated. Susanna bore no male children; Judith's three sons died young; Shakespeare's four grandchildren left no issue. Eventually the property passed to strangers.

Anne Shakespeare is mentioned once in an interlineation, apparently inserted in the will as an afterthought: 'Item, I give unto my wife my second best bed with the furniture,' that is, with the hangings, bed linen, etc. This clause has given rise to endless and often heated controversy over the poet's domestic felicity or lack of it. 'His wife had not wholly escaped his memory,' wrote the great Edmond Malone in the eighteenth century: 'he had forgot her, – he had recollected her, – but so recollected her, as more strongly to mark how little he esteemed her; he had already (as is vulgarly expressed) cut her off, not indeed with a shilling, but with an old bed.' His comment influenced opinion for a long period, but eventually it was pointed out (by Charles Knight in the nineteenth century) that the law entitled a widow to one third of her husband's estate, and that there was no need to mention this disposition in the will. The significance of the bequest can only be guessed, but possibly the bed carried sentimental associations, the best bed being reserved for guests at New Place.

On 23 April 1616 Shakespeare died. About his last illness we have no certain information, although half a century later the vicar of Holy Trinity, John Ward, noted in his diary a story that must then have had currency in Stratford: 'Shakespear, Drayton, and Ben Jhonson had a merry meeting, and it seems drank too hard, for Shakespear died of a fever there contracted.' This story has some plausibility – Jonson enjoyed his cup, and Drayton, who haled from Warwickshire, frequently visited the nearby village of Clifford Chambers. Judith Shakespeare's wedding may have provided the occasion for conviviality. But the anecdote is no more than that; medically it seems dubious, and as a gossip Ward is not entirely reliable.

On the twenty-fifth Shakespeare was laid to rest; so the parish register records. As a notable son of Stratford, he was buried within the chancel of Holy Trinity; more ordinary citizens, including his mother and father, were laid to rest in the churchyard. On the flagstone of the dramatist's grave appears this malediction:

> Good friend, for Jesus' sake forbear
> To dig the dust enclosed here!
> Bless'd be the man that spares these stones,
> And curs'd be he that moves my bones.

We do not know whether Shakespeare himself composed these lines, which are directed not to casual visitors to the church but to the sexton, who sometimes had to disturb the dead in order to make room for a new grave.

Within several years of the interment there was erected, to honour Shakespeare's memory, a monument in the north wall of the chancel, near the grave. A half-length bust of the poet is framed by a niched arch; a pen in his right hand, he is in the act of creation. Above the arch is emblazoned in bas-relief the familiar coat of arms, as described in 1596 by the College of Heralds: 'Gold, on a bend sables, a spear of the first steeled argent; and for his crest or cognisance a falcon, his wings displayed argent, steeled as aforesaid, set upon a helmet with mantels and tassels...' (The words 'non sanz droict', appearing above the trick of coat and crest in two drafts of a Heralds' document, are taken to represent the family motto, but we have no evidence of their use as such by Shakespeare or his heirs.) Small nude figures representing Rest and Labour sit on either side of the arms; a skull forms the apex of the triangular design. The stonemason who carved the monument was Gheerart Janssen, of Dutch origin, whose shop stood in Southwark, a short distance from the Globe. The dramatist and his colleagues perhaps knew it.

In 1623 Heminges and Condell honoured Shakespeare with a monument of another kind by collecting and publishing his plays. They dedicated the volume to the Earls of Pembroke and Montgomery, who, we are told, showed the author much favour while he lived; William Herbert, third Earl of Pembroke, would become a leading contender for the role of the Sweet Boy of the Sonnets, which had been published in 1609 with a dedication to 'Mr W. H.'. On the title-page of the Folio appears a clumsy portrait of Shakespeare engraved by Martin Droeshout; this likeness is commended by Jonson in a verse on the adjoining flyleaf. (The Droeshout portrait and the Stratford bust constitute the only authoritative representations of the poet, although claims have been made for many others, most notably the Chandos painting.) In their preface addressed 'To the Great Variety of Readers', the editors comment on the habits of composition of their colleague: 'His mind and hand went together, and what he thought, he uttered with that easiness that we have scarce received from him a blot in his papers.' To which Jonson rejoined, in his *Timber: or, Discoveries*, 'Would he had blotted a thousand!' But in the fifth preliminary leaf to the Folio he paid noble tribute to the memory of his beloved, the sweet swan of Avon who was not for an age but for all time. Another encomium came from the pen of Leonard Digges, a University College, Oxford, scholar, who was the stepson of Thomas Russell, a Warwickshire squire appointed by Shakespeare as one of the overseers of his will.

The claim of Heminges and Condell that Shakespeare never blotted a line invites scepticism (we know that he revised), but we do not doubt them when they describe their editorial task as a labour of love, designed 'without ambition either of self-profit or fame; only to keep the memory of so worthy a friend and fellow alive, as was our Shakespeare'. Apart from Greene, none of his contemporaries seems to have uttered a malicious word about Shakespeare. Chettle, as we have seen, praised his civil demeanour and uprightness of dealing. From others we hear of good Will, sweet Shakespeare, friendly Shakespeare, so dear loved a neighbour. The actor Augustine Phillips in 1605 remembered him in his will and bequeathed him a thirty shilling piece in gold. Praise did not come easily to Jonson, but in his *Discoveries*, when not under eulogistic obligations, he confessed that he loved the man and honoured his memory on this side idolatry: 'He was indeed honest, and of an open and free nature; had an excellent fancy, brave notions, and gentle expressions.' Aubrey wrote more than half a century after Shakespeare's death, and so his jottings belong to the mythos rather than to the factual record, but we are not inclined to distrust him when he notes, 'He was a handsome well-shaped man, very good company, and of a very ready and pleasant smooth wit.'

Shakespeare's widow lived to see the installation of the monument in Holy Trinity, but not the publication of the First Folio. She died on 6 August 1623. A tradition holds that she 'did earnestly desire to be laid in the same tomb' with her husband, but the injunction against opening the grave prevailed, and she was instead placed alongside. John Hall died in 1635 and his wife in 1649. They too lie in the chancel near the poet. Judith Quiney died in 1662, and Shakespeare's last surviving grandchild, Lady Elizabeth Bernard, in February 1670. New Place, bequeathed to the Bernards by her will, was rebuilt in 1702 and razed in 1759.

2

THE PLAYHOUSES AND THE STAGE

RICHARD HOSLEY

It is convenient to begin this chapter with a brief enquiry into the kinds of temporary playhouse and stage that existed in England on the eve of construction of the first permanent Elizabethan playhouse – that is to say, about 1575. By that time the old medieval stage of Place-and-scaffolds, still in use in Scotland early in the sixteenth century, had fallen into disuse; and the stage of the pageant-wagons, though it would be used in secular contexts until the early seventeenth century, had arrived at the end of its long career as the stage of the great medieval Corpus Christi cycles. Thus the kind of temporary stage that was dominant in England about 1575 was the booth stage of the marketplace – a small rectangular stage mounted on trestles or barrels and 'open' in the sense of being surrounded by spectators on three sides (Fig. 1).

The stage proper of the booth stage generally measured from 15 to 25 ft. in width and from 10 to 15 ft. in depth; its height above the ground averaged about 5 ft. 6 in., with extremes ranging as low as 4 ft. and as high as 8 ft.; and it was backed by a cloth-covered booth, usually open at the top, which served as a tiring-house (mimorum aedes). In typical small examples the booth proper employed four upright posts joined at the top by horizontal poles or timbers, so that the whole booth was constructed as a single bay and the booth front, accordingly, consisted of a single opening in which curtains were hung. In larger examples six or eight or even ten uprights were used, so that the booth was constructed in two or three or even four bays and the booth front, accordingly, consisted of two or three or even four openings in which curtains were hung. The booth stage did not usually employ a 'containing' barrier or playhouse – though because of the lack of such a means of controlling access to the performance the collection of money constituted rather a problem; occasionally, as in the late fifteenth-century morality play *Mankind*, the performance would be stopped briefly at an exciting moment while money was collected from the spectators. But growth in the size of audiences and the experience of having performed in 'rounds' enclosed by a fence or an earthwork 'hill' apparently led the players to investigate ways of controlling access to the performance and thus of collecting charges for admission more efficiently. About 1575 there were two kinds of building in England, both designed for functions other than the acting of plays, which were adapted by the players as temporary outdoor playhouses.

Fig. 1. A booth stage set up in a marketplace

One was the animal-baiting ring or 'game house' (beargarden or bull ring), examples of which are recorded in pictorial and other records as standing on the south bank of the Thames opposite the City of London in the 1560s. The early Bankside baiting-houses were round wooden amphitheatres consisting of (probably) two galleries superimposed one above the other and defining a circular 'pit' some 60 or more feet in diameter. We have no record of the use of a baiting-house for the performance of plays, but the close physical resemblance between the baiting-houses and later 'public' playhouses makes the hypothesis of such use a defensible one. (Compare the later daily alternation of animal-baiting with play-acting in the Hope Playhouse or

Fourth Beargarden of 1614.) Presumably a booth stage was set up against the inner circle of the baiting-house frame, an audience standing in the pit collected around the three sides of the stage, and an additional audience, corresponding to spectators in upper-storey windows of houses in the marketplace situation, watched the performance from seats in the galleries (Fig. 2). Both pit and gallery spectators would, of course, upon entrance to the 'house', have paid fees for the privilege of viewing the performance.

The other kind of building was the inn – or, rather, that particular kind of 'great inn' which consisted of a group of adjoining buildings arranged usually in a rectangular plan so as to define an enclosed 'yard'. Use of inn-yards for the performance of plays is indicated by (among other records) the Act of Common Council of the City of London in 1574 restraining innkeepers and others from permitting plays to be performed 'within the house-yard or any other place within the liberties of this City'. Like the animal-baiting house, the inn-yard constituted a 'natural' playhouse: presumably a booth stage was set up against a wall at one side of the yard (usually one of the 'long' sides), an audience standing in the yard surrounded the stage on three sides, an additional audience observed the performance from seats in windows and galleries overlooking the yard, and, most important, the price of admission was gathered at the moment of each spectator's entrance to the 'house' (Fig. 3).

In one respect the inn-yard may have constituted a better playhouse than the animal-baiting house: if paved, a given yard, unlike the necessarily unpaved pit of the baiting-house, would have afforded protection against the miring of standing spectators during or following wet weather. (Opportunities for an older pastime than the viewing of plays – implied by the reference to 'chambers and secret places' in the Act of Common Council of 1574 – would also have been superior.) But it seems clear that in at least three respects the baiting-house must have been superior to the inn-yard as a playhouse: usually its pit was considerably greater in area than the yard of an inn, it was 'round' instead of rectangular in ground plan (hence more efficient in the accommodation of both pit and gallery spectators), and it had galleries that entirely surrounded the pit as opposed to a gallery here and there and occasional windows overlooking the yard of the usual inn. In this respect it is significant that, in the permanent playhouse constructed in 'the great yard' of the Boar's Head Inn in London in 1598, galleries were apparently built around the four sides of the yard.[1]

The booth stage was essentially an outdoor stage, and the temporary playhouse that accommodated it in a baiting-house or an inn-yard was, despite the location of part of the audience in roofed galleries or upper-storey rooms of an inn, essentially an outdoor playhouse. What was the situation when, during the century ending about 1575, the players performed indoors – in guildhalls, schools or colleges, inns of court, manor houses, palaces, churches, inns, and elsewhere? In most instances what the players did was to convert a domestic (or public) hall into a temporary indoor playhouse. There is some reason to believe that they occasionally set up a booth stage against one wall of the hall in question, and such practice is recorded pictorially in France

Fig. 2. A booth stage set up in the pit of an animal-baiting house

or Italy in the *Andria* illustrations of the Lyons Terence of 1493 – most notably in the frontispiece and the illustration for the opening scene of that play. It also seems probable, however, that English players performing in a hall would generally have preferred to use the already existing 'screens' passage as a tiring-house. In part because of the customary placement of the high table on the dais at the 'upper' end of a hall, plays were normally performed at the 'lower' end – either upon the hall floor or upon a low stage set up against the hall screen (or upon both). At this period the domestic hall screen was normally equipped with two doorways, and these, being without doors, were covered with hangings in order to exclude draughts from the hall. Thus the players, in most situations in which they might undertake to perform a play indoors, found ready at hand, without the necessity

Fig. 3. A booth stage set up in an inn-yard

of preparation, that indispensable convenience of booth-stage production, a pair of curtained entranceways to the playing-area (in this case the hall floor or a low stage set up against the hall screen or both). In a majority of halls, furthermore, use of the screens passage as a tiring-house afforded the players the secondary convenience of a musicians' gallery directly over the passage which could, at need, be put to

19

occasional use as an 'upper station' for the performance of action at an upper-storey window or upon the walls of a town or castle (Fig. 4).

It is customary to distinguish two major classes of permanent Elizabethan playhouse, 'public' and 'private'. The terms are somewhat cloudy, but what they designate is clear enough. In general, the public playhouses were large, 'round', outdoor theatres, whereas the private

Fig. 4. A performance on the floor of a theatrically unmodified domestic hall

playhouses were smaller, rectangular, indoor theatres. (An exception among public playhouses in the matter of roundness was the square Fortune of 1600.) The maximum capacity of a typical public playhouse (the Swan or the Globe) was about 3,000 spectators; that of a typical private playhouse (the Second Blackfriars or the Phoenix), about 700 spectators. At the public playhouses a majority of spectators stood in the yard for a penny (the remainder sitting in galleries and boxes for twopence or more), whereas at the private playhouses all spectators were seated (in pit, galleries, and boxes) and paid sixpence or more. Originally the private playhouses were used exclusively by Boys' companies, but this distinction disappeared about 1609 when the

King's men began using the Blackfriars in winter as well as the Globe in summer. Originally also the private playhouses were found only within the City of London (the Paul's Playhouse, the First and Second Blackfriars), the public playhouses only in the suburbs (the Theatre, the Curtain, the Rose, the Globe, the Fortune, the Red Bull); but this distinction disappeared about 1606 with the opening of the Whitefriars Playhouse to the west of Ludgate. Public-theatre audiences, though socially heterogeneous, were drawn mainly from the lower classes – a situation that has caused modern scholars to refer to the public-theatre audiences as 'popular'; whereas private-theatre audiences tended to be better educated and of higher social rank – 'select' is the word most usually opposed to 'popular' in this respect. Finally, the taste of the audience varied considerably in the two kinds of playhouse, and so accordingly, to a degree, did the kind of play presented.[2]

It has been suggested convincingly that the word *private*, as used by publishers on the title-pages of plays, was designed 'to increase their sales by advertising the fact that the play was of the sophisticated kind written for the indoor theatres', the term merely connoting 'a degree of exclusiveness and superiority'.[3] Thus the opposed term *public* may be interpreted as referring to a playhouse of the outdoor variety that lacked the 'exclusiveness and superiority' of the indoor playhouses. Examples are afforded by Dekker in *The Gull's Hornbook* (1609): 'Whether, therefore, the gatherers of the *public* or *private* playhouse stand to receive the afternoon's rent, . . .'

It should be recognized, however, that the terms *public* and *private* were used also (as one would perhaps expect) in their more usual senses. Thus we find that Heywood's *Love's Mistress* is advertised on its title-page (1636) as having been '*publicly* acted . . . at the Phoenix', Chapman's *Charles Duke of Byron* (1625) as having been acted 'at the Blackfriars and other *public* stages' – both playhouses, of course, being 'private' in the earlier defined sense of that word. This secondary (but more basic) sense of the term *public* is illustrated, about 1619, in a complaint by residents of the Blackfriars precinct against the Second Blackfriars: 'the owner of the said playhouse doth under the name of a *private* house (respecting indeed private commodity only) convert the said house to a *public* playhouse, unto which there is daily such resort of people, . . .' Clearly the term *public* here refers to a playhouse that anyone might attend by virtue of paying the price of admission. The term *open* is apparently a synonym, as on the title-page of Edwards's *Damon and Pythias* (1571), which contemplates performance of that play 'either in *private* or *open* audience'.

Correspondingly, the term *private* in the Blackfriars complaint refers to a playhouse that one might attend only by virtue of belonging to a 'closed' society. Thus the title-page of *The First Two Comedies of Terence* (1627) states that the comedies in question are 'fitted for scholars' *private* action in their schools'. This sense is implied also in the title-page statement (1629) that Carlell's *Deserving Favourite* has been performed 'first before the King's Majesty [i.e. at Court, or *privately*], and since *publicly* at the Blackfriars'. The term was used also in this sense in the Act of Common Council of 1574 in excluding from its ban on performances within the City of London the performance of plays 'in the *private* house, dwelling, or lodging of any nobleman, citizen, or gentleman,...without public or common collection of money of the auditory or beholders thereof'. If, however, visitors were present at a performance given before a usually 'closed' society, the performance, though essentially 'private', could be described as 'public'. Thus in 1605 at St John's College, Oxford, *The Tragedy of Lucretia* was '*publicly* acted...with good commendation and diverse strangers entertained in respect thereof'.

Although both the baiting-house and the inn-yard were used as temporary playhouses before creation of the first permanent Elizabethan playhouse, it seems likely that the physical form of the public playhouse originated mainly in the animal-baiting house. (It is possible, of course, that the rectangular shape of the inn-yard may have been an influence upon the square Fortune.) In accordance with this theory we may suppose that James Burbage, when he built the Theatre in 1576, merely adapted the form of the baiting-house to theatrical needs. To do so he built a large round structure very much like a baiting-house but with five major innovations in the received form. First (though not necessarily immediately), he paved the ring with brick or stone, thus transforming what had been an unpaved 'pit' into a paved 'yard'. In doing this his chief purpose would have been to make possible an efficient system of drains to carry off rainwater falling into the yard. Here his model, both for the thing itself and for its name, may have been the yard of a great inn or the courtyard of a great house or palace. Second, Burbage erected a stage in the yard. Here his model was the booth stage of the marketplace, built rather larger than any recorded example and, since a permanent structure, supported by posts rather than trestles or barrels. Third, Burbage erected a permanent tiring-house in place of the booth which had been set up in front of a few bays of the frame in the earlier temporary arrangement in an animal-baiting ring. Here his chief model was the screens passage of the Tudor domestic hall, modified to withstand the weather by the insertion of doors in the doorways. Presumably the tiring-house, as a permanent structure, was inset into the frame of the playhouse rather than, as in the older temporary situation of the booth stage, set up against the frame of a baiting-house. Thus Burbage produced a structure which, when the leaves of the doors had been opened outward through an arc of 180° and hangings placed in or in front of the open doorways, reproduced that indispensable convenience of the booth stage, a pair of curtained entranceways to the stage; and the gallery over the tiring-house (presumably divided into boxes) was capable of serving variously as a 'Lord's room' for privileged or high-paying spectators, as a music-room, and as a station for the occasional performance of action 'above'. Fourth, Burbage built a 'cover' over the rear part of the stage, supported by posts rising from the yard and surmounted by a 'hut'. The precise origin of such a 'stage super-structure' is difficult to identify, but it must have been designed primarily to house suspension-gear for flying-effects, and such gear had been used in the English street theatre as early as the end of the fourteenth century. And, fifth, Burbage added a third gallery to the frame, for the original Bankside baiting-houses (as recorded in the 'Agas' View of London) appear to have been two-storey buildings. Here Burbage may have been influenced only by normal business acumen, but any of a number of three-storeyed architectural forms might have served as his model.

The theory of origin and development suggested in the preceding paragraph accords with our chief pictorial source of information about the Elizabethan stage, the 'De Wit' drawing of the interior of the Swan Playhouse (*c.* 1596; Fig. 5). This shows a round playhouse frame constructed apparently in 24 bays and measuring presumably about 96 ft. in diameter.[4] Thus the playhouse would have been large enough to accommodate an audience of some 3,000 spectators (the figure given in the notes accompanying the drawing). The playhouse frame, consisting of three galleries superimposed one above the other, defines a circular yard some 70 ft. in diameter. At one side of the play-house yard is a large rectangular stage (*proscaenium*) which extends to about the middle of the yard. The stage is depicted as deeper than wide, but the depiction is probably a distortion in the drawing, for numerous considerations suggest that the stage was wider than deep. The actual size of the stage depends on a number of variable factors: the diameter of the playhouse frame, the depth of the frame, the number of bays of the frame, and the degree of projection of the stage into the yard. In the present case, assuming a 24-sided playhouse frame with an outer diameter of 96 ft., a frame 12 ft. 6 in. deep, and a projection of the stage as far as the middle of the playhouse yard, we may estimate the Swan stage as 43 ft. in width and about 27 ft. in depth (dimensions in a ratio of about 8:5). The height of the stage may be conjectured as 5 ft. 6 in., about the average height of the booth stage.

At the back of the stage in the Swan drawing is a 'tiring-house' (*mimorum aedes*) which appears to project considerably from the play-house frame but which, in actuality, may have projected only a foot or two. The tiring-house is equipped, in the first storey, with two large, round-headed, double-hung doors opening out upon the stage and, in the second storey, with a row of six windows which are presumably the openings of boxes of a 'Lord's room over the stage' (to quote Jonson's allusion in *Every Man out of His Humour*). If the Swan tiring-house was about 40 ft. long, each of the tiring-house doors in the drawing may be estimated as about 7 ft. 6 in. wide and about 9 ft. high; and each of the windows of the gallery over the stage as about 6 ft. square.

In the Swan drawing two large columns in the Corinthian mode rise from the stage (and, of course, from the yard below) to support a 'cover' or 'shadow' or 'heavens' which, running the full length of the tiring-house at the level of its third storey, extends forward from the tiring-house so as to lie directly over the rear part of the stage. And immediately above the stage cover, at the level of what would be a fourth storey of the tiring-house, is a 'hut'. Presumably the fourth-storey hut housed suspension-gear for flying-effects and the third-storey stage cover served as a loading-room for players preparing to 'fly' down to the stage.

The theory of origin and development suggested above accords also with our two chief verbal sources of information about the Elizabethan stage, the builder's contracts for the Fortune (1599) and the Hope (1613).[5] Both contracts call for a three-storey playhouse frame, and the Fortune contract specifies the height of each of the three storeys of the frame: in ascending order, 12 ft., 11 ft., and 9 ft. The Fortune contract also states that the stage in that playhouse is to be 43 ft. wide and that it should 'extend to the middle of the yard'. Thus, since the contract gives the dimensions of the yard as 55 ft. square, the depth of the stage is required to be 27 ft. 6 in., and the dimensions of the stage are in a ratio of about 8:5.

The theory accords also with our second most important pictorial source of information about the Elizabethan stage, Wenzel Hollar's pen-and-ink sketch (*c.* 1640) for his Long Bird's-Eye View of London (1647). The sketch (like the engraving that in part derives from it) depicts a round Second Globe and Hope, both equipped with the exterior stair-towers which the Hope contract requires at that play-house on the analogy of the stair-towers at the Swan. Presumably such exterior stair-towers, whether roofed and enclosed as shown by Hollar or unroofed and open, already existed in the animal-baiting houses of about 1575 and were taken over from them by Burbage when he constructed the Theatre in 1576.

Fig. 5. The 'De Wit' drawing of the Swan Playhouse

The Fortune contract calls for a square playhouse measuring 80 ft. on a side. All the other public playhouses appear to have been 'round' – that is to say, constructed to a ground plan in the shape of a polygon having a large number of sides. Apparently the Swan was constructed in 24 bays, and 24 sides would be an appropriate number if the Swan measured 96 ft. in diameter since in that case the length of horizontal timbers in the outer and inner faces of the frame (12 ft. 6 in. and 9 ft. 3 in., respectively) would have been of convenient length for transportation and handling in construction. That the Swan was at least 96 ft. in diameter is suggested by De Wit's statement that the playhouse could accommodate 3,000 spectators. De Wit's figure has occasionally been scouted as too large, but it is confirmed by the statement of the Spanish ambassador, apropos of Middleton's *Game at Chess* at the Second Globe in 1624, that more than 12,000 people witnessed performances of that play during the first four days of its extraordinary run of 'nine days together'; he says also that more than 3,000 persons were present on the day that the audience was smallest. Presumably, then, it was common knowledge that such playhouses as the Swan and the Second Globe could accommodate a capacity crowd of about 3,000 spectators.

The question arises whether the size of the Swan was typical of Elizabethan public playhouses. An answer is suggested by the general similarity in size of five of the public playhouses. According to its builder's contract, the Hope, built in 1613–14, was to be of 'such large compass, form, wideness, and height as the playhouse called the Swan', built almost twenty years earlier in 1595. Hence we have a class of two playhouses, the Swan and the Hope, which were of the same size. Again, the Second Globe was built in 1614 'upon an old foundation'. Since this would be the foundation of the First Globe, built fifteen years earlier in 1599 and destroyed by fire in 1613, we may suppose that the Second Globe was of the same size as the First. Moreover, the First Globe, as is well known, was constructed of the dismantled timbers of the Theatre. Since the timbers would presumably (through attention to 'carpenter's marks') have been reassembled in their original relationships so as to take advantage of the original cutting and jointing,[6] we may suppose that the First Globe, built in 1599, was of the same size as the Theatre, built some twenty-five years earlier in 1576. It follows that the Second Globe of 1614 was also of the same size as the Theatre of 1576. Hence we have a second class, composed of three playhouses, the Theatre, the First Globe, and the Second Globe, which were of the same size. And the two classes of playhouse were themselves of approximately the same size, for the reason that one theatre from the first class (the Swan) and another

from the second (the Second Globe) were independently described as capable of accommodating about 3,000 spectators. All told, the evidence seems hospitable to a theory that most of the round public playhouses – specifically, the Theatre (1576), the Swan (1595), the First Globe (1599), the Hope (1614), and the Second Globe (1614) – were of about the same size.

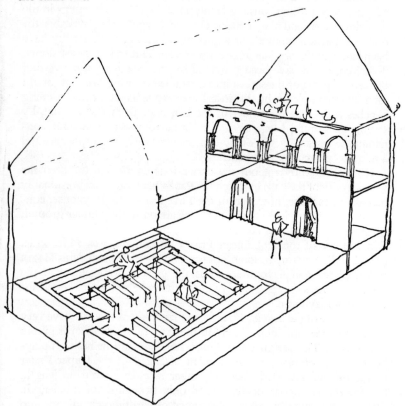

Fig. 6. A reconstruction of a small private playhouse such as the early Paul's or the First Blackfriars

It seems likely that the physical form of the Elizabethan private playhouse originated mainly in the Tudor domestic hall. In accordance with this theory we may suppose that Sebastian Westcott, when he built the unnamed theatre of the Paul's Boys in or shortly before 1575, merely adapted a small hall connected with St Paul's Church to theatrical needs. To do so he may have made only one major innova-

tion, the construction of a low stage (perhaps 4 ft. high) running across the hall from one wall to the other immediately in front of the hall screen. The stage, if the containing hall were (let us say) 26 ft. wide, would have been 26 ft. in width and, presumably, about 16 ft. 6 in. in depth (dimensions in a ratio of about 8:5). The screens passage, if surmounted by a musicians' gallery, could have served without adaptation as a tiring-house, it being possible to fit up hangings in the two doorways, and the 'gallery over the stage' being available for occasional action 'above'; or a gallery, if lacking, could readily have been added to the original one-storey screen. Three tiring-house doors, if desired, could have been provided by the expedient of converting the central panel of the screen into a middle doorway. Westcott might then have completed his theatrical arrangements by merely running benches across the remainder of the hall floor from wall to wall, by setting up ground 'degrees' around a narrow section of floor containing benches (Fig. 6), or by constructing shallow galleries around a narrow 'pit' containing benches.

Nothing is known about the dimensions of the hall (or even the very identity of the hall) in which the Paul's Playhouse was presumably housed. In the case, however, of the First Blackfriars Playhouse, constructed by Richard Farrant in 1576, we are on slightly firmer ground, since we know that the hall in question, an upper-storey room of the Old Buttery of the Dominican Priory of London, was 26 ft. wide. (The building was 95 ft. long, but presumably only part of this length was used for the playhouse.) Thus the general arrangement of the First Blackfriars was presumably much the same as that suggested for the Paul's Playhouse.

In the case of the Second Blackfriars Playhouse of 1596 we have very considerable information, chiefly in the form of verbal records giving dimensions. The designer was James Burbage, and he built his playhouse in the upper-storey Parliament Chamber of the Upper Frater of the priory. The Parliament Chamber measured 100 ft. in length, but for the playhouse Burbage used only two-thirds of this length. The room in question, after the removal of partitions dividing it into apartments, measured 46 ft. in width and 66 ft. in length. In order to convert this room into a playhouse, Burbage made, according to a recently proposed reconstruction,[7] four major innovations. First, since a hall screen (if there was one) could hardly have survived the compartmentation of the Parliament Chamber into apartments earlier in the sixteenth century, he built, at one end of the room, a tiring-house modelled either directly on the screens passage of a Tudor domestic hall or on a tiring-house itself modelled on such a screens passage. The tiring-house, running the full width of the hall, was thus 46 ft.

long and perhaps 12 ft. deep (including the thickness of the tiring-house wall). Probably there were three doorways in the tiring-house façade; in the reconstruction they are given as 7 ft. wide and 9 ft. tall. The second storey of the tiring-house would have been a 'gallery over the stage', the three boxes of which might have been used variously as

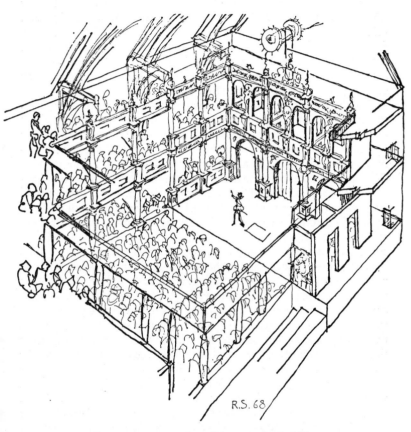

R.S. 68

Fig. 7. A reconstruction of the Second Blackfriars

a Lord's room, as a music-room, and as an upper station for the occasional performance of action above. Second, Burbage built a low stage (perhaps 4 ft. 6 in. high) running across the hall from one wall to the other immediately in front of the tiring-house. Third, he built galleries around the three remaining sides of the room, thus defining a 'pit' which, if the galleries were 8 ft. 6 in. deep, would have measured

29

29 ft. in width and 27 ft. in depth. Presumably the pit was unraked. If the walls of the Parliament Chamber extended 32 ft. above the floor, space would have been available for three galleries (the top gallery perhaps unroofed), and presumably Burbage would have continued these across the stage to join the tiring-house, thus creating upper side-boxes over the stage and side-stage boxes at stage level. Accordingly the stage would have measured 29 ft. in width and 18 ft. 6 in. in depth (dimensions in a ratio of about 8:5). And, fourth, Burbage cut a trap door in the ceiling of the Parliament Chamber so as to make possible descents by suspension-gear housed in one of the 'rooms over the hall'. The proposed reconstruction is illustrated in the accompanying drawing by Richard Southern (Fig. 7).

The theory of origin and development suggested in preceding paragraphs is confirmed by a major pictorial source of information about the Elizabethan indoor playhouse. This is the set of drawings (probably by Inigo Jones) preserved at Worcester College, Oxford.[8] The drawings show a playhouse in a rectangular building with an apsidal end. (The ground plan might be described as in the shape of a closed horse-shoe with parallel sides.) The building is approximately 51 ft. long and 37 ft. wide (interior measure). The tiring-house runs the full width of the building at the rectangular end. The tiring-house is thus 37 ft. long, and it is 11 ft. deep including the thickness of the tiring-house wall. The stage is about 23 ft. wide and 14 ft. deep (dimensions in a ratio of 8:5). The height of the stage above the floor is 4 ft. The galleries, running round the apsidal end of the building, are 8 ft. 6 in. deep. They define an apsidal-ended pit with an unraked floor. Continuation of the galleries across the stage to join the tiring-house has the effect of creating upper side-boxes over the stage and side-stage boxes at stage level. There are three doorways in the tiring-house façade. The second storey of the tiring-house is a gallery over the stage divided into three bays. The two side bays are apparently intended for audience since degrees for seating are indicated. The middle bay, fronted with an arched window, may be interpreted as a music-room, and presumably this served also, at need, as an upper station for the occasional performance of action above. The drawings make no provision for suspension-gear, but such gear could easily have been housed in the attic above the playhouse if a trap door were cut in the playhouse ceiling.

Two parts of the stage in a playhouse like the Swan or the Second Blackfriars require only the briefest comment. Suspension-gear was used for the flying down of a deity from the 'heavens' (Jupiter in *Cymbeline*) or for special lifting effects (heaving Antony aloft in *Antony and Cleopatra*[9]). Since the winch was stationary, descents and ascents were of the bucket-in-a-well variety, the descending or ascending player alighting at or taking off from a central point on the stage a few feet forward of the tiring-house façade. And the trap door was used as a pit (*Titus Andronicus*), a grave (*Hamlet*), or the entrance to a vault or the netherworld. There appears to have been but a single trap door, placed in the middle of the stage.

Fig. 8. Hangings fitted up along the tiring-house façade of a public playhouse such as the Swan or the Globe

Three other parts of the stage, since controversial, require more detailed discussion: the 'discovery-space', the upper station, and the music-room.

The discovery-space was generally an open tiring-house doorway within which curtains (Fig. 7), or in front of which hangings (Fig. 8), had been fitted up.[10] Thus the discovery-space was a foot or two deep, some 7 ft. wide, and about 9 ft. tall. The conception is dependent on three characteristics of the Elizabethan discovery. First, it was extremely rare, there being evidence for only about a dozen discoveries in the several hundred scenes of Shakespeare's thirty-eight plays. Typical examples are the discovery of the dead Horatio in Kyd's *Spanish Tragedy*, of the three caskets in *The Merchant of Venice*, of the sleeping Falstaff in *1 Henry IV*, of the 'statue' of Hermione in *The Winter's Tale*, and of Ferdinand and Miranda playing at chess in *The Tempest*. Second, the Elizabethan discovery is essentially a 'show' or disclosure (usually for the benefit of a character on stage) of a character or object invested with some special interest or significance. That is to say, the discovery-space curtains were not used, as curtains commonly are in the proscenium-arch theatre, as a device to permit the placement of stage-properties out of sight of the audience. In the Elizabethan theatre beds (*Othello*[11]), tables (*Henry VIII*), chairs containing 'sick' characters (*King Lear*), and other such properties were simply carried or drawn on stage at need by attendant players. And, third, the Elizabethan discovery did not involve movement in depth within the discovery-space, for the discovered player usually leaves the discovery-space and comes forward upon the stage immediately or shortly after being discovered.

The upper station was generally the space at the front of one of the boxes of the tiring-house gallery over the stage.[12] Thus the upper station was essentially a box-window which sometimes measured as much as 6 ft. in width. The conception is dependent on three characteristics of Elizabethan action above. First, it was relatively rare, there being evidence for only about three dozen actions above in Shakespeare's thirty-eight plays. Second, Elizabethan action above was essentially an 'appearance' of one character in an elevated place to another character in a place below. The usual situations are the window of a house overlooking the street (Brabantio and Iago in *Othello*) and the walls of a town or castle overlooking the space below (the King and Bolingbroke in *Richard II*). And, third, Elizabethan action above does not involve movement in depth within the upper station, for in most instances the player above remains framed in the window while in dialogue with the player below and sometimes, at the conclusion of that dialogue, descends by way of the tiring-house stairs to stage level and re-enters 'to' the player below.

Like the upper station, the Elizabethan music-room was generally one of the boxes of the second-storey gallery over the stage.[13] (The theory of a third-storey music-room is without foundation.) Presumably the playhouse custom of placing music above originated in use of the musicians' gallery over the screens passage of a domestic hall. In any case, the music room was early a standard appurtenance of the private playhouses, where act-intervals and inter-act music were customary from the beginning. A music-room was at first lacking in the public playhouses, since public-theatre performances did not originally employ act-intervals and inter-act music. (In such playhouses off-stage music was generally performed within the tiring-house at stage level.) About 1609, however, after the King's men had begun performing at the Blackfriars as well as at the Globe, the custom of inter-act music seems to have spread from the private to the public playhouses, and with it apparently came the custom of using one of the tiring-house boxes over the stage as a music-room – compare the requirement of '*a sad song in the music-room*' in Middleton's *Chaste Maid in Cheapside*, a Swan play of 1613. The music-room, whether in a private or a public playhouse, was normally curtained, presumably so that the musicians could be concealed from the audience during the action of the play but readily made visible to them during the performance of inter-act music. And occasionally the music-room curtains were used for a discovery above or otherwise employed, as in the King's spying from an upper-storey window in *Henry VIII*. It may be added that the theory of use of a music-room for action above is confirmed by Jasper Mayne's praise of Ben Jonson (1638) for having, in his plays, generally avoided vulgar theatrical spectacle: 'Thou laid'st no sieges to the music-room.'

It remains to say a few words about the now generally discarded concept of an Elizabethan 'inner stage'.[14] To many investigators it now seems incredible that such a theory could ever have been generally accepted. Two possible reasons may be suggested for the error. The first is that even so recently as thirty years ago most students of the Elizabethan stage were so exclusively accustomed to illusionistic conventions of the then-contemporary proscenium-arch stage that they could not imagine Elizabethan production without something, however small, that would correspond, however approximately, to the proscenium-arch curtain – after all, Elizabethan stage-directions *do* refer to curtains. A simple answer was the 'inner stage', essentially a small proscenium-arch stage at the back of a so-called outer stage which could be used for the setting of stage-properties out of sight of the audience. The other possible reason for the error is that more than one influential scholar has approached the Elizabethan stage (whether consciously or unconsciously) from the point of view of the Restoration stage. Like its predecessor the playhouse of the Stuart court masque, the Restoration playhouse did have, towards the back of its changeable-scenery stage, an 'alcove' which was used somewhat in the manner advocated by modern apologists for the 'inner stage'; and Restoration plays frequently reflect such an alcove in plot-situations and attendant stage-directions. Thus it seems to have been casually assumed that an Elizabethan discovery was the same thing as a Restoration discovery, hence that the Elizabethan discovery-space was the same thing as the Restoration discovery-space. But neither proposition will withstand scrutiny. The origin of the Elizabethan discovery-space is to be found not in the Renaissance stage of changeable scenery but in the curtained scaffold of the medieval *platea*, whose technique of effecting discoveries was transmitted to the Elizabethan stage, in part perhaps directly, in part perhaps indirectly through the media of the booth stage and the domestic hall screen.[15]

3

THE ACTORS AND STAGING

DANIEL SELTZER

Robert Greene, who had very few kind words for actors, condescended to grant them skills which in his opinion were 'a kind of mechanical labour'. What these skills were, however, he did not tell us; and in this, unfortunately, he was not unlike his contemporaries, even those who admired the actors and wrote graceful tributes to the best of them. An age which took so much greatness for granted took few pains to record in detail the action of the 'mechanics' who embodied dramatic writing on stage. Some description does survive, of course. There are many good-natured allusions, and some not so good-natured, to the ranting voices, bad memories, or thumping stage walks of the hacks, to the flamboyant dress of the profession generally, some enthusiastic eulogies of the excellent actors. The paucity of detailed information about acting *styles* points to the truth of the matter: such observations would hardly have informed Londoners of anything they did not know already. If Thomas Lodge, for example, could speak casually of the 'foul lubber' who '[looked] as pale as the visard of the ghost, which cried so miserably at the theatre, like an oysterwife, "Hamlet revenge"', we may be reasonably certain that his readers would place the allusion immediately, and that Lodge thought so too. Four centuries later, we should like to know whether that actor playing the Ghost in the lost *Hamlet* before Shakespeare's moved *as* he cried out, how long he held the sound, how high the voice rose in pitch and volume, and where he stood on the stage platform.

Absence of exact documentation of technique may also indicate that the crafts of the Tudor actor, as they had developed, were relatively new ones. That they were not as specifically described as they were generally praised may very likely be due to the fact that there was in the nature of things no time to do so. The drama of the sixteenth and seventeenth centuries in England was an achievement extraordinary not only for its quality, but for the speed with which that quality, in all its varied forms, seems suddenly to have been achieved. In relative terms, its excellence was short-lived, and aspects of it that survived the closing of the theatres and the Restoration were altered considerably by new styles of performance and staging. We have no way of knowing what sort of actor's 'handbook' might have been produced had Parliament not closed the theatres in 1642, but we have only to note that by the end of the eighteenth century, when the craft of acting was as established professionally as the craft of playwriting, there were many detailed accounts of (and by) famous actors in any number of roles. These accounts attest to the truth that theoreticians generally write after the fact; most critical documents about the performing arts – from Aristotle's *Poetics* onwards – show that when a craft such as acting becomes 'established', in the sense that its conventions can be recognized and named, it is then possible to name those practices maintained by some artists, varied by others, or greatly ignored by a few. Even revolutionary artistic achievement can be described in old terms: rules violently broken or happily altered bear still their convenient names. Vasari had no difficulty in describing in detail the new techniques of Michelangelo and Giotto, nor had Berlioz in extensive and specific description of his own practice of orchestration, nor Lewes of the acting methods of Salvini or Kean. But the passage of three or four highly productive decades allowed no time to record the art of the Elizabethan actor, nor to indicate how this art kept pace – as it must have done – with the extraordinarily quick maturation of modes of dramatic writing. Surely the skills of the actors became more complex between, say, 1590 and 1610, and although all available evidence suggests that these skills during the latter part of the period were mainly different in degree and not in kind from those required by earlier repertory, this complexity of technique must have developed too freely and quickly to attempt to codify them, had any Elizabethan or Jacobean been moved to do so.

Surviving eulogies to the great Elizabethan actors consistently praise them for the realism of their characterizations, but this helps us less than it may seem to do. Every age has always maintained that the goal of its representational arts was to mirror nature accurately. As E. H. Gombrich has observed succinctly, 'What we call *seeing* is invariably coloured and shaped by our knowledge (or belief) of what we see,'[1] and for this reason a study of Elizabethan acting methods can help us understand a little more about habits of perception in general in Shakespeare's time. The important question remains, of course, *how* the mirroring of reality was effected, and this problem has elicited a number of opinions. To date, the body of evidence necessary for an accurate estimate has not been collected and published, but the opinions of the opposing camps are easily summarized. A number of critics hold that Elizabethan acting was highly 'formal', that is, that its range of movement, gesture, and vocal expression was more or less categorical, corresponding to a range of rhetorical attitudes capable of being described objectively, and prohibiting (therefore) factors we might wish to call 'inspiration' or 'individual interpretation'. The opposing opinion maintains that much in the style was specifically 'realistic', even 'naturalistic', that certain details of action would have been executed as they might be today, and that there was every reason for a performance by a great actor to exhibit personal inspiration, in every modern sense of the word (indeed, one of the more important eulogies to Burbage seems to document this to some extent). Other critics believe the acting technique was a mixture of rhetorical forms and precise naturalism; and some suggest that this style gradually changed from the early days of the Theatre to those when Shakespeare's plays were being produced at both the Globe and Blackfriars.[2]

The matter cannot be settled here, of course, but after close examination of over two hundred texts, from the earliest interludes through the late Jacobean period, it seems to the present writer that the proponents of a 'mixed' style (or what a modern audience would see as a mixture of various modes) come closest to the truth. But it is of great importance to observe which components of acting styles appear most variable in the mixture, for some practices appear to have been more or less constant throughout the period, while others changed in interesting relationships to altering methods of *writing* plays. It should be observed in passing, however, that those critics who speak of the 'formal' aspects of Elizabethan acting are only commenting upon ways in which it may have appeared different from ours (that dangerous theatrical adjective, 'stylized' – meaning 'mannered' – has come into use only in our own day, and the Elizabethans would not have known what is meant by it). Critics who find evidence for a 'realistic' style, on the other hand, propose simply that much Elizabethan acting looked like ours. Neither mirror image can be entirely correct. That acting at its best was considered 'realistic' there can be no doubt whatever, but there is no more reason to assume that the craft as a whole would resemble ours, than to expect any other form of Renaissance art to resemble its modern equivalent.

Documentation of acting techniques in Elizabethan plays may be divided in three categories. (1) *Printed stage directions* may tell us how something was done on stage, if one excludes those commonly called 'literary' (which may describe, for example, a setting probably not manifest in the playhouse). (2) *'Implicit' stage directions* may be derived from lines in which a character will actually describe what another on stage is doing, or how he is doing it. (3) *Spatial relationships* among actors on stage – that aspect of staging a modern director calls 'blocking', or the 'moves' of an actor – may sometimes be inferred, although great care must be exercised in drawing conclusions.

Possibilities of movement at any given juncture in stage time are of course numerous, but ultimately there are only so many ways an actor, alone or with one or more others, can move – in address (to them or to the audience) or in silence. Most of the time, this evidence is impossible to isolate; but occasionally one spatial relationship, precisely defined, could have taken place only in sequence with another, usually immediately preceding it. Sometimes, if rarely, it is possible in this way to reconstruct two or three such arrangements, and in these cases a tangible picture of stage movement emerges.

From this body of information one may draw conclusions about four aspects of acting style which, taken together, cover everything an actor can do (physically) on stage: (1) *Stage business*, ranging from small details of action relating to the character's own person to facial expressions and movement carried out on lines; (2) *Voice*, primarily in terms of pitch and volume, but including special uses such as parody, and extending as well to such matters as the pacing of speeches, special pauses, tonal quality, and the like; (3) *Stage movement*, in terms of 'blocking', but also considerations such as which areas of the stage were apparently considered 'strongest' and which were utilized for different kinds of action; (4) *Address*, that is, literally the direction of the actor's speech – when he is alone on stage (as when, in a meditative speech, he may as it were address 'himself' only; or, in an explanatory vein, or comic routine, address the audience; or, in a speech of apostrophe, usually in strong emotions, address an imaginary hearer[3]) or with other actors (when he may speak to one or more at a time, or speak without actually addressing any, or in asides to the audience, or alternate among actors, or between them and the audience; also when his speech covers the exit or anticipates the entrance of another actor). Limitations of space naturally prohibit detailed discussion of evidence relating to all of these categories of action. Examples below will indicate the range of actual practice, particularly in terms of stage business and the matter of address. The extent to which they are typical of practice in general, through the period, will be indicated by summary reference to texts from which individual quotation is impractical.

In *2 The Return from Parnassus*, Kemp is made to criticize bad academic actors who 'never speak in their walk, but at the end of the stage, just as though in walking with a fellow we should never speak but at a stile, a gate, or a ditch, where a man can go no further'. The observation is good evidence that this component of a technique we should regard as 'natural' was common practice. Detailed 'small' business not necessarily relating to the subject matter of lines simultaneously spoken, however, must be considered a category of stage business distinct from action which might – in a more 'formal' mode –

demonstrate an internalized emotion or motivation. Let us examine the former category first.

There is enough evidence in plays from the earlier decades of the period to prove such business no innovation. On an average, in plays with dates of composition falling between 1560 and 1589, there is definite evidence that this convention took place during 4 per cent of the total lines in any given text. Roughly the same percentage applies to plays written between 1590 and 1608, and from 1609 until the closing of the theatres there is evidence that 'small' stage business existed on 6 per cent of the total lines in a play.[4] The convention may be said, therefore, to have been a fairly consistent one throughout the period; the small increase in its frequency during the last three decades under consideration is really not significant. At its most sophisticated, the practice does seem remarkably similar to a modern manner of action. Consider Palamon and Arcite as they talk while involved in the highly detailed business of adjusting each other's armour. One cannot escape the impression of great flexibility and natural pace of delivery:

ARC.   ...Do I pinch you?
PAL.   No.
ARC.   Is't not too heavy?
PAL.   I have worn a lighter,
       But I shall make it serve.
ARC.   I'll buckle it close.
PAL.   By any means.
ARC.   You care not for a grand-guard?
PAL.   No, no! we'll use no horses. I perceive
       You would be fain at that fight.
ARC.   I am indifferent.
PAL.   Faith, so am I. Good cousin, thrust the buckle
       Through far enough.
ARC.   I warrant you.

Shortly after this exchange, they recall battles of earlier days.

ARC.   When I saw you charge first,
       Methought I heard a dreadful clap of thunder
       Break from the troop.
PAL.   But still before that flew
       The lightning of your valour. Stay a little.
       Is not this piece too strait?
             (*The Two Noble Kinsmen* III, vi, 54–62, 82–6)

Not many years earlier, an episode in *Antony and Cleopatra* would have required almost identical business and use of properties, and implies the same ease and natural pacing (apparently as attainable on the stage of the Globe as that of Blackfriars):

ANT.   . . . Come.
CLEO.   Nay, I'll help too.
          What's this for?
ANT.   Ah, let be, let be! Thou art
          The armourer of my heart. False, false; this, this.
CLEO.   Sooth, la, I'll help. Thus it must be.
ANT.   Well, well;
          We shall thrive now. . . .
CLEO.   Is not this buckled well?
ANT.   Rarely, rarely!
                              (IV, iv, 4–11)

Examples from the earlier plays of Shakespeare are of course frequent; Troilus's removal of his armour in his first dialogue with Pandarus would have been accomplished with the same ease with which Hotspur dons his while talking with Lady Percy – and the assumption of various disguises in the comedies provides further parallels.

Evidence is plentiful in plays by Shakespeare's early contemporaries, including those by Marlowe, where stage 'pictures' were perhaps not so static as has often been assumed; Tamburlaine dresses in his captured armour while speaking to Zenocrate (237–47, 250), and in Part Two, Calyphas and his servant play cards while conversing (3740–6) and the hero, in a cumulative description of his victories, uses a map as he speaks (4519–51); and in Faustus's great opening speech, there is no question that the property books – Aristotle, Galen, Justinian, Jerome's Bible, and, finally, those of necromancy – provided opportunity for this category of business on specific lines (33, 40, 55, 66, 77–8) – just as Barabas's money bags and jewels would have been used in the comparable scene of *The Jew of Malta*. The important point about all of these examples is that whether the business simply punctuates and makes vivid the subject matter of the lines, or whether it represents an effort (by playwright or actor) to add realistic details to the stage world of the character (e.g. '*Enter Master Frankford, as it were brushing the crumbs from his clothes with a napkin, as newly risen from supper*' (*A Woman Killed With Kindness*, S.D. at III, ii, 26)), the Elizabethan actors obviously had easy access to an enlargement of a stage personality's realistic world, and that throughout the period that access was absolutely conventional. Indeed, Nashe's complaint about actors not occupied in a crucial action or speech who, too often, 'stroke [their] beards to make action, [and] play with [their] codpiece points',[5] a complaint echoed later by Hamlet, suggests that the bad habits of some actors have remained the same for four centuries.

The second category of stage business – that which to some extent would externalize a psychologically oriented feeling or motivation, actually *demonstrating* to an audience the inner life of a character – is in some ways more interesting than evidence of 'small' business, for it pertains directly to questions of our own staging of the plays. This category of evidence is most revealing of Elizabethan projection of psychology, and is therefore relevant to our own inquiries into such matters as an actor's 'identification' with his stage character. Once again let us begin with a scene representing acting methods late in the period. In *Henry VIII*, a scene with Wolsey and certain nobles, and afterwards the King, provides a complete book of directions for action intended to convey deep emotional turmoil, and indicates precisely a series of gestures which are most suggestive in any consideration of the over-all style of acting. Norfolk, Suffolk, Surrey, and the Lord Chamberlain have been discussing events relative to the King's divorce, when Wolsey and Cromwell enter. Immediately, Norfolk says of the Cardinal, 'Observe, observe, he's moody' (III, ii, 75); nothing has been said, but Norfolk – and the audience – have seen the Cardinal frowning (cf. S.D., III, ii, 203; v, i. 87–8; S.D., v, iii, 113). Wolsey, not observing the others on stage, speaks of the letters Henry has opened, and, dismissing Cromwell, informs the audience of his plans and fears (85–90). The lords who watch have not, of course, 'heard' Wolsey, but Norfolk observes, 'He's discontented' (91). After the others comment, the Cardinal resumes his meditation about Anne Bullen and his fears of Cranmer (94–103). For the third time Norfolk comments on Wolsey's state of mind: 'He is vex'd at something' (103). Here the King enters, reading (as he moves into the acting area) the inventory of Wolsey's possessions, and, not noticing the Cardinal (which suggests that Wolsey has moved to one corner of the stage – probably diagonally opposite whichever door used by Henry for his entrance), asks for him. Norfolk replies:

> My lord, we have
> Stood here observing him. Some strange commotion
> Is in his brain: he bites his lip and starts,
> Stops on a sudden, looks upon the ground,
> Then lays his finger on his temple; straight
> Springs out into fast gait; then stops again,
> Strikes his breast hard; and anon he casts
> His eye against the moon. In most strange postures
> We have seen him set himself.
> (111–19)

Norfolk's catalogue must be accurate, of course; the audience has also seen what the actor did who played Wolsey, and even if Shakespeare is anxious to emphasize the Cardinal's feelings, any added observation in Norfolk's speech would have been built upon the action just ended. Wolsey's business was evidently categorical action for great inner perturbation – 'There is a mutiny in's mind,' Henry says. Biting the lip had long been a standard piece of business (e.g. Catesby, *Richard III*, IV, ii, 27: 'The King is angry; see, he gnaws his lip'; Desdemona, *Othello*, V, ii, 46: 'Alas, why gnaw you so your nether lip?'). In addition we have sudden movement into a fast walk, and sudden stops, quick alternation of looks upward and downward, pressing the finger against the temple, and striking the breast. It would be possible, in fact, following Norfolk's summary, to insert stage-directions for the lines of Wolsey's speech; in any case, the acting style clearly involved more than a few gestures (for a relatively short semi-soliloquy) and apparently eschewed small or over-subtle facial expression. It demanded considerable movement across the stage. It was, to say the least, a 'large' style, and *Henry VIII* is a late play.

At least so far as the evidence suggests, certain emotions did not demand increasingly nuanced stage expression as the years passed. A range of attitudes and gestures very similar to Wolsey's were very likely used by Burbage in early performances of *Othello*. The violence with which Othello's jealousy would have been expressed is unquestionable; it fits too well into an emblematic description – identical to many contemporary analyses of love maladies – to suggest anything less than conventional histrionic treatment. The angry questions Othello puts to Desdemona at the end of III, iv provoke Emilia's question, 'Is not this man jealous?' They have been stock questions, and would have been accompanied by similarly categorical gestures and looks. Generally, Othello's role at this point falls into the type called 'hasty', in the Prologue to a manuscript play, *The Cyprian Conqueror*, requiring 'fuming, and scratching the head, etc.'[6] But there is a more detailed source book for description of the violently jealous hero. After noting that 'your bravest soldiers and most generous spirits are [most readily] enervated with [the passions of Heroical Love] when they surrender to feminine blandishments' (*The Anatomy of Melancholy*, III, 2, 1, 1), Burton goes on to describe the effects of such passions when they become corrupted by jealousy; and it is a very theatrical description:

Besides those strange gestures of staring, frowning, grinning, rolling of eyes, menacing, ghastly looks, broken pace, interrupt, precipitate, half-turns...
[he] will sometimes sigh, weep, sob for anger, swear and belie, slander any man, curse, threaten...and then, eftsoons, impatient as he is, rave, roar, and lay about him like a mad man, thump her sides, drag her about perchance...
his eye is never off hers; he gloats...on her, accurately observing on whom

she looks, who looks at her, what she saith, doth, at dinner, at supper, sitting, walking, at home, abroad...affrighted with every small object; why did she smile, why did she pity him, commend him?...a whore, an arrant whore!

(III, 3, 2)

Desdemona observes her husband's 'fatal' rolling of his eyes (v, ii, 37–8); he weeps, his looks reflect 'a bloody passion', he strikes her, flatters her sarcastically; in short, his action seems to run parallel to Burton's catalogue. It is also very suggestive of the details included in Norfolk's speech about Wolsey. The emotional pressures upon the two men are of course quite different, and yet the evidence in this instance points with some certainty to the fact that the actors who played these characters must have utilized components of physicalization and movement that were all but identical.

Demonstrative business and moves were not always required, of course, to express depth of feeling. Plays from the later years of the period contain many examples of what a modern actor would call business suggestive of 'internalized' emotion, an intensity *felt* by the actor 'in' character. One example must stand for hundreds. At a particularly lovely moment towards the end of *Pericles*, the hero, not yet realizing that his daughter stands before him, pushes Marina from him. He reviews certain phrases she has spoken, and asks her to repeat them. 'I said, my lord, if you did know my parentage, / You would not do me violence,' she replies (v, i. 100–1). 'I do think so,' he says; 'Pray you turn your eyes upon me.' Now Marina has had an aside a few lines previous ('I will desist; / But there is something glows upon my cheek, / And whispers in mine ear "Go not till he speak" ' (95–7)) – and it is possible that the actor was to turn away from Pericles on this; but it is clear in any case that Marina was to speak her next lines still turned from him – which would be the way a modern actress would want to render them.

Plays from the earlier years also reveal a surprising mixture of 'demonstrative' and 'internalized' emotion, as far as may be inferred from stage business. In the old play of *King Leir* (1588–94), a Messenger delivers to Ragan letters from Gonerill; she opens one (1169), and is actually given two lines to cover – in our terms, quite realistically – this detail of business: 'How fares our royal sister? / I did leave her, at my parting, in good health' (1170–71). At this point a stage-direction reads, *She reads the letter, frowns and stamps* (1172), and the Messenger's speech which follows describes her action just as Norfolk's describes Wolsey's:

> See how her colour comes and goes again,
> Now red as scarlet, now as pale as ash:

> See how she knits her brow, and bites her lips,
> And stamps, and makes a dumb shew of disdain,
> Mixed with revenge, and violent extremes.
>
> (1173–7)

The first two lines of this speech are of course 'literary' directions, evoking a reaction no actor, of any period (no matter how skilled in any 'Method'), could effect at will (cf. Brutus' observation to Cassius that an 'angry spot doth glow on Caesar's brow'); the others no doubt tell us exactly what happened. Whatever the relative quality of the writing in each case, the *style* seems hardly more 'primitive' than that documented for Wolsey's action some twenty-three years later.

Moreover, in many texts from quite early in the period under discussion, evidence may be found for internalized emotion – or at least an effort on the playwright's part to achieve it – comparable to many moments in plays written after 1600. A most interesting combination of modes occurs in Marlowe's *Edward II*, whatever its exact date a reasonably early play. Queen Isabel stands silent while her husband's escape and bad fortune are discussed (1831–9, 1841–50), until Sir John of Hainault addresses her, having noticed something about her stance or mood (as rendered by the actor playing her): 'Madam, what resteth, why stand ye in a muse?' (1851). The attitude of a 'muse' (frequently described in the texts as 'a brown study' or 'trance') was very common indeed throughout the period – there are some eighty references to it, in many different dramatic situations, in the plays used for this study. What action it involved is difficult to infer; but at this point in *Edward II* there can be no question that the Queen's silence and her mood, however acted, were meant to convey an *internalized* response. As would be the case in modern production technique, the convention required, apparently, minimal physicalization, or demonstration. Yet earlier in the play, after Isabel's lament on her estrangement from Edward (466–82), various nobles enter, among them Lancaster, who observes, 'Look where the sister of the king of France, / Sits wringing of her hands, and beats her breast' (483–4).

Evidently variations of intensity did not signal categorical forms of stage business, for playwrights frequently intended the actor to reveal in some way that his emotions were too deep not only for words, but for large action indicating those emotions. The 'muse' was a common device for such an effort, but there were others, even in a text as early and as relatively unsophisticated as Pickeryng's *Horestes* (1567). Here Horestes, about to order the execution of his mother, and in conflict of motivation, is directed to '[sigh] hard', although he is given no words to speak; the Vice watches him and observes, 'Jesu God, how still he sits...' (S.D., 891–3; 893). Such deep sighs seem also to have been common practice throughout the period; there are more than sixty examples of them in the plays considered, all of them similar in intention to that 'so piteous and profound', which Ophelia reports that Hamlet 'rais'd', revealing an inner state so intense 'As it did seem to shatter all his bulk'. One cannot escape the impression, in reviewing all of these examples of demonstrated emotion, that Elizabethan practice, while immensely diversified, invariably provided physicalization of some kind, however it might vary in scope, to represent inner feelings – one might almost say, to *describe* them. Pickeryng's effort to deepen our impression of his hero may seem to us shallow and clichéd, but it is really the same in kind as Peele's Edward I, who listens quietly to Eleanor's death-bed confession of her adultery with Edmund – and, *as she speaks*, is directed to turn and [*behold*] *his brother wofully* (2755): a move and an expression that would seem to us 'modern' and full of nuance.

But one must be cautious. Edward's turn and look, Isabel's 'muse', Horestes' sigh, and Marina's aside with its accompanying move all suggest a habit of mirroring reality in fact no more 'internalized' or psychologically oriented in our sense, than were the larger gestures, lip-biting, rapid walks, and breast-thumping of Ragan, Othello, and Wolsey. In the true sense of the word, they were 'representational' artifice; the modern actor would call them 'presentational'. Even the least physicalized of them indicate an acting style which we would consider, if it were unqualified by other components of the art, 'formal' and 'large'. More, this aspect of the over-all style does not seem to have altered as the years passed. In Munday's *John-a-Kent and John-a-Cumber* (c. 1589), certain characters are confused as to the exact location of the invisible Shrimp's voice (1118–24; S.D., 1123–4), and in *Arden of Feversham* (c. 1591) a whole scene must be played as though the characters are moving through fog (1721–98); the stage directions and lines suggest a style neither more nor less 'large' than that used twenty-two or twenty-three years later by the 'charm'd' captives of Prospero, their 'understanding' having been made 'foul and muddy' (*Tempest*, S.D. at v, i, 57; 58 ff.), and their action commensurately demonstrative of their inner state.

The collection of evidence above pertains to acted 'business', and suggests little change of practice over forty or fifty years – years that witnessed a remarkable development in the dramatist's craft. It is important to have a detailed, if summarized, view of stage business, because it is here that one achieves the clearest over-all view of a mixed stylistic practice. But it is in the matter of address that the gradual *change* of style assumed by some critics can be detected. The flexibility with which an actor alters direction of his address implies many other characteristics of his style – for example, a corresponding flexibility of stage movement, individual stance, and blocking of stage 'pictures'. Flexibility of address, however, depends in turn on a more basic element of theatre: the ways in which the texts themselves may or may not require it. The development of acting style during the Elizabethan and Jacobean periods of drama may be said to depend most upon the extraordinary development of the techniques of dialogue by the major playwrights – particularly Shakespeare, Webster, Jonson, Middleton, and Ford. Of secondary importance, though of great interest, is the steadily decreasing emphasis, by these playwrights and others, on the device of soliloquy. Speaking in the most general terms, an examination of the texts dating from 1608 on reveals an increase in the number of 'ensemble' episodes accompanying the decline of soliloquy techniques; and, as has always been the case among professional actors of talent and practicality, crafts of the stage metamorphosed precisely along the lines implicit in the playwrights' dramaturgy. (A comparable phenomenon took place when Stanislavsky transformed the acting styles of the Moscow Art Theatre to answer the immensely complex requirements of Chekhov's new scripts.) When the average number of players on stage in any given episode is only *two* – the average in texts dating earlier than 1585 – the possibilities for flexible alteration of address are of course minimal; similarly, during the earlier period, solo address – whether in an 'apostrophic' or meditative mode, or delivered to the audience – did not require the remarkable nuance of stage practice typical of the later drama. One can locate in the earlier plays long sections of solo speech and dialogue containing many modulations of address, but the consistency with which the texts of later years reveal such modulation is remarkable.

One of the more common forms of such modulation is that alteration which takes place when a character speaks to another who is leaving the acting area (usually covering the exit, and, in fact, sometimes enabling us to know the exact line on which the second actor leaves the individual or group), or sees the entrance of another and comments on it, covering in a similar way the new actor's approach to the acting area. This form of address can be delivered just as easily, of course, by the exiting or entering actor; frequently it would involve address over the shoulder, or coming to a short stop in the exit walk, which would then be resumed after the line or lines. In the earlier period – up to, say, 1580 – this form of delivery covered, when it occurred, on an average, six lines. Usually these lines involved some descriptive comment on the approaching (or departing) character, delivered either to another person already on stage or, in many cases, to the audience. The average number of lines used in such 'anticipatory' or 'covering' address in the period up to 1605–6 is closer to three lines for each occurrence; and – although mathematical exactness is probably not only impossible but subject to varying line readings by each student of the subject – the average seems to drop off still more in plays written between 1606 and the closing of the theatres. The use of the convention itself seems to decrease; in Shakespeare's *Pericles, Cymbeline, The Winter's Tale, The Tempest,* and *Henry VIII,* and in Shakespeare's and Fletcher's *The Two Noble Kinsmen,* the average number of lines used in this category of address is only two – and such address occurs infrequently. In earlier plays, the use of such address was twofold; mainly it served the practical purpose of covering stage-time while a character left or approached the acting area, but occasionally, and more important, it served an expository or narrative purpose. It would lead almost always into solo speech by the actor still on stage, for the joining of episode to episode in most early plays of the period was accomplished purely in terms of explanatory soliloquy. In this sort of speech, action – and thought – would be *described*, and not acted out, or truly 'thought'. But even as the device of the soliloquy became increasingly sophisticated, the convention itself became less and less necessary. If the average of persons on stage, during each episode of a play in the early period, was only two, the average per episode after 1605 is five.[7] Although short asides (averaging, usually, no more than five lines) remain a frequent practice in later years, most of the lines in such scenes require, in one mode or another, flexible alteration of address among the characters present. (This, in turn, would have had an obvious effect on stage movement and positioning.)

Adequate discussion of the techniques of soliloquy would require many pages, and one can only summarize here the development, and subsequent decline, that influenced an over-all acting style. The convention was old even in the early days of Tudor drama, and many critics have observed the range of materials which could be included in such speech. From the early interludes onwards examples of purely introspective or explanatory soliloquies are plentiful; and there are many speeches which one might call 'apostrophic'. Frequently, these modes of address blended. Students of the subject have always wanted to know how often this sort of speech was in fact delivered to the spectators, but the general opinion that such direct address took place very often has never been adequately documented. In the solo speeches of the early 'Vice' characters, the actor would sometimes actually pick out a member of the audience for specific address, referring again and again to 'you' – although equally often this would imply a collective object of his plot descriptions. One suspects that other forms of the soliloquy – a hero's meditations or laments, for example – were also addressed at times to the spectators; but this is harder to prove, especially as dramatic writing gave the characters inner personalities in terms of action instead of purely external description (whether by others or themselves). Nevertheless, there is good evidence of some audience address in introspective speeches from early plays; the writing is unpolished, the machinery creaks, but the manner of the actor is in some cases much clearer. And one may assume that the convention was not entirely dropped with increased subtlety of writing.

In Garter's *Susanna* (*c.* 1568), for example, Joachim comments on the lack of moral government, partly in meditation as he glances about the stage for the judges, but partly in audience address as he prays for blessings upon each spectator as well as for himself (836–51). That part of the speech which is clearly set in direct address is mainly a device to help the actor get off-stage, but even without it, and the explanatory tone in the beginning, one could observe that the sententious tone of the lines rings of explanation to a group of hearers. In an earlier play, *Calisto and Melebea* (*c.* 1527), Calisto prays for Sempronio's good fortune, then says,

> To pass the time now will I walk
> Up and down within mine orchard,
> And to myself go [commune] and talk,
> And pray that fortune to me be not hard,
> Longing to hear whether made or marred;
> My message shall return by my servant Sempronio;
> Thus, farewell my lordis, for a while I will go.

> (306–12)

The tone here is not sententious but personal. The character *presents*, in fact, the subject matter for a soliloquy which the playwright did not wish – or did not know how – to compose. Although the speech is, in its own terms, 'introspective', it rings of explanation, and it may be said that Calisto *announces* what his emotions are, but does not actually express them. They are presented much as Joachim, in *Susanna*, presents *sententiae* upon moral government.

These examples have been chosen arbitrarily, but even though they come from the very early period they indicate roughly certain conventional practices. In many cases, speeches which one might ordinarily categorize as addressed to an 'imaginative rather than actual, mute rather than responsive' auditory,[8] actually contain some evidence that at least part of the lines were oriented toward the audience. Speeches from *Clyomon and Clamydes*, from *Cambises*, *Horestes*, and *Appius and*

Virginia, from plays performed in schools, in the University halls, at court, and upon public stages, suggest direct address in all types of soliloquies – usually with the Vice's common intention of explanation, but more and more often in purely introspective, meditative speech. Indeed there is every reason to assume a certain amount of direct address *whenever* a character was alone on stage, that it frequently took place in the execution of asides, and that there is no evidence for less use of the convention in the great plays of Shakespeare, whenever soliloquy might occur. Indeed, Joachim's observations on the insolence of office require direct address neither more nor less than Hamlet's do; and Poverty's walk about the platform, and his speech to the audience as he moved (*Impatient Poverty* (*c.* 1547), 994–5 ff.), may be the mould not only for all the prodigal sons of the Tudor interludes, hawking their wares as Mater and Pater occupy another part of the stage, but also for such soliloquies as Ferdinand's, as he bears Prospero's logs, while the magician and the princess stand nearby. It is well to remember John Russell Brown's observation that any sort of direct speech in this drama was not addressed to the audience 'as if it were in another world'[9] – but that a sense of reality in these plays moved in both directions across the edge of the platform. Since an actor will usually project speech to a listener as though some sort of response were possible, and even forthcoming, we may perhaps conclude that audience address in the plays of this period placed the spectator in a truly creative relationship with the actor. This relationship existed not only during solo speech on stage, but also would have been reinforced as actors directed asides to the audience during ensemble scenes. Thus the total action of the play would be punctuated at frequent intervals with speech literally including the audience in narrative action or introspective thought.

In the early period of Tudor drama, a conservative estimate indicates that about 8 per cent of each play was addressed either entirely to the audience, or contained speeches beginning with audience address which were then directed back to a stage area. This estimate is based upon a figure of 1,900 lines, on the average, in each play, with some manner of solo speech in which direct address occurred taking place (again on the average) five times in the course of each play, each speech averaging about thirty lines. This set of figures does not change much as one moves into the greater period of the drama, although of course certain texts, considered individually, range far from the norm. Nor is there any evidence, as the years pass, that direct address was associated more or less with solo speech than it had been in the earlier period. What does take place, as I have suggested, is that the frequency of the convention of soliloquy itself diminishes dramatically. When it occurs, even in the late plays of Shakespeare, and the later plays of his contemporaries, it is usually possible to recognize the category of solo speech that is in each case the archetype – almost always recalling a form used in the very early years of the period; but it occurs much less often.

Nor does the less frequent appearance of the device coincide with the availability, to Shakespeare's company or others, of private theatres. Although Shakespeare's art in the composition of soliloquies reached its height during the period 1600–6, when the major tragedies were written, there was already some indication that *certain kinds of action did not require the convention as often*. Except perhaps for Angelo's rather short *tour de force*, we do not remember *Measure for Measure*, *Troilus and Cressida*, or *All's Well That Ends Well* for their soliloquies; in *Troilus and Cressida*, in fact, there are no speeches of great importance which really qualify to be so called. In *Othello*, Shakespeare maintained and polished the oldest of the old categories of solo speech – that of the Vice – in distributing Iago's brilliant soliloquies of explanation and anticipation (many of them couched quite explicitly in a form of direct address; e.g. 'And what's he, then, that says I play the villain...?'), but the hero really has only one speech which may be called a soliloquy (III, iii, 262–81). There may be much audience address in *King Lear* which takes the form of asides or short speeches that bridge episodes of action, and a large part of I, ii is given over to Edmund's solo speeches, one apostrophic (1–22) and one a prose speech of character 'explanation' (111–27). Considering the text as a whole, however, there is little use of the device. *Macbeth* and *Hamlet* are different matters, of course, for the action of the play moves in direct proportion to the development (or disintegration) of the hero's mind. In both plays, about 10 per cent of stage time is consumed by the solo lines of each hero. In *Antony and Cleopatra*, the way in which the device is used in the last plays of Shakespeare, and in many of his contemporaries writing after 1610, begins to take shape. The play has only one big set-piece – Enobarbus' lament on his desertion – but such meditative moments as Antony's 'I must from this enchanting queen break off' pass quickly into another sort of action; this, for example, is embedded in a nine-line speech on the death of Fulvia – subject matter which, in an earlier play, might have suggested to the playwright a full-blown soliloquy. An examination of *Pericles*, *Cymbeline*, *The Winter's Tale*, *The Tempest*, *Henry VIII*, and *The Two Noble Kinsmen* reveals on the whole a further diminishing of emphasis upon soliloquy. Counting all speeches spoken by a character alone on stage – including Prologues, Epilogues, and Gower's choruses – and by characters in asides longer than five lines each, there are in *Pericles* 389 lines of solo speech, 401 in *Cymbeline*, 146 in *The Winter's Tale*, 87 in *The Tempest*, 69 in *Henry VIII*, and – a wholesome warning against quick judgements! – 210 in *The Two Noble Kinsmen*. For what the observation is worth, there are only 14 lines of solo speech, aside from Gower's, in the last three acts of *Pericles* (the acts generally agreed to be Shakespeare's); the relatively few lines of solo speech in *Henry VIII* occur as often in the so-called 'Shakespearian' scenes as in the 'Fletcherian'. The question of authorship in *The Two Noble Kinsmen* is too complicated to make many distinctions; but whichever playwright is responsible for the mad scenes of the Gaoler's daughter is responsible for the sudden alteration in the pattern.

One must not underestimate the theatrical effect of this gradual change in the later plays of the period. It occurs, in plays by Shakespeare's contemporaries, in roughly the same proportion as in the last romances, and it is an alteration in the very texture of stage artifice, in the means used by dramatists to advance action. The actual response of the spectators, taken in sum, would be altered commensurately, for a special habit of response was rendered less and less central to the actor's projection of plays with fewer soliloquies, each of them, therefore, containing less direct address – and *more* modulation within scenes of ensemble and dialogue. In the last plays of Shakespeare, there remain of course several soliloquies, some of them truly in the old style (e.g. Posthumus', on women, *Cymbeline* II, v, 1–35), and many half-soliloquies, usually spoken with reference to others actually on stage (e.g. Leontes' in the second episode of *The Winter's Tale*). But considered as a whole one's impression of these plays as theatrical pieces has a distinctly new emphasis.

This emphasis corresponds to the critical opinion, widely held, that the last Shakespearian plays have 'lost' a focus and concentration typical of the major tragedies, and that this concentration is replaced by other dramaturgical factors. At least part of the focus in the major tragedies was achieved, speaking for a moment purely in stage terms, through the skilful use of soliloquy. This device aided in gradual concentration inward upon the mind of the hero, always shown to strive painfully towards understanding, always true to the agony of a vision limited by mortality. The hero's *self*-exposition at regular points in the course of the play, especially true of Hamlet and Macbeth, actually effects one element of action, and simultaneously the acting methods required to embody it. In later plays – and not only those by Shakespeare – the dramaturgy concerns itself with a fabric of action at once shallower and more complex: shallower in point of 'character', since the sequence of cause and event is now more important than internalized motivation; and more complex in plot-line, which must spread more widely, with greater speed, involving as it does so many more characters. And of these characters it is often more important to know where they are geographically, and where they are about to go, than to know at length what they are thinking. Shakespeare's development – beginning perhaps most noticeably with *King Lear* and *Antony and Cleopatra* – had been towards a more generalized vision, a fabric in which the total effect would be more important than the probing in depth of an individual mind. He began to practise, then, as to a lesser extent did many of his contemporaries, ways to compress the rhythms of human speech so that much of the elongation implicit in the device of soliloquy was now not only unnecessary, but would have changed his new characters into the sort of personalities destructive to the dramaturgy of romance.

Leontes' soliloquy (*The Winter's Tale* I, ii, 109–46) is the best example of the developed form late in the period. Really a half-soliloquy, it is spoken with other actors on stage – and in part to one of them, the boy, Mamillius. In its physicalization it would perhaps not have varied greatly from many others, earlier in the period; but vocally and in terms of the actor's stance, corresponding to extraordinary requirements of modulated address, it is entirely different. In its first part, it requires modulation from attention to the scene across the stage area to a stance of meditation, then to the child standing nearby. As the speech progresses, its tempo and stress change suddenly, and the rhythm and diction mirror the chaos of Leontes' mind, much as the tortured syntax, paralleling the disjointed sequence of thought, becomes an implicit stage direction for Hamlet, in his first soliloquy. But the process in the *Hamlet* soliloquy is one of self-interruption, the subject matter moving from the specific to the general and back again. To render it adequately required – as is true today – an ability to modulate tone and tempo within the individual line; nevertheless there is a regularity about it that is missing from Leontes' speech. Here there is a swifter alteration of specific address, with interruption representative not simply of a change of subject, but of *degree* in the character's very ability to articulate it. When this articulation is meant to be more difficult, the diction itself becomes more abstract; and to render this theatrically, implying the concentration of idea in the character's mind, must have required – as, again, it does today – an entirely new approach on the part of the actor.

It will be seen, in summary, that certain aspects of Elizabethan acting style remained more or less the same throughout the decades of greatest production. Always there had been conventional ways to enlarge the detailed reality of a stage personality's physical world, by means of 'small' stage business carried forward on lines; and always there seem to have been recognizably categorical practices for 'demonstrating' various levels of inward emotional states – some of them, in our terms, 'large', and some amazingly modern in their minimal physical manifestations. An over-all impression, however, conveys a sense of style we should probably call 'formalized'. On the other hand, the details of address – absolutely organic to details of play-*writing* – must have metamorphosed very greatly between, say, 1580 and 1595; and as dramaturgical fashions and preferences changed after that year, such details continued to alter accordingly. The skills of the players had to keep up with the requirements of their scripts, and the phenomenon of their training – about which we know next to nothing – must have been truly extraordinary. The actor chosen to play Cambises, for example, must have been an excellent artist, in terms of the repertory companies then at work; but one wonders if the young Marlowe would have attempted *Tamburlaine* had there been no Alleyn to render the totally new requirements of that script! But the development of which I have spoken may be seen, perhaps, most clearly if one wonders how actors trained as Alleyn may have been could approach the new vocal techniques implicit in such roles as Ferdinand, in *The Duchess of Malfi*, or Prospero. We have said little about characters in plays written for the boys' companies; but it is fascinating that the evidence collected for this study comes as frequently, in the later years of the period, from the children's texts as from the public repertory – and hardly ever does it present new or categorically different documentation of acting style. The devices of theatrical style inevitably change from year to year, but stage abilities and physical development of adolescent and pre-adolescent boys do not – and this leads one to assume, if only as a general conclusion, that the remarkable nuance of address (for example) that is implicit in the late plays of Shakespeare or Fletcher, and which requires for adequate presentation now not only an actor of talent but a man of experience and even wisdom, was beyond the children's abilities: *if* we also assume that such nuance would have been rendered as we think it should be today. The truth of the matter is that the very tonality, pace, and general characterization of a children's production in the Jacobean period can never be grasped through any evidence available to us, and is one aspect of Renaissance acting in England lost in the flux of time.

Of the actors themselves – Greene's 'mechanics' – it must be said that they must have been unlike most actors at work today. If in nothing else, they were remarkable for the spectrum of their perceptions and physical abilities, for even if they failed frequently (as they must have done) their successes were responsible for the survival of the theatre's most valuable possessions. Their memories must have been

phenomenal and their stamina – physically and vocally – unlike anything required of repertory actors, anywhere, today. Whatever the
categorical devices may have been that helped them learn the action
that suited their roles, they obviously achieved – to the satisfaction of
the most demanding Elizabethan spectators – a truth to life that graced
their scripts just as greatly as the achievement of those scripts ennobled
and dignified them.

4

SHAKESPEARE'S READING

G. K. HUNTER

An inquiry into 'Shakespeare's reading' is difficult to confine within manageable bounds unless, of course, it is stopped short of any interpretation and confined to book titles, quotations, and a list of the stories that Shakespeare is presumed to have used. And even in such a truncated form the inquiry is bedevilled by the problem of what constitutes evidence. The game of literary parallels is one that can be played with dashing but irrelevant freedom. As will be suggested later, the wisdom of the Elizabethans was nearly all traditional wisdom; the point in the tradition that the modern critic selects as a 'source' is often arbitrary and tendentious. Such publications as M. P. Tilley's *Dictionary of the Proverbs in England in the Sixteenth and Seventeenth Centuries* (1950) may help to curb the wilder excesses of the past; but the ambition to discover new things must continue to operate, and no doubt will continue to metamorphose the similar into the identical.

On the other side of the subject lies the opposite danger: of finding oneself claiming to describe Shakespeare's mind – a task that might seem best left to clairvoyants. And yet the reading habits of any man are an important aspect of his mental habits. Shakespeare's mind was certainly no mere waiting-room in which quotations marked time between one book and another. The evidences of his reading are fragmentary and discontinuous; it is obvious that he absorbed and modified whatever he read. It may be dangerously facile to apply straight to Shakespeare the evidence about Coleridge's creative reading that Professor Livingston Lowes assembled in *The Road to Xanadu* – for Shakespeare was not a nineteenth-century poet but an Elizabethan playwright – but Lowes's image of the hooks and eyes of Coleridge's imagination may provide the best picture of Shakespeare's mental processes that is available to us. And that such a process was involved somewhere in Shakespeare's creative mind seems to be proved by the recurrent associative patterns discussed by Walter Whiter and by E. A. Armstrong.

ELIZABETHAN READING HABITS

The Coleridgean image of Shakespeare's reading has the disadvantage that it seems to isolate Shakespeare from many of his contemporaries. There may be some advantage therefore in taking a brief preliminary glance at Elizabethan reading habits in general, to suggest the background of expectations about reading against which Shakespeare lived his professional life.

Reading was one of the skills to which the Humanists, like other educators, devoted a great deal of energy. They were, of course, largely concerned with the new materials for reading – Greco-Roman literature – but the question 'How should we read these books?' was an integral one which had to be faced and answered. And it was answered in a surprisingly medieval way. The medieval imitation of the classics, writes Karl Burdach (quoted by Roberto Weiss), 'proceeds according to the method of the glossator, that is to say it takes details, choice and beautiful sentences, with a collector's precision; it is a matter of indifference to the collector where they came from'. In the Elizabethan period the names of the classical authors had become important, but it was a long time before the spirit of the work from which quotations came controlled the use of the quotations.

The obvious and standard method of using one's reading to collect information and details of rhetorical structure (and in consequence, the educators hoped, a classical style of life) was by way of a commonplace book. This was a collection of wise sayings, similes and other materials, under moral headings: 'Abstinence', 'Adversity', 'Affection', 'Ambition' etc. And here, as in so many other fields, it seems as if the method of the schools dominated the whole cultural scene. We find Sir Philip Sidney urging his brother Robert to keep up his collections:

And so as in a table, be it a witty word, of which Tacitus is full, sentences, as of which Livy, or of similitudes, whereof Plutarch, straight to lay it up in the right place of his storehouse.

As late as 1720 Swift feels it necessary to dissuade a 'young gentleman lately entered into holy orders' from relying on his commonplace book, lest he produce 'a manifest incoherent piece of patchwork'. This points to the obvious danger. Much Elizabethan writing is, in fact, related to reading as patchwork is to rags; but that patchworks or (less pejoratively) mosaics need not be manifestly incoherent may be suggested by Jonson's *Sejanus* and Webster's *The Duchess of Malfi* – works largely made up of quotations.

The copiousness of the Elizabethan style was often capable of absorbing within an exuberant unity the multitude of quotations it contained. The danger that Swift points to seemed unimportant. Indeed there was a constant demand for further aids to *copia*. A steady stream of epitomes and digests, anthologies, nosegays, gardens of wisdom and wellsprings of witty conceits flowed from the press. These, already digested and broken down under topics, saved one the labour of making one's own commonplace book. Under certain circumstances they might save altogether the labour of consecutive reading.

SHAKESPEARE AND THE CLASSICS

The extensive use of books of quotations has an obvious bearing on the long-debated question of Shakespeare's classical attainments. This was an age which loved the panache of classical display more than the understanding of authors. Sir Jack Daw in Jonson's *Epicoene* who 'pretends only to learning, buys titles, and nothing else of books in him' is only an extreme case of the foppery that pressed on 'polite learning', and continued to press on it through the eighteenth century. Dr Alice Walker's detailed study of the reading of Thomas Lodge makes the point that in Lodge's work 'full value is given to anything that bore the hall-mark of Greece or Rome, while greater debts to more modern writers are passed by unacknowledged'. Many of Lodge's references turn out to have medieval sources – the same is true of Thomas Dekker – but this is revealed to the researcher not to the reader.

Shakespeare's 'classicism' cannot be wholly described in these terms. Dr Farmer, anxious to disprove Shakespeare's direct acquaintance with the classics, quoted Bishop Hurd to the effect that

they who are in such astonishment at the learning of Shakespeare forget that the Pagan imagery was familiar to all the poets of his time; and that abundance of this sort of learning was to be picked up from almost every book that he could take into his hands.

This is unsatisfactory; it does not allow for the extent to which Shakespeare's allusions are submerged in the context which they serve. Shakespeare was neither a flamboyant name-dropper nor a scholar in any modern sense; but he was not either the simple representative of 'Nature' that seventeenth and eighteenth century criticism made of him (in antithesis to Jonson). His work is erected on a consciousness of literary conventions and literary methods, derived from the study of the classics in Grammar School. Classical allusion was not simply a decoration to his style, but an integral part (however derived) of a whole mode of writing. Moreover it is reasonably certain that his 'small latin' included an ability to get sense out of works not translated, and a continuing memory of some texts that he read in Latin. This ability does not seem to have deserted him at any point in his career, for as late as *The Tempest* (v. i. 33 ff.) he can augment Golding's translation of Ovid by reference to the original (or by memory of it).

But the onset of Neo-classicism made it increasingly difficult to see Shakespeare's Renaissance skills as connected with the 'real' classics. As early as 1640 Leonard Digges – the stepson of the executor of Shakespeare's will – made it his peculiar glory that

> Nature only helped him, for look through
> This whole book thou shalt find he doth not borrow
> One phrase from Greeks, nor Latins imitate,
> Nor once from vulgar languages translate.

On the most literal level this seems not to be true. Moreover I suspect that in the period when Shakespeare started writing it would not have seemed possible as praise. Francis Meres, writing in 1598, seems closer to the actual relationship between Shakespeare and the classics:

As the soul of Euphorbus was thought to live in Pythagoras, so the sweet witty soul of Ovid lives in mellifluous and honey-tongued Shakespeare.

In this view of the matter the classical author is still an influence and an authority; but his power is derived from his capacity to release Shakespeare's own faculties. Renaissance schoolmasters insisted that the end of imitation was to learn to make something of one's own; and Shakespeare's classicism seems best regarded in these terms of creative affinity. The explicit presence of Ovid is most noticeable in Shakespeare's early work; but the Ovidian characteristics – the facility and copiousness of mellifluous rhetoric and of verbal wit – remain Shakespearian throughout his career.

A COMMUNAL CREATIVENESS

These methods of acquiring knowledge did not cease to seem appropriate when the reading moved away from classical to modern texts – or modern experiences; we remember how Hamlet calls out for his table-book when he learns from the ghost that 'one may smile, and smile, and be a villain'. The authors of the period shared a common school-experience and a common style of learning. Even more important, they shared a common world of creative methods. The acquisitiveness they had learned in relation to Cicero or Virgil, and the common stock of adages, similes, apophthegms, jests, situations they all acquired at second-hand – these led to a communal creativeness in which copying from one another or censuring the inventions of another were part of the artist's life. And nowhere does this community of creativeness seem more important than in the drama. To most of them the drama seemed (and was) of ephemeral worth. In many cases several dramatists worked together, often under great pressure of time. It was a frankly commercial area of writing, designed for quick effects and quick profits. Sequels and continuations abounded; formulae that worked well were liable to be worked to death. Moreover several of the most successful dramatists were also actors; the experience of acting in other men's plays was obviously one way of absorbing their techniques. We should not forget this mode of absorption when we think about Shakespeare's 'reading'. Undoubtedly he learned more about plays by living among players and playwrights than he did from any other source. Nor should we forget the amount that Shakespeare copied from himself. The relationship of *Twelfth Night* to *The Comedy of Errors* and to *The Two Gentlemen of Verona* is a good example, which has been skilfully explored by L. G. Salingar and by Harold Jenkins.

This community of creative interests, this absence of search either for originality of material or fidelity to individual experience – this was a European rather than an English phenomenon. And it was not only jests and adages that swelled the teeming folio collections of the period. Stories attracted the collector no less, and 'good' stories appear throughout Europe in one collection after another. Take the slander story which forms the basis of the Hero/Claudio plot in *Much Ado About Nothing*. This appears in two of the great poetic collections of stories – Ariosto's *Orlando Furioso* and Spenser's *Faerie Queene*. It also appears in prose in Bandello's *Novelle* (1554), in Belleforest's *Histoires Tragiques* (1574) – translated from Bandello – in Whetstone's *Rocke of Regard* (1576), in Peter Beverley's poem *Ariodanto and Jenevra* (1566). Presumably it appeared also in a lost play, *Ariodante and Genevra*, acted at court in 1583. Another lost play, acted in 1575, may have been based on Bandello's version. In addition there are various Italian plays on the same subject. The source-hunter is faced by an embarrassing wealth of potential sources, and only minutiae (often untrustworthy) can suggest preferences. Sometimes indeed the author seems to have been well aware of the variety of tellings to which the tale was liable and to have used the dialectic that is thus set up as part of the imaginative world of the play. Shakespeare's *Troilus and Cressida*, for example, may be seen as the product of a collision between the medieval versions of the Troy story (Chaucer, Lydgate, Caxton all seem to have contributed) and Renaissance handlings of the same material, such as Chapman's Homer, Robert Greene's *Euphues his Censure to Philautus* together with (perhaps) the thirteenth book of Ovid's *Metamorphoses*. It is worth noting that Shakespeare seems to have been more assiduous in collecting variant sources than were his fellows. Kenneth Muir remarks: 'Shakespeare, as a general rule, took more pains than his contemporaries in the collection of source material.'

SHAKESPEARE'S HISTORY

One of the recurrent problems for the modern critic dealing with Elizabethan writings is to define what 'originality' can mean inside the framework of strictly traditional ways of creating literature. Shakespeare's use of the best-known books of the period, the Bible (in both the Bishops' and the Geneva versions) and the official Homilies (appointed to be read regularly in all churches) gives a good example of the way his mind seems to have held a great reservoir of stories and phrases and ideas, always available and yet never determining his thinking. His handling of multiple sources and the freedom this gives him for a creative use of source material should also be noted. Another example of his originality, more easily understandable in modern terms, can be seen in the divergence from traditional play-material he seems to have made when he turned (very early) from the classics he read at school to the chronicles of his own country. This strongly suggests a man following his own bent rather than his schoolmaster.

So long as it was supposed that Shakespeare had begun his career with plays that were made out of other men's imaginings it could not be supposed that he was a serious and *original* reader of the chronicles. But when *The Contention betwixt the two famous houses of York and Lancaster* (1594) and *The True Tragedy of Richard Duke of York* (1595) were shown not to be the sources of Shakespeare's *Henry VI* plays but derivatives from them, the way was open for F. P. Wilson's hypothesis: 'for all we know there were no popular plays on English history before the Armada and Shakespeare may have been the first to write one'. This has important implications for a review of Shakespeare's reading; it means that Shakespeare may have been the first man to make serious use of the chronicles, as he is the only dramatist to make sustained use of them.

When Shakespeare picked up the 1587 edition of Holinshed's chronicles he made himself heir to continuous and cumulative labour of more than seventy years. It is not without significance that this was in the main citizen labour. That the knowledge of the past is a key to the present and that the observation of great events teaches immediate lessons – these were attitudes easily assimilated by a mass audience, and there is no reason to suppose that Shakespeare did not share them. His work in English history should be seen as the crown of that bourgeois effort that runs through Fabyan, Hall, Stowe and Holinshed.

What Shakespeare did not find in the chronicles but had to draw out of his creative imagination was unity of theme and structure in individual plays, a power of balancing cause against cause and individual against individual. T. W. Baldwin has argued at great length that Shakespeare's debt to his schooldays was not only a knowledge of authors but also a knowledge of rhetorical and constructive methods, based on a study of the *Ars Poetica* and Terence and of their commentators. The skill already in Shakespeare's possession at the time of writing the first four history plays seems to bear this out.

The process of writing nine history plays did not leave Shakespeare's reading of history entirely unaffected. As he moves back in time from the chaos of the Wars of the Roses into the more ordered period that set up the conflict, he seems to become more concerned with the private lives of the public figures, with personal entanglements and alternative systems of value. But an exploration of the tension between integrity and power could not be taken very far in the terms provided by Hall and Holinshed; Shakespeare's interests drive him, almost inevitably, from the history that the chroniclers purvey (what happened when) to the history that is told by 'that grave learned philosopher and historiographer, Plutarch of Chaeronea' (as Sir Thomas North calls him). Plutarch describes his own intent as:

not to write histories, but only lives. For the noblest deeds do not always show men's virtues and vices; but oftentimes a light occasion, a word or some sport, makes men's natural dispositions appear more plain than the famous battles...

(*Life of Antonius*)

Plutarch provides Shakespeare with a dramatic framework that seems to fit his purpose more completely than anything else he ever used. The plays he bases on Plutarch – *Julius Caesar*, *Coriolanus*, *Antony and Cleopatra* – are more continuously faithful to their source than any other plays in Shakespeare.

OTHER SOURCE MATERIALS

As early as 1582 Stephen Gosson, playwright turned stage-scourge, characterized the favourite source materials of the contemporary theatre:

I may boldly say it because I have seen it that the *Palace of Pleasure*, the *Golden Ass*, the *Ethiopian History*, *Amadis of France*, the *Round Table*, bawdy comedies in Latin, French, Italian and Spanish have been thoroughly ransacked to furnish the playhouses in London.

(*Plays Confuted in Five Actions*)

By the time Shakespeare was an established dramatist the list had been modified a little, but not really changed. Medieval Romance (*Amadis de Gaule*) and Greek Romance (the *Aethiopica*) had begotten hybrid forms of romantic narrative, and it is from these (Greene's *Pandosto*, Lodge's *Rosalynde*, Montemayor's *Diana*, Sidney's *Arcadia*) that Shakespeare derives his plots. Shakespeare certainly knew the *Aethiopica*; and he turns to another classical romance for the story of *Pericles*; but he shows no interest in medieval Romance though it is like enough that he knew *Guy of Warwick* and the *Amadis de Gaule* (from which he may have taken the names of Florizel and Perdita). William Painter's *Palace of Pleasure* remained a favourite source throughout the period; but the novelle reached Shakespeare in a range wider than Painter's selection; it seems probable that he drew on Italian texts of *Il Pecorone* (for *The Merchant of Venice*), of Giraldi Cinthio's *Hecatommithi* (for *Othello*), and of Boccaccio (for the wager plot in *Cymbeline*). He may, of course, have turned to French translations of the Italian; the French puns in *Love's Labour's Lost* suggest a fair facility in that language.

The third element in Gosson's list – 'bawdy comedies' – also lasted into Shakespeare's day as an important class of source material, but again in a modified form. By the last decade of the century the comic form of erotic intrigue, to which I take it Gosson is referring, had been largely naturalized, in novelle as well as in plays. Shakespeare had no need to read Ariosto's *Suppositi* when he could find the Bianca plot of *The Taming of the Shrew* already englished in Gascoigne's *Supposes*. None the less John Manningham's famous comment on *Twelfth Night* indicates that as late as 1602 there remained in educated circles in England a lively awareness of European comedy:

At our feast we had a play called *Twelfth Night or What You Will*, much like *The Comedy of Errors* or *Menechmi* in Plautus, but most like and near to that in Italian called *Inganni*.

The plot of *Gl' Ingannati* (1531), to which Manningham is probably referring, could have been known to Shakespeare through the French *Les Abusez* (1543), or the Latin *Laelia* which was performed in Cambridge in 1547 and again in 1595. Alternatively it might have reached him in Bandello's novella version, or in Belleforest's translation of Bandello, or in Barnaby Rich's story in *Riche's Farewell to Military Profession* (1581), probably based on Belleforest.

The status of 'old plays' is one that has much vexed the problem of Shakespeare's sources. As noted above it was at one time supposed that Shakespeare had begun his career as a botcher of other men's plays. This not only seemed to fit the textual evidence (as interpreted at that point) but even more compellingly it tallied with the image of a Shakespeare who relied on nature rather than art. The desire to protect our national bard from too much learning, to avoid the Casaubon-like image of a studious collator of texts, a collector of evidences, a burrower among manuscripts, has often led the signs of these activities in the extant plays to be laid at the door of an 'old play'. The 'old playwright' can then take up the mask of Casaubon, and Shakespeare can revert to the ideal outlined in 'Dr Furnivall's golden words':

I see a square-built yet lithe and active fellow, with ruddy cheeks, hazel eyes and auburn hair, as full of life as an egg is full of meat, impulsive, inquiring, sympathetic; up to any fun and daring; into scrapes and out of them with a laugh; making love to all the girls; a favourite wherever he goes – even with the prigs and fools he mocks, etc.

(Introduction to the 'Leopold' Shakespeare)

Dr Dover Wilson has discovered evidence, he believes, that *Richard II* contains information derived from Hall's chronicle, Holinshed, Samuel Daniel's *Civil Wars*, Berners' translation of Froissart, the manuscript play of *Woodstock*, and two other historical manuscripts in French. He is unwilling to believe that Shakespeare read all these, and so he saddles another with the task:

Was Shakespeare a profound historical scholar or merely the reviser of such a scholar's play?...He may have dipped into the opening paragraphs of Hall or turned up Holinshed here and there...His unknown predecessor [sc. the 'old playwright'], soaked in the history of England, had read the chronicles for him and had digested what they had to say upon the downfall of Richard II into a play-book...are we not justified in supposing, from everything we know about him, that Shakespeare followed the line of least resistance, whenever he could?

'Old plays' have a further attraction for the modern critic of Shakespeare: they help to explain the 'carelessness' of much of Shakespeare's dramaturgy (when measured by Ibsenite standards) and so exempt Shakespeare from full responsibility for plays that the critic can only approve in part. *Hamlet* is the classic instance of this. It is known from Nashe's preface to Greene's *Menaphon* (1589) that a Hamlet play existed at that point; but the extant *Hamlet* cannot have been written before 1600. (The ghost of the *Ur-Hamlet* haunts our sense of the play; it is difficult to deal honestly with the actual body of the text when this invisible double is so available for blame.

The cases of *King Lear* and *Measure for Measure* are less dangerous to discuss, for the old plays have survived, and we can see what Shakespeare has made of them. *The True Chronicle History of King Leir and his three Daughters* was certainly known to Shakespeare; but it provided no more than a general outline of one possible route through the story. It contains no Fool, no madness, no Poor Tom (who is derived, of course, like the rest of the Gloucester plot, from Sidney's *Arcadia*), no storm, no banishment or disguise for Kent. Cordelia wins the battle at the end; the wicked dukes and the wicked daughters run away; Lear and Cordelia are restored to power and happiness. *King Lear* is nearest to the old play in the opening scene, but even here Shakespeare abandons the credible motivations of the source and gives a quite different quality to the action. It is as if Shakespeare had read or remembered the old play in the context of the other versions of the Lear story – in Holinshed, in *The Mirror for Magistrates*, in Spenser, perhaps even in the context of the recent scandal of Brian Annesley and his three daughters (the youngest called Cordell). But most of all he seems to have seen all these in terms of a vision of what they could come to mean, and so to have combined and remembered (drawing in improbable 'sources' like Samuel Harsnet's *Declaration of Egregious Popish Impostures* (1603)) and made what he willed out of what he found.

Whetstone's *Promos and Cassandra*, the 'old play' behind *Measure for Measure* is again placed by Shakespeare in the context of the many other versions of the story available to him. He changed fundamental aspects of the plot, making Isabella a novice and sparing her any defilement in the bed of Angelo. To this end he invented the figure and the stratagem of Mariana. Not only so, but by repeating the motif of the substituted victim not only for Claudio but also for Barnardine he gives it a thematic importance it does not have in any of the sources. The pretended departure of the Duke, and his return to observe the vices he suspects, is also new. Shakespeare may have got the idea from Middleton's *The Phoenix* or Marston's *The Fawn*; but he chose to apply it to this story, and he augmented the effect by making the disguise that of a friar and confessor, largely because of a leading idea which controlled the selection and connection of all the elements involved. The interrelation of mercy and justice is something which can be seen to lie latent and half-buried in the turgid rhetoric of *Promos and Cassandra*. It was no doubt this that attracted Shakespeare to the story. But in working out a structure which would release the dramatic potential of this theme, in its political, personal and theological aspects, he was obliged to recast entirely the relationship of the parts. The 'old play' is like the grain in the wood which may suggest to the carver the contours his chisel will follow, but whose 'meaning' is his invention and entirely at his discretion.

SHAKESPEARE'S CONTEMPORARY READING

It is one thing to note that Shakespeare was well read in contemporary English writing – in the works of Lyly and Marlowe and Greene, and Daniel and Chapman and Sidney; most of these were colleagues whose innovations were tied into his professional life as his innovations were tied into theirs; but the question whether or not Shakespeare 'kept up' with contemporary intellectual life in the larger sense raises quite different issues. This was, of course, a European culture, though by Shakespeare's time most of the basic books were available in English. Once again the question of actual reading is difficult to prove, and seems less important than a general acquaintance with the kind of material involved. If Shakespeare is not to be seen as a learned man, reading many books, remembering what they contain, being led from one reference to another, comparing what different authors say about similar problems, synthesizing their approaches, we must suppose he reached the same point by a different and less probable route – by living inside the intellectual problems of his own age and working out possible attitudes to them in splendid isolation (or in talk with any real intellectuals he happened to know). Certainly (and this is what matters) his dramatic conflicts reflect intellectual concerns that other men in his period focussed upon through books. The plays in the period of *Hamlet*, *Julius Caesar* and *Troilus and Cressida* show men having to make their heroism out of the accidents and insufficiencies of real experience, precisely in the manner of Montaigne:

To whom are Caesar and Alexander beholding for that infinite greatness of their renown, but to fortune?...A man is not always upon the top of the breach, nor in the front of an army, in the sight of his general, as upon a stage. A man may be surprised between a hedge and a ditch...

(II, xvi, 'Of Glory')

Does this mean that Shakespeare had read Montaigne? The germ of much of it is in Plutarch, and we know that Shakespeare had been reading Plutarch. Did Shakespeare, reading Plutarch as Montaigne read Plutarch, and responding to Plutarch's view of heroism as Montaigne responded to it, push Plutarch's view in precisely the direction that Montaigne had already followed? It is quite possible; and we cannot prove it true or untrue. The problem of the Ghost in *Hamlet*, as Dover Wilson has unravelled it, implies awareness of a Renaissance controversy about the status of ghosts. Which of the controversialists had Shakespeare read (if any)? We do not know. It is fairly clear that Edmund's soliloquy on bastardy comes from Ortensio Landi's 'paradox in the defence of bastardy'; but what understanding of libertine thought drove Shakespeare to fasten on 'besides it seemeth as a certainty that nature hath some peculiar respect of bastards' as the key to a coherent libertine philosophy? Had he been reading Montaigne or Machiavelli or Lipsius or Bodin? We do not know.

It seems inevitable, however, that the modern critic should act as if Shakespeare knew these authors, drawing on them to expand the meaning of his intellectual positions and academic conflicts. Their eloquence helps to involve the modern reader in what Shakespeare did not bother to say completely; but there is a corresponding danger that we may over-intellectualize both the plays and the author, implying that the plays were written to exemplify the intellectual positions they contain, or that Shakespeare read up this material to give himself ideas. It seems more proper to suppose that Shakespeare read Montaigne and others because they dealt with matters that already fascinated him, because he took an active part in the intellectual life of his time, seeking challenge or confirmation. Who would read through Harsnet's *Declaration of Egregious Popish Impostures* just to give a few devils names like Flibbertigibbet or Hoppididance? We must suppose, I think, that Shakespeare read widely, perhaps desultorily, but with a keen exploratory interest in the intellectual world in which he moved and to which he contributed.

5

SHAKESPEARE AND THE
ENGLISH LANGUAGE

RANDOLPH QUIRK

In this chapter we shall be concerned less with the facts of language than with attempting to establish the kind of language study that is most significant for students of Shakespeare. The title seeks to dissociate itself on the one hand from the 'language of Shakespeare's time' (which might concern contemporary archives of a remote area having no necessary connection with Shakespeare), and equally on the other hand from the 'language of Shakespeare' (which too often seems to imply that the poet is a sort of linguistic island). It should be superfluous to point out that the language of Shakespeare is an amalgam of the language that Shakespeare found around him – together with what he made of it. And these need to be painstakingly separated for the intelligent appraisal of Shakespeare to an extent that is quite unnecessary for the intelligent appraisal of Yeats or Eliot or Pinter. In other words, over and above the dense complexities that must have been difficult for the Elizabethans too, there are for us in reading Shakespeare difficulties that did not exist in Shakespeare's own time. These are paradoxically aggravated by our very familiarity with the plays: as witness our 'institutionalizing' some expressions in a usage as foreign to Shakespeare as Spenser's *derring do(e)* was to Chaucer. When Iago pretends to relieve Othello's feelings with the assurance that Cassio had spoken his passionate words to Desdemona only in his sleep, Othello says 'But this denoted a foregone conclusion' (III, iii, 432) and however carefully we have studied Elizabethan English, it is very hard for us to remember in the theatre that this does not mean what we have since taken the phrase *foregone conclusion* to mean. And Iago goes on, ' 'Tis a shrewd doubt, though it be but a dream,' using *shrewd* in the sense 'grave, serious' which is now archaic. The extent to which we love Shakespeare (as we love the Authorized Version) for the familiar but exalted language is a measure of our inability to respond to Shakespeare as his contemporaries did. We miss the chance of sharing an Elizabethan audience's savouring of old and new, slang and formal, pompous or fashionable, hackneyed or daring: the chance therefore of achieving the shock of pleasure comparable with what is possible for us in hearing, say, *Under Milk Wood*. But not only that: we are actually in danger of not grasping what is said. Let us remember, for example, that in the very frequent wordplay, it is often the case that one of the meanings is dead and hence, for us, no word-play at all: Leontes' words to his little son (*The Winter's Tale* I, ii, 123), 'We must be neat – not neat, but cleanly', will illustrate this; he replaces *neat* because of its bovine sense which suggests horns and hence cuckoldry.

It is important, therefore, to study the language of Shakespeare's time and then to distinguish Shakespeare's language within it. But even this is to proceed too fast. There is an important consideration which must occupy us between these two, and that is Shakespeare's interest in and reaction to the language around him: narrowly – his interest in the linguistic fashions and controversies of his time, and more broadly – his interest in the nature of language itself. What we need is thus a study involving a three-fold distinction:

(1) English as it was about 1600;

(2) Shakespeare's interest in his language;

(3) Shakespeare's unique use of English.

In speaking of Shakespeare's 'unique' use of English it will be realized that one is speaking in linguistic terms and not in bardolatry. Every individual has a unique *parole*, a unique realization of what is possible in the language of his time and place. But at the same time this is not to deny that the *parole* of some individuals is more interesting than that of others: William Shakespeare's than Nahum Tate's, for example.

Now the language of any period can be considered as comprising three aspects: *vocabulary* – the word-stock; *grammar* – the organisation of vocabulary into sentences; and thirdly *transmission* – the means of transmitting language from one person to another, either directly by the sounds of speech or indirectly by the marks of written representation.

In many respects the English of 1600 has remained unchanged in all three aspects. Many words sound the same, and are spelt the same; many grammatical patterns have remained unchanged; many words have stayed in use and in the same use, that is, with the same meaning. Our reason for studying the language of 1600, however, is that in many respects the language has changed quite sharply, and we are confronted by two difficulties. The first is the discipline of recognizing these differences. The second is the much more acute difficulty of deciding whether these differences are purely those between our time and 1600 (features which would not seem striking to Shakespeare's audience) or whether they are differences which result from Shakespeare's creativeness (and which would therefore seem individual in his own time).

So far as transmission is concerned, the complications are both less and more troublesome. Less because – *pace* those critics who have written about individual poets' 'voices' – it is doubtful whether much can be done to distinguish an author's pronunciation – still less *voice quality* – from that of his time in general. Here is one area, in fact, where confusion has been perpetuated through such terms as 'Shakespeare's pronunciation' – even used as the title of an important book – where little attempt is made to distinguish Shakespeare from his time and where mainly the latter is meant. In addition, these problems are less troublesome, one might suggest, because it is equally doubtful whether a great deal is to be gained from a closer knowledge of transmission differences. Now that we have the technical ability to put on a play in roughly the pronunciation of 1600, the desirability of so doing has become less apparent. Since so many of the features of Elizabethan pronunciation have remained in twentieth-century use with utterly different sociological connotations, it is exceedingly difficult to avoid farcical overtones in ways that do not arise with original versions in French or German, or even in Chaucerian English.

The complications are *more* troublesome inasmuch as the two modes of transmission – sound and spelling – are necessarily confounded in dealing with an earlier time where the language is couched (as to substance) in only one of these. And while both spellings and sounds have changed, they have not changed in the same ways and we obviously cannot infer the sound changes from the spelling ones. Editing and interpretative scholarship have gained (and undoubtedly can continue to gain) from the close study of both aspects of transmission. We would rarely think of accepting an emendation today without close reference to the ways in which a given word was spelt in 1600 and the ways in which that spelling could have given rise – whether from manuscript or from print – to the corruption that we suspect. And the study of the sounds, despite the spellings, has led to a far fuller knowledge – particularly of word-play: 'I am here,' says Touchstone to the bucolic Audrey, 'I am here with thee and thy goats, as the most capricious poet, honest Ovid, was among the Goths' (*As You Like It* III, iii, 4). The connection between *goats* and *capricious* on the one hand and *Goths* on the other is obscured alike by Elizabethan spelling, our own spelling, and our modern pronunciation. It is only when we know that the pronunciation of *Goth* was different in Shakespeare's time that the full connection, the full range of the pun, can become apparent. Spelling and modern pronunciation disguise a pun similarly in Hotspur's 'That roan shall be my throne' (*1 Henry IV* II, iii, 67); cf. Kökeritz, pp. 320 f, Dobson, p. 1010.

To turn now to grammar, we find here very great and significant differences from the habits of our own time, but at least we are helped by the fact that they are for the most part obvious to us. They are not obscured by spelling as in transmission or by continuity of form as with vocabulary. Not usually, at any rate but there are snares here too, even in so seemingly innocent a form as *his*. In *Hamlet*, III, iii, the King's soliloquy presents him considering the relative ease with which justice can be evaded in 'the corrupted currents of this world'. But, he goes on (60–2),

'tis not so above:
There is no shuffling; there the action lies
In his true nature.

During the summer of 1966, at the Stratford production by Peter Hall, I heard the player heavily emphasize *his*, apparently under the impression (and certainly conveying the impression to the audience) that the reference was to God's nature, thus convicting Shakespeare at once of woolly expression and bad theology, if not of actual nonsense. Yet *his* as the genitive of *it* (here referring to *action*) was a contemporary commonplace, however much the salt has subsequently lost his savour. Abbot dismisses the point as too well-known to merit more than a single line, though he spends a page examining exceptions such as *its* and *it*.

Scarcely less firmly 'trodden under foot of men' is our former awareness of another pronominal usage, the distinction between *you* and *thou*, though many studies have been published on this point, some of them noted below (p. 266). Even when we are intellectually aware of the distinction, however, it is hard to school ourselves to the appropriate reaction when we are in the theatre, and in any case there remain misconceptions among scholars themselves. It is often said that the old singular and plural are used in Shakespeare as they are used in Chaucer: and this is quite untrue; it is often said that in 1600 *you* was polite, formal usage but *thou* was familiar or insulting. This is a gross oversimplification: cf. McIntosh, Mulholland. The modern linguistic concept of contrast operating through *marked* and *unmarked* members can give us a truer picture. *You* is usually the stylistically unmarked form: it is not so much 'polite' as 'not impolite'; it is not so much 'formal' as 'not informal'. It is for this reason that *thou* can operate in such a wide variety of contrasts with it. At one extreme we have the solemnity and formality of religious discourse as in Edmund's 'Thou, Nature, art my goddess; to thy law My services are bound' (*King Lear* I, ii, 1 f). Then again we have the very antonym of this in pure contempt: there is Sir Toby's advice to Sir Andrew Aguecheek in drafting the challenge to his rival, 'Taunt him with the license of ink; if thou thou'st him some thrice, it shall not be amiss' (*Twelfth Night* III, ii, 40 f). But we need to notice that in this instance the device draws attention to the fact that while Andrew and Fabian are using the unmarked *you* to each other and to Sir Toby, Sir Toby is using *thou* to Sir Andrew with more than a suggestion of the contempt he is advising Sir Andrew to use with the count's serving man. It is important to realize that it is not Sir Toby's use of *thou* as such which conveys his lack of respect; it is the fact that he is doing so in a social context which makes it appropriate for other speakers to use *you*. If we compare the exchanges between Falstaff and Prince Hal in *1 Henry IV*, we see sharply different values given to *thou* because the contrasts in which it operates are different. Both pass back and forth between the unmarked *you* and the marked *thou* of anger or intimacy: but there is no distancing between them in the pronoun usage and so no social opposition enters the situation. At a given moment both are using either *you* (as in Hal's 'How now, woolsack! What mutter you?' and Falstaff's 'You Prince of Wales!...Are you not a coward?' II, iv, 127 ff) or else, as a little later in the same scene, they are both using *thou* (Falstaff's 'Dost thou hear me, Hal?' and the Prince's 'Ay, and mark thee too, Jack' *ibid.* 202).

The importance of the active contrast betwen *you* and *thou* is brought out excellently in the first scene of *King Lear*. Kent, Gloucester, Edmund and Lear all use *you* in speaking to each other: as we should expect. Goneril, Regan and Cordelia address their father as *you* – again as we should expect. Lear addresses Goneril and Regan as *thou*, and again – from father to daughter – this is what we should expect. Against this background of perfect decorum and the fully expected, it should no doubt come as a surprise to us that Lear addreses Cordelia at first as *you*: 'what can you say to draw / A third more opulent than your sisters?' (I, i, 84 f). So also 93 f. It seems unlikely that these uses of *you(r)* are without significance in indicating a special feeling that Lear has for the girl he calls 'our joy', who has been, as France says, Lear's 'best object', the argument of his praise, the balm of his age, the best, the dearest (*ibid.* 214–6). When, however, he is shocked by what he takes to be her lack of love, he uses *thou* – not now the *thou* of father to daughter but the *thou* of anger: 'But goes thy heart with this?' 'Thy truth, then, be thy dower!' (104, 107). This is what is meant by saying the importance lies in *active contrast*. Although *you* is the general unmarked form beside which the use of *thou* is conspicuous, the position is that in a relationship where *thou* is expected, *you* can likewise be in contrast and conspicuous. This becomes important again and again in the scenes that follow: Lear grows cool to Goneril and the change is reflected in the use of *you*: 'Are you our daughter?' 'Your name, fair gentlewoman?' (I, iv, 218, 235), and he turns to Regan with his customary affectionate paternal *thou* for these two daughters: 'Beloved Regan, Thy sister's naught' (II, iv, 131 f). The Fool addresses the disguised Kent as *you*; Regan conspiring with Goneril's steward expresses her ultimate acknowledgement of their partnership by coming down the intimacy scale from *you* to *thou*: 'So fare you well...Fare thee well' (IV, v, 36, 40).

If it is only with difficulty that we today can respond to this contrast of *you* and *thou*, our sensitivity is still less in relation to the use of the second person pronoun with imperatives. The pronoun may have subject form or object form or it may be absent, and in some cases – 17, according to Millward – all three possibilities can occur with the same verb:

> Come thou on my side. (*Richard III* I, iv, 263)
> Come thee on. (*Antony and Cleopatra* IV, vii, 16)
> Come on my right hand. (*Julius Caesar* I, ii, 213).

While it would be idle to pretend that these three forms of imperative were always carefully distinguished in meaning at this time, we must not assume that they were usually synonymous. Leaving out of account reflexive use like *calm thee*, it would seem that, beside an 'unmarked' imperative without any pronoun, the form with *thou* was emphatic; this is frequently clear from the metre or the context, as when the Second Murderer refuses to profit from the death of Clarence:

> Take thou the fee, and tell him what I say. (*Richard III* I, iv, 275)

The pronoun subject becomes especially contrastive when the *do* auxiliary is also used, as when Queen Margaret begs for death:

> What, wilt thou not? Then, Clarence, do it thou.
> ...sweet Clarence, do thou do it. (*3 Henry VI* v, v, 71, 73)

Or, in a different vein, Falstaff's plea:

> Do not thou, when thou art king, hang a thief. (*1 Henry IV* I, ii, 60)

On the other hand, the imperative with the objective form of the pronoun (which may be better explained as an unstressed form of the subject pronoun) seems rather to seek the personal involvement of the addressee. We may compare Polonius' farewell to his son:

> Farewell; my blessing season this in thee (*Hamlet* I, iii, 81)

with the Ghost's to his son:

> Fare thee well at once...
> Adieu, adieu, adieu! Remember me. (*ibid.* v, 88, 91)

It is naturally especially common with verbs used to summon attention, such as *look* and *hark*: for example,

> But hear thee, Gratiano:
> Thou art too wild.... (*The Merchant of Venice* II, ii, 165 f)

Mention has been made of the *do* auxiliary (p. 72). Shakespeare witnessed the increasing association of this auxiliary with questions, negation and emphasis (*Do you go? I don't go, I DO go*), but for the most part a choice remained which could be used for stylistic contrast. As Mrs Salmon (1965) has pointed out, Jacques Bellot was among Shakespeare's contemporaries one of those most plainly aware of the use of *do* to confer a weighty and sonorous rotundity, observing that people 'doe adde commonly the verb Faire, before the other verbes, for the replenishing and sounding of their tongue with more grace' (*Le Maistre d'Escole Anglais*). It is in this knowledge that we must savour Falstaff's coloured rhetoric when he plays the King:

> This pitch, as ancient writers do report, doth defile.
> (*1 Henry IV* II, iv, 400)

or when he exults in Mistress Page's passion for him:

O, she did so course o'er my exteriors with such a greedy intention that the appetite of her eye did seem to scorch me up like a burning-glass.
> (*The Merry Wives of Windsor* I, iii, 62 ff)

The purpose has been to show that even the minutiae of grammar present important differences in Elizabethan English; it goes without saying that such differences are no less important in larger matters such as clause and sentence structure. But it is time we glanced at the remaining aspect of language, vocabulary. The difficulties here – as in transmission – are often disguised. That is to say, we really do not come upon many entirely strange words in Shakespeare that hoist a danger signal warning us to consult Onions or the *N.E.D.* When Salerio in *The Merchant of Venice* says 'Slubber not business for my sake' (II, viii, 39), we are compelled to look up *slubber* ('treat carelessly'). Later in the play, Portia says that she speaks too long, 'to peize the time' (III, ii, 22), meaning to weigh it down and make it slow. The problem of entirely strange words is not, of course, to be underrated, and there are plenty in Shakespeare 'stranger' than *slubber* and *peize*: *chopine* (a kind of shoe) and *eisel* (vinegar) occur in *Hamlet*, *kecksy* (a wild plant) and *sutler* (camp-follower) in *Henry V*. And generations of editors, let alone readers, have been puzzled by Petruchio's

> Sit down, Kate, and welcome. Soud, soud, soud, soud.
> (*The Taming of the Shrew* IV, i, 125)

Many have taken it to be a nonsense-word, part of the snatch of song that has just preceded, or an exclamation; some have preferred to emend *s* to *f*. This is a good illustration of the great scope still remaining for work on Shakespeare's problem words and Dr Hulme has argued in favour of reading *u* as *n*, the word *sonde* in the sense of 'food' having been certainly still current in the mid-fifteenth century.

But the problem of overtly strange words is less than the problem of words which disguise their strangeness. We meet a large number of words more or less familiar in their graphic substance, but with different meanings which we can easily ignore, to our loss, since very frequently the modern meaning will make some kind of sense in the Shake-spearian context. For example, Polonius tells Reynaldo to 'breathe' his son's faults 'quaintly' (*Hamlet* II, i, 31) and we may link Polonius with quaintness in the modern sense without surprise; but Polonius means the insinuation to be done *artfully*. Iago's *shrewd doubt* quoted earlier would also make sense in terms of the present-day meanings, but we are the losers if we do not realize that *shrewd* means 'serious'. We are still further misled if we do not understand Edmund's 'pretence of danger' in its Elizabethan sense, 'dangerous or malicious purpose' (*King Lear* I, ii, 84). Similar examples will spring to mind: *important* often meant 'importunate', *perfection* 'performance'; *humour, frank, kind, husband, sad, safe, quick, respect* – one could make a very long list of words which are among the commonest today but whose modern meaning is, as C. S. Lewis categorized it, the 'dangerous' one when we meet them as common words also in Shakespeare.

All these differences – in transmission, grammar, and vocabulary – are part of the normal linguistic process. Similar differences can be found in comparing the language of Chaucer or of Dr Johnson with our own: change is unchanging, so to say; only the examples of lin-guistic change differ from comparison to comparison. But each age has its special linguistic preoccupations too: in Chaucer's time, for instance, the co-existence with a largely popular English of a largely courtly French; in Dr Johnson's the problem of reducing the language to teachable rule in the light of enlightenment and rationalism, and in the face of a growing middle class that was literate. In Shakespeare's time, too, there were special preoccupations – the post-Renaissance experimentation with language, a fluidity of linguistic fashion and a new literary self-consciousness on the part of writers in the vernacular; an ambition to achieve a literature in English to match that of the classical languages or at any rate that of French or Italian.

I have just used the word *fluidity*, but we must be cautious here. I applied it to linguistic fashion, not to the language itself. Again and again, one finds writers on Shakespeare's language describing a rule-less norm-less flux – a bright chaotic galaxy only constellated by the bard's genius, who created patterns that were entirely original and *sui generis*. We all know this to be wholly distorted, but despite our intellectual awareness of this, its effect as a piece of critical rhetoric (not to say folklore) on our imagination seems unavoidable from time to time. All languages (we must continually remind ourselves) are always in a state of flux. And when we consider the linguistic originality with which English has been used in the past eighty years by men like Hopkins, Joyce or even Dylan Thomas, we must see that the artist of our own time is no more restricted by a rule-ful, norm-ful language than Shakespeare was. The ways in which Shakespeare is seen as being defiantly independent often (if not usually) concern word-formation and in particular 'conversion' from one part of speech to another: but of course this is a property of English in all periods not merely of Shakespeare's period, still less of Shakespeare alone. Again, only specific examples of the process are Shakespeare's.

'Chaos and fire-new, unharnessed energy.' 'A buccaneering spirit in language as well as on the high seas.' Gross, romantic distortions? Not entirely, we must admit. There was less *sense of fixity* about the language in 1600 than in some other periods, and also more outspoken controversy and overt interest in the medium. The cult of the hard word as a necessity and indeed a virtue is something which runs through the whole period. *Ovids Banquet of Sence* (1595) shows Chapman delighting in obscure new words and elegant conceits; *disparent* seemingly used by no one else, appears on the second page. He says in his preface: 'that Poesie should be as perviall as Oratorie, and plainnes her speciall ornament, were the plaine way to barbarisme... it serves not a skilfull Painters turne, to draw the figure of a face onely to make knowne who it represents; but hee must lymn, give luster, shaddow, and heightning; which though ignorants will esteeme spic'd, and too curious, yet such as have the judiciall perspective, will see it hath motion, spirit, and life... Obscuritie in affection of words, and indigested concets, is pedanticall and childish; but where it shroudeth it selfe in the hart of his subiect, uttered with fitnes of figure, and expressive Epethites; with that darknes wil I still labour to be shaddowed; rich Minerals are digd out of the bowels of the earth, not found in the superficies and dust of it.'

In 1595 we have had the fashion for augmenting the language as it flourished with Thomas Elyot, the countermovement against excess augmentation from the inkhorn as fought by Thomas Wilson and Puttenham, and now with Chapman and others the rejoinder that, yes, *affected* and *pedantic* obscurities for their own sake are to be repudiated, but a high degree of ornamentation and precision is required and to this end 'rich Minerals' must continue to be 'digd out of the bowels of the earth'.

One needs to stress this tug of war because it is commonly said that Shakespeare scorned the inkhorn, and one can cite many passages which seem to support this. 'I have receiv'd my proportion, like the Prodigious Son,' says Launce in *The Two Gentlemen of Verona* (II, iii, 3), and as Silvia says in the following scene (line 30), 'A fine volley of words' can be 'quickly shot off'. Shakespeare is aware that the un-learned can be injudiciously attracted by high-sounding language with his Hostess Quickly's *honeysuckle* for 'homicidal', *honey-seed* for 'homicide' (*2 Henry IV*, II, i, 47 f), his Dogberry and Verges, and his Costard ('welcome the sour cup of prosperity! Affliction may one day smile again': *Love's Labour's Lost* I, i, 291). Launcelot's *impertinent* (*The Merchant of Venice* II, ii, 124) confuses 'pertinent' and 'important' in its contemporary sense of 'urgent'. Benvolio mocks the Nurse by using *indite* for *invite* (*Romeo and Juliet* II, iv, 125), a malapropism elsewhere used by Hostess Quickly (*2 Henry IV* II, i, 25). But this is not to scorn augmentation and the inkhorn: there was no disagreement on this point – that the uneducated would make ridiculous errors. John Hart, the Chester Herald, had pointed this out in his *Methode* of 1570, when he gave examples such as *temporal* for 'temperate', *certisfied* for both 'certified' and 'satisfied', *dispense* for 'suspense'. It was an undoubted fact, to which George Baker had testified in 1576 (*The New Jewel of Health*), that some people, 'more curious than wyse, esteeme of nothing but that which is most rare, or in harde and unknowne languages', and we recall Don Adriano de Armado and his 'posteriors of this day', which 'the rude multitude call the afternoon' and which is an expression that seems to Holofernes 'liable, congruent, and measurable' (*Love's Labour's Lost* V, i, 76–8). Again, there was no disagreement on this: as in the passage quoted from Chapman above, the use of learned language for obscurity's sake was ridiculous and Shakespeare shows it to be so, just as he shows the ignorant *attempt* at learned language to be so. From Armado to Polonius and beyond, we have characters who draw out the thread of their verbosity finer than the staple of their argument, as Holofernes puts it (*Love's Labour's Lost* V, i, 14), and it is not only he and Nathaniel who are laughed at for having 'been at a great feast of languages and stol'n the scraps' (*ibid.* 34). Nathaniel may speak of abrogating scurrility (*Love's Labour's Lost* IV, ii, 51), Touchstone of abandoning the society of this female, 'which in the boorish' is leave the company of this woman (*As You Like It* V, i, 42 ff), and this is ridiculous. But when Macbeth likewise pairs a learned expression with its 'boorish' equivalent, as in:

>   this my hand will rather
>   The multitudinous seas incarnadine,
>   Making the green one red,   (II, ii, 61–3)

or earlier:

>   If th' assassination
>   Could trammel up the consequence, and catch,
>   With his surcease, success; that but this blow
>   Might be the be-all and the end-all here,   (I, vii, 2–5)

he is not being ridiculous. Here is the inkhorn used in deadly earnest,
deliberately, as an expressive virtue. And this is the position taken up,
as we saw, by Chapman and this was even the ultimate position of
Cheke and Wilson: augmentation was necessary, the language was
deficient in aureate expression. A generation before Shakespeare was
born, Skelton was pointing out that the language was so 'rude' and
lacking in 'pollysshed tearmes'

>   That if I wold apply
>   To write ornatly
>   I wot not where to finde
>   Tearmes to serve my mynde.

As poets felt particularly acutely the language's need, so it was they
who supplied the need most discriminatingly. Puttenham (*The Arte of
English Poesie*, 1589) acknowledges the services that poets have rendered in 'their studious endevours, commendably employed in enrich-
ing and polishing their native Tongue'. Nash (*Pierce Penilesse*, 1592)
praises 'the Poets of our time' for having 'cleansed our language from
barbarisme' and Gervase Markham (*The Gentlemans Academie*, 1595)
praises them for having given English its new 'glory and exact com-
pendiousness'. Francis Meres lists Shakespeare and Chapman among
the poets by whom 'the English tongue is mightily enriched, and
gorgeouslie invested in rare ornaments and resplendent abiliments',
and speaks specifically of 'Shakespeares fine filed phrase' (*Palladis
Tamia*, 1598).

While Shakespeare laughed at the excesses of augmentation, therefore, he was himself deeply engaged in the process and was acknowledged to be so. He was similarly ambivalent about euphuism. There
is the burlesque of Launce and Speed in *The Two Gentlemen of Verona*
(for example, III, i) or of Osric (*Hamlet* V, ii). There is Falstaff: 'for
though the camomile, the more it is trodden on the faster it grows,
yet youth, the more it is wasted the sooner it wears' (*1 Henry IV*, II,
iv, 388). Yet the forced ingenuity of symmetry and image characteristic
of euphuist prose can be detected in serious verse too: in *Richard III*,

in *Othello*, not least in *1 Henry IV*. Two scenes after Falstaff's burlesque, we have the King speaking somewhat in the ridiculed vein:

> whereof a little
> More than a little is by much too much.
> So, when he had occasion to be seen,
> He was but as the cuckoo is in June,
> Heard, not regarded, seen, but with such eyes
> As, sick and blunted with community,
> Afford no extraordinary gaze,
> Such as is bent on sun-like majesty. (III, ii, 72–9)

One final facet of linguistic fashion deserves a mention. Robert Cawdrey's *Table Alphabeticall* of 1604 echoes the well-known condemnation by Thomas Wilson fifty years earlier of those who 'pouder their talke with oversea language'. The fashion has been sustained over half a century whereby 'He that commeth lately out of Fraunce, will talke French English...An other chops in with English Italienated.' Indeed, said Wilson, 'I dare sweare this, if some of their mothers were alive, thei were not able to tell what they say' (*Arte of Rhetorique*, 1553). 'The pox of such antic, lisping, affecting fantasticoes; these new tuners of accent,' says Mercutio; 'these fashion-mongers, these pardon me's' (*Romeo and Juliet* II, iv, 27, 32).

Small wonder, then, if engaged so deeply in the linguistic foibles, fashions, controversies and creativeness of his time, that Shakespeare's interest should extend also to the scepticism about the linguistic sign itself which was current if far from dominant in Elizabethan and Jacobean thought. Every man's language 'is eloquent ynough for hym self', writes a translator of Peter Ramus in 1574, countering the argument of the superiority of Latin, 'and that of others in respect of it is had as barbarous'. 'That which we call a rose By any other name would smell as sweet', and if Juliet (*Romeo and Juliet* II, ii, 43 f) cannot claim the poet's sanction any more than Falstaff with his 'What is honour? A word' (*1 Henry IV*, v, i, 132), it can be fairly claimed that they both have greater sanction than Juliet's nurse to whom primitive word-magic is attributed in 'Doth not rosemary and Romeo begin both with the same letter?' (*Romeo and Juliet* II, iv, 201).

The word-magic game is one that Cordelia refuses to play in reply to Lear's 'what can you say to draw / A third more opulent than your sisters?...mend your speech a little' (*King Lear* I, i, 85, 93); cf Mahood. It may seem ironical but it is no contradiction that the man who could use words to greatest effect was one who saw most clearly and sophisticatedly the distinction between 'words, words, mere words' and 'matter from the heart' (*Troilus and Cressida* v, iii, 108), and was able to frame so sardonic a speculation for Bolingbroke on the power of words:

> How long a time lies in one little word!
> Four lagging winters and four wanton springs
> End in a word: such is the breath of Kings.
> (*Richard II* i, iii, 213 ff)

But it is time to say a few words – and space alone forbids more – on the last leg of my proposed tripos. First, the language of Shakespeare's time; second, Shakespeare's interest in the language of his time; and only then shall we, thirdly, be in a position to attempt useful observations about his own use of the language of his time.

And how many there are to make! When all is done to get things into perspective, to see the rich texture of the language in Shakespeare's time, there is still a great deal of individuality in Shakespeare's usage. In word-formation, for instance, and particularly in verb-formation. The dynamic element in Shakespeare's clauses is characteristically the most sharply pointed, and he is particularly fond of verbs with the prefixes *be-* and *en-*. Albany tells his wife 'Bemonster not thy feature' (*King Lear* iv, ii, 63), Kent speaks of Lear's 'unnatural and be-madding sorrow' (iii, i, 38), and it is worth considering the verbal force that *bemadding* has retained here beside the comparatively static, attributive value acquired by *maddening*, which was coined later. As for verbs with *en-*, one need only cite Cassio's lines in *Othello*:

> The gutter'd rocks, and congregated sands,
> Traitors ensteep'd to enclog the guiltless keel.
> (ii, i, 69 f)

(or, with Kenneth Muir in the Penguin edition of 1968, *enscarped* 'abruptly shelved', in place of *ensteep'd*). And highly charged verbs emerge also from the direct-conversion process: 'The hearts That spaniel'd me at heels' (still more if with Hulme we prefer *pannelled* to Hanmer's emendation) in *Antony and Cleopatra* iv, xii, 20 f, or Edgar's tightly compressed 'He childed as I father'd' (*King Lear* iii, vi, 110).

Even his noun units often have a dynamic, verbal character as we see from 'gutter'd rocks, and congregated sands' just quoted from *Othello*. This is no less noticeable in many of the image-decked nominal groups in the Sonnets: 'your own dear-purchas'd right' (Sonnet 117), 'your ne'er-cloying sweetness' (118), 'fore-bemoaned moan' (30), 'his sweet up-locked treasure' (52), 'the time-bettering days' (82), 'proud-pied April' (98), (Time's) 'bending sickle's compass' (116). And as these complex, clause-embedding modifiers may turn our minds to Hopkins, one may also cite 'the world-without-end hour' in Sonnet 57.

Perhaps because grammatical patterning had so recently been exploited *ad nauseam* in the euphuistic style, lexical patterning may be presumed to be nearer the centre of Shakespeare's interest. We may quote from Mortimer's speech to his keepers in *1 Henry VI* to illustrate what is meant:

> Weak shoulders, overborne with burdening grief,
> And pithless arms, like to a withered vine
> That droops his sapless branches to the ground.
> Yet are these feet, whose strengthless stay is numb,
> Unable to support this lump of clay,
> Swift-winged with desire to get a grave. (II, v, 10 ff)

Hardly the bard at his best, yet there is very considerable complexity in what he is attempting, a complexity in lexicology not syntax; or, rather, in that kind of 'lexical syntax' in which some modern linguists are becoming increasingly interested. *Weak* has a grammatical link (as modifier) with *shoulders*; *shoulders* is linked lexically to *burdening*, since there is a traditional collocation *burden – shoulder*; 'weak with grief' is thus achieved through the network of lexical and grammatical links. From *shoulders* to the lexically connected *arms*; but *arms* is grammatically linked to *pithless* which then lexically connects with *vine*, while conversely the grammatical modifier of *vine* (*withered*) works back to *arms* which become the *sapless branches* of the following line, though the direct lexical congruence is with *vine*. The *feet*, as part of a lexical series with *shoulders* and *arms*, have a grammatically specified *stay* which is *strengthless* and *numb*; at this point we may notice the morphological as well as semantic links between *pithless*, *sapless* and *strengthless*, the first two collocating most naturally with *vine* but (especially with the help of the third) working well with the human limbs. The *stay* has both a grammatical and a lexical link with *support*, and the latter looks back to *shoulder* and *burden* lexically as well as forward to *lump of clay*, the lexical link in addition to the grammatical one working to counteract any feeling of 'mixed' metaphor. The last line, apart from a lexical connection between *clay* and *grave*, sees a lightning antithesis to the heavily endorsed overburdened weakness of the preceding lines, an antithesis that is Mercurial in two senses as the feet become swift-winged with desire to get a grave.

Lexical congruence working through, without, or in defiance of syntactic structure is, of course, the stock machinery of imagery, and characteristically the Shakespearian image is developed in a pairing of lexical items through syntax or collocation or both. The latter – the most straightforward – is seen, for example, in the adequacy with which Ulysses' musical image is established in the words, 'untune that string' (*Troilus and Cressida* I, iii, 109). Syntax and collocation working independently produce more complex images; we may compare with the Ulysses example the following:

> Unthread the rude eye of rebellion.
> (*King John* v, iv, 11)

In addition to the grammatical (verb – object) connection between *unthread* and *eye*, there is a discontinuous lexical connection between *eye*'s premodifier *rude* and postmodifier *rebellion*, the transverse arrangement helping to remove the danger of destroying the image by an unwelcome mixture. A somewhat similar effect can be observed in

> Heaven stops the nose at it, and the moon winks
> (*Othello* IV, ii, 78)

where the two clauses are grammatically related by co-ordination, by subjects that collocate (*heaven* and *moon*) and by predicates that are lexically congruent also: closing nose and eye. But it is the transverseness of these lexical links that minimizes the incongruence in the image of heaven stopping its nose. In the following example from *As You Like It* there is a discontinuous linkage with a different arrangement:

> . . . weed your better judgments
> Of all opinion that grows rank in them.   (II, vii, 45 f)

The two verbs *weed* and *grows* are lexically congruent, and to this set belongs also the complement *rank* (for *weed* and *rank*, compare *Hamlet* I, ii, 135 f; III, iv, 151 f). Nested between *weed* and *grows* are two nouns which likewise collocate; the fact that both are equally and analogously incongruent with the verbs to which they are grammatically linked (as object and subject respectively) helps to establish and empower an image that depends upon an 'unlexical' sequence.

But given the phenomenon of multiple meaning, a single lexical sign can self-collocate and produce the congruent collocation in more than one direction from itself. There is an example of this in Portia's well-known 'mercy' speech, the pivotal word being *strain'd* (*The Merchant of Venice* IV, i, 179). Shylock has just asked 'On what compulsion must I?' and so *strain'd* in Portia's reply has an obvious backward link to this: there is no compulsiveness in mercy. But then it works forward also to the dropping of the gentle rain: mercy is not filtered, drop by drop, from heaven; cf. Mahood (1957), p. 22. It is worth considering the *sullied – solid* crux in this light too (*Hamlet* I, ii,

129). Thus it would seem that the phonological experts can allow us a neutralized phonetic contrast; cf. Dobson (1968), pp. 581 ff, 592 f and notes. At the same time, the semantic span is well motivated, so that while at the point of utterance the word's relations are backwards to the pollution by the Queen's incest (cf. Clemen (1951), p. 114), thereafter it seems perverse to ignore the lexical congruity of *solid* with the *melt* that leads to *thaw, resolve,* and *dew* in the next line (cf. Mahood (1957), p. 16).

There is a more obvious 'syntactic' movement through lexical interaction when multiple meaning is allowed to emerge in the course of repetition. Leontes' reaction to *neat* may be adduced again, 'We must be neat – not neat, but cleanly' (*The Winter's Tale* I, ii, 123), in which only the first occurrence may be said to collocate with *cleanly.* But his use of *play* is a better illustration:

> Go, play, boy, play; thy mother plays, and I
> Play too; but so disgrac'd a part...   (*ibid.* 187 f)

The second instance of *play* is in part colloquial repetition but it is partly also the sinister turning point, a lingering over the word which releases the sexual sense (*N.E.D.* 10c) in which the third instance occurs, indicated collocationally by the female subject; the fourth instance again shows by collocation (*part*) its ironically different use.

There are of course many aspects of Shakespeare's use of English and many approaches to his language that can sharpen and enrich our reaction to the plays and poems. It would not have been practicable here to explore more than a meagre selection of the possibilities, and equally it has not seemed appropriate to attempt a wider coverage at the expense of depth. The concentration on certain facets reflects my belief that it is especially through further study of the interrelations of grammatical and lexical patterns that linguists can in the immediate future offer contributions most readily compatible with and contributory to the insights of literary scholarship.

6

SHAKESPEARE'S USE OF RHETORIC

BRIAN VICKERS

I

Rhetoric was for over two thousand years the most important discipline to anyone interested in literature. It was in existence as an art several centuries before Aristotle and it extended its influence on Western literature right up to the time of Wordsworth (see, in the Reading List, books by Abrams, Stone). It began life as a practical tool, in the law-courts, for our earliest knowledge of rhetoric is as an aid to litigation (Kennedy) and it was developed and applied to politics in Greece and still more so in Rome. The Romans took especially seriously the importance of rhetoric in education, and although they derived the principle and much of their system from Hellenistic schools (Marrou) it was thanks to their thorough establishment of the rhetorical education throughout the Roman Empire that rhetoric established itself in both secular and Christian contexts strongly enough to survive the fall of that Empire and continue in vigour through the Middle Ages (Curtius, C. S. Baldwin, Faral), indeed gathering momentum in the Renaissance partly through the separate developments in Byzantium and their influx into Florence (Bolgar). In England rhetoric was pursued with the same fervour as in other Humanist cultures (Howell) perhaps more so, because of the increasing role it played in education (Curtius, T. W. Baldwin). Indeed the English rhetoric-books of the late sixteenth century seem more inventive, more imaginative in their realization of the literary applications of rhetoric than their continental counterparts. (A concise history of rhetoric, with further references, can be found in Vickers, 1970.)

Rhetoric was rejected by the Romantic movement as an 'artificial system' which hampered the expression of individuality, and much abuse was attached to its supposedly 'rigid', 'sterile' nature. Today we still live with the post-Romantic animus to rhetoric, an animus which has passed into the language: 'rhetorical', 'oratorical', 'rhetorician', are words with ineradicable connotations of falseness and specious display. But curiously enough the same prejudice is attached to many words deriving from the drama: 'theatrical', 'stagey', 'acting'

(Barish), and I would like to suggest that while in both cases the words we use betray a certain suspicion of display we should be able to detach rhetoric from these connotations as easily as we detach the drama from them.

But the issue of 'system' needs more discussion, for unless we settle it satisfactorily there is always the danger that readers unconvinced of the literary importance of rhetoric will regard Shakespeare's indisputable mastery of that art with suspicion, and may transfer to him the unenlightened animus which they attach to rhetoric. The 'art of speech', the 'art of speaking well' was indeed developed into a system with its own conventions, but it was no more harmful to expressiveness in literature than those conventions which we all accept in the other arts, the laws of perspective in painting, the laws of harmony in music: rhetorical figures are to be regarded as artistic conventions of the same order as rhyme or metrical patterns in poetry, sonata-form or fugue in music. The paradox is that by subordinating himself to artistic conventions, to agreed limitations and shorthand modes of expression, the artist working within a traditional system was then able to achieve a freedom and spontaneity which had a universal relevance, for the language of art was understood by all. One of the fascinations of studying the development of writers using the rhetorical tradition is to trace just this process of assimilation, from an external form to something lived through, imbued with life. Some of the most knowledgeable rhetoricians have been the greatest poets: Virgil, Dante, Chaucer, Shakespeare, Racine, Herbert, Milton, Pope. Considering this fact few would want to accuse them of rigidity or sterility, and many might consider the possibility that rhetoric, instead of being a hindrance, was a creative help.

II

Although rhetoric began as a tool for public life, its relevance to literature was soon realized. The eloquence of the lawyer or orator was a quality which the poet also needed, and at a very early date (aided of course by the dominance of rhetoric in education) rhetoric was regarded as the repository of all eloquence, and both poetry and prose were equated with rhetoric and with each other. Poetry merely had the extra complication of metrics, and indeed throughout the life-span of rhetoric poetry was seldom granted an autonomous existence (fleetingly in Tasso). Hence the methods of rhetoric, originally developed for the needs of the orator in a law-court or political assembly, were adapted to literature, not always with relevance. For instance the five stages of composition were *inventio, dispositio, elocutio, pronuntiatio, memoria*: invention (that is, 'finding' one's material, usually with the corollary that one 'found' it in the various places where one had stored it, the *loci* or 'places, seats' in one's notebooks), disposition or arrangement, elocution or style, delivery and memory. Evidently the last two stages were relevant to the orator memorizing his speech and delivering it with appropriate gestures, but they were not much use to the dramatist, nor indeed were invention and disposition except in the generalized sense of the selection and ordering of plot-material. But since this 'material' was the stuff of human life, the interaction between human beings, then the various rhetorical techniques for 'invention' and structure were of little relevance.

Thus it would seem, in theory as in practice, that the relevant teaching for the poet or dramatist was that contained within *elocutio*, style. Several historians of rhetoric lament the prominence given to style in rhetorical handbooks, preferring some more 'philosophical' attitude to communication. But if one surveys the history of rhetoric it becomes evident that despite the occasional exhortations of an Aristotle, a Cicero or a Quintilian that rhetoric should become more a way of life, a culture, a public and private ethic even, rhetoric had a kind of centre of gravity which kept pulling it back towards style (Vickers, 1970). The most influential classical rhetoric-books were not Aristotle's *Rhetoric*, Cicero's *Orator*, Quintilian's *Institutes of Oratory*, but Cicero's early and schematic *de Inventione* and the pseudo-Ciceronian *Ad Herennium*, Book Four of which consists simply of a list of figures. The medieval rhetoric-books are most often organized around a list of the figures, usually taken straight from the *Ad Herennium* (Faral, C. S. Baldwin), and the most popular compilations in the Renaissance, whether continental Latin ones by Susenbrotus and Trapezuntius or English ones by Wilson, Peacham and Puttenham, gravitate towards a list of the figures which was often the most thumbed part, as surviving copies show. For nearly two thousand years what the student and budding writer most wanted from rhetoric-books was a list of the tropes and figures, set out as clearly as possible, and this fact seems to me good evidence for man's intuitive recognition that rhetoric was fundamentally different from logic or philosophy: it was a literary discipline, and it was properly concerned with the details of language and expressiveness.

Shakespeare's main interest in rhetoric lay in the tropes and schemes, and we must re-create, re-experience that interest if we are properly to understand his poetic development. This is easier said than done, for several reasons. The terminology of the figures is not their most attractive aspect, and even the rhetoricians were sometimes confused by variations of terms (Sonnino is a useful guide here). Then there are so many figures (any moderately complete list looks frightening), for since rhetoric presented a formalizing of all possible linguistic effects then a large proportion of the figures refer to rare or unusual structures. In her pioneering study, *Shakespeare's Use of the Arts of Language*, Sister Miriam Joseph assembled from various sources a list of two hundred odd figures and showed that Shakespeare indeed used them all at one time or another: but we must discriminate here, and even some one as committed to rediscovering rhetoric as I am must feel doubts concerning such peculiarities as *bdelygmia* or *onedismus*. The hundred or so figures in the *Ad Herennium* are already sufficient, and for most critical purposes a central corpus of about the forty most frequently used figures is adequate. But even these names look forbidding – *polyptoton, epanorthosis, epistrophe*. One can only plead that the Greek or Latin names are etymologically descriptive of the specific effect created by each figure and that it seems better to master the most important names rather than invent new ones or try to anglicize them (as in Puttenham's ill-fated attempt: '*Syllepsis* or the double supply', '*Parison*, or the figure of even', '*Ploce*, or the doubler'). One thing is certain, that every person who had a grammar-school education in Europe between Ovid and Pope knew by heart, familiarly, up to a hundred figures, by their right names. As Puttenham's best editors have said

A well-educated modern reader may confess without shame to momentary confusion between *Hypozeuxis* and *Hypozeugma*, but to his Elizabethan prototype the categories of the figures were, like the multiplication-tables, a part of his foundations...We are all aware of the patterning in Elizabethan verse of this period, but we are generally content to name the *genus* – balance, antithesis, repetition, and so on. The educated Elizabethan could give a name to every *species*.

(pp. lxxvff)

And although we may continue to have difficulty distinguishing the figures, even an hour's practice will make it surprisingly easy.

All rhetorical devices were thought of as deviations made from the norm of 'plain' communication (strictly conceived) for some emotional or structural purpose. These devices were divided into *tropes* and *figures* (figures were sometimes called *schemes*). A trope (or 'turn') involves a change or transference of a word's meaning: from the literal to the imaginative plane, in such devices as metaphor, allegory, irony, *litotes* (understatement), *hyperbole* (overstatement), *synecdoche* (substituting the part for the whole), *metonymy* (substituting greater for lesser). Modern criticism has rediscovered the tropes extremely well, and there are many valuable studies of Shakespeare's imagery, but the figures have yet to be generally accepted, and it is on these that I shall concentrate. The figures sometimes involve changes of meaning, but they are primarily concerned with the shape or physical structure of language, the placing of words in certain syntactical positions, their repetition in varying patterns (to make an analogy with music, tropes exist in a vertical plane, like pitch or harmony; the figures exist in a horizontal plane, like rhythm or other stress-devices). It will be convenient, perhaps, to define the most popular figures, and for convenience I take all my illustrations from *Richard III*.

First, the very familiar group of figures which create symmetrical structure, often found together. *Anaphora*, the most common of all rhetorical figures, repeats a word at the beginning of a sequence of clauses or sentences:

> Then curs'd she Richard, then curs'd she Buckingham,
> Then curs'd she Hastings.   (III, iii, 18–9)

That example also used *parison*, in which within adjacent clauses or sentences word corresponds to word (either repeating the same word – 'curs'd' – or else grouping noun with noun, adjective with adjective, etc.). A more exact use of *parison*, putting great ironic stress on the final word, is this:

> Was ever woman in this humour woo'd?
> Was ever woman in this humour won? (I, ii, 227–8)

Both these examples increase the effect of symmetry by using *isocolon*, which gives exactly the same length to corresponding clauses, as again in the Duchess of York's catalogue of a family's distress:

> She for an Edward weeps, and so do I:
> I for a Clarence weep, so doth not she.
> These babes for Clarence weep, and so do I:
> I for an Edward weep, so do not they.   (II, ii, 82–5)

The obverse of *anaphora* is *epistrophe*, the same word ending a sequence of clauses. Shakespeare rightly chooses this figure to spotlight the sinister effect of Richard's 'planted' prophecy

> which says that G
> Of Edward's heirs the murderer shall be. (I, i, 39–40)

As intended, suspicion falls on Clarence, who protests that the King

> hearkens after prophecies and dreams,
> And from the cross-row plucks the letter G,
> And says a wizard told him that by G

His issue disinherited should be;
And, for my name of George begins with G,
It follows in his thought that I am he.   (I, i, 54-9)

That is a rather special use of *epistrophe* but it conforms to the theoretical justification of the figure as stressing a word of importance. Symmetry is also invoked for *antimetabole*, which repeats words but in an inverted order:

Since every Jack became a gentleman,
There's many a gentle person made a Jack.   (I, iii, 71-2)

Next a group of figures which repeat individual words in various ways. *Ploce* is one of the most used figures of stress (especially in this play), repeating a word within the same clause or line:

...themselves the conquerors
Make war upon themselves – brother to brother,
Blood to blood, self against self.   (II, iv, 61-3)

Epizeuxis is a more acute form of *ploce*, where the word is repeated without any other word intervening:

O Pomfret, Pomfret! O thou bloody prison.   (III, iii, 8)

Epanalepsis repeats the same word at the beginning and end of the same line, as with 'themselves' in the example for *ploce* above, or again with Richmond's reflections on Hope:

Kings it makes gods, and meaner creatures kings.   (V, ii, 24)

A related figure is *anadiplosis*, which gives the same word the last position in one clause and the first (or near the first) in the clause following. It rightly expresses causation, as in Richard's impatience:

Come, I have learn'd that fearful commenting
Is leaden servitor to dull delay;
Delay leads impotent and snail-pac'd beggary.   (IV, iii, 51-3)

If *anadiplosis* is carried through three or more clauses, it became a figure known in Greek as *climax* ('a ladder'; in Latin *gradatio*), and is again suitably used for causation in Richard's despair:

My conscience hath a thousand several tongues,
And every tongue brings in a several tale,
And every tale condemns me for a villain.   (V, iii, 193-5)

A more cutting type of repetition is the figure *polyptoton*, which takes a word and echoes it with another word derived from the same root:

Thou bloodless remnant of that royal blood!   (I, ii, 7)

This figure is sometimes said to be a pun, and can be grouped with the four main types of pun distinguished by rhetoric: *paronomasia* repeats a word similar in sound to one already used (and in its mature applications with an ironic distinction of sense):

> Not my deserts, but what I will deserve.   (IV, iv, 415)

or – a favourite Elizabethan pun, this –

> Cousins, indeed; and by their uncle cozen'd.   (IV, iv, 222)

Antanaclasis has a similar effect, in that it repeats a word while shifting from one meaning to another, as in Anne's curse on Richard for having killed her husband:

> O, cursed be the hand that made these holes!
> Cursed the heart that had the heart to do it!
> Cursed the blood that let his blood from hence!   (I, ii, 13–5)

By contrast *syllepsis* uses a word having two different meanings, without repeating it (an 'ambiguity', in modern terms), as when Richard promises Clarence 'your imprisonment shall not be long; / I will deliver or else lie for you' (I, i, 115), where 'lie' means (a) go to prison or (b) tell lies about. This is an especially apt figure for the double-faced Richard, and Shakespeare makes him comment on the fact:

> Thus, like the formal vice, Iniquity,
> I moralize two meanings in one word.   (III, i, 82–3)

The last type of pun is *asteismus*, particularly useful in drama, in which a word is returned by the answerer with an unlooked-for second meaning, as when Gloucester converts Brakenbury's defence into a bawdy joke.

> – With this, my lord, myself have nought to do.
> – Nought to do with Mistress Shore! I tell thee, fellow,
> He that doth nought with her, excepting one,
> Were best to do it secretly alone.   (I, i, 97–100)

or in Gloucester's later outrageous pun on 'Humphrey Hour' (IV, iv, 175). There is no need to illustrate a group of figures which are in general circulation: *zeugma* (the same verb for two disparate objects), *periphrasis*, *ellipsis*, *apostrophe*. If one reader's experience may be trusted to begin with, I would think that the figures listed here would provide the minimum necessary technical knowledge for an appreciation of a great deal of rhetorical usage.

But I am conscious that some readers may have another objection to the figures which I must briefly deal with before coming to discuss Shakespeare's developing use of rhetoric in prose and verse. The objection has indeed been made even by historians of rhetoric and scholars who have helped to reclaim other aspects of rhetoric for serious humane literary study, the objection that the figures are mere toys, 'husks', 'dry formulae', sterile patterns with no imaginative function. This is still the most serious objection to rhetoric, and if it were true then two thousand years of teaching and writing were disastrously wasted. But in fact rhetoricians of Greece, Rome and Renaissance England all argued that the figures had definite emotional and intellectual effects (see Vickers, 1970, ch. 3, for a fuller account). Rhetorical figures were conventions which had an important rationale, for theory held that by using them writers could best express feeling, could express it most naturally. This is an essential point to grasp, and if the illustration of it must be limited to the rhetoricians who were Shakespeare's contemporaries the functional nature of the figures will nevertheless be seen clearly.

Thus for the enlarged (1593) edition of his *Garden of Eloquence* (1577) Henry Peacham added a section on each figure giving 'The Use' and 'The Caution', stressing the need for the rhetorical device to be related to the sense and not to be over-used. So he urges that in figures like *anaphora*, *epanalepsis*, *ploce* and *epistrophe* the word chosen for repetition must be one vital to the sense (e.g. *epistrophe* 'serveth to leave a word of importance in the end of a sentence, that it may the longer hold the sound in the mind of the hearer', p. 43). Peacham picks out the 'figures of sentence' as being 'very sharp and vehement' (pp. 61–2) and says that such figures 'do attend upon affections (i.e. the passions), as ready handmaids at commandment to express most aptly whatsoever the heart doth affect or suffer' (p. 120): rhetoric re-enacts feeling. In his brief but intelligent *Directions for Speech and Style* (c. 1599), John Hoskins accepts that the word repeated be an important one, but seeks a psychological explanation for it: 'as no man is sick in thought upon one thing but for some vehemency or distress, so in speech there is no repetition without importance' (p. 12). Like all rhetoricians he holds that the figures not only re-create feeling in the character or action portrayed but therefore directly affect the feeling of the reader or playgoer: *anaphora* 'beats upon one thing to cause the quicker feeling in the audience' (p. 13). Like Peacham he urges the writer to tie the figure to sense and structure (the use of a figure should 'come from some choice and not from barrenness', p. 17), especially having regard to the organic needs of the whole: 'In these two sorts of amplifying you may insert all figures *as the passion of the matter shall serve*'; *polyptoton* 'is a good figure, and may be used *with or without passion*' (pp. 21, 17; my italics). Finally, an equally sharp awareness of decorum and of the functional nature of the figures is shown by Puttenham in his *Arte of English Poesie* (1589). For Puttenham, as for many Renaissance men, the figures are essential to literature: 'the chief praise and cunning of our Poet is in the discreet using of his figures' (p. 138) (without them language is 'but as our ordinary talk'), yet they must be organically related to sense and feeling, and not extraneous, as in such clumsy repetitions as

'To love him and love him, as sinners should do.' These repetitions be not figurative but fantastical, for a figure is ever used to a purpose, either of beauty or of efficacy...(p. 202)

Elsewhere he shows what varied functions can be obtained by using *aposiopesis* (pp. 116–17), and reveals a remarkable awareness of the relationship between sound and sense in poetry (p. 196: on 'figures of sentence'). He concludes his account, as I mine, by pointing to the relationship between rhetoric and reality, Art and Nature: we all use rhetorical figures 'by very nature, without discipline' (teaching) according to our individual personalities, and rhetoric exists to refine and intensify their effect. 'Nature herself suggesteth the figure in this or that form: but Art aideth the judgment of his use and application' (p. 298). Rhetoric is not simply an imitation of nature, but almost a re-creation of it, in its own terms: 'rather a repetition or reminiscence natural, reduced into perfection, and made prompt by use and exercise' (p. 306).

I have cited some of the evidence from Renaissance rhetoricians here, despite the limitations of space, because for so long the historians and specialists in rhetoric have rejected the figures as irrelevant. This essay can only provide an outline of its subject, and it is for that reason especially important to establish an enlightened and humane attitude to the rhetorical figures, for without this further detailed work on rhetoric could not take place with any conviction of its literary validity. Shakespeare, like Puttenham or Longinus, evidently regarded the figures of rhetoric as having each their own range of relevance to states of mind or feeling. Rather than 'dry formulae' they are channels for feeling, pockets of energy, powerful and flexible according to the mind using them.

III

In his use of rhetoric as in other ways Shakespeare developed from stiffness to flexibility. He does not move away from rhetoric, rather he absorbs it into the tissue of living dramatic speech until it re-creates thought and feeling with a freshness which conceals its art. It is sometimes thought that there is less rhetoric in the later plays, but although we do not yet have an exhaustive study of his rhetorical development it seems to me unlikely that this is so. One can already see that of the many rhetorical figures in Shakespeare quoted by Sister Joseph the majority come from the mature plays, and this is not surprising, for it means that – as one might expect – Shakespeare only gradually learned to use the full resources of rhetoric. The same is true within Milton's development, for rhetoric only comes into its own in *Paradise Lost* (the early poems show a mastery of metaphor but not of the more expressive figures), and this points to a further truth in Shakespeare, that rhetoric is only stretched to its fullest when the action and characters themselves are of a depth and force to draw on the whole resources of language. J. M. Manly's early study of Chaucer's rhetoric was prepared to find the figures used frequently but did not expect to find them in the greatest poetry: 'that some of Chaucer's freest and most delightful work should contain twice as much rhetoric as some of his least inspired compositions is a puzzle that demands investiga-tion.' It is not a puzzle: once we have grasped the functional potential of rhetoric it is self-evident that the greatest poetry may have often been based on the greatest use of rhetoric.

It would take many years to study Shakespeare's stylistic develop-ment with the attention it deserves, but a few examples can be given here, drawing by comparison on some of the figures already cited (I need hardly add that the discussion of individual figures taken out of their dramatic context is a crude and preliminary stage; the challenge facing students of rhetoric is to integrate the appreciation of stylistic detail into a response to the whole). One might juxtapose the rather stiff uses of rhetorical symmetry quoted from *Richard III* with a few lines in *Othello* which also combine *anaphora, isocolon, parison* and *epistrophe*, but to show Othello's trapped mind:

> By the world,
> I think my wife be honest, and think she is not;
> I think that thou art just, and think thou art not.
> I'll have some proof.   (III, iii, 388–90)

An external analysis would record that the same figures are used here as earlier, but evidently they now contain a much more intense and a much more personal kind of feeling, a feeling which is controlled by the symmetry because it is trapped by the action at this point. With the two correct but stiff uses of *gradatio* by Richard compare Othello's:

> No, Iago;
> I'll see before I doubt; when I doubt, prove;
> And, on the proof, there is no more but this –
> Away at once with love or jealousy!   (III, iii, 193–6)

Now the figure is again used for causation but it also expresses a whole view of life, that absolutist tendency in Othello to move to extremes once he is given an 'acceptable' basis which Iago can exploit to the full. And when it reaches its climax, the figure *antanaclasis* (repeating a word or phrase with a shift of meaning) has an incomparably sad and sinister effect:

> Put out the light, and then put out the light.   (v, ii, 7)

As the realization of his act begins to break through, Othello's awareness is rightly conveyed with *ploce* on the key word:

> If she come in she'll sure speak to my wife.
> My wife! my wife! what wife? I have no wife. (v, ii, 99–100)

And having punished himself Othello's dying words fall into the mould of *antimetabole*, without any sense of unnaturalness:

> I kiss'd thee ere I kill'd thee. No way but this –
> Killing my self, to die upon a kiss.   (v, ii, 361–2)

Such a brief juxtaposition of early and late is unsatisfactory as it necessarily fragments, but if taken further it could provide rewarding insights into Shakespeare's realization of the potential expressiveness of particular figures.

The more important task is to evaluate the development of his rhetoric within prose and verse, considering the whole dramatic context. I have elsewhere attempted such an analysis for the prose (Vickers, 1968), and I shall not duplicate my findings here. One important general point, though, which has bearings on Shakespeare's over-all development and on the problems of studying rhetoric in his poetry, is that I showed that his development in prose was not towards either a less extended use of rhetorical figures or a more speedy and brilliant interplay between diverse schemes, but rather that he continued to use the central corpus of figures to create passages of prose which are structurally similar but have an almost infinite range of dramatic functions. That is to say that if one rearranges the many rhetorical prose-speeches into their basic patterns the shape on the page is not fundamentally different between a Dromio and a Timon of Athens: both use *anaphora, parison, isocolon, epistrophe, antimetabole,* and so on. But the function of symmetry as a stress device within the stylistic and dramatic pattern of the play as a whole varies enormously. In the early clowns the speeches are basically catalogues of ridiculous behaviour, but the 'catalogue' later serves both as a satirical description of Ajax (limited in reference but dramatically organic), and for those extraordinary speeches of Poor Tom which refract so much of the

'Reason-in-Madness' of the later stages in *King Lear*. Proficiency in rhetoric can show the excellence of a character, whether for Henry V arguing with his soldiers on the eve of Agincourt and wooing Kate after the battle, or for the matching brilliance of Touchstone and Rosalind; but a fondness for symmetry can also show up the pomposity of Armado, the unsuitably formal political rhetoric of Brutus, and the varying degrees of frankness and deception within Falstaff. Rhetorical symmetry in prose is a tool for which Shakespeare found endless and unpredictable uses.

I would imagine that a chronological study of the development of his verse-rhetoric would reveal an analogous flexibility of reference, and although I do not have room to attempt it here a few points can be made. In the early work one will not be surprised to find that, as rhetoric had been the basis of both prose and verse since Gorgias, Shakespeare applies it to both media with equal stiffness and formality, so that the specific resources of verse tend to get swallowed up by the dominance of rhetorical patterning. Compare these two passages from *The Comedy of Errors*: first, Dromio of Ephesus complaining at the way his master treats him:

> When I am cold he heats me with beating;
> when I am warm he cools me with beating.
> I am wak'd with it when I sleep
> rais'd with it when I sit;
> driven out of doors with it when I go from home;
> welcom'd home with it when I return...   (IV, iv, 29 ff)

Secondly, Adriana complaining that Antipholus neglects her:

> The time was once when thou unurg'd wouldst vow
> That never words were music to thine ear,
> That never object pleasing in thine eye,
> That never touch well welcome to thy hand,
> That never meat sweet-savour'd in thy taste,
> Unless I spake, or look'd or touch'd, or carv'd to thee.
> (II, ii, 112 ff)

Of course, the moods are widely different, but if anything the prose passage shows more inventiveness because it is free from the oppressive regularity of the decasyllabic line, which at this stage Shakespeare is using like building-bricks. (Study of his verse-rhetoric must be combined with that of all the other facets of verse – rhyme, metrics, use of varying line-lengths).

The nature of the development of his verse-rhetoric can be hinted at by the juxtaposition of early and late styles, this time in longer excerpts, relying on the reader's knowledge of the dramatic context.

First a part of the impassioned speech by Queen Margaret to Queen Elizabeth in *Richard III:*

> Where is thy husband now? Where be thy brothers?
> Where be thy two sons? Wherein dost thou joy?
> Who sues, and kneels, and says 'God save the Queen'?
> Where be the bending peers that flattered thee?
> Where be the thronging troops that followed thee?
> Decline all this, and see what now thou art:
> For happy wife, a most distressed widow;
> For joyful mother, one that wails the name;
> For one being su'd to, one that humbly sues;
> For Queen, a very caitiff crown'd with care;
> For she that scorn'd at me, now scorn'd of me;
> For she being fear'd of all now fearing one;
> For she commanding all, obey'd of none.　　(IV, iv, 92–104)

The figures are so obvious that one hardly need name them – two long stretches of *anaphora*; *epistrophe* between lines ('thee' – 'thee') or within them ('at me' – 'of me'); *isocolon* and *parison* throughout, sometimes inventively (e.g. in line 3 the parallel verbs imitate the physical movement – 'sues' – 'kneels' – 'says'); *polyptoton* to help point up the ironic reversal of fortune ('su'd' – 'sues'; 'fear'd' – 'fearing'); *ploce* likewise ('scorn'd' – 'scorn'd'), and two witty uses of antithesis in the last two lines (especially the surprise echo to 'fear'd of all': 'now fearing one', i.e. Richard). It is a vigorous, dramatic speech which still makes its effect in the theatre, and rhetoric is certainly closely associated with feeling. But it is stiff, static, or in the more specific terms of this discussion, Shakespeare is manipulating the feeling *via* the rhetoric, from the outside. Nature has not yet digested the Art.

By contrast, as a parallel example at a similar level of mental excitement we might consider one of Leontes' speeches from *The Winter's Tale*. He is attacking Camillo, who has been trying to assure him that his 'diseas'd opinion' is groundless. Earlier in this tremendous scene Leontes' jealousy has been expressed in the most sinister word-play, as he teased unlooked for meanings out of words to convince himself that there had been a similar doubleness in deeds. But now the structural figures take over, as Leontes attacks with a devastating series of questions, the pressure being increased by *parison* linking the clauses together in a fixed mould, while the verbs are placed savagely at the beginning of each clause and in the form closest to action, *'doing'*:

> Is whispering nothing?
> Is leaning cheek to cheek? Is meeting noses?
> Kissing with inside lip? Stopping the career

Of laughter with a sigh? – a note infallible
Of breaking honesty. Horsing foot on foot?
Skulking in corners? Wishing clocks more swift;
Hours, minutes; noon, midnight?

The symmetry, the very structure of the verse shows the progressive
breakdown of Leontes' mind; he is increasingly obsessed with the
act, with what they might have done together (despite the confident-
sounding questions he has no evidence – each is a figment of his
imagination, given a definite-seeming status by the syntactical structure). The fast growth of the obsession is wonderfully conveyed by
the figure *zeugma*, one verb doing duty for several objects, so speeding
up the clock and the adulterers' imputed impatience: 'Wishing...
Hours, minutes; noon, midnight', from the communal time to the
time for private assignation.

Now to convince himself finally Leontes presents them deceiving
everyone, with an effective use of *anadiplosis* ('but theirs, theirs only'):

And all eyes
Blind with the pin and web but theirs, theirs only,
That would unseen be wicked.

So far, from the first sentence onwards at the end of each question has
been suspended the word 'nothing' (the parisonic structure makes it
evident that this is understood at the end of each clause): 'Is whisper-
ing nothing?/Is leaning cheek to cheek [nothing]? Is meeting noses
[nothing]?' Having been held in reserve for so long the word finally
comes bursting out, with a quite devastating use of *epistrophe*:

– is this nothing?
Why, then the world and all that's in't is nothing;
The covering sky is nothing; Bohemia nothing;
My wife is nothing; nor nothing have these nothings,
If this be nothing.   (I, ii, 284–96)

In the penultimate clause indeed the word forces its way into the
language before its time (*ploce*). We recall Peacham's caveat that the
function of *epistrophe* is 'to leave a word of importance in the end of
a sentence, that it may the longer hold the sound in the mind of the
hearer', or better still John Hoskins' account of linguistic obsession:
'as no man is sick in thought upon one thing but for some vehemency
or distress, so in speech there is no repetition without importance.'
Both points are validated here, and there is a further irony that the
'word of importance' should be 'nothing', for indeed the answer to
Leontes' questions is 'Yes, they are all nothing.' But for him it is
a searing progression of certainties, and rhetoric channels it through

the figures. Here Shakespeare is experiencing the feeling from the inside, his intuitive grasp of human experience finding apparently natural outlet in the shapes of rhetoric.

Finally another example of verse-rhetoric from this play but in a very different mood, to show the variety of which the figures are capable when used creatively. In the sheep-shearing scene, at the end of the great flower-speech, Perdita regrets not having 'flow'rs o'th' spring' for the young, unmarried people, especially for Florizel 'To strew him o'er and o'er!' He protests at this passive role prescribed for him – 'What, like a corse?' – and Perdita denies it:

> No, like a bank for love to lie and play on;
> Not like a corse; or if – not to be buried,
> But quick, and in mine arms.

Already we see how rhetoric (*anaphora, parison*) can be used as a formal device to contain the fluid life of feeling, but in Florizel's response rhetoric both contains and displays his feeling and her unique and endless delight:

> What you do
> Still betters what is done. When you speak, sweet,
> I'd have you do it ever. When you sing,
> I'd have you buy and sell so; so give alms,
> Pray so; and, for the ord'ring your affairs,
> To sing them too. When you do dance, I wish you
> A wave o'th'sea, that you might ever do
> Nothing but that; move still, still so,
> And own no other function. Each your doing,
> So singular in each particular,
> Crowns what you are doing in the present deeds,
> That all your acts are queens.   (IV, iv, 134–46)

To anyone with even a smattering of rhetoric it will be evident that much of what modern critics describe as the 'texture' of verse is in fact the product of a skilful use of rhetoric – density, smoothness, recurrence, fluidity. Here are many of the most formal schemes of rhetoric; three sentences are exactly symmetrical in structure ('When you speak. . . When you sing. . . When you do dance') but *anaphora, parison*, and *isocolon* perfectly convey Florizel's awe at her perfection in all her doings. 'Her doings' is the theme of the whole speech, so it is only right that *ploce* should put constant stress on 'you', and that *ploce* and *polyptoton* should wring every variant from the key verb, 'do': 'do, done, do, do, doing, doing, deeds' until she is crowned: 'all your acts are queens.' Other figures express the perfection of Perdita as she is: *anadiplosis* links together 'sell so; so give alms', or if we take it into the next line 'so' also ends that clause (*epanalepsis*).

At the comparison of Perdita to a wave, the verse takes on a wave-like motion, as several critics have noted, but it does so largely through rhetoric, by the cyclic repetition of 'you' and 'do', and again by *anadiplosis*: 'move still, still so.' And the figures are subtly played off against the verse-movement, with the symmetry now corresponding (lines 2–4), now diverging, using the line-division to accentuate the break within a symmetry (lines 4–5, 7–8). Here the mature Shakespearian style absorbs the structures of rhetoric to produce new and expressive structures of feeling. The early poetry displays its rhetoric stiffly, the mature style absorbs it: therefore modern criticism has been able to ignore the rhetorical framework in the mature style and discuss the life and feeling direct. But it seems at least likely that an awareness of the forms of rhetoric can enlarge our understanding of the poetry, for in Shakespeare's time and in Shakespeare's poetry rhetoric and feeling were one.

7

SHAKESPEARE'S POETRY

INGA-STINA EWBANK

> Nature her selfe was proud of his designes,
>   And ioy'd to weare the dressing of his lines!
> Which were so richly spun, and wouen so fit,
>   As, since, she will vouchsafe no other Wit.

Ben Jonson, 'To the Memory of...Mr. William Shakespeare'
(1623)

We should expect a dramatic poet like Shakespeare to write his finest poetry in his most dramatic scenes. And this is just what we do find...The same plays are the most poetic and the most dramatic, and this not by a concurrence of two activities, but by the full expansion of one and the same activity.   T. S. Eliot, 'A Dialogue on Dramatic Poetry' (1928)

I

Three hundred years separate Ben Jonson's and T. S. Eliot's statements, but they are united in their assurance that Shakespeare's poetry was above all a superb means of dramatic expression. Eliot had to rediscover what Jonson could take for granted: that in Shakespeare the Poet and the Dramatist were, like the Phoenix and Turtle in his own poem, 'single nature's double name'. This is of course only one out of a multitude of possible ways of talking about Shakespeare's poetry. I have chosen it because I believe it to be the most important way, and also because it is impossible in a single essay to deal fully with even a single aspect of Shakespeare's poetry – let alone with them all. One might attempt to give an account of the wide range and scope of his verse as well as its fine nuances and precise and evocative details; of the way his rhythms and imagery altered as he gained ever-greater control of his medium; of his sense of decorum, in the widest application of the word, which means that each of his works has its own poetic qualities and raises its own problems. But to do this – to face all these and many more issues, all of them interrelated – would, as in Milton's poem 'On Shakespeare', tend to 'make *us* marble with too much conceiving'. The reader must regard this essay as an introduction to the dramatic poet rather than an exhaustive examination of Shakespeare's poetry.

Eliot's view of the poet and dramatist as 'two distincts, division none' heralds, in time if not in fact, the generation of scholars and critics to whom present-day students of Shakespeare owe so much. Critics like G. Wilson Knight, Caroline Spurgeon and Wolfgang Clemen – to mention only the pioneers – have taught us to see Shakespeare's poetry as integral to his dramatic fabric. At worst, and in the wrong hands, the approach to each Shakespeare work as 'an expanded metaphor' (G. Wilson Knight) has meant undue concentration on the verse alone, or on iterative imagery, or on Shakespeare's verbal symbolism as a sort of quasi-philosophical system. At best it has meant seeing the poems – especially the sonnets – and the plays as products of the same imaginative process.

Shakespeare himself was reticent about the nature of that process. No doubt most of us feel that he, if anyone, justifies Coleridge's exalted definition of the 'primary Imagination' as 'a repetition in the finite mind of the eternal act of creation in the infinite I AM'; but the nearest he gets to the description of such a creative act is in Theseus' account of how

> The poet's eye, in a fine frenzy rolling,
> Doth glance from heaven to earth, from earth to heaven;
> And as imagination bodies forth
> The forms of things unknown, the poet's pen
> Turns them to shapes, and gives to airy nothing
> A local habitation and a name.
> (*A Midsummer Night's Dream* v, i, 12–17)

And in the dramatic context Theseus is dismissive, even derisive, of the Romantic visionary, placing the poet with the lunatic and the lover as men 'of imagination all compact'. Closer to the Renaissance ideal of the poet as an eloquent teacher is the Poet in *Timon of Athens*, who is also given finer lines about the nature of poetic inspiration –

> our gentle flame
> Provokes itself, and like the current flies
> Each bound it chafes – (i, i, 25–7)

than his opportunist approach to writing, as demonstrated in the play, deserves. But the limitations of a view of poetry as the art of giving outward form to an inner moral are exposed when the Painter tells the Poet: A thousand moral paintings I can show
> That shall demonstrate these quick blows of Fortune's
> More pregnantly than words. (i, i, 93–5)

Shakespeare's whole corpus testifies to the fact that he believed in the pregnancy of words over 'a thousand moral paintings', in the power of imaginative poetry to reach further than any merely visual image. Hamlet, for one, expresses this belief when he rebukes his mother,

> 'Tis not alone my inky cloak, good mother,
> ....
> That can denote me truly...
> ....
> But I have that within which passes show –
> These but the trappings and the suits of woe,
>
> (*Hamlet* I, ii, 77–86)

and then proceeds, through the rest of the play, to use all the resources of language to demonstrate 'that within'.

Unlike his fellow-sonneteer Sidney, Shakespeare left no Apology for Poetry; unlike such of his fellow-dramatists as Nashe, Greene, Jonson, Chapman or Webster, he left no comments outside his plays on what he thought good drama and good poetry should be like. From the plays we can learn something of what he thought they should *not* be like. Mocking of 'taffeta phrases, silken terms precise, / Three-piled hyperboles, spruce affectation, / Figures pedantical' plays a large part in *Love's Labour's Lost,* and most of the other love comedies contain references to literary affectations and mannerisms. Not many agree that *Titus Andronicus* is a parody on 'the height of Seneca his style' as practised by the tragic dramatists of the late 1580s and the early 90s, but the verse of the Mousetrap in *Hamlet* certainly is; and the 'very tragical mirth' of the Pyramus and Thisbe interlude in *A Midsummer Night's Dream* takes off the cruder forms of contemporary dramatic and non-dramatic literature – even, some would say, Shakespeare's own *Romeo and Juliet.* But in none of these cases is the literary satire the main point: it is part of and subordinated to a dramatic exploration of the false as against the genuine, fiction as against reality. Deliberately 'bad' Shakespearean poetry is sometimes functional *rather than* parodic. The nurse's mock-Senecan fulminations against the 'woeful, woeful, woeful day' in *Romeo and Juliet* IV, v, serve to set Juliet's mock-death here off from her real one in the last scene. Othello's departure from his real self, at the point where he definitely succumbs to Iago's persuasions, is measured by his assumption of the voice of the conventional Revenger:

> Arise, black vengeance, from the hollow hell.
> Yield up, O love, thy crown and hearted throne
> To tyrannous hate! Swell, bosom...
>
> (*Othello* III, iii, 451–3)

If the 'poetic' of the plays is often negatively stated and always embodied in the dramatic whole, the sonnets more clearly show

Shakespeare reflecting on his own poetic practice and comparing it with that of others. For example, Shakespeare refuses to 'glance aside / To new-found methods, and to compounds strange' (76), and he has ambivalent feelings about 'the proud full sail' of the Rival Poet's 'great verse' (86). As Joan Grundy has pointed out, Shakespeare and Sidney alone among Elizabethan sonneteers question the aims and methods of the Petrarchan convention which they inherited. But Shakespeare's, unlike Sidney's, questioning is not so much a literary quarrel as part of a larger concern with rendering the real image of the person he is writing of and to and for – the Youth (1–126) and the Dark Lady (127–152). His poet's prayer is: 'O, let me, true in love, but truly write' (21); and to write truly means to show 'that you alone are you' (84). Even in the best-known piece of mockery of Petrarchan love-poetry, 'My mistress' eyes are nothing like the sun' (130), the mockery itself is the staircase by which we climb to the real point of the poem, the celebration of the 'rareness' of the Lady:

> And yet, by heaven, I think my love as rare
> As any she belied with false compare.

Explicitly, then, in the sonnets, Shakespeare is striving for a subordination of the style to the subject matter. Ideally, the style *is* the subject:

> O, know, sweet love, I always write of you,
> And you and love are still my argument;   (76)

> In others' works thou dost but mend the style,
> And arts with thy sweet graces graced be;
>   But thou art all my art.   (78)

That this is not merely an echo of Sidney's 'Look in thy heart and write', but is meant as well as said, is shown by the texture and structure of the individual sonnets. Whatever the 'true' facts behind the 1609 volume of *Sonnets* – and this is not the place to enter into the controversy about the identities of Mr W.H., the Fair Youth, the Rival Poet and the Dark Lady – it remains a poetically true record of two different love relationships, with the fluctuations of mind and mood involved in each. In the first 126 sonnets the Youth is re-created, not in static perfection but dramatically pitted against the enemies that threaten: the flatterers without, his own unfaithfulness within and – all around – the very condition of man as he is subjected to inexorable Time. The greater the threat, the keener the imaginative realization of the enemy's attack and the poet's counter-attack:

> Like as the waves make towards the pebbled shore,
> So do our minutes hasten to their end;
> Each changing place with that which goes before,

In sequent toil all forwards do contend.
Nativity, once in the main of light,
Crawls to maturity, wherewith being crown'd,
Crooked eclipses 'gainst his glory fight,
And Time that gave doth now his gift confound.
Time doth transfix the flourish set on youth,
And delves the parallels in beauty's brow,
Feeds on the rarities of nature's truth,
And nothing stands but for his scythe to mow.
    And yet to times in hope my verse shall stand,
    Praising thy worth, despite his cruel hand.   (60)

J. W. Lever, in a particularly fine analysis of this sonnet, has shown how it 'achieves its own poetic miracle by taking an entire chain of images from the speech of Ovid's Pythagoras [in the *Metamorphoses*] and fusing them at white heat with the themes of the sonnet sequence'. In sonnets like this we have the implicit application of Shakespeare's explicit poetic. But we have it in lesser sonnets, too. Even in the lines which I quoted from Sonnet 78, the style embodies the meaning. The pretty pattern of sound and sense in 'arts with thy sweet graces graced be' resolves itself into the monosyllabic plainness of 'but thou art all my art', where yet the crucial pun on 'art' shows that the plainness is carefully controlled artifice. It is artifice of a lower imaginative order than that behind the careful structuring of evocative images in Sonnet 60; but in neither poem does the style simply illustrate or decorate a thought. The greatest sonnets, whether to the Youth or to the Lady, *enact* the impact of the beloved on the poet, through their diction, their imagery, their rhythm and their structural pattern – whether it be the rise from despondency to jubilation through 'thy sweet love rememb'red' in Sonnet 29, or the downward movement to the realization that 'Time will come and take my love away' of sonnet 64, or the tug-of-war impulses of 'Th'expense of spirit in a waste of shame' in Sonnet 129.

Already we have seen that when Shakespeare sets about applying his sonnet poetic – the fusion of subject and style, matter and manner – this involves qualities which are dramatic as well as poetic. It involves the arrangement of words and images into a pattern which is formal, not merely in the external sense that it consists of three quatrains and a clinching couplet, but in the sense that it imitates an action. And it involves the rendering of the general through the particular, so that the beloved's image, 'most rich in youth', is part of the consciousness that 'every thing that grows / Holds in perfection but a little moment' (15). Both these are essential, and common, to all great dramatists. But there is also another, perhaps peculiarly Shakespearean, quality involved. Read as a whole, the *Sonnets* show an apparently paradoxical combination of a tremendous interest in words and belief in their power with a kind of humbleness about the possibilities of language.

The very desire to show 'that you alone are you' makes the poet conscious of the inadequacy of poetry:

> Who will believe my verse in time to come,
> ....
> If I could write the beauty of your eyes
> And in fresh numbers number all your graces,
> The age to come would say 'This poet lies;
> Such heavenly touches ne'er touch'd earthly faces.'
> So should my papers, yellowed with their age,
> Be scorn'd, like old men of less truth than tongue. (17)

The truth-tongue opposition in that last line reminds us of a key *motif* in *Richard II*. Richard D. Altick, in an important study of 'symphonic imagery' in this play, shows how

that words are mere conventional sounds molded by the tongue, and reality is something else again, is constantly on the minds of all the characters.

Most critics agree that *Richard II* is a milestone in Shakespeare's poetic–dramatic development, and that the play – like its poet-hero – is uniquely self-conscious about the power *and* limitations of language. But the sonnets' questioning of language reverberates right through to the end of Shakespeare's career. In Sonnet 23, the intensity of the poet's emotion outruns words altogether:

> O, let my looks be then the eloquence
> And dumb presagers of my speaking breast;
> Who plead for love, and look for recompense,
> More than that tongue that more hath more express'd.
> O learn to read what silent love hath writ!
> To hear with eyes belongs to love's fine wit.

Shakespeare is here talking about what in *The Winter's Tale* he puts into a stage-image, when he makes the reunion of Leontes and Hermione wordless. In that scene he shows his awareness, as a dramatist, of realities which language cannot get at, not even the subtle tool of his own poetry.

Part of Shakespeare's poetic belief is that what *is* cannot always be said. In this context one should mention his enigmatic poem *The Phoenix and Turtle* – his contribution to the miscellany called *Loves Martyr* (1601) – for it represents his furthest reaching out in words towards what cannot be articulated. It is an incantatory celebration of a love so great and pure and mysterious as to be able to transcend nature and reason, and it is in that sense an extension, in one particular direction, of the sonnets as well as an anticipation of central themes in the Romances. But in its structure and handling of language it strangely anticipates the dramatic rhythm of the closing scenes of *King Lear*, from IV, vi, onwards. The death and victory of Phoenix and the turtle is represented through the 'anthem' of the mourning birds and the 'threnos' spoken by Reason:

> Beauty, truth, and rarity,
> Grace in all simplicity,
> Here enclos'd in cinders lie.
> ....
> Truth may seem, but cannot be;
> Beauty brag, but 'tis not she:
> Truth and beauty buried be.

So at the height of his agony – albeit this is suffering and victory of a different kind – Lear is surrounded by characters who sympathetically participate in what they cannot fully comprehend. There, too, we have statements of utter simplicity in the face of the unbearable, the too great, too complex; and that simplicity has, as in the poem, a kind of imperious finality, as in Edgar's aside at IV, vi, 141–2:

> I would not take this from report. It is,
> And my heart breaks at it.

As in the poem, whatever the central action means, '*it is*'; and all that the survivors can ultimately say is that 'we that are young / Shall never see so much nor live so long'.

The Phoenix and Turtle, because of its purity of diction and lyrical form, has often been compared to the songs in Shakespeare's plays, although of course it is much more intellectual and metaphysically complex than any of the songs. With the songs it also shares the quality of expressing through simple juxtaposition of images or statements, through the combination of words into an incantation rather than an argument, what more logically structured dramatic dialogue cannot express. Shakespeare's songs have increasingly been recognized as dramatically functional, and one of their functions – in the mature plays at least – is to say what could otherwise not be said in the plays where they occur. We need only think of Feste's concluding song which by illogic draws together the discordant elements in *Twelfth Night*; or Ophelia's mad songs; or Desdemona's willow-song, which is the only form in which she can articulate her sense of what is happening.

It would be very wrong to give the impression that Shakespeare, like some modern dramatists, was preoccupied with the non-meaning

of language and the impossibility of communication. The plays themselves, through to Prospero's eloquent farewell to his art, are evidence
enough to the contrary. Through the sonnets there surges a powerful
belief in his own verse, gathered into explicit assertion in the group
that deals with the immortalizing of the Friend by his poetry –
supremely in Sonnet 55:

> Not marble nor the gilded monuments
> Of princes shall outlive this pow'rful rhyme;
> But you shall shine more bright in these contents
> Than unswept stone, besmear'd with sluttish time.

In this sonnet he makes new a commonplace conceit which Renaissance poets took over from Ovid (thus proving his point by the very
writing of the poem). In other sonnets, such as 'Let me not to the
marriage of true minds / Admit impediments' (116), it is by the perfect
handling of some of the simplest words in the language that he makes
his assertion of belief both in his subject and in his poetry. The reason
why it is important to stress Shakespeare's sense (to us perhaps
unwarranted) of the limitations of his poetry is that it is part of the
poetic, in the deepest sense, of the sonnets and of the plays. The poetry
not the poet matters, and the poetry matters as the true image of its
subject. The reason why the sonnets are the greatest love poems in the
language is also the reason why Shakespeare is the greatest poetic
dramatist. We could call it selflessness – and critics have often drawn
attention to the lack of self-assertion in Shakespeare's sonnets, compared
to those of his contemporaries. We could borrow Keats's phrase and
call it 'negative capability'. In either case we are talking of the man
whose 'nature is subdu'd / To what it works in, like the dyer's hand'
(Sonnet 111). And perhaps that is the nearest we can get to a generalization about the poetic *and* dramatic 'activity' which T. S. Eliot spoke of.

II

In making this generalization one is of course cutting across all those
variations within sonnets and between sonnets, within plays and
between plays, that we usually sum up as Shakespeare's development.
How did Shakespeare find his own idiom?

Talking about 'development' within the sonnets is dangerous, for
it is unlikely that the scholarly debate about the dates of individual
sonnets, and about the time-limits within which the whole sequence
was written, will ever be settled. But, whatever their chronological
position (and one would like to think that they are apprentice work),
there are sonnets which do not rise above the level of the conventional

Petrarchan exercise, cleverly refurbishing old conceits and playing the
fashionable game on the themes of sleeplessness, absence or the war
between eye and heart. For extreme examples one may turn to Sonnets
153 and 154, the anticlimactic conclusion to the 1609 volume. They are
variations on a theme borrowed from the *Greek Anthology*: a nymph
steals the arrow of sleeping Cupid and quenches its 'love-kindling
fire' in a cool well, which thus becomes

> a bath and healthful remedy
> For men diseas'd; but I, my mistress' thrall,
> Came there for cure, and this by that I prove:
> Love's fire heats water, water cools not love.   (154)

It is difficult to see anything 'Shakespearean' about this – and
indeed Dover Wilson thought these two poems 'early essays, if indeed
they are Shakespeare's at all'. What the poem is communicating is not
so much the paradoxical impulses of a love relationship as the poet's
pleasure at his own ingenuity: at the verbal pattern of the last line and
the way this clinches, with a q.e.d. finality, the argument of the conceit.
The poets of the 1590s were often intoxicated with word-patterns; and,
unless this is a cynical exercise, Shakespeare, when he wrote it, had
yet to learn how to make such patterns expressive rather than exhibi-
tionist. (One might compare Peele's use of a similar patterning, on
a similar subject, to make a sensuous and moving impact in the opening
song of *David and Bethsabe*.)

But one does not have to read far to discover that Shakespeare could
make verbal ingenuity a means of communicating a sense of life. Thus
in this passage from a sonnet on an apparently conventional subject,

> When most I wink, then do mine eyes best see,
> For all the day they view things unrespected;
> But when I sleep, in dreams they look on thee,
> And, darkly bright, are bright in dark directed;
> Then thou whose shadow shadows doth make bright,
> How would thy shadow's form form happy show
> To the clear day with thy much clearer light,
> When to unseeing eyes thy shade shines so,   (43)

the style is not simply drawing attention to itself. The pattern of
accumulating paradoxes and antitheses becomes an enactment of how
the vision of the beloved gives new content to old words. The meaning
of shadows and forms, brightness and darkness, is, as it were, revalued;
until the dramatic sense of life deserves a comparison with the last
line of Milton's sonnet on his deceased wife:

> I waked, she fled, and day brought back my night.

But where in Milton the reversal of meanings embodies personal tragedy, the mood evoked here is of joy; and G. K. Hunter has nicely described the line 'And, darkly bright, are bright in dark directed' as 'a triumphant dance of words expressing the lover's delight'.

In what we presume to be later sonnets, obvious artifice gives way to the kind of realism which consists in prosaic diction, 'unpoetical' imagery and a rhythm approaching that of the speaking voice. Shakespeare is reflecting, or anticipating, the general stylistic development that we tend to think of as a movement from an Elizabethan to a Jacobean mode of writing; and, in so doing, he is serving his own expressive needs. It is not a question of realistic writing in a modern sense. Sonnets 118 ('Like as to make our appetites more keen') and 147 ('My love is as a fever, longing still / For that which longer nurseth the disease') are as ingenious in their use of metaphor as are sonnets 153–4; but the artifice is now so carefully controlled as to give an impression of nature. While the Cupid-nymph-lover poems fail to communicate the torments of a love where one has 'garner'd up' one's heart, 118 and 147 render, respectively, the agonized experience of a beloved's unfaithfulness and the 'frantic mad' passion for a woman who, the poet *knows*, is 'as black as hell, as dark as night'. Word-patterns in sonnets like these take on a precision which, supported by the movement of the verse, follows the curve of feeling:

> Enjoy'd no sooner but despised straight;
> Past reason hunted, and, no sooner had,
> Past reason hated, ...
> ....
> Had, having, and in quest to have, extreme;
> A bliss in proof, and prov'd, a very woe.   (129)

Shakespeare did more than any other sonneteer to enlarge the human content and expand the thematic range of the sonnet. Even so, the sonnets' scope for action and character is necessarily limited; and they can only give us an outline map of Shakespeare's development as a poetic dramatist. But if they show us Shakespeare moving from a kind of group style, characterized by rather self-conscious use of verbal artifice, through an individual use of elements of that group style, to an individual style in which artifice and nature are so blended that – in Polixenes' words – 'the art itself is nature'; then they also give us a paradigm – not of course to be used too rigidly – for the development of Shakespeare's dramatic poetry.

Elizabethan tragedy of the 1580s and 90s was trying to combine the epic structure of native drama with the unified form of Senecan tragedy in which the hero contemplates his suffering. The result, in terms of style, tends to be a language written for orators, to comment on tableaux, rather than for actors, to make particular dramatic situations and characters alive to the audience. Speeches are often structured on a rhetorical scheme, supported by heavy (and at worst mechanical) alliteration; the imagery tends towards self-conscious similes; the lines are stiffly end-stopped. The language tends to make the impression of having an action of its own, counterpointed to the human reality within the drama. Take, for example, the speech of the dying Mortimer in *1 Henry VI*:

> Even like a man new haled from the rack,
> So fare my limbs with long imprisonment;
> And these grey locks, the pursuivants of death,
> Nestor-like aged in an age of care,
> Argue the end of Edmund Mortimer.
> These eyes, like lamps whose wasting oil is spent,
> Wax dim, as drawing to their exigent;
> Weak shoulders, overborne with burdening grief,
> And pithless arms, like to a withered vine
> That droops his sapless branches to the ground.
> Yet are these feet, whose strengthless stay is numb,
> Unable to support this lump of clay,
> Swift-winged with desire to get a grave,
> As witting I no other comfort have.　　(II, v, 3–16)

In its way, this is a moving speech, but it has to be a long one, for it can make its impact only by accretion. The Elizabethans were triumphantly aware of what Richard Carew, in *The Excellency of the English Tongue* (*c.* 1595), termed 'our tongue's copiousness' and particularly of its richness in 'fruitful and forcible' metaphors. Yet even when Mortimer has taken an inventory from his locks down to his feet, he has left us with a list of items which, however 'forcibly' each is illustrated, do not merge to prove an experience upon our pulses. The scheme of the speech is not so rigid as Hieronimo's notorious outburst of grief ('O eyes! no eyes, but fountains fraught with tears', *The Spanish Tragedy* III, ii, 1 ff), but it has the same basis in a linguistic, rather than experiential, pattern, pointed by alliteration, word-play ('aged in an age of care') and the accumulation of adjectives with similar endings ('pithless', 'sapless', 'strengthless'). We may compare this with the speech of another character who also feels that he belongs with the rack and the grave:

> You do me wrong to take me out o'th'grave.
> Thou art a soul in bliss; but I am bound
> Upon a wheel of fire, that mine own tears
> Do scald like molten lead.　　(*King Lear* IV, vii, 45–8)

Lear needs four lines to communicate infinitely more than Mortimer in his fourteen, and the 'more' is to be measured not in quantity but in quality. Where Mortimer's poetry plays as a kind of decoration over the dramatic situation, Lear's *is* the situation, truly proving upon our pulses what this particular debilitated body feels like and what its spiritual condition is. The language is shaped by the structure of the human experience: literal and metaphorical levels have merged (Lear thinks he *is* in Purgatory, not that he is 'as if'), and the alliteration measures the gulf which he senses between himself and Cordelia ('Thou art a soul in *b*liss; *b*ut I am *b*ound...'). The single metaphor ('like molten lead'), which also contains the single adjective of the passage, renders the intensity, rather than the structure, of the experience. These features are related to the whole poetic quality of *King Lear*, brilliantly analysed by Winifred Nowottny, of being so concerned with simply underlining the intensity of suffering made manifest in the dramatic action that there is little need for analytical imagery to communicate 'what it feels like'. Stage-directions – like '*Enter* Lear, *with* Cordelia *dead in his arms*' – or references to what we can see for ourselves – like 'a head so old and white as this' – become more eloquent than similes or metaphors in a play which concludes on Edgar's exhortation to 'speak what we feel, not what we ought to say'. Mortimer remains articulate, indeed a very systematic chronicler of past history, to his end; and Richard Plantagenet's conventional epitaph on him turns his experience into a generalized allegory:

> And peace, no war, befall thy parting soul!
> In prison hast thou spent a pilgrimage,
> And like a hermit overpass'd thy days.
> (*1 Henry VI* II, v, 115–17)

Lear's dying moments are verbally as broken and tormented, torn to shreds between hope and despair, as the man himself; and as Kent speaks on his death, his words keep the attention riveted on Lear's specific agony:

> Vex not his ghost. O, let him pass! He hates him
> That would upon the rack of this tough world
> Stretch him out longer.   (v, iii, 313–15)

While we thus perceive Lear's individual fate more keenly than Mortimer's, we are yet at the same time more keenly aware of its universal dimension. This is very largely the achievement of the poetry, and partly of the imagery. In making Kent return to the image of the rack, Shakespeare not only reminds us of the earlier scene (IV, vii) but also introduces, in a climactic fashion, a *motif* dominant throughout the play. Ever since Miss Spurgeon's exposition of leading motives in the imagery of Shakespeare's plays, and since Professor Clemen's study of the *dramatic* function of imagery, we have been able to appreciate the way in which iterative imagery spreads a whole network of subterranean connections, often in defiance of ordinary logic, between passages, linking them structurally, fitting them into the whole imaginative fabric of the play, and so expanding issues that the play as a whole asks questions and makes statements larger than a mere plot-paraphrase would suggest. Every student now knows, for example, that disease and poison are dominant images in *Hamlet*; evil, darkness and babes in *Macbeth*; that cosmic and food imagery renders the polarity of *Antony and Cleopatra* – and, indeed, that *King Lear* is dominated by the image of 'a human body in anguished movement, tugged, wrenched, ...tortured and finally broken on the rack' (Miss Spurgeon). We can also now more readily appreciate the effect of recurring key-words – like 'see' in *King Lear* – which cumulatively gain the dramatic and thematic power of images.

But not only imagery links Kent's speech with the poetic and dramatic whole of *King Lear*. The very mode of his speech – his two initial exclamations and the aggressiveness of 'He hates him...' – is that predominant in the play as a whole. ('Blow, winds, and crack your cheeks; rage, blow.' 'Come not between the dragon and his wrath.') It has been pointed out how the plays of Shakespeare's maturity tend to have their typical speech-modes – the questions in *Hamlet*; the ambiguities and equivocations in *Macbeth*; and the exclamations and very simple but also very basic questions in *King Lear* – which not only set the mood for the play but express in epitome its spiritual core. The rhythm of Kent's speech is in itself so close to the speaking voice, and the syntax so expressive of the character Kent at this particular moment, that no superimposed art is apparent (or perhaps even conscious on the part of the author). But here is another way in which the single speech is subordinated to the over-all form of the play; and one is reminded of M. C. Bradbrook's description of 'the central core' of each Shakespeare play as 'an informing power radiating and glowing through every tissue and fibre of the whole, down to the single word'.

If, on the paradigm of Shakespeare's utilization of his poetic gifts, Lear's and Mortimer's speeches represent the two extremes of art and artifice, then the speeches of Richard II, and especially his prison speech in v, v, might represent a mid-way point. Here we have elaborate and self-conscious verbal artifice – extended metaphors, carefully balanced antitheses, intricate word-play – but here, too, the artifice reflects the very nature of the hero and of his tragic dilemma. He is a man who can control words, but not reality. Furthermore,

Shakespeare is not simply letting Richard indulge himself in verbal wit for the sake of character revelation. The speech contains the climactic occurrence of many key-words and image patterns which have been weaving through the play in a 'symphonic' fashion. Its poetry creates a structural as well as thematic resolution for the play as a whole. Guided by Richard Altick, to whose essay I have already referred, we may see *Richard II* as pointing the continuity between the exuberant and often uncontrolled word-play of Shakespeare's earlier plays and the highly controlled use of great image-themes in the plays of his mature period. Both characteristics testify to his associative poetic power; the difference between them testifies to his development from a dramatic poet to a poetic dramatist.

In concentrating on a few chosen passages, I have obviously begged many questions and excluded vast areas of Shakespearean dramatic verse. The qualities to be found in the *Henry VI* plays could, to a large extent, be paralleled in *Titus Andronicus*; but already *Romeo and Juliet* shows Shakespeare discovering new dramatic possibilities within con-temporary poetic conventions – such as using a love sonnet for the dialogue of Romeo and Juliet's first meeting. The early, middle and 'Problem' comedies present their own features and problems, which the scope of this essay cannot hold. The poetry of *King Lear*, like that of all the great tragedies, is not typical of anything but itself. The longer and more analytical speeches of Hamlet or Macbeth would have provided better examples of Shakespeare making rhythm, diction and imagery expressive of a character's inner life, while also suggesting the general through the particular – so that in Macbeth's 'If it were done...' we both *know* his state of mind and sense something about good, evil and damnation in general. The poetry of the Roman plays, and especially of *Coriolanus* with its 'public' use of language and its deliberately non-evocative imagery, would have illustrated the shaping power of Shakespeare's sense of decorum. (Students of the Roman plays are indebted to Maurice Charney for his analysis of their style, or styles.) And, finally, the poetry of the Last Plays defies generaliza-tions as much as that of the others, but in different ways. They contain passages as tense and expressive as anything in the tragedies (one thinks, for example, of Leontes's jealousy); but there are also passages that seem to return to an earlier, decorative or artificial mode. Granville-Barker even spoke of 'a new euphuism of imagination' in these plays. And there is, too, a new kind of elliptical writing which James Sutherland has discussed in a provocative essay. It is as if Shakespeare were at times forcing the situation to yield meanings which it can barely sustain, or as if the metaphysical mode were swamping the dramatic.

With all these qualifications made (and many not made that should have been), the passages on which I have been concentrating yield a few simple truths about Shakespeare's development. They show that it is a matter of the way language is subordinated to subject matter. The artistic growth here is obviously to be seen in terms of both language and subject. The *King Lear* passage is better than the one from *Henry VI* not simply because it contains better poetry – or, as Mrs Nowottny has put it,

With Shakespeare, the language that 'makes' the play depends in the first instance on his making the kind of play in which it is possible and proper to speak it.

What is involved, is an ever-growing sensitivity to language, inextricably tied up with an ever-larger sensitivity to human experience. That Shakespeare was interested in life can be proved (if it needs proving) from all his poetry: one could point to the almost obsessive urge in the sonnets to give the beloved life within the medium of language; or to the way abstracts come alive in his language; or one could simply refer to Miss Spurgeon. However much one doubts her biographical interpretation of Shakespeare's imagery – Shakespeare's feelings about dogs or the eddy under the Clopton bridge – one must believe her when she says that 'it is the life of things which appeals to him, stimulates and enchants him, rather than beauty of colour or form or even significance'. And clearly different aspects of life interested him more or differently at different times in his career. However mythical his sorrows, when he wrote *Troilus and Cressida* he needed, and found, a language for the violence of sex and the destructiveness of Time which he had not found when he wrote *The Two Gentlemen of Verona* and did not need when he wrote *The Winter's Tale*. It is the amount of felt life in his dramatic poetry which first and last moves us; and this is proved at the simplest level by the way our own experiences modify our reactions to his lines. It does not matter how many children Lady Macbeth had, but every woman who has nursed a baby will ever afterwards feel more strongly about her 'I have given suck' speech, as about Cleopatra's 'Dost thou not see my baby...'. At another level it is proved by the effect which his characters produce of being – in Eric Bentley's phrase – 'in the world'. Through the verse we perceive the dynamism of ideas passing in and out of their minds: Macbeth is probably the clearest example. We see their minds being coloured by an event or an idea (Hamlet), or even usurped by someone else's vision of life, as is the case with Othello in III, iii. We see the dialogue developing into a record of the interaction of minds, so that the last fifty-five lines of *Macbeth* I, vii, become a living image of how

Macbeth's will feeds upon Lady Macbeth's and is spurred by it, until he can speak the final couplet with what is virtually her voice. (Irving in fact gave the last two lines to Lady Macbeth, thus spoiling the point.) We see the formalized stichomythia of early tragedy translated into the head-on clash of alienated and opposed sensibilities –

> QUEEN   Hamlet, thou hast thy father much offended.
> HAMLET Mother, you have my father much offended.
> QUEEN   Come, come, you answer with an idle tongue.
> HAMLET Go, go, you question with a wicked tongue—
>
> (*Hamlet* III, iv, 9–12)

or, at the opposite extreme, into the complete and sympathetic sharing of experience at the end of *King Lear*:

> KENT   Is this the promis'd end?
> EDGAR   Or image of that horror?
> ALBANY   Fall and cease!
>
> (*King Lear* V, iii, 263–4)

There can hardly be a more obvious example in dramatic literature of the audience off and on stage participating in a moment of only-too-keenly felt life.

But no amount of felt life in single and separate moments will make a play. For the dynamic and sustained, and yet concentrated, rendering of life that is drama, there must be a coherent relationship between all the moments: a form. If one part of Shakespeare's unique gift is a genius for language that expresses human experience, the other part is a genius for form that organizes words and experience into an imaginative whole.

It may, finally, be a hallmark of his art that within each play this imaginative unity co-exists with a greater variety of styles than we find in any other major dramatist. In no play is that variety more striking, nor more functional, than in *Antony and Cleopatra*. It is a play where we are constantly being asked to move through dimensions: of time (the Antony that was *versus* the Antony that is), of space (Rome *versus* Egypt), and of language (the cosmic *versus* the human, the heroic *versus* the humorous, the superlative *versus* the very ordinary). Cleopatra's image has room for the barge-speech *and* for the nurse being sucked asleep by the babe at her breast; for 'Royal Egypt, Empress!' *and* for 'e'en a woman, and commanded / By such poor passion as the maid that milks / And does the meanest chares'. The play's poetry delights in defying expectations, using the simplest imagery at the most exalted moments. When Antony dies in Cleopatra's arms, what starts as a 'high' speech turns quietly towards a sense of personal loss and a feeling that:

> Young boys and girls
> Are level now with men. The odds is gone,
> And there is nothing left remarkable
> Beneath the visiting moon.   (IV, xv, 65–8)

In Act V Cleopatra presents to Dolabella her vision of Antony in imagery of breath-taking grandeur, looking up and down the Great Chain of Being and all through the cosmos for terms of comparison:

> His face was as the heav'ns, and therein stuck
> A sun and moon, which kept their course and lighted
> The little O, the earth.
> ....
> His legs bestrid the ocean; his rear'd arm
> Crested the world. His voice was propertied
> As all the tuned spheres,...
> ....
> .... His delights
> Were dolphin-like.   (V, ii, 82–9)

Who but Shakespeare would dare to puncture such a speech thus:

> CLEOPATRA   Think you there was or might be such a man
>   As this I dreamt of?
> DOLABELLA   Gentle madam, no.

And who else would leave us with the feeling that Cleopatra's vision both is and is not true? The play's vision of the *range* of possibilities within a single human life cuts across the simply ethical dimension – which, of course, is amply represented, too, as in 'the triple pillar of the world transform'd / Into a strumpet's fool'—and no analysis can exhaust the reasons why we are so moved at 'a lass unparallel'd'.

Antony and Cleopatra shows Shakespeare's awareness that human experience is often intangible and ultimately, at its highest reaches or lowest depths, mysterious. It is amorphous and chaotic. 'The web of our life is of a mingled yarn, good and ill together.' We look to our poets to illuminate the mysteries and to our dramatists to make order out of the chaos. It was the achievement of the greatest poet-dramatist to create such order without destroying the mystery of human personality and human fate. His lines were indeed 'so richly spun, and wouen so fit', but, as in Desdemona's handkerchief, there was also magic in the web.

8

SHAKESPEARE'S NARRATIVE POEMS

J. W. LEVER

In all editions of Shakespeare's collected works, his poems appear after the entire body of thirty-seven plays, making up a kind of non-dramatic appendix. Tradition alone explains this position, with its suggestion of second-class matter. Down the centuries editors have respectfully followed the broad lay-out of the First Folio, which included only the dramas; when in 1778 the poems were added, it seemed inevitable that they should be tacked on at the end of the familiar sequence. There they have since remained. Yet as an introduction to Shakespeare's complex genius, the narrative poems at least might have been more suitably placed at the head of his works. In order of composition *Venus and Adonis*, published in 1593, was not likely to have been what Shakespeare in his dedication termed 'the first heir of my invention', but it was certainly his first work to appear in print. *The Rape of Lucrece* followed in the next year, when the only plays yet published were *Titus Andronicus* and the unauthorized quarto of *2 Henry VI*. More important than matters of chronology, these poems give a striking impression of the energy and range of the early Shakespeare; more so, indeed, than his first experiments on the stage. Written at a time when the theatres were closed on account of plague in the capital, they belong to a phase of rapid maturing and awareness of latent powers. Into them was poured a ferment of intuitions, perceptions, speculations and fancies that had not yet found dramatic expression. Many of the sonnets have these qualities and often show close resemblances in attitudes, imagery and turn of phrase; but as a personal medium they stand at a further remove from the plays. The narrative poems were, in the truest sense, the 'first heirs' of Shakespeare's literary creation.

Both *Venus and Adonis* and *Lucrece* were widely read and admired in their time; both, however, can mislead a modern reader who comes to them unprepared. Their unchecked exuberance, ornamentation and profusion of trope and conceit were characteristic of the younger Shakespeare and the age he grew up in: they were not, as they might be in a present-day writer, marks of a superficial talent. Also the poems need to be seen in their respective settings if their tone is to be understood. *Venus and Adonis* has been thought at once too sensuous and too cold, too fleshly and too abstract, too absurd in its situations and yet too tragic in nuance. *Lucrece* has seemed an undramatic drama, too static for the stage, too rhetorical for narrative verse. Such reactions, sincere as they may be, arise from a half-conscious application of standards foreign to the poems themselves. These poems are not 'dramatic', nor are they 'narrative' in the usually accepted sense. They work through their distinctive modes, mythological romance in the case of *Venus and Adonis*, tragical morality in that of *Lucrece*. Through the channels of these Elizabethan forms they aimed at reconciling a variety of effects. Success was not total, but by and large the medium of myth in *Venus and Adonis* brought a wide range of attitudes into accord. Elements of humour and pathos, sensuous and intellectual perceptions combined. With some minor and local flaws, the poem is a triumphant example of diversity in unity. In *Lucrece* the results were less even. The morality form was not so flexible as that of myth, and structurally the poem was unwieldy. There are nevertheless passages of remarkable power, and the first part at least is an outstanding achievement.

Mythological romance gained marked popularity in the last years of the sixteenth century. Introduced by Lodge in *Scilla's Metamorphosis* (1589), it was taken up by Marlowe, Drayton and others. The common inspiration was Ovid's *Metamorphoses*, which offered not only a wealth of story material but also a form that crystallized an acute awareness of the beauty, sensuousness and multiplicity of nature. Ovid's tales presented a virginal world without history or morality. It was inhabited by figures who were creatures of impulse embodying divine or natural forces, archetypes rather than many-sided human beings. Their pursuits, flights, ardours and recoils not so much reflected as prefigured the behaviour of social man. Loveliness and horror, desire and death, were part of their world, but these were regarded with a calm, half-ironic detachment that held the reader's interest, while keeping him at a distance from full imaginative participation. Happenings that in other mediums would evoke pained, erotic or amused responses followed in smooth sequence without arresting the unperturbed narrative flow. In this realm of myth the springs of human experience could be descried and mapped out with a clarity no other medium could provide.

Shakespeare borrowed the outline of *Venus and Adonis* fom Ovid's tale in *Metamorphoses* x, but took details from some of the other stories. Adonis was described by Ovid as a willing young lover with whom Venus enjoyed the pastoral life for an unspecified period, dressing herself as a huntress and joining in the chase against timid hares and deer, though warning him against dangerous beasts. In Shakespeare the events were compressed into a single summer's day and night. At dawn the immortal goddess visited an 'earthly son' and proceeded to woo him with all her charms. Adonis, a coy, self-regarding adolescent, rejected her through the hours of daylight. Aspiring to another kind of manly prowess, he chose that night to hunt the boar, and was killed for his pains. Next morning Venus discovered his body: in her grief she forsook the world and laid a curse on human love, henceforth to be linked with perverseness, cruelty and suffering. As a model of how the spirit of Ovidian narrative might be carried over into English verse, *Scilla's Metamorphosis* set a good formal precedent. Lodge's six-line stanzas had grace and poise; they kept the action moving easily, while allowing scope for elaboration. Early in the poem the story of Adonis was alluded to, with the death of 'the sweet Arcadian boy' and Venus's agonized laments:

> How on his senseless corse she lay a-crying,
> As if the boy were then but new a-dying.

And there were clear hints for the courtship of Adonis in the description of a disdainful Glaucus wooed by the enamoured sea-nymph Scilla:

> How oft with blushes would she plead for grace,
> How oft with whisp'rings would she tempt his ears:
> How oft with crystal did she wet his face:
> How oft she wiped them with her amber hairs:
> So oft, methought I oft in heart desired
> To see the end whereto disdain aspired.

Shakespeare's imagination was engaged on a variety of levels, and the story as he reconceived it had a complexity of its own. Ovid's Arcadian landscape merged insensibly with the English countryside, its downs and woodlands, pastures and hedgerows, foxes and hares, with the noises of hunting dogs and lark-song up on high. There was inherent comedy in the situation of the love-sick goddess of love, frustrated by a callow boy who pouted and turned away his face from her kiss. Setting and situation came together happily in the escapade of Adonis's horse, the paragon of its kind, who breaks his rein and gallops away to answer the call of 'A breeding jennet, lusty, young and proud'; the natural courtship of the animals supplying implicit comment on the waywardness of the young human male. Lovers' follies, and the worse follies of those who rejected love, would be matter for future romantic comedies teaching the lesson 'Make the most of the present time'. In the Arden of *As You Like It* and the woods of *A Midsummer Night's Dream* a range of perverse attitudes would be explored. The plight of Venus prefigured Titania's love for a mortal; Adonis's self-regard looked ahead to that of Bertram in *All's Well*. As in these plays, intellectual issues are also joined. At times the dialogue becomes a set *débat*, with the goddess condemning 'fruitless chastity' in arguments drawn from Erasmus's *Encomium Matrimonii*, and the boy countering with a moralist's diatribe against lust, broken off as he remembers that 'The text is old, the orator too green'. Shakespeare was raising questions of major concern in his approach to life and love. The conception of Increase as the only answer to 'never-resting time', as well as concern with the workings of lust in action, would recur throughout the plays and were directly linked with the themes of the sonnets.

Permeating the poem, underlying its romance, its comedy, its fresh descriptions of nature, its theoretical discourses, is a sense of elemental tragedy. The keynote is struck in the opening lines of Venus's first address to Adonis:

> Nature that made thee, with herself at strife,
> Saith that the world hath ending with thy life.

In all Shakespeare's writing, 'Nature with herself at strife' was the deepest apprehension, that no received concept of world order, no Platonist or Christian idealism, could altogether dispel. At the quick of experience no individual could escape the co-presence of beauty and destruction, love and death, creation and chaos. Awareness of this gives a special urgency to Venus's wooing, and her presentiment of the death of Adonis mirrors a universal pessimism:

> For he being dead, with him is beauty slain,
> And, beauty dead, black chaos comes again.

The vision of destruction takes in not only the central figures of the poem, but also its natural setting. Terror is the lot of all creatures. The startled hare who 'Cranks and crosses with a thousand doubles' in a desperate attempt to outrun the hounds; the injured snail struck on its 'tender horns' who

> Shrinks backward to his shelly cave in pain,
> And there, all smoth'red up, in shade doth sit,

share a common experience with the goddess on earth and her human love. The snail's fearful retreat images Venus's eyes shrinking from the sight of dead Adonis. In gruesome contrast, the frothy mouth of the boar after its kill, 'Like milk and blood being mingled both together', resembles the white and red complexion of the living boy. Significantly, Venus in the presence of death has no more serenity than any country girl who has lost her lover; she shares the helplessness of all creatures. Such insights foreshadow the great love tragedies, anticipating Othello's premonition 'Chaos is come again', and Cleopatra's 'No more but e'en a woman, and commanded / By such poor passion as the maid that milks'.

Shakespeare's rehandling of Ovid's myth gives it a new breadth and universality, through which the diverse perceptions are integrated. Venus is not just one more tenuous figure of pastoral, indistinguishable from others in her disguise as a huntress. The poem draws attention to her many attributes as the great goddess of love. Her arrival on earth is sudden and mysterious. She has put on a woman's form, yet she is strangely incorporeal, neither naked nor clothed, neither young nor old, with perennial beauty that 'as the spring doth yearly grow'. The sensuality of her courtship is only apparent: her hand if touched would 'dissolve, or seem to melt'; the primroses she lies on support her 'like sturdy trees'; when the time will come for her to leave earth, two 'strengthless doves' will draw her through the skies. As Venus Genetrix, her wooing proceeds on various levels: through direct sensuous appeal; through charming the intellect and the fancy,

> Bid me discourse, I will enchant thine ear,
> Or, like a fairy, trip along the green,
> Or, like a nymph, with long dishevelled hair,
> Dance on the sands, and yet no footing seen. . .

through yoking erotic sensations to the pleasures of hillock and brake, making her body a source of delight on the vegetable plane of existence – 'I'll be a park, and thou shalt be my deer'; – through evoking the precedent of fierce animal desire set by the runaway horse. As for Adonis, the commonplace adolescent is transformed in the eyes of Venus, as the friend of the sonnets was transformed in the eyes of Shakespeare the poet, becoming 'the very archetypal pattern and substance of which all beautiful things are but shadows'.[1] The essence of all that was lovely and transient in nature,

> his breath and beauty set
> Gloss on the rose, smell to the violet.

Conversely, the boar that slays Adonis is no common beast like the many wild animals against which he had been warned in Ovid's story. Unique in its blind ferocity, it is presented as the antitype of destruction, unmotivated, brutishly unaware of the death it carries. At the end, Shakespeare keeps Ovid's metamorphosis of Adonis into a wind-flower; but this is subordinate in importance to the universal change in the nature of love itself. As Venus yokes her doves and despairingly flies back to Paphos, she leaves behind her the fallen world of everyday life.

In terms of Ovid's medium, Shakespeare had created a myth to end myths. But seen in a wider frame of reference, *Venus and Adonis* has affinities with the more elemental Greek myths of nature and human passion. In its tragical aspect it recalls the story of Hippolytus and Phaedra, which Shakespeare must have known from Seneca. There, however, both protagonists were fully human, and Aphrodite had become less a divinity than desire personified. In the purer form of a pagan nature myth, Bion's *Lament for Adonis* had the universality of Shakespeare's poem. Adonis was a superhuman figure, the demigod of vegetation whose death was accompanied by the fall of the season, and who was mourned by all living things. But the treatments differed basically as much as the outlook of the Greek world differed from that of the Renaissance. Bion's elegy described the whole of nature grieving in sympathy with the divine lovers:

Woe, woe for Cypris, the mountains all are saying, and the oak trees answer, *woe for Adonis*. And the rivers bewail the sorrows of Aphrodite, and the wells are weeping Adonis on the mountains.[2]

In *Venus and Adonis*, nature does not go into mourning; on the contrary, there is total indifference. The world knows nothing of its loss; the echoes do not, as in Bion's *Lament*, grieve of their own accord, but senselessly repeat Venus's cries. Summer preserves its outward charm; only in the deeper insight of the bereaved is its beauty seen to be empty:

> The flowers are sweet, their colours fresh and trim,
> But true-sweet beauty liv'd and died with him.

Shakespeare's myth draws its validity not from the outer world but from the human imagination only. All through his poem there is a disparity between physical sight and the vision of the inner eye. Venus might be the embodiment of beauty and love, but to the literal-minded Adonis she is no more than an infatuated older woman. The reader for his part is inclined to see Adonis objectively as an uninteresting youth, callow and self-absorbed; only through the eyes of Venus does he appear as 'The field's chief flower...more lovely than a man'. The ambivalence of truth and seeming was the mainspring of both comedy and tragedy in Shakespeare; only in the imagination of lovers and poets is the transcendent worth of the individual affirmed.

The expression of such antinomies through complex human experience belonged to Shakespeare's life-work as a dramatist. The development was from myth to history, from fictional paradigms to

many-sided individuals. Maturity brought an ever more intense awareness of the duality of life, but also a growing belief in the capacity of
love to transcend it. In the love tragedies the characters were exposed
from all quarters to the disparities of truth and seeming, the destructive
action of time, the chaos that underlay order. *Antony and Cleopatra*
was, in this sense, a vast reworking of *Venus and Adonis*. Not Ovid's
pastoral world but an empire torn by civil war formed the setting.
Instead of one day of frustrated courtship between the goddess of love
and a boy with a mind bent only on hunting, the rival claims of love
and ambition were fought out over years in the souls of a great queen
and a military hero. The desires, ardours and caprices of the immortal
Venus were realized in an all too human Cleopatra. Adonis's youthful
dreams of prowess became the exploits of an ageing Antony who would
at last be caught in 'the world's great snare'. Yet in the realm of the
imagination both lovers at death attained to the rank of demigods. In
Shakespeare's later drama myth was not abandoned, but built itself
a new validity through the workings of whatever was godlike in
human nature.

The Rape of Lucrece, Shakespeare's second narrative poem, was
conceived on a different basis. Again the outlines were taken from Ovid,
but from the *Fasti*, not the *Metamorphoses*; a prose account by Livy
was also consulted, as well as Chaucer's rendering in *The Legende of
Good Women*. The story was of crime, suffering and retribution;
legendary indeed, but rooted in the world of history, not myth,
describing the passions of human beings, not projections of fancy. In
the dedication to *Venus and Adonis* 'some graver labour' had been
promised. *Lucrece*, carefully printed and again dedicated to Southampton, lived up to the description. What Ovid had told in 131 lines of
compact hexameters was expanded into a poem of 1855 lines, composed
in 'rhyme royal' that produced a more weighty effect than the six-line
stanza and lent itself to even more elaborate treatment. Every device
of rhetorical amplification, patterned imagery and intricate conceit
was worked into the texture. Action alternated with reflection; inner
conflicts were set over against generalities; minute detail and large
abstractions both found a place. From start to finish, a strong rhythmic
drive carried the narration on through its varying tempos.

To understand these qualities, some recognition of Shakespeare's
artistic problem is called for. Clearly he was undertaking an essay in
the tragic mode, and on lines very different from the treatment he
found in his sources. The primary object in *Lucrece* was not to portray
a virtuous woman, or to relate a great historical event, but to show
the workings of evil on a universal scale. The theme of creative love
in *Venus and Adonis* was here to be replaced by that of 'lust in action',

vicious, destructive, and serving to typify the dark forces in man and nature alike. *Venus and Adonis*, too, had conveyed a profound sense of the tragical side of existence, but the Ovidian style of narration had maintained an overriding elegance and detachment. For *The Rape of Lucrece* a form was required that would allow the destructive and chaotic elements to predominate. At this stage of Shakespeare's development, the inevitable course was to make use of such models as the poetry of his age could offer.

The form chosen was neither drama nor simple narrative, but stemmed from the Elizabethan 'tragical morality', where an exemplary story, based on history, was made to drive home a moral principle. 'Tragedy' here was essentially rhetorical and didactic, unrelated to drama, and typically defined as 'a lofty kind of poetry, shewing the rueful end of royal personages and their fall from felicity'.[3] The most celebrated work of its kind was *A Mirror For Magistrates* (1555–87), presenting stories of the fall of rulers and statesmen. Written for the most part in solemn stanzas of 'rhyme royal', they served as a series of contemporary warnings against the sins of ambition and lust. Daniel's *Complaint of Rosamund* (1592) continued the tradition, with less concern for teaching a political lesson and a centring of interest in the female victim of corruption amongst the great. Shakespeare's poem was structurally a broad amalgam of the two kinds, and might, in sixteenth-century fashion, have been termed 'The Tragedy of Tarquin and the Complaint of Lucrece'. Instead of monologues interspersed with prose comments there was a framework of third-person narrative, though in the second part much of the poem was devoted to Lucrece's laments. The didactic tone was preserved, but directed not so much to rulers as to persons of high social rank. In momentary recoil from his intended crime Tarquin is made to exclaim:

> O shame to knighthood and to shining arms!
> O foul dishonour to my household's grave!

Historically, as was made clear in the sources and indeed the 'Argument' to the poem,[4] Tarquin was the son of a usurper who had murdered his own father-in-law and practised many tyrannies; he had no family honour to lose. But such anxieties would have been fitting enough for a young Elizabethan nobleman of high lineage. As an example to shun, the Tarquin of this poem was a 'mirror' for individuals like the Earl of Southampton, heir to his dead father's estate, who came of age in the year *Lucrece* was published.

Shakespeare's treatment, however, ranges far beyond the rather narrow limits of the conventional forms. He borrows the rhetorical style; indeed, he heightens it; but he also infuses a stream of complex imagery sprung from his own tragic perceptions. Individual crime and suffering are given a universal resonance. Lust becomes an aspect of that predatory nature implied in *Venus and Adonis* but here made fully explicit. Darkness, clouds, beasts and birds of prey take the place of sunshine, starlight, flowers and innocent animals. Reinforcing the violence in nature are images of aggression and conquest in the human sphere, as well as suggestions of the guilt-ridden psyche of the wrong-doer. In the latter part of the poem Lucrece's laments reach out to indict nature, society, and the very structure of creation. The long account of the picture of Troy presents a sustained metaphor of war and its evils, centring on the treacherous Sinon and Hecuba, 'Time's ruin, beauty's wrack, and grim care's reign'. The morality form, less flexible than myth, is strained to breaking point by the vast creative energy it is made to hold. So long as action carries the poem forward, a remarkable sombre power is generated; but after the first part has reached its climax, an increasing imbalance sets in between the traditional mode for expressing tragedy and Shakespeare's wide apprehensions of what the tragic state involves.

In the dedication, *Lucrece* is described as 'this pamphlet without beginning'. The poem makes no attempt to provide a historical background to events. Nor is mention made of Tarquin's first visit to Lucrece in company with her husband, when her beauty and modest bearing had aroused his desire. Political setting and plausibility alike are sacrificed for an intense concentration on the primary moral theme, the assault of irresistible lust upon innocent chastity. Plunging at once *in medias res* with the furious ride of 'lust-breathed Tarquin', the poem makes headlong action the correlative of the wild urge of desire. Outer and inner realities correspond through images of fire and smoke, torches, coals and darkness. Antithetically Lucrece is introduced, not as in Ovid's realistic description of her, spinning with her maids and weeping at Collatine's absence, but abstracted in a heraldic conceit depicting her face as an emblem of beauty and virtue reconciled. In keeping with the didactic medium, the vanity of lust is explicitly stated in Tarquin's tortuous mental debates ' 'Tween frozen conscience and hot-burning will'. The thing he seeks is 'A dream, a breath, a froth of fleeting joy'; it would bring shame and self-hatred; the scandal would blot his escutcheon and disgrace his descendants. Alternating with debate, the chaos in Tarquin, the calm in Lucrece is presented through patterned imagery that sets up a universal opposition between the two states. Night as an enveloping presence accompanies Tarquin in his movements and meditations. With night go its creatures, owls, wolves, vultures, hawks; types of all that is predatory in animal nature. On the human plane, Tarquin's lust, the 'uproar' in his veins, his 'drumming' heart, even his hand that 'marched', become troops of a squalid army of invasion, 'In bloody death and ravishment delighting'. His thief-like progress towards the bedchamber is punctuated by impediments and alarms: the door grating on the threshold, the shriek of weasels, the successive locks to be forced, the glove with the needle that pricks his finger. The vivid details, charged with dreamlike evocativeness, serve as projections of anxiety and guilt in the soul. In contrast the sight of Lucrece peacefully asleep gives rise to images of another order. Her presence suggests a dazzling beam of sunlight, a 'virtuous monument', 'an April daisy on the grass', symbolizing bright chastity, cold virtue and vulnerable innocence. Rhetoric again supervenes as she awakes and calls reason to her aid with measured arguments. Briefly the assault is held back, but soon desire rudely breaks up the flow of words, and the rape is accomplished. As in the sonnets, lust is 'Enjoy'd no sooner but despised straight'. Like 'full-fed hound or gorged hawk' it withdraws, tame at last, leaving Tarquin's soul defiled. Evil has run its course; but not before its work of destruction and self-destruction has been consummated.

The second and longer portion of the poem is dominated by the figure of Lucrece lamenting her woes and making the decision to end her life. In the 'complaint' medium the heroine usually recounted her story and the circumstances that led to her fall. The line of development led on to full-scale characterization in the manner of Defoe and Richardson. But here the one important action left to relate is Lucrece's suicide. The laments lack narrative constraint and expand in a vacuum. As for character, the intense concentration on Tarquin as a moral example has reduced Lucrece in the first part to an emblem of virtue; in the latter portion she becomes little more than a declamatory voice. Here lies the basic weakness, rather than in the rhetorical style itself, though the opportunities for conscious eloquence tempted Shakespeare's facility and led to a piling up of tropes in imitation of the Senecan grand manner. It was even difficult to manipulate sympathy with the act of suicide, an ethically dubious course for Christian readers who accepted the maxim that 'compelled sins were no sins'. Only in brief phases of action, addressing her maid or giving her letter to the groom, does Lucrece engage interest. On the other hand, the extensive monologues allow Shakespeare to enlarge on major themes implicit in the imagery of the Tarquin section. The properties of evil and the workings of chance and mutability are explored on a cosmic scale. Tarquin's crime is presented as an aspect of the nature of things, challenging any optimistic belief in 'world order'. Night, the accomplice of Tarquin, is a 'vast, sin-concealing chaos'. Opportunity or chance is seen as an autonomous force able to corrupt innocence and frustrate virtue both in nature and man. The view of a tainted world comprehends a society that is heartless and cruel, where 'The orphan pines while the oppressor feeds'. Time, in one aspect the universal healer, in another brings decay and oblivion, destroys monuments and spoils antiquities. On all planes of being duality prevails. The enormous indictment amounts to a statement of the major premises of Shakespearean tragedy.

The Rape of Lucrece has been generally seen as a striking anticipation of *Macbeth*. Actually the resemblance lies mainly in the first part. The conflict in the wrongdoer's soul, the demoniacal drive to evil, the setting of darkness, the imagery of war and creatures of prey closely link the 'tragedy of Tarquin' to the mature drama. The morality form here collaborated fruitfully with Shakespeare's own perceptions and pointed a way forward in his development as a tragedian. No simple reworking of Ovid's narrative technique could have brought about such results. Moreover, in its own right this portion of the poem was a fine achievement. Its kinetic qualities, its use of internal dialogue, its sharply focused details of sight and sound, give it distinctive properties, often outside the scope of drama and in some ways analogous to the art of film. If the heightened rhetoric and emotive imagery are alien to our conceptions of poetry, they have found their modern equivalents in other, non-literary mediums. For Shakespeare's age their recognized place was in narrative verse. After the first powerful episode, however, *Lucrece* loses momentum and formal cohesion. The gap opens ever wider between the poem as an artifact and as a repository for Shakespearean concepts and themes. Yet in this respect, at least, the poem remains of absorbing interest. The great addresses to Night, Opportunity and Time may add little to Lucrece's stature, but they prefigure Shakespeare's vision of tragedy more clearly than anywhere else in his early writing. The detailed description of Troy, though awkwardly linked to the subject matter of the poem, was the first presentation of a recurrent theme, to be returned to in *2 Henry IV* and *Hamlet*, and treated at length, as the archetype of 'wars and lechery', in *Troilus and Cressida*. Indeed, the brief sketches of 'sly Ulysses', the senile Nestor, and 'despairing Hecuba' seem like notes for the stage characters of that play. At the end, the strangely inapposite description of Brutus, with his 'folly's show' disguising 'deep policy', looks ahead to the Antony of *Julius Caesar*.

With its poise, clarity and varied appeal, *Venus and Adonis* is a more successful poem than the over-ambitious but ill-balanced *Rape of Lucrece*. Yet both poems have outstanding merit in their different but complementary modes. Together they are unique forerunners of Shakespeare's fulfilled dramatic powers.

9

SHAKESPEARE THE ELIZABETHAN DRAMATIST

DAVID BEVINGTON

The division between Shakespeare's Elizabethan phase and his Jacobean phase is real and significant. Whatever his reasons, Shakespeare did in fact seek a new direction and emphasis during the second decade of his career as a practising dramatist. By and large, one can say that during the decade of the 1590s, Shakespeare wrote English history plays – the *Henry VI* trilogy and *Richard III* (1590–3), *King John* (*c.* 1594–6), and the famous tetralogy from *Richard II* (1594–5) through *Henry IV* in two parts (*c.* 1596–8) to *Henry V* (1599) – and farcical or festive comedies: the experimental and imitative beginning (*c.* 1589–94) in *Love's Labour's Lost, The Comedy of Errors, The Two Gentlemen of Verona,* and *The Taming of the Shrew*; the mid-decade lyric vein in *A Midsummer Night's Dream* and *The Merchant of Venice*; mature romantic statement in *Much Ado about Nothing, As You Like It,* and *Twelfth Night* (1598–1600); and a late farce in *The Merry Wives of Windsor* (1597–1602). During the 1600s, he wrote the darker 'problem' comedies, virtually all the great tragedies, and finally a group of predominantly tragicomic 'romances'. Even the apparent exceptions to this generalization help confirm a pattern. The late history play *Henry VIII* (1613), written in probable collaboration with Fletcher, lacks the triumphant battle oratory, comic exuberance, and thoughtful analysis of the monarchy so characteristic of Shakespeare's earlier patriotic dramas. Conversely, Shakespeare's two early sporadic attempts at tragedy are an unsuccessful apprenticeship in Senecan blood revenge (*Titus Andronicus, c.* 1589–90) and a touching love story (*Romeo and Juliet, c.* 1594–5). This recognizable distinction between the Elizabethan and the Jacobean Shakespeare is a tribute to the extraordinary intellectual and artistic consistency of this dramatist as he sought constantly to develop new forms.

It is easy to oversimplify the possible motives underlying Shakespeare's change of direction, and to speak knowingly of Shakespeare 'on the heights' or entering the valley of despair, as though the plays might represent little more than his own spiritual odyssey. Or one can pluck out the heart of Shakespeare's mystery by seeing a political reflection in his plays, an indication of a shift from the great Elizabethan compromise (however shaky during its last years) to an era under James I of political and religious confrontation, impasse, and eventually drift toward civil war. More broadly, it is tempting to invoke a change of cultural and philosophic outlook from 'Elizabethan optimism' to 'Jacobean pessimism', which, although gradual rather than sudden, did comprise the challenge of many medieval orthodoxies in such fields as astronomy, geography, medicine, logic and rhetoric, Biblical learning, and political theory. John Donne lamented that the 'new philosophy casts all in doubt'; its apostles were Galileo, Bacon, Montaigne, Machiavelli. Some element of truth may well lie in all these generalizations.

When we view Shakespeare as an artist and man of the theatre, at any rate, we can affirm that he did devote himself to the perfection of certain genres before moving on to new areas of endeavour, and that in doing so he both reflected and influenced the trend of dramatic art generally in the London of his day. When he wrote English history plays and bright comedies, these forms were the stock-in-trade of the London popular stage. The 1590s belonged to the adult companies, such as Shakespeare's the Chamberlain's men and their rivals the Lord Admiral's men. Juvenile theatre was in eclipse, forced to close at the start of the decade and not permitted to reopen until 1599. Competing only among themselves, the adult companies enjoyed an extraordinary financial success, and purveyed entertainments to a widely diversified national audience. Under these conditions, the mores and artistic forms of their plays veered towards popular consensus: England's military and cultural supremacy patriotically defended, the monarchy upheld, Catholic plotting disdained, love and marriage wholesomely affirmed as inseparable, and the like. When on the other hand the boys' theatre reopened in 1599 (significantly the very year of *Henry V*), drama began to gravitate towards the more exclusive precinct of the court. Satire became the fashion, if not the rage. Tragicomedy flourished. The adult companies were compelled to follow suit, especially when their Puritan-leaning audiences began to fall away in the deteriorating atmosphere of court versus London populace.

Shakespeare began his dramatic career, then, at an auspicious moment: the adult companies were about to enter the period of their greatest success, and the English history play was in its merest infancy. Scholarship used to maintain that Shakespeare was a great follower of conventions, perfecting what others had begun – in this case, learning the rudiments of the history play from such contemporaries as George Peele, Robert Greene, Thomas Lodge, and Christopher Marlowe.

The Globe Theatre. From Claes Jans Visscher's 'Long View of London'

Now it seems more likely that Shakespeare was a pioneer as well. To guide his earliest efforts, he may have had little more to go on than *Gorboduc* (1562), the anonymous *The Famous Victories of Henry V* (1583–8), and some experimenting with history in late morality plays such as *Cambises* (1561) or Robert Wilson's *The Three Lords and Three Ladies of London* (1588–90). The popularity of Shakespeare's *Henry VI* plays and *Richard III* may well have figured prominently in establishing a new vogue for patriotic drama, and in prescribing its literary form.

The time was also auspicious for the emergence of Shakespeare's historical genius because of England's recent Armada victory over the Spanish (1588). At least in part, the English history play satisfied a current need for celebratory triumphs of England's national greatness, and conversely for warnings of the dangers to be found in international conspiracy abroad and decadent complacency at home. In this hour of challenge, English dramatists (with Shakespeare in the vanguard) ransacked the nation's annals for illustrations from her glorious past – Crécy, Poitiers, Agincourt – as well as more sobering and instructive instances of political disaster. A new edition of Holinshed's *Chronicles* (1587) was appropriately at hand for source material.

Thus it was that Shakespeare turned first to the saga of Lancaster versus York, England's prolonged agony of civil war during much of the fifteenth century. The Lancastrian claim to the throne belonged to Henry IV and to his heroic son Henry V, since Henry IV's father had been Duke of Lancaster and son of Edward III. But Henry IV had won the throne by the deposition and murder of his cousin, Richard II, and the illegality of this act left the Lancastrian regime vulnerable to rival dynastic claims. These claims emerged with a vengeance after the untimely death of Henry V in 1422, and the accession of his underage and weakminded son Henry VI. The Yorkist family of Richard Plantagenet and his sons Edward (later Edward IV), Clarence, and Richard (later Richard III) could argue a prior descent from Edward III, and consequently seized the opportunity of a minority kingship, squabbling at court, and French hostility abroad. The struggle led to England's loss of her French territories and almost total anarchy at home. It strained to the limit England's ability to exist as a nation, and ended only with the accession of the Tudor Henry VII, Elizabeth's grandfather, in 1485. A century later, it was appropriate to give thanks for the continued stability of Tudor rule, and at the same time to foresee the spectre of renewed dynastic instability under an aging virgin queen with no appointed successor and with many Catholic enemies plotting a return to power.

In the first play of the series, *1 Henry VI*, a chief conclusion seems to be that political division at home leads to military defeat abroad.

The scene shifts rapidly back and forth from the English court to the French camp. The English, normally invincible and contemptuous of the cowardly French, are their own worst enemy. At home, the young King Henry is bedevilled by the aspirations of his closest relatives, such as his corrupt ecclesiastical uncle the Bishop of Winchester, and his conspiratorial Yorkist cousin Richard Plantagenet. The king's ineffectual attempt to appease both Yorkist and Lancastrian factions produces divided responsibility for the French campaign, and the victimization of the valiant general Talbot. This general, Shakespeare's first popular stage hero, appears larger than life. He is martyred in the name of personal and family honour, devotion to God, and service to his country. His old-fashioned virtues contrast not only with the machinations of the English courtiers, but with the devil-worshipping and profligate French. He is everything that the French Dauphin Charles is not: courageous, self-controlled, putting reason above passion in his relationship with women, courteously forbearing and yet stern with the enemy. Even more he is opposite to Joan of Arc, unsympathetically portrayed as a wanton and trafficker in evil spirits. Thus the play derives its thematic focus from a metaphoric conflict between good and evil. England is a family divided against itself, disobedient to the will of heaven, paying for the sins of usurpation and fratricide. The manifestations of this moral enervation are to be found at all levels in the triumph of selfish whim over right reason. Not coincidentally, the play ends with the king's own surrender to the imperious will of a Frenchwoman, Margaret of Anjou.

This Margaret, Henry's French bride, becomes an ever more ominous presence in the subsequent *Henry VI* plays. In concert with her paramour, the conniving Duke of Suffolk, she engineers the downfall of the good Humphrey Duke of Gloucester. He is the victimized hero of the second play. The chief virtue for which he must die is his role as intermediary between the commoners' just complaints and the prerogative of the throne. Royal authority cannot be challenged, in his view, but it must be receptive to petitions and willing to amend injustices on its own authority. This humane view affronts those who insist on despotic absolutism, and he is mercilessly cut down. Without his sane guidance, the commons take matters into their own hands. The communistic rebellion of Jack Cade, with its ludicrous antics, is a fearful reminder of what will happen when the people are goaded too far. Yet the responsibility for their disobedience rests primarily with a defaulted aristocracy. Richard Plantagenet, for his part, cynically whets the ambitions of Cade in order to further the breakdown of civil authority, by which Richard hopes to seize power. Popular unrest is only a prelude to outright civil war among feuding nobles.

And in that war it is Margaret, not Henry VI, who serves as Lancastrian commander-in-chief. By expending frightful vengeance on Richard Plantagenet and his family, she invites an escalation of violence on both sides. After most of the carnage is done, after Margaret herself has lost husband and son, we see her in *Richard III*, withered and impotent, a prophetess of the retaliatory plan by which an angry God exacts an eye for an eye, a Yorkist prince for a Lancastrian prince, until England's penalty for insurrection is fully paid.

It is thus in *Richard III* that providential meaning finally emerges from the chaos of England's suffering. So many deaths are necessary because England's rulers have grown insolent and must be purged to satisfy heaven's wrath. Richard III himself, youngest son of his namesake father Plantagenet, is the scourge appointed by heaven to cleanse a moral wilderness. Richard is the epitome of all of England's wrongs: he is ambitious, ruthless, diabolically inspired, hypocritical, and – in a central theatrical metaphor – he is a masterful actor of many roles. In a superb irony that sustains the play, we see Richard reaching for the throne, gloating in his own success that seems to confirm his godless faith in the unlimited power of the individual will – whereas we know that in fact Richard unwittingly fulfils providential destiny. Most of his victims fittingly condemn themselves out of their own mouths for the wrongs they have committed, or ignore plain warnings of impending disaster. Others, like Richard's pitiful nephews, must pay the price of their fathers' sins. Richard clambers to the throne over the fallen bodies of his kinsmen only to lose it to Henry Tudor, God's appointed minister of the renewed state. Shakespeare minimizes the dubiousness of Henry's own claim to the throne, the usurping manner of his accession, and the historical unattractiveness of his character; instead, Henry is an emblem of rightminded devotion to duty and to God.

In literary form these plays do not conform to any classical ideal. They are neither comedies nor tragedies, but segments of chronicle in sequence. Unity is achieved, as we have seen, by thematic means rather than by single focus of the action. Indeed, the plot lines are numerous, the array of characters vast. Episodic incidents frequently introduce personages whom we never see again. The acting company, following a native homiletic tradition going back to the morality plays and religious cycles, does its utmost to produce multiplicity and panorama. In staging, especially, Shakespeare's early history plays revel in gymnastic feats of scaling operations against the façade of the 'tiring house' or dressing room, actual firing of cannon, alarums and excursions in profusion, appearances 'on the walls'. The scene moves epically from country to country and battlefield to battlefield with the easy fluidity of the open Elizabethan stage. Violence is displayed whenever possible. Comedy is raucous, often anti-foreign; conversely, big scenes of political seriousness do not flinch from revealing the secret counsels of kings and emperors.

Shakespeare's later histories, although vastly superior as works of art, are really continuations of the same popular dramatic genre. In the opening of *1 Henry IV*, for example, we experience the same juxtaposition in alternating scenes of high seriousness and practical joking, the court and the Boar's Head Tavern, wakeful counsellors of the king and a gluttonous, mischief-loving counsellor of the prince. Unity of theme provides the common point of reference; and the theme, stated with growing maturity, bears a close relation to that of the earlier plays. Once again, Shakespeare examines the strengths and potential weaknesses of the English monarchy, and searches for a definition of the ideal ruler through positive and negative example. *King John* obviously provides a negative instance. Shakespeare refuses to glorify this king's reign into anti-Catholic defiance, as more rabidly Protestant dramatists had done. Instead, he portrays a whimsical tyrant and murderer of his kinsman, so evil that well-meaning Englishmen must actively consider the prospect of overthrowing him. Yet the desperate recourse to armed rebellion is invoked only to reveal its ultimate fallacy. The choric Bastard Faulconbridge, instinctively loyal to John, must experience fully the appeal of disaffection so that he can conscientiously transcend it. Rebellion is the worst alternative, for it must rely on foreign alliances and so play into the hands of England's cynical enemies. The violent displacement of the worst of kings (apart from Richard III, who, as predecessor of the Tudors, had to be viewed as an exception) merely teaches others to rebel.

This sad lesson plagues the Henry Bolingbroke who forces his way to the throne in *Richard II*. His reasons for opposing Richard are manifold. Richard is a spendthrift and incompetent ruler, despoiling his subjects for his own decadent luxuries. As his watchful uncles Gaunt and York observe in choric exasperation, Richard subverts the very law of primogeniture by which he rules when he illegally seizes Bolingbroke's birthright. Henry returns to England from exile solely to claim his lands and titles so wrongfully misappropriated. Yet the choric moderates of the play are equally insistent that Henry must not resort to force: God's is the quarrel. They see the far-reaching consequences of rebellion that Henry ignores. Once Henry has defeated Richard in battle, what alternative has he but to assume the throne? And once king, how can he allow his rival to continue alive? The logic of these silent questions leads to regicide and an illegal regime. In the *Henry IV* plays, the new king tastes the bitter fruit of his having taught others to employ revolution.

The paradox of rule is carefully balanced in *Richard II*. Richard himself is unfit to govern and yet is graced by a regal bearing that never deserts him, especially in his brave death; Henry is an expert administrator and politician, and yet can never achieve the style or charisma of a born monarch. Our sympathies are divided, and the dominant metaphors of the play convey a structure of antithesis – such as the image of two buckets in a well, one rising as the other is lowered. Richard's is the poetic temperament, and his plight is rendered in an interrelated set of cosmic and natural metaphors. He is the neglectful father of an unruly family, the ailing physician of a sick body politic, the indolent gardener of a paradise choked with weeds. His cosmos is disordered by comets, drought, a weeping universe, and a sun in decline. In his death he sees himself as a martyr and saint, and his moving depiction of life as a prison or shadow invokes an ideal of contemplative withdrawal by which Henry's worldly achievement appears crass and vain. Who has in fact triumphed, the rejected poet or the successful but tormented worldling? A latter-day poet, Yeats, has tellingly contrasted these two figures as a vessel of porcelain, exquisite but impractical, and a vessel of clay, hardy but graceless. To put the question thus is to wonder if Shakespeare sees an inherent contradiction in political rule, whereby the polarities of vision and pragmatism can never wholly coalesce.

The question remains central to the education of Prince Hal as he prepares to become Henry V. Can he retain the breadth of compassion and *joie de vivre* he has known under Falstaff's tutelage, and still attain dignity and the calculating, efficient use of power incumbent upon any great administrator? The struggle is posed for Hal by a series of foils, or contrasting yet parallel characters, whom he must both emulate and surpass by avoiding their fatal weaknesses. Falstaff embodies the camaraderie of youth and mirthful escape from responsibility, but is for that reason dangerously akin to licence, rebellion, and anarchy. Hal's own true father, unlike Falstaff, would have Hal grow up preternaturally wary and discreet; but Henry IV's counsel is marred by the insincere expediency of his political cunning. Still another foil character, Hotspur, so close to Hal in age and energy, holds out to the prince the ideal of bright honour. Yet Hotspur is a rebel, humourless, fanatic, so obsessed with honour that it tarnishes into egomania and leads him into a trap created by the Machiavellian intrigues of his own allies. Falstaff can easily puncture the hollowness of this honour, yet is himself deficient in the opposite extreme. Hal must find the middle course between Falstaff and Hotspur, Falstaff and Henry IV.

In *2 Henry IV* the foil to Falstaff is the Lord Chief Justice, and the issues are justice and reputation. Here, however, the structural equation is altered, for the Chief Justice is a man of complete probity whereas Falstaff's genius is on the wane. No longer the constant companion of the prince, Falstaff spends his time with prostitutes, rowdies, or corrupt Justices of the Peace. He fears death, and his hopes of attaining great dignities under Henry V are outlandish and pathetic. Hal's ultimate rejection of his companion seems both inevitable and somewhat heartless; it is incumbent upon him, and he finally accepts the consequences of maturity and kingship. The free play of his winsome personality must dwindle as he embraces the public and ceremonial role of leader; his choice of friends, as of wife, can no longer be simply his own. Still, the choice is made compassionately, on behalf of England's public weal, and is a sacrifice for which the prince too must feel some regret. We cannot seriously charge him with having used Falstaff merely to cultivate the myth of the prodigal son. The love between them, though brief, was too real for that. At least Hal is no replica of his cold-blooded brother, Prince John.

The concluding portrait in *Henry V* is not without its ironies. The war against France, furthered by all the slogans of patriotic fervour, has its seamier underside. The church hopes for war in order to avoid a heavy tax, and Hal chooses war as an instrument of uniting a discordant populace. Under martial law he eliminates political rivals with dispatch. We see him manipulating emotions with his great public speeches and his sportive visits in disguise to his soldiers' firesides. Notwithstanding, he is courageous, generous, and charismatic. He is amusedly condescending yet fond toward Fluellen, the cantankerous and old-fashioned Welshman who upholds the finest traditions of a unified British army. Although Hal's marriage with Katharine of France is a political alliance, he courts her with genuine relish and affection. Perhaps even an ideal English king is the prisoner of 'idol ceremony', since his chief contribution to society is a kind of play-acting, but Hal at least carries it off with style.

In his early comedies, as in his histories, Shakespeare experimented with genres that had only recently made their appearance on the Elizabethan popular stage, and, by the late 1590s, synthesized them into his own successful formula. Even at the very outset, he revealed a genius for transforming his models or sources, often classical or continental in origin, into an unmistakably English humour. *The Comedy of Errors*, for example, is a farce of mistaken identity, derived chiefly from Plautus's *Menaechmi*, or *The Twins*. Shakespeare has preserved from the original what suited him most: the swiftly-paced action and dialogue, the hilarity and improbability of the plot, the compression of events into one place and brief span of time, the farcical consistency of tone, and above all the ingenious structuring of the action whereby the initial error of mistaken identity is elaborated into every conceivable misconception, reaches a climax of confrontation, and then is neatly resolved with virtually every character brought to a suitable account. Shakespeare is indebted to classical tradition, in other words, for rhetoric, dramatic form, and decorum. The form is much unlike that of English popular romance of the period, with its sequential action, episodic multiplicity of event, and loose handling of time and place. Yet the English spirit is also dominant in the moral decency of Shakespeare's characters, the emphasis on the marital bond and on the need for public order.

In *Love's Labour's Lost*, Shakespeare gives us unmistakably English portraits of a hedge-priest, pedantic schoolmaster, small-town constable, clown, and country wench, complete with a rustic dramatic rendition of 'The Nine Worthies'. The main action, contrastingly, is a highly embroidered and courtly debate on love versus contemplative study, in the style of John Lyly. Similarly in *The Two Gentlemen of Verona*, the disputations on love versus friendship are periodically offset by the vaudeville-like clowning of the servants, Speed, and Launce with his dog. *The Taming of the Shrew*, in its double plot, juxtaposes the exquisite neoclassical structure of Ariosto's original, *I Suppositi* (*Supposes*), with the thoroughly English hilarity, slapstick violence, and facetious antifeminism of the wife-taming episode. Even in the neoclassical plot, the love relationships and satiric sketches are modestly expurgated to suit English popular mores.

A Midsummer Night's Dream, for which no extensive source has been found, skilfully interweaves not two but four distinct groups of characters, each with its own plot line and distinctive tone: the royal party of Theseus, the four lovers who flee into the woods, the fairies, and the rude mechanicals of Athens. Furthermore, Shakespeare introduces a structural motif of profound consequence to many of his later romantic comedies: the contrasting of two dramatic worlds, one earthbound, rational, legalistic, and competitive; the other distant, improbable, sylvan, and regenerative. It is 'the sharp Athenian law' urged by the prudent father, Egeus, that compels the lovers to flee from repressive civilization to the mystery and freedom of the forest. There they experience a transforming vision under the whimsical tutelage of the fairies, whose mad love quarrels are not so very different from those of mortal men. The fatuous tradesman, Bottom, also undergoes an enchanted pilgrimage, ludicrous in fashion because of his asininity but nonetheless wondrous. Who among us, after all, can boast that we have been the lover of the Faery Queen? This childlike faith in dream bears fruit in the mechanicals' play of 'Pyramus and Thisbe', so fearfully real to them that they must apologize for the power of artistic creation and so lay bare their contrivances. Theseus and his queen, who laugh at this simplicity, have alone been untouched by the magic of the forest; and Theseus' sardonic rationalism at the expense of all poetic vision, or madness, suggests that he is the poorer for being so worldly-wise. The pattern of this delicate play, and of the imaginative experience in its essence, is one (as in Keats's 'Nightingale') of brief and fantastic journey into the realm of the unseen, borne on the wings of frenzy and intoxication, from which one must awake as though haunted, uncertain what is real and what is not. As the fairies explain in the epilogue, the play itself has been but a shadow. Still, as Theseus knows, 'The best in this kind are but shadows' – the best of art is like a dream.

In *The Merchant of Venice*, the two contrasting worlds are those of Venice and Belmont. The city, dominated by the evil genius of Shylock, is commercial and cut-throat, a place of harsh law and sudden disasters, a man's world. Portia's Belmont is, like its mistress, enchantingly feminine and mysterious, in rarified and pure mountain air, reached only by a journey across water, a place of caskets, rings, fairytale riddles, harmonious melodies, nocturnal quietude. Bassanio's quest for Portia is like Jason's quest for the golden fleece, an adventure in which those who risk all deserve to win all. Shylock, contrastingly, holds to the letter of the law, the old dispensation lacking in grace and charity; it is his paradoxical fate to lose all because he has clung to those things dearest to him (even his daughter Jessica) as though they were merchandise. From Belmont, Portia must descend into the sultry and feverish arena of Venice to untangle those problems for which human institutions appear to offer no solutions. Antonio, who has risked all for friendship, is carried off to the regenerative company of Belmont, where he joins Jessica, Lorenzo, and all those who have practised *caritas*. Shylock, however sympathetically portrayed as a persecuted man, is cast by the comic structure of the play into the role of villain.

Much Ado about Nothing does not offer two diverse worlds that can be spatially located. There is, however, an important thematic contrast between appearance and reality, between the masks we show to others and our inner state of mind. The action of the play abounds in masking and overhearing scenes, in which the characters abuse one another with false surmise. Shakespeare characteristically employs a double plot, comparing two sets of lovers who must learn to understand one another as best they can. Claudio and Hero, the more conventional pair, fall easily in love but are only superficially acquainted; accordingly, they are prone to misconceptions based upon stereotyped attitudes. When rumour has it that Don Pedro, Claudio's superior officer and close friend, is wooing Hero for himself, Claudio jumps *a priori* to the predictable but wrong conclusion: all's fair in love and war, and so the rumour must be true. Claudio lacks faith, in other words, in Hero's unseen qualities. He cannot perceive simply that she couldn't do such a thing. The rumour is 'much ado about nothing', for it was based on mere fantasy. Yet it is potentially destructive. The second such delusion, cynically plotted by the villain Don John, is equally baffling to the young lover who has failed to learn his lesson. This time the charge of adultery is grave indeed, and would produce tragic results except for a providential intervention ludicrously appearing in the disguise of an inept police force. Justice stumbles on truth, and offers Claudio a third chance that he scarcely deserves. His Hero, whom he has apparently killed with his accusation, is brought back to life as though by miracle. The other lovers, Benedick and Beatrice, follow a different and more hopeful course to genuine rapport. Although they sardonically abuse one another with insults and swear never to marry, they are in fact idealists about love who need only to be convinced of the other's constancy and true worth. This time the deceptions practised on them take a benign turn, for they are fooled into believing what in fact has always been true. The exposure of one's deepest feeling is painful, because it leaves one vulnerable to callousness or indifference. Benedick and Beatrice struggle to retain what they consider to be the integrity of their personalities, but eventually discover that the most precious things involve risk and demand faith.

In *As You Like It* we again find contrasting worlds, of Duke Frederick's court and the Forest of Arden. The court is above all a place of envy, resenting the fair Orlando, Rosalind, and the banished elder duke for the goodness by which they outshine the practitioners of tyranny. When these fugitives from social oppression band together in the communal fraternity of the forest, they find a restorative natural order that will not reward hypocrisy or grasping ambition. They find also, as Jaques and Touchstone observe, that the forest has its defects: it is indifferent to suffering, and it lacks the graces of civilization. The forest is a means to regeneration, not a final resting place. It has a strange ability to move the hearts even of Frederick and of Orlando's churlish brother Oliver, who, by envying the virtuous, have shown their secret longing to be better than they know how to be. The forest, by stripping away the pretensions of social intercourse, enables man to free himself from the prison of his own insincerity. Still, when Orlando and his old servant Adam are threatened by starvation in the pitiless wilderness, it is the compassion of their fellow-creatures that saves them; and this sudden appearance of Orlando at the rustic banquet prompts the banished duke to think, not of man's ingratitude to man, but of the church-bells and other institutional conventions they have all known in better days, and to which they will return.

Twelfth Night is, like its near contemporary *Henry V*, the triumphant culmination of a popular form Shakespeare had shaped to his own particular genius, and which he was about to lay aside. In its types of comic appeal this play characteristically blends farce (the familiar Plautine business of mistaken identity) with coarse buffoonery (Sir Toby and company), and most of all with Shakespeare's 'philosophic' comedy of love and marriage raised to a Platonic perspective of eternal joyousness. The subplot of Sir Toby and Malvolio also uses the comic device of satirical exposure, so much in vogue on the boy actors' newly-reopened private stage. Yet the genial Shakespeare cannot let satire have the last word: the outraged Malvolio is entreated to a peace, and his compassionate mistress Olivia thinks he has been 'most notoriously abused'. Like its unattractive apologist Jaques, in *As You Like It*, satire is too destructive and potentially sadistic a form of expression to dominate the festive character of *Twelfth Night*. Rather, in a Saturnalian mood of post-Christmas celebration, Malvolio's churlish gospel of denial must be answered by the positive ideal of release. 'Youth's a stuff will not endure', sings the Fool, and Viola echoes this innocently hedonistic spirit when she urges Olivia to give up sterile mourning and embrace the proper uses of beauty. Sin or madness in this play is equated with Malvolio's wish to spoil others' happiness, a madness graphically portrayed through a pervasive metaphor of inversion. We see Malvolio, the apostle of sobriety, imprisoned as a madman for his erratic behaviour in yellow stockings, while the Fool roams freely abroad and is mistaken by Malvolio for a learned clergyman. Illyria thus becomes a joyously improbable world where appearance and reality are wholly reversed. The lovers undergo experiences as though in a dream, and are transformed.

To comment briefly on the tragedies of the Elizabethan period is to underscore the relative lateness of any central artistic preoccupation with this genre. *Titus Andronicus* is hardly an auspicious start. *Romeo and Juliet* is exquisite, but in ways that more resemble the lyric comedies than the late tragedies. Its lovers come from ordinary rather than exalted backgrounds, and are almost totally innocent of the catastrophes engulfing them. In a tragedy of circumstance and family feuding, they are the sacrificial victims. The lessons of their ill-fated passion – the poignant brevity of love, the obstinacy of parents, the misunderstanding of society at large – are those of such comedies as *A Midsummer Night's Dream*; and indeed the deaths of Romeo and Juliet bear a striking resemblance to those of Pyramus and Thisbe.

In poetic texture as well, *Romeo and Juliet* is permeated with hilarious bawdry and elaborate Petrarchan metaphors.

Julius Caesar (1598–1600), although approaching tragic maturity, has important affinities with Shakespeare's history plays of the same period. As in *Richard II*, we find a lack of focus on a single protagonist, and witness instead the carefully balanced confrontation between political rivals. Whose actions are more justified, Caesar's or Brutus'? Because the scene is Rome, English standards of monarchical heredity do not apply; nonetheless, in Brutus' eyes Caesar is a usurper, unfit to govern because he has violated senatorial tradition. Yet what can Brutus hope to accomplish by Caesar's death, other than another illegitimacy of rule and an invitation to civil strife? Shakespeare ironically characterizes Brutus as not unlike the very man he would supplant: deaf to counsel, fatally prone to flattery, and proud. Even though Brutus is truly noble, he cannot command a noble revolution; for revolution itself plays into the hands of less scrupulous politicians such as Antony and Octavius.

With *Hamlet* (1599–c. 1601), Shakespearean tragedy comes triumphantly into its own right, and in a way that hauntingly depicts the sombre cosmic preoccupations of the 1600s. The recurrent imagery of *Hamlet* is of unweeded gardens, ulcerated sores filmed over, inward poisons, garments of hypocritical seeming. Claudius impresses Denmark with his watchful diplomacy; Polonius is all sagacity; Rosencrantz and Guildenstern are loyal, earnest subjects. Only Hamlet knows the truth, and it is his dreadful secret that alienates him from all the rest. The courtiers think Hamlet mad, and analyse his infirmity in ways that tellingly reveal their own: to Rosencrantz and Guildenstern Hamlet is politically ambitious, and so on. This alienation provokes Hamlet to mistrust exceedingly his erstwhile friends, and to generalize about human nature and the universe in profoundly pessimistic terms. His behaviour is indeed antisocial and his response to Claudius' villainy ineffectual, as he himself observes; but on balance we blame not Hamlet but his corrupted world. Even the Ghost's command is riddling, for it involves cold-blooded murder, and to a man of Hamlet's poetic sensibility such crass action is indefensible. Hamlet is confronted above all with the inherent absurdity of action in an imperfect world. Only when he subscribes to a providential view of destiny is an answer unexpectedly provided him. Truly, as John Donne said, the 'new philosophy' of the 1600s has cast all in doubt.

10

SHAKESPEARE THE JACOBEAN
DRAMATIST

M. C. BRADBROOK

His Jacobean decade (1603–13) includes Shakespeare's major tragedies beyond *Hamlet*, the Roman plays, the last romances, *Timon of Athens*, *King Henry VIII*. In 1609 his sonnets were first printed. By 1613, both Shakespeare and Beaumont left the stage, and the decade had seen also the chief masterpieces of Jonson, Tourneur, Webster and Chapman.

A period of relative social stability permitted the indulgence of creative instability in the arts. In the drama, whilst new Italian influences were brought to bear at court yet London players, and especially Shakespeare's company, were at the height of their prosperity. Practised and confident, the craftsmen had evolved their own native standards to challenge both ecclesiastical opponents and academic legislators. Alleyn and Henslowe, Burbage and Shakespeare, were gentlemen, each with his coat of arms; a truce had prevailed in the war against the sinfulness of the stage which had been waged earlier and was to be resumed later.

Playwrights felt confident enough to turn to self-questioning, which sharpened into satiric comedy or darkened into the tragic mode. In the new intimacy of a closed theatre, the subtlety of the actors brought them and the audience together to study personal conflicts, so that 'to the new age, so often sceptical, tentative and self conscious in its exploration of hidden motives, a new style was necessary, a style that could express the mind as it was in action, could record thought at the moment it arose in the mind'.[1] A theatre rooted in traditional social rituals was being replaced by an art at once more critical and more individual, more sharply divided from popular entertainment. This was the age both of Shakespeare and of Jonson; the deeper probings came from the more traditional craftsman. While Jonson's interests were social and 'politic', and led him towards analysis of a 'Machiavellian' kind, Shakespeare with Montaigne turned from social issues to the proper study of Mankind, a being 'ondoyant et divers'.

In a theatre, the form of the building itself expresses and conditions social response. This period saw a revolution in stage technique, the transition from what was essentially still the medieval open stage, to the ancestor of the closed modern house. It saw also a great development in spectacular staging, in which court productions led the way. But the popular theatres also developed new and better 'machines'.

The general temper of the first Jacobean decade was satiric and critical. With Italian sets, Italianate tragedies also became fashionable; the second wave of Revenge plays – that of Marston, Tourneur and Webster – showed the great influence of *Hamlet*, while Shakespeare himself moved on from the Revenge tradition. Satiric city comedy, and political tragedy were Jonsonian forms designed for the more sophisticated part of the audience; but as the cheats and rogues of the comedy were caricatures, drawn within a set convention, so the evil world of Italy was seen as an aspect of England. As G. K. Hunter has pointed out, it bore little resemblance to the Italy of the Counter Reformation, of Spanish hegemony and Baroque art.

The dark negations of Webster are perhaps finally less disquieting than the new melodramatic art of Fletcher.

a more relaxed drama, which in its character-types mirrored a stable world and yet in its language maintained and indeed further developed the informality of the earliest Jacobean years. The essential property of the new Beaumont and Fletcher drama consists in its dislocation...There is no firm ground for reverence, or for a cosmic scheme, in the great majority of the plays which deeply bear John Fletcher's impress. Neither Fletcher nor Beaumont was ever a declared revolutionary, yet few dramatists can have written plays so fully destructive in implication.[2]

Shakespeare, fifteen years older than Fletcher, evolved no single form. In the space of four years, 1604–8, he appears to have composed *Othello*, *King Lear*, *Macbeth*, *Antony and Cleopatra*, *Coriolanus* and perhaps some lesser works. The form of each is distinct from the rest, to a much greater degree than had been the case with his Elizabethan comedies and histories. The English history play, to which Shakespeare had given such predominance, passed into rapid decline.[3] Even when it depicted tragic disorder, the history had rested on assumptions of social order reaching back to the great providential history of creation which the craft guilds had presented from Chaucer's time until the Reformation. Of course, the pieties and assurances that sustained civic pageantry had not gone unquestioned in the theatre that saw Marlowe's *Edward II*; and Shakespeare's own sequence reveals a deepening scepticism. The emblematic framework was never quite as stable as critics like Tillyard tend to suggest, and Ulysses' famous speech on degree is a lament for its passing.

Although the presence of the aged Queen Elizabeth had sustained the providential legend of the coming of the Tudors, yet even before her death it had faded. James I was not the stuff of which public images are made, so that the British Solomon was soon replaced in popular idolatry by the youthful Prince Henry. Loss of the royal image symbolized much deeper loss, which on the stage can be registered in scenic terms:

For centuries kings had been presented to the public, whether real kings in public ceremonies, or actor kings in plays and pageants, in a throne backed by a symbol of the realm. That symbol combined elements from the pageant-castles, from the city gates, from triumphal arches, from the choir screen of the church. The throne was framed by columns supporting a canopy, a 'heavens' – exactly the same kind of pavilion-canopy used to frame an altar or a tomb...Its background structure resembled a castle, a throne, a city gate, a tomb, or an altar. It was a symbol of social order and of divine order – of the real ties between man and king, between heaven and earth.[4]

The tomb of Shakespeare's master, Baron Hunsdon, in Westminster Abbey, its black altar shape flanked by gilded obelisks and wreathed trophies is one of the more splendid examples of this kind. Hunsdon died in 1597. After 1603, Shakespeare can show only the vacated throne of Lear, Macbeth's haunted chair. Perhaps the ghost of King Hamlet represents more than the demise of a single royalty.

As a historian, Professor Christopher Hill accepts this as evidence of a change:

All old conventions are being challenged. We could tell simply by reading the literature of the time that two sets of standards were in conflict. In *King Lear*, the traditional feudal patriarchal loyalties are challenged by the blind individualism of Goneril, Regan and Edmund...in later Jacobean and Caroline drama the tension is lost.[5]

The shift from English history to the Roman tragedy of *Julius Caesar* and the Trojan tragedy of *Troilus and Cressida* freed Shakespeare of certain presuppositions. 'Roman society lacked a divine sanction, or at least it seemed to the Christian tradition to have done so; it was therefore a fit ground in which to explore the political behaviour of men empirically, freed from the assumption of a providence shaping their ends.'[6] Ralegh's *History of the World* was to show the conflict still unresolved; and by the time he wrote *Antony and Cleopatra* Shakespeare had enlarged humanity to almost godlike state – though the descendant of Hercules and the incarnation of Isis fall among the defeated.

Meanwhile, however, politics considered as an autonomous activity subjected the greatest heroes to a scrutiny which patriotism had withheld from the hero of Agincourt – Caesar is godlike and ailing, Hector gallant but without a princely sense of responsibility. Hamlet behaves outrageously to Ophelia, yet we believe her when she cries 'O, what a noble mind is here o'erthrown!'

Maynard Mack has distinguished the two voices of Jacobean tragedy as those of the hero and his foil – Hamlet and the gravedigger, Emilia and Desdemona, Cleopatra and the countryman each speak in languages which do not commune; their dialogue can never be finally adjudicated, but the opposites must somehow be reconciled. We believe in Othello's nobility – and we believe Emilia when she calls him 'ignorant as dirt'; Goneril terms Lear an 'idle old man' and Cordelia kneels to the madman as 'my royal lord'. Both command assent, but as a saint has said, we must first believe in order that we may understand.

The complexity of character as it is shown directly, and the complexity of its conflict-relations with others presupposes a much finer meshed form of acting established between members of the company. After 1608, Shakespeare worked for the closed theatre at Blackfriars as well as for the open stage of the Globe, which marked a decisive break with the old 'playing place' or 'game place' of medieval times. Yet, far from supporting Glynne Wickham's view that this was a move towards the modern stage of naturalism and prose, Shakespeare turned in his final plays towards the old romances and 'drama of the gaps', adapting the purely theatrical trends that were now in ascendancy.

Growing sophistication in the audience altered their relation with the actors and playwright; by 1611, Fletcher was offering a virtuoso display of passion to the judgement of connoisseurs, while at the end of his life, victim of habits he had inculcated, Jonson bitterly caricatured the critic Damplay.

As social confrontation hardened, leading up to the Civil War, the theatre was to shrink to a vehicle for courtly views, dependent on courtly favour. Social cross currents were still swirling and eddying through the early Jacobean theatre; the turbulence assured its greatness. Shakespeare's power of synthesis established some community of theme between a popular romance like *Pericles* and the delicate courtly masquing of *The Tempest*, so that modern writers tend to forget that they belong to totally different kinds of theatre.

As in the golden decade, Shakespeare's company dominated without overwhelming the others (in Caroline times it stood far ahead), so it has recently been argued that Shakespeare dominated the playwrights.[7] By the second decade of James's reign, both Fletcher and Massinger, writing for his company, were capable of stagey writing, that is, of utilizing a theatrical success by borrowing situations, to use as a series of properties. Such a labour-saving device, not unwelcome in a repertory company, perhaps, offered short cuts to the actors, and was quite different from the rhetorical borrowings of Elizabethan times, which were more literary. The plot situation and some key lines of *Othello* were used by Massinger in *The Emperor of the East*, but for the court were given an incongruous happy ending.

Shakespeare's Jacobean tragedies are full of scenes which imprint the character in action upon the minds of the audience. Such great stage moments as Lear on the heath, Othello at Desdemona's bedside, Macbeth and the witches radiate symbolic potency – they have often given themes for painting – yet they do not belong to a ritual tradition like the earlier tourneys, coronations, challenges; they are not loaded with memories of other like events, but are at once representative of the human condition yet stamped with the specific mark of a particular plot and a master craftsman. Free from old emblematic forms, and as yet without a trading stock of melodramatic images, Shakespearian tragedies result from a balance of interest between playwright, actors and audience.

At a much humbler level such a balance can be seen in the collaborative work on city pageants, which Shakespeare's contemporaries were engaged in;[8] and the final proof of it is the collaboration which he engaged in during the composition of his latest plays, *Pericles*, *Two Noble Kinsmen*, the lost *Cardenio* and possibly *King Henry VIII*. In these latest plays, a new kind of emblematic scene is established; it is the language of the poet that validates the stage image, not the image which carries the words as accompaniment. Enobarbus' description of Cleopatra in her barge justifies the abruptness of Antony's 'I will to Egypt' though he himself has not heard the words; to him the soothsayer only appears as an emissary of Egyptian magic power. The statue scene of *The Winter's Tale*, the masques of *The Tempest* provide the climax of action; yet, as I have indicated elsewhere,[9] they evoke the scenic emblems of Shakespeare's youth – the Living Statue, the Ship, the Cave, and other 'devices'. Some of the ancient rôles, the May Queen, Monster and Magician are used to explore an interior world where fine and delicate sensibilities alternate with 'imagination foul as Vulcan's stithy'.

Any attempt to discuss Shakespeare's Jacobean achievement which is not swamped in generalities must be highly selective. Its specific qualities will be more clearly brought out by a consideration of the first Jacobean tragedy, *Othello*, and the first romance, *Pericles*.

Othello was performed at court on 1 November 1604; it captivated the popular stage, where ever since it has been central to the Shakespearian repertory. In Jacobean times, the characters are more often referred to than any others save Hamlet and Falstaff. The story was new to the stage; its bold and splendid roles inverted traditional ones.

All stage Moors were wicked demi-devils; Aaron of *Titus Andronicus*, 'a Moor that has damnation dyed upon his flesh' shares the diabolic gaiety of Marlowe's Ithamore, who like many a later Moor or Turk, is associated in complots with a Machiavellian. Crude atrocity plays depicting such a pair, atheist or infidel, treacherous and parricidal, mechanical bogeymen of the most automatic gesticulations, lasted till Caroline times.[10]

Even in Webster the disguise of a Moor often covers a diabolic 'second self'; but in Shakespeare all the characteristics expected for these familiar figures are transferred to Iago. The tempter is marked, by his malicious wit and Mephistophelian contempt for virtue, as the hero's foil. Iago 'is *homo emancipatus a Deo*, seeing the world and human life as self-sufficient on their own terms...[man] is the king of beasts, crowned by his superior faculties. And society, by the same token, is the arena of endless competition...To the kind of love existing between hero and heroine,...the ancient is the dark counter-type, the adversary...nothing engrosses him so much as the subject of love or receives from him so mordant a negation.'[11] Yet the betrayed Othello sees no cloven hoof – 'I look down towards his feet; but that's a fable' – and turns back with animal cries to the body of his 'girl', all ceremony lost. The spiritually human and the animal blend; behaviour, dominant over doctrine, shapes belief. Othello, a baptised Moor, uses the votive candle as symbol of his earthly saint – 'Put out the light, and then put out the light'. Heaven and Hell gleam through the play, as when Othello and Iago kneel to make their deadly compact:

> Arise, black vengeance, from the hollow hell.
> Yield up, O love, thy crown and hearted throne
> To tyrannous hate!   (III, iii, 451–3)

Yet the play turns on the magic of the lost love token; if the one lover is the descendant of kings, the other daughter of a Venetian senator, a domestic love story challenged the traditional view that high tragedy involved 'the growth, state, and declination of Princes, change of Government and lawes, vicissitudes of sedition, faction, succession, confederacies, plantations, with all other errors, or alterations in publique affaires.'[12]

There is a marked indifference to what every Elizabethan would feel the chief interest of Cyprus – the history of the Turkish attack, their defeat at the Battle of Lepanto, their subsequent conquest.

> When I love thee not
> Chaos is come again.   (III, iii, 92–3)

makes love and not society the regulative principle of Othello's life.
He tells Emilia

> had she been true,
> If heaven would make me such another world
> Of one entire and perfect chrysolite,
> I'd not have sold her for it. (v, ii, 146–9)

The flawless talismanic stone that no force could crack or break is
symbolized in the fragile web of her soul and body; there was magic
in *this* web. To Desdemona Othello also is a world: 'My heart's sub-
dued / Even to the very quality of my lord' (i, iii, 250–1). When
she hears that Cassio has been killed, Desdemona's cry 'Alas,
he is betrayed and I undone!' implies that she herself cannot be
betrayed for she takes Othello's mistakes and guilt on herself. Though
she knows herself to be falsely murdered and to die guiltless, when
Emilia cries 'O, who hath done this deed?' she can reply 'Nobody;
I myself', for it is herself, her other self, who is guilty. Othello at once
intuitively recognizes and cannot endure the truth of the words, which
assert their unity as one flesh, if not entirely of one mind and heart;
so he repudiates it in a great burst of self-directed rage:

> She's like a liar gone to burning hell;
> 'Twas I that killed her. (v, ii, 132–3)

To that same hell Emilia at once consigns him:

> O, the more angel she,
> And you the blacker devil! (v, ii, 134–5)

The angel and the devil are yet one flesh and this is what each is
asserting behind the frantic words.

When a middle-aged alien, honoured yet but a denizen of the state,
wins a love that is hazardous and vulnerable because only imperfectly
in accord with social habit, the Doge endorses the act of free election,
in spite of social disapproval. A warrior among merchants, Othello
had chosen his Venetian masters and served freely; like Desdemona,
he belonged to a new society of chosen and contractual individualism.

Desdemona thereby assumes a servant's obedience ('I will not stay
to offend you'). A wife owed fealty to her husband; if she murdered
him, she was guilty not only of murder but of treason also. To one
bred in the habit of command, wedded to the daughter of his 'very
noble and approved good masters' the revolt from obedience destroyed
the foundations of his being:

> They have the power to hurt us whom we love,
> We lay our sleeping lives within their arms.

A year earlier than this play, in 1603, Thomas Heywood had shown a betrayed husband who could yet allow tenderness full play, banishing his guilty wife – 'It was thy hand cut two hearts out of one'. Her penitent death restored the marriage tie:

> My wife, the mother to my pretty babes!
> Both these lost names I do restore thee back,
> And with this kiss I wed thee once again.[13]

The new principle of character introduced is one of growth and change, felt as a change in relationships. Compared with Heywood's scene of conversion and reconversion, the temptation of Othello in Acts III and IV constitutes a new way of making plays. Organic psychological growth or degeneration, central to Shakespeare's four great tragedies, distinguishes them from his own later plays as from his earlier ones.

The shame of a noble nature is itself a kind of expiation in Cassio and Othello. The hero has become one to be cursed by Emilia, ordered about by Ludovico, disarmed by Montano:

> Soft you; a word or two before you go:
> I have done the state some service and they know it.
>
> (v, ii, 341–2)

This might be a defence plea; the Venetians halt to hear their prisoner. But that he 'forsake the room and go with them' is impossible. Recalling his act of almost suicidal loyalty against the malignant Turk in Aleppo, he looks on his stricken life and his own 'Turkish' self – the theatrical image which Shakespeare has so firmly repudiated – and divides it cleanly from him. Executing the judgement of the court, he fulfils another role of the black-visaged man (as in Peacham's scene from *Titus Andronicus*, he is familiar). For Othello is a soldier, absolute and decisive, used to letting his muscles take over from his mind in crisis. The tears he sheds are like the fruit of the myrrh tree, emblem of death; but they are healing. In death he ventures to kiss his wife, nor does he feel any longer divided from her:

> No way but this:
> Killing myself to die upon a kiss.

The nineteenth century's view of Othello as entirely noble ('there is none we love like Othello', said Swinburne) produced its reaction; few would go so far as the critic who thought Desdemona so guilty in deceiving her father, as to call down a deserved fate. But it has been suggested more than once that Othello is damned for committing suicide, or that his lack of insight alienates. T. S. Eliot's influential words on the final speech set the tone for a whole generation of critics:

I...have never read a more terrible exposure of human weakness...What Othello seems to me to be doing is *cheering himself up*. He is endeavouring to escape reality...dramatizing himself...He takes in the spectator, but the human motive is primarily to take in himself.[14]

Enlarging on this, Leavis thinks Othello's 'habit of self approving dramatization' is often 'a disguise' for 'obtuse and brutal egoism'.

It is significant that Eliot talks of 'reading' the speech. Such an interpretation could never be used in the theatre. It simply is not actable.

Moreover this view, it has been remarked, is quite close to Iago's view of Othello; it is also quite close to that of Shakespeare's source. It is what then might have been expected in such a story, particularly by theatregoers; but the power of Shakespeare's drama is generated by departure from the stock action for an Eleazer, a Muly Mahomet. The conflict and sympathy of this play depends in the first place on the character of the hero contradicting a stereotype, and secondly in the slow poisoning and quick final recovery, the change of speed in his development. Jacobean spectators were used to hearing speeches from the scaffold, in which a dying man put off his guilt.

J. I. M. Stewart sees both Iago and Othello as 'abstractions from a single and, as it were, invisible protagonist...It is less a matter of Othello projecting concealed facets of himself upon Iago...than of the dramatist's abstracting these facets, and embodying them in a figure substantially symbolic.'[15] For W. H. Auden, on the other hand, Iago is far more significant and interesting than Othello; there are as many Iagos as there are characters for him to deceive, and he must display every trick for which great actors are praised. Everything he sets out to do he accomplishes, including his own self-destruction. He exists to play with the lives of others, producing a ruinous change, like that of a cancer cell, in the organic body of relationships; for he could say, with the Serpent of Valéry, 'Je suis Celui qui modifie'.[16]

These divergent views show with what variety it is possible for individuals to identify with each of the characters, and to project the conflict *in toto* rather than single aspects. When A. C. Bradley found in *Othello* 'a certain limitation, a partial suppression of that element in Shakespeare which unites him with the mystical poets and with the greatest musicians and philosophers' he did not recognize that this lack of the symbolic, or of a cosmic dimension was itself a great act of emancipation, a shedding of the taboos and irrational supports which some critics are eager to put back. Shakespeare had gone off the gold standard of conventional judgements, and had gained a floating position where the audience must follow with its own judgement the natural pulses of sympathy. Crowds thronged to see 'kind Lear' and 'the grieved Moor'.[17] It was less than thirty years since feeling had been blocked out by the stage direction for Tamburlaine when he sees Zenocrate with his rival; 'he goes to her and takes her away lovingly by the hand, looking wrathfully on Agydas, and saying nothing'. Othello never holds anything back; his words are always ready to command. In his madness he gains no deepened insight such as comes to Hamlet or Lear. But the sharp orders and animal cries, the hero's fit of delirious rage belong with a new sympathetic acting technique; the feminine part of the audience would have been as responsive to the appeal of the exotic as was Desdemona herself. The sensuous warmth and opulence of the language, the firm rhythm, the sustained simplicity of action join together the leading parts in their interaction on each other and on the audience. In the eavesdropping scene, for instance, Bianca acts the part of a whore, while Cassio responds and Othello interprets the whole thing in terms of his wife (IV, i, 120–44).

Othello's fury at being offered his own love-token to soothe the pain of his brow's 'injury' not only causes Desdemona to drop the handkerchief but to forget where she lost it. The 'faith, half asleep' with which she excuses her half-fainting condition after the brothel scene, her fearful noting in the death-scene of Othello's rolling eyes and the gnawing of his lip demand interpretation and participation from the audience. After the brawl, honest Iago 'looks dead with grieving' (II, iii, 173). The pleasures of variety are joined with firm 'conceit' – or 'conception' – of each part. This 'Method' style must have emanated from Burbage who was famous as a 'Protean' actor, living entirely inside his role, and never putting it off, even in the tiring house. Younger actors, trained by him, would conform – as in modern times, they conformed to Stanislavsky. The chameleon poet, as Keats observed, has as much delight in conceiving an Iago as an Imogen; the poet, like the actor, has no identity. Yet, fundamentally, we talk always out of our own experience; and as this play inverts some conventional stage roles, it reflects – but also inverted – the bitter story of betrayal that is told in the sonnets. The clever servant who so thoroughly dominates his master, who by his talent for acting the blunt man acceptably gets his own way, might have been a role with which Shakespeare in his darkest moments could identify, no less than with the unconditional generosity of forgiveness in Cassio and Desdemona. Physical facts are acknowledged in the sonnets with the very pun that maddens Othello:

> When my love swears that she is made of truth,
> I do believe her, though I know she lies...
> Therefore I lie with her, and she with me,
> And in our faults by lies we flatter'd be.
>
> (Sonnet 138)

'Lie with her! lie on her! they say lie on her, when they belie her!'
cries Othello at news of the 'confession' (IV, i, 36–7). If part of the
sonnet situation appears in the grief of Othello, the nausea of the
sonnets on the Dark Lady, and the straight sexual abuse of others,
sounds like Iago's voice; the invisible protagonist in whom Iago and
Othello are united wrote the sonnets. Othello's social insecurity, his
hesitation about his age, his peculiarly flat use of an emblematic heaven
and hell conceived as stage locations could be paralleled, with agonized
sense of a metamorphosis in the beloved image:

> Her name, that was as fresh
> As Dian's image, is now begrim'd and black
> As my own face: (III, iii, 390–2)
> But I have sworn thee fair and thought thee bright
> Who art as black as hell, as dark as night.   (Sonnet 147)

Buried at a deep level, with the relation of friendship and love inverted,
the older experience, already once shaped in the alembic of the imagination, may have assisted in *Othello*'s deep catharsis, unaccompanied as
it is by strain or complexity or the reverberation of further unresolved
conflicts. The eloquence and unity of this play, the close relation of all
characters in one great household might suggest that behind it lies
the old emblem of the Tree of Life, with its many branches:

No man is an island, entire of itself; every man is a piece of the continent,
a part of the main; if a clod be washed away by the sea, Europe is the less,
as well as if a promontory were, as well as if a manor of thy friends or of
thine own were; any man's death diminishes me, because I am involved in
mankind. And therefore never send to know for whom the bell tolls; it tolls
for thee.[18]

Unity behind the rending divisions, which derives perhaps from the
underlying unity in a conflict projected from a personal experience is
endorsed by the ease and power of rhythm and movement in the play,
its shapeliness and order. Based on natural relations, as expressed by
the actors in their sense of an ensemble, this kind of unity is far less
direct and obvious than one based on hierarchy and degree, or on
social analysis and 'humourous observation' of Jonson's kind.

As social ritual, the Jacobean court masque replaced the Elizabethan
history play. Celebrating unity and concord, but designed for the few
rather than the many, it depended on those assumptions of order and
degree which, whatever their philosophic validity, were no longer
socially at the centre. The Platonic assumptions of a great festive poem
like Spenser's *Epithalamium* were challenged by a scepticism and

pessimism which found its most powerful expression on the public stage, above all perhaps in the world of *King Lear*.

Shakespeare's final plays are related to the masque and also to the older emblematic stages of his youth. Their relation to the masque is attested by their effect on Milton, whose own masques are his most Shakespearian writings. The structure is poetic, but goes well beyond the poetry to spectacle and presentation, and draws on a great range of social and theatrical habit. With a striking unity of theme they offer a range of audience appeal and of staging as wide as the tragedies that precede them. *Coriolanus* and *Antony and Cleopatra* can be contrasted as a play of strict and severe control, and one of great opulence and variety. When Antony sums up his story in the speech to Eros 'Sometimes we see a cloud that's dragonish' he anticipates Prospero's speech on the ending of the revels; the underlying principle has been a succession of pompous and baroque pageants melting into each other. The pageant of Cleopatra as Venus, described by Enobarbus, is directly presented by her in her death scene. A river pageant and a royal performance by a Queen, African and richly robed in pearl and blue and silver, had been seen as early as 1605 on the Whitehall stage. In Ben Jonson's *Masque of Blackness*, Anne of Denmark had appeared in person, seated in a great shell with her maids of honour, and surrounded by sporting Tritons. This masque, in which for the first time the Queen of England appeared as a player, could not have failed to move the imagination of the King's servants who would – including Shakespeare – have been in attendance. It joined perhaps with memories of Elizabethan pageantry on the Thames.

The Winter's Tale and *The Tempest* appear connected in some way with the marriage of Princess Elizabeth, later Queen of Bohemia. The tale of *Cymbeline* reshapes British history, giving a romantic and distanced view of Roman and British elements. But *The Winter's Tale* also refashioned a romance of Shakespeare's old stage enemy, Robert Greene, dead some twenty years; *Cymbeline* recalls other early plays of those far-off times such as *Clyamon and Clamydes*. In *Pericles* and *The Two Noble Kinsmen* Chaucer and Gower, poets of an older time, are invoked as supporters; the second may reshape that famous early lost play, Edwards' *Palamon and Arcite*, and it certainly contains echoes of Shakespeare's own *A Midsummer Night's Dream*.

A popular and perennially attractive romance, *Pericles* incurred the scorn of Ben Jonson, who dismissed it as a 'mouldy tale' a relic of a feast of language, left for alms like 'the shrieve's crusts'. However, in 1619 it was given at a court performance in honour of the departing French ambassador. The performance was divided into two halves – after Act II – the point at which Shakespeare took over the writing.

During this interval especially sumptuous refreshments were served in china dishes, and the late-night show ended at two in the morning. On such an occasion a 'mouldy tale' would seem no fit offering.

Dryden who adapted and improved on *The Tempest* in his *Enchanted Island*, thought *Pericles* 'a ridiculous incoherent story'. Dr Johnson found *The Winter's Tale* 'with all its absurdities, very entertaining' but coming to *Cymbeline*, refused to 'waste criticism upon unresisting imbecility, upon faults too evident for detection and too gross for aggravation'. The popularity of *Pericles* puzzled contemporaries, as it still puzzles critics, for poetry of the gaps is always bewildering. Many references suggest that it had no right to be as popular as it was; though included in the projected edition of Shakespeare's works for 1619, it did not appear in the First Folio of 1623, where *Timon of Athens*, another puzzling play, was inserted only to fill a printer's need. *The Two Noble Kinsmen* was never formally acknowledged; these may represent only a portion of Shakespeare's minor uncompleted work, in which he reverted to the older habit of working with a collaborator.

These 'tales, tempests and such drolleries' as Jonson scornfully termed them, combined shows (or drolleries) of great splendour with violent action, and passages of concentrated writing, sometimes delicate, sometimes ferocious. The disturbed imagination that confers insight on a Hamlet, a Lear, a Macbeth is here presenting the play. The intuitive linking of character with character – so that, for example, in *King Lear* the Fool 'serves as a screen on which Shakespeare flashes readings from the psychic life of the protagonist' – now extends itself so that the total drama is seen from outside the normal range of view by one, like Gower, 'assuming man's infirmities' but not really subject to them. Imogen waking beside the headless trunk of Cloten dressed in her husband's garments produces an effect like that of the modern Theatre of the Absurd in its violence and incongruity. The devouring of Paulina's husband by the bear is reinforced in its comic horror by the clownish jocularity of the shepherd: 'I have not winked since I saw these sights; the men are not yet cold under water, nor the bear half din'd on the gentleman; he's at it now' (*The Winter's Tale* III, iii, 101–4).

The Two Noble Kinsmen is sprinkled with images of horror to parallel the tableau of slain knights at the opening of *Pericles*; an unburied king that

> I' the blood cizd field lay swoln,
> Shewing the Sun his teeth, grinning at the moon   (I, i, 103–4)

and women that have

> sod their Infants in (and after eat them)
> The brine they wept at killing 'em.   (I, ii, 24–5)

The colloquial violence of the brothel scenes in *Pericles* stands out from the homespun texture of the rest no less than does the poetry of the final recognition scene, for which perhaps the whole play was devised. In the beautiful trance-like calm of this 'Ship' scene, silence is broken only by deliberately inadequate words till Pericles finally hears the music of the spheres, inaudible to mortals:

> Such harmony is in immortal souls,
> But while this muddy vesture of decay
> Doth grossly close it in, we cannot hear it.
> (*Merchant of Venice* v, i, 63–5)

The presenter, Gower, from whose *Confessio Amantis* the story comes, stands 'i' the gaps to teach you / The stages of our story' and promises the audience

> What's done in action, more if might,
> Shall be discover'd; please you sit and hark.

His final trite moral summary, like the even more trite summary concluding *The Two Noble Kinsmen*, underlines how little can be discovered. Sudden transforming of humanity into puppets, or *vice versa*, as if charmed by Prospero's rod, constitutes the shock treatment of these plays; the jagged join of old and new styles, the turbulence of subtle feelings and preposterous violence is made explicit by the presenter.

The framework of a medieval Romance or tale of adventure had been provided by those fixed and regular habits from which it gave a momentary escape. The struggle to retain and transform the old form is part of the history of Elizabethan literature. In the theatre, romance had been decried from the time of Philip Sidney, with his mocking account of adventurous stage journeys. Shakespeare returned to these old forms (being himself already mocked in *The Knight of the Burning Pestle* for the inflated rhetoric of his Hotspur). He could only attempt to invoke something beyond the ordinary framework.

The 'play within a play' was by this time familiar enough; what is presented in these plays is something like 'the play beyond the play' – those larger and unheard harmonies of which it is an echo.

Cervantes had found another way to this humane achievement of reconciliation; but it is to Cervantes that anyone in search of a comparable imagination must turn. As *Othello* gains its effect by concentrating upon the natural and shutting out cosmic reverberations, the romances are designed to reverberate and vibrate in accordance with what is brought to them. In a doctrinal and critical age, they appeal, they charm or sometimes repel, but 'the poet never affirmeth and therefor never lieth'. And yet, as one of Shakespeare's jesters knew, 'the truest poetry is the most feigning'.

The unity of time and place in *The Tempest* is masterly, a direct evidence of control; but it does not, compared with the other romances, give the sense of relief of a dislocated joint falling into place; for the logic of Time as chorus in *The Winter's Tale* works in a different way. The speedy fall and slow recovery of faith may be contrasted with the movement of Othello's mind; and in that play, the 'double time' skilfully controls the tension and response. Nowadays, being used to working with two-clock systems, even analytic pedants may accept what was perhaps, originally, the craftsman's intuitive cunning.

A Caroline defender of the poet, feigning disapproval of both Jonson 'the Dagon-poet' and Shakespeare, declares:

> Shakespeare, the Plebeian Driller, was
> Founder'd in's *Pericles* and must not pass.[19]

To drill could mean to *whirl, twirl,* or *churn*, i.e Shakespeare devised this popular whirligig of a plot and 'founder'd' in the turbulence he created. At the time, a number of plays had appeared with such titles as *Cupid's Whirligig*, or *A Woman is a Weathercock*, but Shakespeare worked and reworked this same theme many times; and to the end in *The Tempest*, it images forth a conflict only partly resolved.

In positive terms, this suggests that the audience was meant to reach a state which cannot be defined, a state of being overwhelmed. It had sometimes been described as 'rapture' or 'delight' and perhaps it is what the fastidious but susceptible young Milton was trying to describe when he wrote for the Second Folio:

> Thou in our wonder and astonishment
> Hast built thyself a live-long Monument...
> Those Delphick lines with deep impression took,
> Then thou our fancy of itself bereaving,
> Dost make us Marble with too much conceiving.

To judge by *Comus*, Milton must have received the deepest impression from *The Tempest*, which in spite of its classic design, has received such diversity of interpretation that it remains 'deliberately enigmatic'. The most notable thing about the hero is 'the impossibility of charting the movements of his mind', and 'it is rarely possible to be sure what is going on inside these people, or that there is one right way of acting the parts'.[20] The play is susceptible of almost any interpretation that the audience chooses to put on it; it is a *new* myth, with all the openness, the invitation to personal variety that is characteristic of the older rituals. Its simplicity is deceptive, and won perhaps at great cost.

Even its shows, the plays within the play, are profoundly unclear; the audience seem to move through such a country as Othello described

to Desdemona. Caliban is as strange as the anthropophagi. It is also
a dream country; the slanders and plots of Antonio and Sebastian, who
speak with the accents of Iago – the sneering and derisive confederacy
of 'the joker in the pack' – are silenced. Yet, like Iago, they do not
repent. The play is truly 'Delphic'.

The enigmatic and puzzling nature of the latest products of Shakespeare's Jacobean workshop would seem to indicate that he was
experimenting to integrate old and new conventions of the stage,
conscious of the widening gap between the forms of his youth and
that of his age. He could use the old framework – but always to some
new purpose. A coronation earthly and heavenly are built into a plot
that replaces the old Wheel of Fortune by the personal fiat of Henry VIII,
determining the rise and fall of Buckingham, Katherine, Anne, Wolsey
and Cranmer.[21] In the whirligig that shifts the characters of *The Two
Noble Kinsmen* and *Pericles* some symmetry is kept; the comic madness
of the jailer's daughter, like that of the madmen in Middleton's
Changeling, is based on an immediate sense of the 'difference of men'
whereas the heroine cannot distinguish Palamon from Arcite, and
prefers school-girl friendships to either. Pericles' love for Marina and
Antiochus' incestuous relation with his daughter are contrasted by
Gower, whose motto, if not wholly acceptable, is not wholly irrelevant
either:

Et bonum quo antiquius, eo melius.   (Prologue 1, 10)

Accepting, as Chaucer had done before him, the role of an unlearned
writer, combining all the arts of the theatre with a full sense of their
range, Shakespeare in these latest plays yet implies that actors, audience
and poet share an event brought only into being by full action. Words
can only bear witness to silence, as shadows bear witness to light. He
did not seek to print his plays, perhaps from assurance as much as from
humility.

In the first phase of his Jacobean writings, Shakespeare set against
the analytic and critical drama led by Jonson the 'esemplastic power'
of a tragedy built on principles of growth and change in human relations. Against the purely spectacular and theatrical display of Fletcher's
baroque theatre, and the court masque, he worked for continuity.
Of Wisdom, it is said, that remaining in herself, she makes all things
new.

11

SHAKESPEARE AND MUSIC

F. W. STERNFELD

In order to assess the employment of music in Shakespeare's plays we must remember that a wealth of dramatic music was available to him both in England and abroad as model and analogue. The tragedies and comedies of native dramatists were not lacking in sung lyrics or instrumental pieces, and there were moreover the influences, whether direct or indirect, of the Italian *intermedio* and the French *ballet*. It will be seen that no mention has been made of Italian opera which existed contemporary with Shakespeare. In this respect one must remember that Shakespeare's characters speak naturally and predominantly in verbal cadences, whereas in Italian opera song is the natural and exclusive mode of utterance.

From time immemorial, however, men of the theatre have found it useful to intersperse spoken plays with music since audiences subjected to an exclusive diet of speech, much of it in verse, tend to get restless. Music (in addition to stage machinery and other spectacular effects) seems one of the means to alleviate that condition. Apart from this practical consideration, many theatrical artists have felt that music adds another dimension to the play, conveys ideas which cannot be as well set forth in verbal discourse. Certainly, many of Shakespeare's predecessors and contemporaries shared these practical and aesthetic doctrines.

The obvious place to insert music in a spoken play is between the acts. For one thing, competence to declaim and competence to sing are not too frequently combined, and this comparatively simple device gives one group of performers, namely, the actors, a chance to rest, while another group, namely the musicians, keep the audience amused. Italian spoken comedies were sometimes punctuated by musical *intermedi* between the acts, notably in performances at court, given in the second half of the sixteenth century. And similarly, in Sackville's and Norton's *Gorboduc*, a tragedy in blank verse acted before Queen Elizabeth in 1562, each act is preceded by a dumbshow to the accompaniment of instrumental music. But with the rapid development of dramatic art in the later sixteenth century and its growing independence of Senecan and other humanist models, no such neat division was attempted, and music crept into the very body of spoken plays to an increasing degree. In later Elizabethan and Jacobean drama the dumb-show became an integral device of the play, as witnessed by Kyd's *Spanish Tragedy*, Shakespeare's *Titus Andronicus* and *Hamlet*, and Webster's *Duchess of Malfi*. Altogether, strains of instrumental music were frequently employed to endow a particular sequence with especial, if not magic significance. It is music's sound to which the ghost of Helen of Troy is conjured up in Marlowe's *Doctor Faustus*. On the other hand, the *intermedio* tradition, where music framed the play, survives somewhat in the musical finale which sometimes concludes a play, notably a comedy. Here Feste's epilogue to *Twelfth Night* offers a distinguished example. No doubt there were many precedents: the spring and winter song at the end of *Love's Labour's Lost*, the tradition of the Elizabethan jig which often concluded plays, and the related Italian tradition of the joyous choral dancing finale at the conclusion of *intermedi*.

Before proceeding to a more detailed examination of vocal and instrumental music in Shakespeare's plays, it may be well to enumerate the major categories into which these various cues can usefully be divided. (One would hesitate to call these musical cues 'insertions', for to term them thus in the mature and late plays would be to deny them their chief value: to be an integrated part of the drama itself.)

There is, first of all, what may be called stage music: an action on the stage which functionally demands music, for example, a banquet, serenade, or call to battle.

The second category may, for the sake of brevity, be termed magic music, employed, for instance, to make someone fall in love, or fall asleep, or be miraculously healed. Naturally, these classifications may overlap; a call to battle may be functional stage music, but it may also steel the nerves of the faltering. It is, perhaps, fair to say that scholars in the first half of this century have paid a good deal of attention to the magic function of music in Elizabethan plays, and well they might in view of the numerous examples extending from the way in which Glendower's daughter sings Mortimer to sleep in *Henry IV* to the manner in which Ariel entices Ferdinand 'to these yellow sands' in *The Tempest*. Of course, some magic effects on the stage are brought about by human cunning and suggestion, but frequently these events are supernatural, and both Lady Mortimer and Ariel are aided by the supernatural powers commanded by Glendower and Prospero respectively. Glendower's musicians who

> Hang in the air a thousand leagues from hence,
> And straight they shall be here:

are clearly concealed, perhaps behind a curtain, as are the spirits who accompany Ariel, as well as the Masque of Shapes in Act III of *The Tempest*. At other points this concealment of supernatural, magic music seems to be brought about by placing music under a trap-door, as when the strange sound of oboes which presages the fall of the hero in *Antony and Cleopatra* is accompanied by the stage direction

[Music of the hautboys is under the stage].

In this instance nobody would wish to draw a neat line between the magic, the superstitious and the prophetic; but it is a fair generalization to say that magic music, when supernatural, is as a rule concealed and invisible. Frequently it is also inaudible to the rest of the cast and heard only by those to whom it is addressed, as in the Music of the Spheres in *Pericles*.

A third category could be described as character music, that is to say, as music which portrays or reveals the character of one of the protagonists. In *Troilus and Cressida* the nature of Pandarus, the provider of soft luxuries, the pander, is characterized by the sophisticated lecherous song which he sings

Love, love, nothing but love, still love, still more!

Beyond that it also portrays Paris and Helen for whom he sings, as well as the Elizabethan gentry whom Shakespeare satirizes. Sometimes the character expressed through music is assumed rather than real. In *Othello* honest Iago pretends to conviviality and kindliness when he sings:

And let me the canakin clink, clink.

Fondness for music is usually a criterion of kindliness in Shakespeare; in Pandarus this trait may degenerate into excessive sweetness and softness; in Iago it is merely the disguise behind which he hides. Lack of fondness for music (and plays), as in the case of Cassius who 'has a lean and hungry look', is taken as a symptom of lack of charity, and so this attitude toward music may become a negative characterization. There is nothing lean and hungry about clowns, and when Feste in *Twelfth Night* sings

O Mistress mine, where are you roaming?

this easy-going gospel of *joie de vivre* marks both him and his audience, Toby and Andrew. When he asks them whether they want 'a love song, or a song of good life' for their sixpence, they clearly demand the former, because they 'care not for good life', that is, Puritan restrictions. Often it is desirable and dramatically economical that a character be portrayed in song, but there are times when Shakespeare's characters are good at verse but not at singing; at other times their social station requires that they don't sing themselves but bid a servant to do so. Duke Orsino's excessive melancholy and love-sickness is marvellously portrayed by Feste's recital of

> Come away, come away, death;

a lyric the Duke expressly commands to be performed for his gratification. A similar case of self-indulgence occurs in *Measure for Measure* when the unhappy and deserted Mariana asks a boy singer to recite the melancholy

> Take, O take those lips away,

to 'please her woe'. But probably the supreme example of characterization, of revealing a protagonist's true mind beneath the surface, occurs in Ophelia's famous mad scene. When the heroine sings numerous songs (and snatches of songs) before the King, the Queen and Horatio; when she breaks into song spontaneously without being urged to perform by the others and without polite protestations on her own part, she betrays to the audience several crucial facts. First, that her mind is deranged, for the object of the devotions of the Prince of Denmark should not break into song in a manner quite unbecoming to her social station. (On that point the etiquette books, whether Italian or English, are quite clear. Note that Shakespeare is careful to insert polite disclaimers in the surrounding dialogue when a member of the nobility does sing, as Balthasar does in *Much Ado About Nothing* and Pandarus in *Troilus and Cressida*.) Secondly, Ophelia's lyrics are a clear indication of the profound grief over her father's death:

> White his shroud as the mountain snow,
> Larded with sweet flowers;
> Which bewept to the grave did not go
> With true-love showers.

Here the insertion of the monosyllable 'not' in the third line illustrates a method much employed in Shakespeare's use of song. In a popular lyric he departs from the text, presumably well-known to the audience, to convey the state of mind of the singer. The syllable 'not' is metrically superfluous and its omission would agree with the over-all sense of the stanza (for which reason older editors often emended 'to the grave did go'). But by singing 'to the grave did not go' Ophelia indicates her sense of shock at the absence of pomp and circumstance on the occasion of her father's burial. If one of the strands of Ophelia's consciousness, or subconsciousness, is concerned with her filial grief, the other is her love for Hamlet, and in that connection concern for her chastity 'not too delicately avowed by her father and her brother', as Coleridge puts it. Whether she sings a mere snatch, such as

> For Bonny sweet Robin is all my joy

or four entire stanzas of a St Valentine's Day song, her concern with love, moreover extramarital love, is quite clear. Both the fact of her singing and the subject matter of her songs characterize her state of mind and her preoccupations.

A fourth category of music is distinctly present. It foretells a change of tone within the drama; from suspicion to trust, from vengeance to forgiveness, from hate (or coldness) to love. The employment of music to indicate to the audience a general change of tone is a most economical way of indicating the different style of the proceedings ahead. It obviates tiresome verbal explanations and asides and has been used in this capacity both in ritual and in drama from time immemorial. The most felicitous examples in Shakespeare occur in his last comedies where the miraculous element functions not so much in its own right than as a token of expiation and happiness. In *The Tempest*, the wedding masque in Act IV and Ariel's song in Act V

> Where the bee sucks, there suck I;

certainly prefigure

> ...calm seas, auspicious gales.
> And sail so expeditious that shall catch
> Your royal fleet far off.

To be sure, the functions of the music overlap, the wedding masque is also stage music, and Ariel's lyric serves also, in a manner of speaking, as a character song. The airy spirit sings to himself about his future life, revealing his bent of mind. Yet the larger aesthetic meaning is unmistakable. The intervention of music in *The Winter's Tale* to prepare for the denouement is similarly timed. There is a masque in Act IV and the sheep-shearing in Bohemia is followed by a striking musical interlude in Act V. When Paulina commands

> Music, awake her: strike

and the statue comes to life, we know that the complete reconciliation within the older generation will soon follow that between Florizel and his father. This instrumental music, to the sound of which Hermione descends from the pedestal, is some mere fifty lines from the end of the play. It may be that Shakespeare, who concluded both *The Tempest* and *The Winter's Tale* with spoken verse and thereby deprived himself of a musical finale effect, wished to place near the conclusion of the drama pieces of incidental music, fairly prominent within the play's frame. From what we may infer about the playwright's methods from the extant plays, such a combination of mundane and lofty considerations would not be alien to his customary procedure.

So far this discussion of Shakespeare's employment of music has dealt with the manner in which songs or instrumental passages are woven into the spoken text, without reference to the notes themselves or to their instrumentation.

In regard to the actual music, our knowledge is fairly scant though it must be granted that, in particular since the Second World War, modern bibliographical methods, extensive concordances of incipits and their variants have filled several gaps in our knowledge. By reference to the monographs cited at the end of this book the interested reader will find numerous musical settings for the songs in Shakespeare's plays. In a few instances it is more than likely that these represent the actual notes employed by the King's men, if not in a first performance, at least in an early revival. But more often than not we cannot be certain that a particular tune was used on the stage, as when a melody with the appropriate title, or incipit, or rubric occurs in a commonplace book or other source of the period, and the setting represents a likely hypothesis. In still other cases no certainty of any kind exists, but an Elizabethan or Jacobean tune has been found which fits the text metrically and whose melodic contours suggest an atmosphere not at odds with the dramatic situation. Here we deal with a working hypothesis which, at least on historical and stylistic grounds, seems acceptable *faute de mieux*. If we count all the songs in Shakespeare, including quotations of mere snatches, and if we include lyrics that were, perhaps, only declaimed but might have been sung, the total is fairly near to a hundred. In about forty instances we have music, extending from near certainty to a hypothesis that is historically not unacceptable.

Once more, the music which provided the setting for these lyrics covered a wide range. At one end we have simple, ballad-like ditties, presumably well known to contemporary audiences. These tunes easily fitted a variety of lyrics composed of lines of three stresses or four stresses or an alternation of the two. We must assume that these melodies, accommodating various texts, were well enough known so as not to require musical notation, for in the broadsides of the period one usually meets merely such verbal rubrics as 'To the tune of Greensleeves' or 'To the tune of Walsingham'. In the few instances where melodies are given in musical notation it is a one-staff notation, that is to say, a melody without accompaniment. Indeed, most of these melodies, although capable of being harmonized, do not require harmonization. A person calling them to mind could sing them spontaneously or hum them without carrying an instrument, such as a lute or a cittern, which is rarely carried about unless one plans a musical performance. Of such a nature are most of the ballad-like ditties sung by the Fool in *King Lear*, by Silence in *Henry IV*, and by Ophelia in *Hamlet*. True, the first quarto of *Hamlet* has the stage direction

Enter Ophelia playing on a lute, and her hair down, singing.

But this stage direction does not occur in the second quarto or the Folio, and there is no reference to a musical instrument in the surrounding dialogue. Certainly, Ophelia's songs do not require accompaniment, though a few strummed chords would do them no harm. In *Othello*, on the other hand, it would be extremely awkward for Desdemona to accompany herself on a lute when she sings the Willow Song and while Emilia undresses her. The lyric which she recalls is an old song, which survives in two commonplace lute books of the sixteenth century (one in Dublin, one in Washington, D.C.). As she remembers, she sings, and to search at this point for a musical instrument would break dramatic continuity and spoil the impression of spontaneity.

In modern literature these ditties are sometimes referred to as ballads, sometimes as folksongs. The term folksong is unobjectionable provided it does not imply anonymity but conveys the fact of popularity with 'folk', regardless of whether or not we know the name of the composer. A case in point is the song of Peter (enacted by Will Kemp, who preceded Robert Armin as the company's clown) in *Romeo and Juliet*. The verbal text of Peter's lyric was first printed in an anthology in 1576 and attributed to Richard Edwards. The music survives in two manuscripts, unattributed, but is probably also by Edwards. To all intents and purposes, then, Shakespeare has the clown quote a lyric by Edwards, a playright and poet of an older generation. But functionally the song sounds like a ballad, not like a humanist poem in praise of music (as which it is revealed when one contemplates the entire lyric and not merely the lines quoted by Peter). Its four-stress lines, its simple, fairly syllabic melody which is easily sung or hummed without accompaniment, the puns and jokes to which its content is subjected in the surrounding dialogue, all of these aspects combine to make the clown's song the equivalent of a ballad or an anonymous folksong, if there be such a thing except in the minds of nineteenth century scholars.

These simple ditties, then, provide music for many of Shakespeare's lyrics. In contrast there are also songs that might be described as art music rather than quasi folk music. These are characterized either by the prosodic complexity of the verbal text or simply by the dramatic context. A protagonist sings a song, not spontaneously as it springs to his mind, but as a studied and considered performance, either after entreaties by his friends or at the express command of his master. As a rule the singing requires an instrumental accompaniment, and this accompaniment is often referred to in the dialogue surrounding the lyric. In *Julius Caesar* Brutus refers three times to the 'instrument' with which Lucius accompanies himself, and in *Henry VIII* Queen Katherine commands, 'Take thy lute, wench'. Pandarus's song in *Troilus and Cressida* is another example. Before beginning he says at one point, 'Come, give me an instrument' and at another 'I'll sing you a song now'. And when Helen commands, 'Let thy song be love', Pandarus obliges with a lyric which in finesse and sophistication is far removed from the metrical simplicity of the songs and ditties sung by Autolycus in *The Winter's Tale*. Ariel in *The Tempest* is another artful singer of whom professional skill is demanded, notably in 'Full fathom five' and 'Where the bee sucks'. Of these songs we fortunately possess settings from the early seventeenth century, attributed to the lutenist Robert Johnson (*c.* 1582–1633) and printed by John Wilson (1595–1674) in the latter's *Cheerful Ayres*, MDCLX (*recte* 1659). It is impossible to establish whether these settings were composed for the first performance in 1611 or for the revival in 1612–13 or later, but there seem to be no good historical or stylistic grounds for doubting that Johnson's music was expressly composed for Shakespeare's play and that the date of composition falls within Shakespeare's lifetime. It is also possible that Thomas Morley, next to William Byrd Shakespeare's most famous musical contemporary, was connected with two other lyrics which were performed on the stage by professional musicians, each consisting of several stanzas. In *As You Like It* two singing boys sing four stanzas of 'It was a lover and his lass'. When one of them asks

Shall we clap into't roundly, without hawking, or spitting, or saying we are hoarse, which are the only prologues to a bad voice?

he is poking fun at the polite disclaimers of aristocratic amateurs. A musical setting for single voice and lute appears in the printed edition of Morley's *First Book of Ayres*, 1600, and can easily be adapted for two voices. In *Twelfth Night* Feste sings two stanzas of 'O Mistress mine, where are you roaming?' Feste is clearly a professional musician who gives a professional performance for pay. An instrumental piece entitled 'O Mistress mine' was printed in Morley's *Consort Lessons*, 1599, and its melody fits Shakespeare's words very well. In both cases, though, Morley's music requires adaptation, which Johnson's does not, and for a variety of reasons collaboration between Morley and Shakespeare is less likely, though by no means impossible.

A word must be said about the 'scoring' of Shakespeare's vocal and instrumental resources. A modern audience listening to a Bach cantata or mass performed by a choral society of men and women experiences a sonority greatly at variance with that envisaged by the composer who wrote for boys and countertenors (as did Byrd and Palestrina), rather than female sopranos and altos. Similarly, the modern theatre-goer must remember that the only performers for Shakespeare's songs were men and boys, a fact which makes a crucial difference to the sonority and overtones of the lyrics of Ophelia and Desdemona. A thin, sexless sound in contrast to a reverberant and chesty tone will stress the aspects of pathos and helplessness of a deserted or cruelly dis-appointed heroine. It will also help to accentuate interest on the turns and twists of the plot rather than on the sensuous aspects of the action. In this regard a comparison between Shakespeare's *Othello* and Verdi's opera *Otello* is illuminating. But boys by no means sang only the lyrics of the heroines, they also performed the songs of the fairies in *A Mid-summer Night's Dream*, the children disguised as fairies in *The Merry Wives of Windsor*, and the music of Ariel and his troupe in *The Tem-pest*. Clearly, in these and other instances their size and the tone colour of their voices added to the illusion of the supernatural. In this regard the Chamberlain's/King's men had little advantage over the St Paul's and Blackfriar's boys. On the contrary, the group of 'little eyasses' would contain a greater number of musically trained boys. But Shakespeare's troupe of adult players had one cardinal advantage: it could offer, within the same drama, in addition to boys, an adult singer who in size, maturity and sonority was a welcome contrast. To watch the playwright developing this resource over the years within his 'orchestra' is a fascinating spectacle. Naturally, it was the clown who was most easily available as a trained musician among the adult personnel and in the chronological progression from Balthasar to Amiens, to the gravedigger (in *Hamlet*) to Feste to Pandarus to Lear's fool to Autolycus, some of the best parts belong to clowns. Notwith-standing, the part of Pandarus is not to be despised and Pandarus's song has been called by Richmond Noble 'one of the very greatest dramatic masterpieces in our language'. In any event, it is obvious that after Armin succeeded Kemp Shakespeare steadily increased both the importance of the speaking part and the singing part of the adult singer until, in the role of Autolycus, he created a figure which is both essential to the theme and at the same time adds another dimension to the play through its music. This dimension has a great deal to do with the turn from farce to 'romance' as Shakespeare's last plays are usually designated. By the time the function of the boy-singer had reached a somewhat similar apotheosis, as in the part of Ariel, the perfection of the vocal resources in Shakespeare's orchestra is complete.

As to the instrumental forces, these greatly contributed to the atmosphere the playwright wished to evoke by virtue of the symbolism attached to various families of instruments. Whether a scene was military or courtly or domestic, whether the influences at work were divine or diabolical, whether the outlook was one for peace or for bloodshed, all these and many other matters could be suggested to an audience by the sound of certain instruments and instrumental combinations. It did not matter so much what was played as rather how it was played: harsh versus still, fast versus slow, loud versus soft, wind instruments versus stringed instruments, and so forth. In themselves the instrumental pieces did not command a great deal of intrinsic musical interest, it was the overtones of their sonorities that mattered. In that regard Shakespeare and Milton were perhaps the last poets who could still count on a fairly wide knowledge of certain traditions stretching back to the Middle Ages and even Antiquity. Not that Dryden and Johnson and Keats and Yeats were less knowledgeable, but with the exception of a few cognoscenti familiarity with these concepts could no longer be counted upon on the part of their listeners and readers. Very little instrumental music for the stage has survived, and such little that has suggests dances, marches and other pieces of great brevity and simplicity, homophonic in nature, posing no problem of comprehension. (It would be naïve to expect in the theatre music of the length and complexity of a Dowland Fantasia, a Bach Fugue, a Beethoven Quartet.) At the most obvious level trumpets (and sometimes drums) connoted a military or courtly scene, whereas plucked instruments such as the lute and cittern suggested domesticity. The contrast between the silver strings of Apollo and the Muses and the pipes (wind instruments) of Pan and Marsyas was steadily employed in medieval and Elizabethan drama, but it is probably less immediately apparent to a modern audience. Shakespeare's groundlings, even if they could not read and write, were familiar with the 'lute' of the Biblical David and the classical Orpheus, the 'silver-tuned strings' of the Muses from many an Elizabethan play. Again, the music of the spheres and its 'invisible fiddlers' occurs in many a stage play, and the popular picture books of the sixteenth century contain instances of teaching the beholder the contrast between the aristocratic lute and the plebeian pipes. No classical education was required, therefore, to grasp the symbolism of musical instruments to which Shakespeare frequently resorts at crucial stages of his plot.

The belief that heavenly music rewards the good, punishes the bad, heals the sick, and foretells divine plans to anguished mortals operates in the masque-like episodes in *Pericles*, *Cymbeline*, *The Winter's Tale*, and *The Tempest*. On the stage this heavenly music is usually represented by the soft music of strings, gentleness being a commendable quality not only in the speaking voice of women (witness Cordelia) but also in the tone colour of instruments. By contrast, the harsh squealing of oboes and the brazen din of trumpets usually connotes excessive egotism, unnecessary bloodshed, and civil strife. This contrast between instruments 'haut' and 'bas', to use the medieval terms, is noticeable in those scenes where music plays a therapeutic role to assist an ailing patient. In *2 Henry IV* the dying king appeals for quiet

> KING   Let there be no noise made, my gentle friends;
> Unless some dull and favourable hand
> Will whisper music to my weary spirit.
> WARWICK   Call for the music in the other room.

Clearly, strings are called for on this occasion, as in *King Lear* when soft music restores 'the untuned and jarring senses' of the King. When Cordelia agrees to have her father awakened, the doctor commands

> Louder the music there![1]

And when in *Pericles* Cerimon employs music to revive Thaisa he again has recourse to the tradition:

> The still[2] and woeful music that we have,
> Cause it to sound, beseech you.
> The viol[3] once more. How thou stirr'st, thou block!

Opposed to these healing strains was the sound of oboes. (The oboes of the sixteenth and seventeenth centuries were much harsher and louder than those encountered in a modern symphony orchestra.) The banqueting scenes in *Titus Andronicus* and *Macbeth*, and the ominous music, under the stage, in *Antony and Cleopatra* are instances. Between these two extremes is a wealth of passages from short alarums and dead marches to morris dances and masques, illustrating the playwright's discriminating utilization of instrumental passages; always, to be sure, in the greater service of his central objective: poetic drama.

12

THE HISTORICAL AND
SOCIAL BACKGROUND

JOEL HURSTFIELD

A historian who is not himself a literary critic is perhaps too ready to see Shakespeare's plays as historical sources rather than in terms of their form, plot, language and imagery. He may indeed be guilty of putting Shakespeare too much in his time and too little in the context of the historical development of English drama. Yet so handicapped, and perhaps also helped, the historian does see in Shakespeare's work reflections of the two societies in England or, to anticipate the phrase of Disraeli, the two nations. If this conclusion is correct, and not merely a subjective discovery in literature of what the historian finds in Elizabethan and Jacobean society, then the plays – whether histories or not – show over and over again the insecure grasp of crown and government upon the authority they have inherited and claim. The crown which sits so uneasily on the head of Henry IV is a burden to all Shakespeare's rulers. 'To be a King and wear a crown', said Elizabeth I to her parliamentarians in 1601, 'is a thing more glorious to them that see it, than it is pleasant to them that bear it.'[1] The force which destroys Julius Caesar, Coriolanus, Richard II, Richard III is a force which threatened the Tudor and Stuart monarchy. 'I am Richard II,' said Elizabeth on another occasion to the historian Lambarde, when referring to Shakespeare's play, 'know ye not that?'[2]

For here was a monarchy which rested on two claims: that it was of divine origin and that it governed by consent of the whole people. These claims were not inherently contradictory since, in sixteenth century political thought, representation did not imply election. The overwhelming majority of Englishmen in the time of Shakespeare did not possess the right to vote; and of those who had it, few ever had the opportunity to use it. Direct patronage, or agreement between factions, usually determined who should sit in Parliament. The basic assumption was that the leading men of the shire, however they were elected, spoke for their whole community; and this was not questioned until the middle of the seventeenth century when, in the tumult of revolution, a small minority called for a wider suffrage. But what was becoming a significant issue was whether the monarch made policy in the light only of divine guidance, or modified it where necessary on the advice of some four hundred men gathered in the House of Commons and some sixty in the House of Lords. Was James I answerable for his policy in the next world only, as he believed, or could he be called to a reckoning in this?

It is often assumed that in Ulysses's plea for order and degree in *Troilus and Cressida* is an account of the Elizabethan form of social hierarchy as it existed. Yet what Ulysses is saying is that the Greek camp is sick because order and degree no longer prevail. In Shakespeare's England order and degree, where they existed at all, existed much more in form than substance; and so it had been throughout the sixteenth century. Indeed the real malaise was not because order and degree were in dissolution but because they were being imposed upon a society which had in many respects broken free from their rigidities. The tragedy of the Stuarts was that Charles I took degree, with monarchy at its apex, more seriously than had any of his predecessors, and far more seriously than would any of his parliamentarians.

For Tudor society was fluid and pressing against the narrow channels into which church and state would confine it. To grasp this is fundamental to any understanding of Elizabethan or Jacobean society. It is not that the old order was dissolving. It was that a new more rigid order and degree were being imposed. It is not that the Tudor monarchy was fighting to retain its inherited powers, but it had enlarged these powers in a measure never enjoyed by its predecessors.

The central event which was to dominate the history of a whole century occurred a generation before Shakespeare's birth. In the 1530s Henry assumed on behalf of the monarchy powers which no other king of England had ever possessed. We call this event the English Reformation and the term is valid provided it is taken to describe a profound change in the constitution and society, perhaps more important than the religious change with which the term is associated. (I am not referring to the administrative 'revolution' associated with the name of Thomas Cromwell, which turns out to be less significant than was at one time thought.)

Henry assumed the headship of the English church; and one uses the word assumed deliberately because the king did not derive his authority from parliament – which did not possess the power to give it – but as he stated, from God alone. Parliament was there simply to confirm, not grant this title, and to impose the penalties for disobedience. 'The King's Majesty,' says the Act of Supremacy of 1534,

'justly and rightfully is and oweth [ought] to be the supreme head.'
The truth or otherwise of this statement could only be known when
its author got to heaven; but in practice it became increasingly difficult
for Henry VIII's successors to treat the whole religious settlement as
if it were a private treaty between himself and the Almighty. The changes,
first to Anglicanism under Henry VIII, then to radical Protestantism
in the course of Edward VI's short reign, then sharply back to Catholicism during Mary's equally short reign, then back again to a moderate
Protestant Anglicanism under Elizabeth I, had been too fundamental
and too swift to permit a monarch to carry through by himself.
Parliament came to see its own role, not simply as that of confirming
the king's claims and executing his policy, but also as advising and
commenting upon, criticizing and modifying the shape and content of
the English church. It is the fashion to speak of a 'partnership' between
crown and Parliament in the Tudor period. By the end of Shakespeare's
lifetime this 'partnership' resembled much more the unsettled relationship between one firm, the crown, which had overvalued its assets, and
another, a more aggressive consortium, the parliamentarians, which
was thinking in terms of a take-over bid, so that it could run the
business of government more efficiently and according to modern
managerial techniques, in a new partnership.

When Shakespeare came to London much of this struggle lay in the
future, but it was not very far away at the time that he left. What,
however, we are seeing from Henry VIII's day onward is the emergence
of the unitary, sovereign, state, the state seeking supremacy in secular
and spiritual things alike, and which was trying to reach into every
crevice of men's thoughts and actions. Recognizing this process, More
resigned his office of Lord Chancellor and then renounced life itself.
We who can see the full-length Holbein portrait of Henry VIII with
his legs astride his gorgeous costume, his arrogant, beady eyes staring
out on the world, see the visual image of the Leviathan state, sparing
no man in its inexorable advance to power. Order and degree formed
part of the new concept of the state, pressed on the nation by the crown
and its servants.

But below the flamboyant language of Henry VIII, the supreme
head, the more modest language of Elizabeth I, and the renewed
extravagance of James I, there was, in fact, an unstable and shifting
balance of power. For though parliament was, in the design of
Henry VIII, no more than a ratifying and enforcing instrument for
carrying through his revolution, the parliamentarians were beginning
to think otherwise. To understand the basis and framework of these
advancing claims we must look beyond the court to the few million
people who were Shakespeare's fellow countrymen.

It so happens that we have the work of two of Shakespeare's contemporaries to guide us in this. The first is Sir Thomas Smith, scholar, politician and diplomat, who wrote his *De Republica Anglorum* – only the title is in Latin – in 1565, the year after Shakespeare's birth. The second is Thomas Wilson, a minor figure in government circles, who wrote a survey of English society in about the year 1600, roughly halfway between the time of Shakespeare's arrival in London and his return to Stratford.

Smith wrote his book, which is enormously interesting as the only contemporary account of English government and society, while he was ambassador at the Court of the Valois. He distrusted the French government and loathed the conditions of political and religious disorder which he saw all around him. By contrast, as he looked homeward, he saw indeed an ordered society secure in its internal peace, with each man acknowledging his appointed place in this happy commonwealth. (Even the criminals sentenced to death did not complain because they realized that the sentence had been lawfully given).[3] Monarchy, aristocracy, gentry, burgesses, yeomen, all of them lived in settled, stable conditions, and performed duties appropriate to their rank. Smith even found a 'fourth sort of men which do not rule';[4] and these, by the way, though he does not say so, were the overwhelming majority of the queen's subjects. It is indeed, he argues, possible to identify each class by its very appearance: 'a gentleman (if he will be so accounted) must go like a gentleman, a yeoman like a yeoman, and a rascal like a rascal.'[5] But what is a gentleman? It is here that Smith lets reality break through the smooth surface of his two-dimensional survey. Gentlemen, he says, are being made 'good cheap' in England;[6] and the College of Heralds was always available to discover or invent an ancient lineage. Unkind critics, he acknowledges, scornfully call these *arrivistes* 'gentlemen of the first head'. Anyone, he says, who can afford to behave like a gentleman – 'who will bear the port, charge and countenance of a gentleman' – can soon be acknowledged as one.[7] Smith accepts that the *nouveaux riches* can make good their claim to gentility.

Thomas Wilson, writing about 35 years later, is less sure than is Smith about the ordered stability of England. Smith, of course, knows perfectly well that Tudor society is far more complex and indeterminate than his ordered hierarchy would imply. He gently tilts at the new families but assumes that they will rapidly adopt the postures of their class. Wilson's comments are not gently ironic but bitter. He was himself a younger son whose lot he laments, one of those, as he says, who inherit no more than 'that which the cat left on the malt heap'.[8] He is without land and without prospects. But he sees all around him the discouraging signs of an aggressive expansionist class from among whom he selects the upstart yeomen and lawyers for his most caustic comments.

The yeoman, he complains, 'must skip into his velvet breeches and silken doublet and, getting to be admitted into some Inn of Court or Chancery, must ever after think scorn to be called any other than gentleman.'⁹ (It is good to be reminded of the somewhat different kind of yeomen from those to whom Shakespeare's Henry V and Richard III addressed their memorable words.) 'Prithee, nuncle,' asks the Fool of King Lear, 'tell me whether a madman be a gentleman or a yeoman' (III, vi, 9–13). To Lear's reply that the answer must be a king, the Fool retorts: No, a madman is 'a yeoman that has a gentleman to his son; for he's a mad yeoman that sees his son a gentleman before him'. Often these ambitions of the yeoman class are snuffed out in extravagance, but, says Wilson, the lawyers do better.

Many lawyers, says Wilson, are 'grown so great, so rich and so proud, that no other sort dare meddle with them'. The most eminent lawyers were, indeed, getting most of the profitable business, and the rest of the members of this overcrowded profession had to 'live by pettifogging'. So they pry into records and provoke litigation with the result that they 'undo the country people and buy up all the lands that are to be sold'. These parasites are to be found everywhere, except perhaps in the Isle of Anglesey 'which boast they never had lawyers nor foxes'.¹⁰ It was, of course, not only the gentry who suffered.'The first thing we do,' says Dick, the crony of Jack Cade, the rebel, 'let's kill all the lawyers' (*2 Henry VI* IV, ii, 73–7). 'Nay, that I mean to do,' replies Cade, 'Is not this a lamentable thing, that of the skin of an innocent lamb should be made parchment? That parchment, being scribbl'd o'er, should undo a man?'

Though England, of course, was not populated solely by lawyers, gentlemen and yeomen, we hear much of them in contemporary literature and politics because England was still essentially a rural country, and land the measure of a man's wealth and standing. Cloth, the only English industry of major importance, was still mainly a rural industry. But most men did not possess land, for example, the agricultural labourer, the textile worker in town and country, the retailer, the seaman, the schoolmaster and many others. It is true that the enclosure movement, much of it for converting corn-land to sheep rearing, accompanied often by depopulation, had passed its peak by the time that Shakespeare was born; but its effects were still felt and remembered. Wealthy merchants and civil servants did own land for, as ever, the wealthy townsman sought to take root in the country. But, wherever they lived, they were alike acutely subject to the violent fluctuations of climate and harvest, of famine and plague, of commercial boom and slump, of war and peace.

During the whole of Shakespeare's lifetime there was not a single year when Europe was not engaged in war. England was not itself involved the whole time. From his birth until 1585 – roughly the time when he came to London – England was at peace, apart from isolated skirmishes. But for the rest of Elizabeth's reign, that is, for more than half the time that he spent in London, she was at war, deeply committed, and at a prodigious cost, to a stubborn struggle in the Netherlands, in Ireland and on the high seas. The new reign brought peace; but there could have been no period during Shakespeare's adult life when he would not see broken men returning from battle to which they had gone as volunteers or conscripts in defence of their own country, or as soldiers of fortune in foreign wars. 'What! a young knave and begging!' exclaims Falstaff. 'Is there not wars?' (2 *Henry IV* I, ii, 68–9). One should not be surprised that there are few plays of Shakespeare, whether history, comedy or tragedy, in which the sounds of war are not heard either on the stage or from the wings.

But far more widespread in their effects and implications were the threats of hunger and disease. The primitive state of English agriculture, and the inaccessibility of alternative supplies, meant that a wet summer and a ruined harvest brought high prices and hunger. Three wet summers in succession spelled out a major disaster as happened in the period 1594–6 and is best described in Titania's speech in *A Midsummer Night's Dream*. The price of corn, as compared with wages, has never been as high, before or since. London could sometimes import urgently needed corn via Danzig; other places using waterborne supplies might gain some relief. But inland transport, whether by water or land, was subject to all sorts of climatic hazards and was expensive for bulky commodities. Corn could double its price over relatively short distances.

Severe as these physical handicaps were, they were worsened by the sharp rise in population which extended for about a century after the 1530s. Probably, the population doubled during this period, rising from about two and a half to five million, though the pace was uneven; and the population of London may have quadrupled, reaching a quarter of a million by the end of Shakespeare's life. Historians have not yet taken the measure or discovered the cause of this upward trend; but about its existence there is no doubt. Men like Hakluyt saw it clearly enough and used this evidence to urge emigration and colonial settlement. Again, the effects of this growth were intensified by the backward state of the economy. Industry had neither the capital, nor the markets, nor the raw materials, nor the technical resources to absorb this increased labour; nor had farmers the knowledge to force up production to meet the pressure of demand. Hence England faced the situation, familiar enough to us today in the West Indies and India, of a population outgrowing its industry and its subsistence, and forced therefore to leave. It gives us some insight into both Shakespeare's age and our own to reflect that England today, with some fifty million people is, in certain respects, underpopulated while his England, with some five million, was threatened with overpopulation.

The other consequences of this are also familiar: unemployment, underemployment and inflation. Underemployment, as we can see today in Spain, southern Italy and some of the emergent nations, was more widespread than unemployment. It is a condition in which men are not wholly without work, but work only part of the week or part of the day. In the earlier centuries this was in some respects masked by two characteristics of medieval life: a part of the population was taken out of the labour market into monasteries and nunneries; and secondly, the large number of saints' days in any case reduced the length of the working week. When Protestant England abolished monasteries and drastically reduced the saints' days, the implicit conditions of underemployment became explicit.

But even more widespread were the effects of inflation. This, as always, affected the whole population. But it did not affect the whole population in the same way. It is a common enough phenomenon, in any time of inflation, that some of the rich grow richer and some of the poor grow poorer. So it was in Tudor England. Fortune, says Henry IV

> ...either gives a stomach and no food –
> Such are the poor, in health – or else a feast,
> And takes away the stomach – such are the rich...
>
> (2 *Henry IV* IV, iv, 105–7)

Many lost, for example, tenants (including copyholders) whose legal insecurity of tenure, or sheer weakness, made it possible to evict them; those landlords who found no means of raising rents to meet a changed situation, or had to bankrupt themselves to meet the heavy cost of litigation, or even dowries for a string of daughters; artisans whose labour was more plentiful than the food they ate; and the crown whose income simply could not be enlarged to meet the increased cost of living, administration, diplomacy and war. Who gained? Many merchants who sold on a rising market; those landlords who could force rents up and generally modernize their estates; many lawyers whose services are always needed in time of rapid change. All the evidence points to the increasing importance of these classes in society. We ask, therefore, what was their role in government?

The provincial gentry supplied the justices of the peace and the sheriffs. They served as amateurs but many of them had spent a year or more at either Oxford or Cambridge, or at the Inns of Court in London, the third university of England. They had both judicial and administrative duties, including the maintenance of order, the supervision of roads and bridges, the apprenticing of poor children, the fixing of wages and the organization of poor relief. A proportion of them worked hard and conscientiously but others were slack and easily responded to favour or gifts. They were not as bad as Shallow and Silence but some were probably not much better. The provincial administration for military affairs was no better. Under a leading nobleman as lord lieutenant it was factious, sometimes corrupt and thoroughly amateur.

Any study of Tudor provincial administration displays the great gap between the claims and the powers of the crown. Its writ ran only as far as the gentry cared to obey it. Behind the writ lay the threat; and a summons to appear before the Star Chamber in London was not lightheartedly received by justices who corrupted administration or juries who falsified verdicts. Many a great person in his shire was cut down to size by the government in London. But there were limits to the amount that it could do against the pressures of vested interests or just simply idleness or stupidity in the shire. Hence it is nowadays said by many historians that this was not an autocracy and that 'Tudor despotism' is a nineteenth century myth.

Yet this ignores one important element in government power: its control over communication. If the printing press in one sense weakens central authority because it makes possible the dissemination of minority opinions, in another it comes to its aid. Certainly, the government used pamphlets and homilies, addresses by high court judges at the assizes, sermons, proclamations, preambles to statutes to expound and popularize its aims to all who could read, write or listen. And the royal progress provided a dazzling, theatrical cavalcade through the towns and villages of southern England – these costly, elaborate processions never got to the north – and helped to implant in the popular imagination the divine attributes of the sovereign. Meanwhile, on the negative side, the strong censorship exercised over all forms of literature, secular no less than divine, did much to uphold the sacred virtues of the established order. The penalties for dissent were heavy and they grew heavier in the generation after Shakespeare's death as the fundamental dispute within the nation intensified and the country drifted into civil war. The dispute centred upon the nature of authority, and it dominates many of his plays.

The Tudor crown under Henry VIII had absorbed too much power over church and state, over thought and action. Divinity might hedge a king – if there were also arms to defend him; but it could not shield him from the doubts of his critics, or provide him with the necessary funds to govern. By the end of the sixteenth century, even the relatively austere Elizabeth was being forced to sell land to meet the exhausting costs of war. The more she lived on capital, the more she and her successors would have to call on parliamentary support. But it was the same kind of men who were influential in the shires who were also influential in Parliament, and Parliament was unwilling to grant money without a direct influence on government policy. Yet this control no monarch of the day was willing to accept, least of all the goddess Elizabeth or the kingly Solomon, James I. Hence the conditions of deadlock which were developing during Shakespeare's last decade in London. The anointed king held the spiritual and constitutional titles and the authority to determine policy, without the economic power to carry it through. The Commons possessed the economic power without the constitutional right to make policy.

'The state of monarchy', James I once told his faithful parliamentarians, 'is the supremest thing upon earth. For kings are not only God's lieutenants upon earth and sit upon God's throne, but even by God himself they are called gods.'[11] These parliamentarians were many of them astute, experienced men of the world who were hearing one thing and seeing another. They looked upon this man, ungainly, undignified, impoverished. They saw a patronage system which under Elizabeth, in spite of her mistakes, was usually used skilfully to distribute power and to bring the ablest men to the top. They had seen the whole system shudder at the end of the reign when the Earl of Essex had declined to submit to the controls essential to monarchical rule. The Essex rebellion, in which the Earl of Southampton, Shakespeare's patron, was involved, had it succeeded, would have put the clock back to the Wars of the Roses. Elizabeth regained control; and royal patronage remained the only viable system of government between the decline of medieval feudalism and the rise of modern party government. But James never grasped its full purpose. To him the criteria for the elevation of his public servants were not their wisdom and statecraft but their physical charms and his personal affection. The monarch who declared that kings were called gods by God himself could thus write to his favourite, the Earl of Somerset: 'Do not all courtesies and places come through your office as Chamberlain, and rewards through your father-in-law as Treasurer. Do not you two as it were hedge in all the court with a manner of necessity to depend upon you?'[12] Patronage was debased into favouritism; and it was there for all men to see. Was divinity enough to hedge a king?

Decay and division spread out from the court to the upper ranks of society and on through the shires. So, too, contempt and resistance began to find voice among those who had always measured monarchy against the divine criteria of the Bible. For Puritanism was now a force to be reckoned with.

When it first emerged under that name, early in Elizabeth's reign, the term was applied to a minority of churchmen, Members of Parliament and others who felt that the Anglican Reformation had stopped short of its goal. It had not established anything resembling a biblical commonwealth, now developing in Geneva, nor had it purged the English church of Romish rituals and organization. Some of the leaders of Puritanism were to be found in the upper ranks of church and state, and among the *jeunesse dorée* of the age, of which the best example was the Earl of Essex. Some of these political leaders had a deep and fervent interest in religion, as had the Earl of Huntingdon, others saw it much more as part of a political alignment. Many M.P.s saw it also as a great force for resisting the alien power of Spain, and the alien influence represented by Mary, Queen of Scots.

From our point of view, however, a new and important element became apparent, late in the reign, in the shape of moral puritanism and, more especially, sabbatarianism. Since Puritans used the Bible as a guide to conduct, not simply to faith, but to political and social life, and since they could read it in their own language, it took on for them a greater importance than it had ever held. They made a serious attempt to recreate some of the conditions and standards of behaviour which had been adopted by the biblical Children of Israel. Part of this was the Mosaic injunction to remember the Sabbath day and keep it holy. In 1595 the publication of Nicholas Bound's *Doctrine of the Sabbath* gave formal exposition to this developing theme; but this was only part, albeit an important part, of the increasingly rigid moral stance assumed by the Puritans. The long struggle between the Puritans and the theatre had begun. To be virtuous was to renounce cakes and ale. The controversy over sabbatarianism was bitterly fought for decades with the result, said Thomas Fuller, that 'the sabbath itself had no rest'.[13] Puritan dissent challenged the fundamentals of church, state and society.

Catholic dissent was less dangerous though the government was bound to take it seriously in the light of the whole European situation of national and civil war. Catholicism in England, it is true, collected its own extremists who played dangerous political games with foreign powers, but they were a tiny minority. The crown for its part tried to stamp out Catholicism by increasingly severe penalties. Yet in spite of this, the overwhelming majority of the Catholics remained loyal subjects of the crown in the time of its danger, as during the threat of the Spanish Armada in 1588, and Gunpowder Plot in 1605. Only in Ireland, where Catholicism formed part of a domestic desire for self-expression and independence, did it become a truly hostile movement. But in England Puritanism was more of a threat than Catholicism, partly because the Puritans functioned *within* the governing class, and partly because their whole philosophy found its source and authority, not in monarchy and hierarchy, but in a quasi-egalitarian biblical commonwealth.

Here then was evidence that the elaborate, gilded superstructure of a divine royal order rested insecurely on its religious foundations. And when the House of Commons became the sounding board for religious criticism and political discontent, as it did during the last years of Shakespeare's life, the whole system was under severe strain. Yet it would be wrong to paint these later years of Shakespeare's life in sombre colours. For the growing intensity of the debate was itself a sign of the intellectual vigour, independence and adventurousness distributed widely within the nation.

It was a time, too, of the growth of a social conscience. In the early sixteenth century Hythlodaye in More's *Utopia* could write bitterly: 'When I consider and weigh in my mind all these commonwealths which nowadays anywhere do flourish, so God help me, I can perceive nothing but a certain conspiracy of rich men procuring their own commodities under the name and title of the commonwealth.'[14] There was still the division between the two nations; and Smith's 'Fourth sort of men which do not rule' lived often in dire poverty at the edge of starvation. Yet Elizabeth's reign had seen the emergence of imaginative policies for social welfare, and the formulation of good machinery for carrying them through. There was at last the open recognition that innocent and hardworking men could be caught up in the harsh consequences of an economic slump. It was now acknowledged that somehow work must be found or relief given. The state too, in the shape of the county or town, was assuming some degree of responsibility for the orphan, the sick and the aged. Unevenly, pragmatically, the governing classes saw that their own strength and the survival of their society were bound up with the recognition of social responsibility for their fellow Englishmen. One unforeseen result of this was that the civil war of the seventeenth century was not a social revolution as well.

London had been a pioneer in welfare matters, as in so much else. And here in the capital, in the years when Shakespeare was turning his thoughts towards London, was gathered the greatest talent in politics, law and administration. Here were the palace, its law courts, Parliament, the city gilds and companies; here was diversity, a teeming thrusting population, a questing interest in novelty. Here were poets, churchmen, politicians, lawyers, pamphleteers. Here was money seeking an outlet in commerce, piracy and the gentler arts of peace. Never before in English history had there been such a concentration of wealth, talent and opportunity. Here, then, was a 'wide and universal theatre' embracing the whole capital, with an audience in their places waiting for the play to start.

13

SHAKESPEARE AND THE THOUGHT
OF HIS AGE

W. R. ELTON

Shakespeare's works, formed in the changing thought of his age, require a recognition of Renaissance intellectual conventions. These conventions, also, affected the attitude of Shakespeare's audience. This outline will identify some Renaissance conceptual modes which may usefully be recalled to the twentieth-century reader.

Despite an influential portrayal of 'the Elizabethan world picture' as unaltered from the medieval, its notable features were complexity and variety, inconsistency and fluidity. Similarly, the recently reiterated 'frame of order' may be regarded, for our purposes, as, to a large extent, a background of Elizabethan commonplaces against which Shakespeare played complex and ironical variations. While his dramas assert the 'great chain of being', for instance, and the hierarchy of order, they also as frequently act out the opposite, the reality of disorder. Considering the rapidity of Renaissance change, moreover, generalizations about Shakespeare's age, or about such complex patterns as Renaissance Christianity, should ordinarily specify, with as much precision as possible, the time and place in question.

Transitional beyond many eras, mingling divided and distinguished worlds, the Shakespearian age witnessed numerous revaluations and reversals. Not unexpectedly, a favourite metaphor was the 'world upside down'; while a repeated mode of a central Renaissance work such as *Hamlet* is the interrogative. In view of Elizabethan complexities, the present condensed notes are thus subject to their own appropriate qualifications.

I ANALOGY

Most generally, for Shakespeare and his audience, a prevailing intellectual mode differing from our own was the analogical. Though an analogical world-view relating God and man, inherited from the Middle Ages, was in process of dissolution, the analogical habit of mind, with its correspondences, hierarchies, and microcosmic–macrocosmic relationships survived. Levels of existence, including human and cosmic, were habitually correlated, and correspondences and resemblances were perceived everywhere. Man as microcosmic model was thus a mediator between himself and the universe; and knowledge of one element in the microcosm-macrocosm analogy was knowledge of the other. Blending faith with knowledge, actuality with metaphysics, analogy also joined symbol with concept, the internal with the external world. Analogy, indeed, provided the perceiver with the impression of aesthetically and philosophically comprehending experience.

While medieval analogical thought, including 'analogy of being' which likened man and God, had been largely regulated within the Church, Reformation and Renaissance currents tended to transform it. The Reformers' re-emphasis on man's fallen nature and darkened reason denied such human-divine likeness (at best, an analogy of faith). In the Renaissance revival of antiquity, including Stoic, Pythagorean, neo-Platonic, and hermetic influences, analogy became increasingly a syncretic and secularized instrument for unlocking what Paracelsus called the 'great secret wisdom'. Through this unified theory of the human imagination, poets sought with scientists to interpret the Book of Nature and to discover the harmonious, ordered, and interrelated universe.

In the Shakespearian theatre, analogy, in this sense a momentary leap between levels, correlated the disparate planes of earth (the stage), hell (the cellerage), and heaven (the 'heavens' projecting above part of the stage). Upon that stage, moreover, were spoken lines which might, through analogy, simultaneously allude to the universe, to the state or body politic, to the family, and to the microcosmic individual. Without awareness of analogical (rather than, e.g., allegorical) Christ-allusions, Shakespeare's auditors might have condemned as blasphemous Richard II's comments upon himself:

> Did they not sometime cry 'All hail!' to me?
> So Judas did to Christ; but he, in twelve,
> Found truth in all but one; I, in twelve thousand, none.
> (IV, i, 169–71)

Or, among other instances, in *King Lear* they might have missed the relevant overtones of Cordelia's reference to her father's 'business' (IV, iv, 24).

Shakespearian analogy connected a scale of creation which ordered the world's diversity. From Aquinas to Richard Hooker (d. 1600) that pattern, it has been held, comprised such principles as plenitude, or the view that the universe, created by God out of nothing, was, by the Creator's desire, to be populated through all possible kinds.

A second principle was hierarchy or unilinear gradation; upon this scale, each of God's diverse creatures, in accordance with his distance from divine perfection, had an allotted position, observing 'degree, priority, and place' (*Troilus and Cressida* I, iii, 86). The final principle, continuity, implied regular, rather than uneven or saltatory, progression in this universal chain of being. Thus, from God and the angels, man, woman, the lower animals, vegetation, to the most inferior 'stones' or 'senseless things' (*Julius Caesar* I, i, 36), creation was unifiedly and uninterruptedly graded.

Because he possessed both soul and body, man occupied a pivotal place in the great chain of being. Externally, his individual actions found their implications echoed in macrocosmic nature. Macbeth's murder of Duncan reverberates through hell and heaven; Lear's madness embraces an inner and outer storm; and even contemplation of a crime, or the prospect of moral choice, might affect the outward world. Brutus observes, meditating on the cosmic correlatives preceding 'the acting of a dreadful thing', that

> The Genius and the mortal instruments
> Are then in council; and the state of man,
> Like to a little kingdom, suffers then
> The nature of an insurrection.
>
> > (*Julius Caesar* II, i, 66–9)

As moral choice brought into focus the cosmos, it simultaneously brought into question the identity of the chooser. Internally, man's mingled nature was expressed in a conflict between his divine soul or reason, and his baser appetites or passion. Precluded by the Fall from ascending in perfection to the angelic level, he might easily be tempted to descend to the bestial plane. In contrast to the more modern idea of human goodness, consciousness of Original Sin was uppermost. Shakespearian drama ponders the extremes of human possibilities, as in *The Tempest*'s magically learned Prospero and bestially ignorant Caliban. Recalling Pico della Mirandola's admiration, Hamlet's wonder at man's workmanship (II, ii, 304–5) is, however, contrasted by the murderous Captain's conception in *King Lear* of 'man's work' (V, iii, 40).

Inwardly, sinful predisposition, marked by pride, predominance of passion over reason, and neglect of degree, was outwardly analogous to political disorder, as well as to the decay of nature. The primitive Edenic 'golden age' was irrecoverable; and the predicted end of the world – 'The poor world,' notes Rosalind, 'is almost six thousand years old' (*As You Like It* IV, i, 83–4) – was imminent. Natural degeneration, in contrast to our optimistic idea of progress, was everywhere evident: physically, man was a pygmy compared to his longer-lived progenitors; artistically, the ancients had been superior; and even in suffering, as the closing lines of *King Lear* declare, the young 'Shall never see so much nor live so long' (v, iii, 325–6). While above the moon all had been considered permanent, below the moon ordinary matter, such as the body – 'this muddy vesture of decay' (*The Merchant of Venice* v, i, 64) – was subject to mutability. Mutability itself was ruled with fearful, eroding effect by Time: life, the dying Hotspur observed, was 'time's fool' (*1 Henry IV* v, iv, 81) – man was also, like Romeo, the unpredictable 'fortune's fool' (*Romeo and Juliet* iii, i, 133). For many Elizabethans, despite their religious beliefs, 'injurious time' (*Troilus and Cressida* iv, iv, 41) was obsessively a murderer. Except for such figures as Giordano Bruno (1548?–1600), on the other hand, it was left to the later seventeenth century, to John Milton and Blaise Pascal, to emphasize the fearful immensities of Space.

In addition to cosmic correspondences, analogical thinking implied hierarchy and order in the political realm. Proceeding from the idea of God as ruler of the macrocosm to the idea of monarch as ruler of the political world, argument by correspondence had evident royalist implications. That mode of argument led inevitably to the widespread Renaissance employment, derived largely from Aristotle's *Politics*, of the analogy of the body politic. The latter corresponded to the human body, whose heart or head corresponded to the king, and whose lower members resembled the lower members of the social organism. As the body obeyed the soul, and the world the Creator, so subjects were to obey the king. In *Coriolanus* a variation of the body analogy occurs in which the belly, compared by Menenius to the senators, is said to sustain the ungrateful and 'mutinous parts', including the 'great toe of this assembly' (i, i, 94–153). That the body-politic correspondence was natural could be verified, in turn, by analogy with the family and its patriarchal head, as well as with the animal kingdom. Throughout the divine creation were primacies of various orders: like God in the macrocosm and the sun in the heavens were, for instance, the eagle among creatures of the air, and the lion among beasts of earth. Within all mankind, moreover, innately implanted by God, was an absolute 'law of nature', by which his rational creatures everywhere recognized right and wrong. In the scholastic tradition, the habitual knowledge of natural law, or the willingness to recognize right reason – synderesis – is the faculty of Macbeth's conscience implicitly dwelt upon in the tragedy after his murder of Duncan.

Hierarchically, the human soul, of which Malvolio professed to 'think nobly' (*Twelfth Night* iv, ii, 53), was threefold: the highest, or rational soul, which man on earth possessed uniquely; the sensible,

sensitive, or appetitive soul, which man shared with lower animals –
its concupiscible impulse drove him towards, and its irascible away
from objects; and the lowest, or vegetative (vegetable; nutritive) soul,
distributed still more widely and concerned mainly with reproduction
and growth. Further, the rational soul was itself divided into two kinds:
the intuitive or angelic, whose knowledge was immediately infused,
without any intervening process; and the discursive, involving rational
effort and sense data. The soul was facilitated in its work by the body's
three main organs, liver, heart, and brain: the liver served the soul's
vegetal, the heart its vital, and the brain its animal faculties – the last
contained motive, sensitive, and principal virtues (i.e. involving commonsense, fantasy, and imagination, as well as reason, judgement, and
memory).

Central to earth, lowest and heaviest planet in creation, man himself
was formed by the natural combination within him of the four elements:
in ascending hierarchical order, 'the dull elements of earth and water'
(*Henry V* III, vii, 22–3), both tending to fall to the centre of the universe,
and air and fire, both tending to rise. At point of death, Cleopatra
exclaims,

> I am fire and air; my other elements
> I give to baser life.   (v, ii, 287–8)

While, if unmixed, the elements would separate into their proper
spheres, in a mixed state they both abetted terrestrial instability and
shaped man's temperament. Antony's eulogy of Brutus's qualities
observes the exemplary mingling in him of the elements (*Julius Caesar*
v, v, 73–5). Each element possessed two of the four primary qualities
which combined into a 'humour' or human temperament: earth (cold
and dry: melancholy); water (cold and moist: phlegmatic); air (hot
and moist: sanguine); fire (hot and dry: choleric).

Like his soul and his humours, man's body possessed cosmic
affinities: e.g. the brain with the Moon; the liver with the planet
Jupiter; the spleen with the planet Saturn. Assigned to each of the
planets and the sphere of the fixed stars, and guiding them, was a hierarchy of incorporeal spirits, angels or daemons – intelligences which
may be alluded to in Lear's proposal to Cordelia that they 'take upon'
them 'the mystery of things' as if they were 'God's spies' (v, iii, 16–17).
In parallel fashion, on earth, the fallen angels and Satan, along with
such occult forces as witches, continued to tempt man and lead him
on to sin. For a time, Martin Luther (1483–1546), for example, was
afflicted by doubts whether his calling to reform the Church was, in
inspiration, divine or diabolic. Hamlet expresses such fears of the Ghost,
since 'the devil hath power/T'assume a pleasing shape' (II, ii, 595–6).

Macbeth finds himself all too susceptible to the weird sisters. And the disillusioned Othello suspects Satan's presence in Iago:

> I look down towards his feet – but that's a fable.
>
> (v, ii, 289)

Although controversial, belief in the influence of the stars upon man's life was held by a majority of Shakespeare's audience. Indeed, distinguished astronomers, such as Tycho Brahe (1546–1601) and Johannes Kepler (1571–1630), were practising astrologers, and the eminent physicist, William Gilbert (c. 1540–1603), physician to Queen Elizabeth, maintained astrological views. Natural astrology (useful, e.g. for meteorological predictions governing such matters as the influence of planets on crops) was widely credited, but differentiated from judicial astrology (more suspect, as involving details of personal lives and political prognostications). While astrologers agreed that man's fate was determined by his planetary conjunctions, they continued to dispute whether the determining moment was that of conception or that of birth. Rejecting his father's supernatural determinism and astrological notions, the illegitimate and naturalistic-deterministic Edmund voices the attitudes of sceptical Renaissance spectators (*King Lear* I, ii, 98–127). Opposed to primogeniture and exclusion by accident of birth, Edmund's anti-legal and anti-social view holds that the heat of the conceptual moment itself determines the natural superiority of bastards (I, ii, 11–12).

Renaissance astrological views operated within a finite universe of spherical shape – the circle was regarded as perfection in form and motion – and the very small planet earth was at its centre and lowest point. Motionless itself, earth was at the centre of a series of moving concentric crystalline spheres, those of the Moon, Mercury, Venus, the Sun, Mars, Jupiter, and Saturn. Beyond Saturn were the fixed stars; beyond these was the *Primum Mobile* or First Mover; and beyond that was the void, containing neither time nor space. As the planets revolved, they produced, inaudible to mortal sense, the Pythagorean 'music of the spheres':

> There's not the smallest orb which thou behold'st
> But in his motion like an angel sings,
> Still quiring to the young-ey'd cherubins.
>
> (*The Merchant of Venice* v, i, 60–2)

Recognizing Renaissance uses of analogy, the modern student should also note the radical differences between the philosophical preconceptions of our scientific age and those of the Shakespearian era. In addition to such influences as those of Francis Bacon (1561–1626) and

Thomas Hobbes (1588–1679), as well as those of Kepler and Galileo Galilei (1564–1642), a major cleavage between the Shakespearian world-view and our own was effected by René Descartes (1596–1650). Towards the mid-seventeenth century, Cartesian dualism separated off mind from matter, and soul from body. While influential, this body-soul dichotomy was hardly new, and Descartes, as Professor Ryle reminds us, 'was reformulating already prevalent theological doctrines of the soul in the new syntax of Galileo. The theologian's privacy of conscience became the philosopher's privacy of consciousness, and what had been the bogy of Predestination reappeared as the bogy of Determinism'. For Descartes, all nature was to be explained as either thought or extension; hence, the mind became a purely thinking sub-stance, the body a soulless mechanical system. Exalting philosophical rationalism and evicting mystery, casting doubt on the objective reality of the outside world, Cartesianism held that we can know only our own clear and distinct ideas. Putting aside, like Bacon, as unknowable or uncertain, final causes – the 'why' or purposefulness of things – Descartes considered objects as intelligible only as we bring our judgements to bear upon them. If only such knowledge alone were possible, it would follow that the analogical method of knowing the universe was thenceforth outmoded. Further, from the Cartesian preference for clarity and its suspicion of our illusory and sensory judgements resulted in turn the misprising of feeling and the affective life as no more than a confused idea. Such Cartesian scepticism and subjectivism led to the rejection as meaningless or obscure of the previous centuries' Aristotelian perspectives.

For, in contrast to the Cartesian disjunction and its dissolution of the world of correspondences, the Elizabethan universe still held to the Aristotelian premises of teleology, or purposefulness, and causal action. According to Aristotle, to know the cause of things was to know their nature. Familiar to Shakespeare's contemporaries were the Aristotelian four causes: the final cause, or purpose or end for which a change is made; the efficient cause, or that by which some change is made; the material cause, or that in which a change is made; and the formal cause, or that into which something is changed. Renaissance concern with causation may be seen in Polonius' labouring of the efficient 'cause' of Hamlet's madness, 'For this effect defective comes by cause' (II, ii, 101–3). Reflecting the controversy over final versus natural causes, Lear's pagan interrogation of the 'philosopher' con-cerns the 'cause of thunder?' (III, iv, 150–1), traditionally a divine manifestation, like the 'cause in nature that make these hard hearts' (III, vi, 77–8). Ironically, Othello's 'causeless' murder of Desdemona is prologued by a reiteration of 'cause':

It is the cause, it is the cause, my soul –
...It is the cause.   (v, ii, 1–3)

Further, in Shakespearian use of the language of formal logic may be found remains of the Aristotelian and scholastic modes: e.g. 'syllogism' (*Twelfth Night* I, v, 45); 'discourse of reason' (*Hamlet* I, ii, 150; *Troilus and Cressida* II, ii, 116); 'dilemma' (*The Merry Wives of Windsor* IV, v, 78; *All's Well that Ends Well* III, vi, 67); 'major', i.e. premise (*1 Henry IV* II, iv, 478); 'premises' themselves (*All's Well that Ends Well* II, i, 200; *Henry VIII* II, i, 63); 'fallacy' (*The Comedy of Errors* II, ii, 185); 'accident' (*Troilus and Cressida* III, iii, 83); etc. In Hamlet's 'Sense, sure, you have, / Else could you not have motion' (III, iv, 71–2) and in his 'forms, moods, shapes...denote' (I, ii, 82–3), among other of his expressions, may be found further echoes of the Aristotelian tradition.

In the Aristotelian view, change involves a unity between potential matter and actualized form. Although matter in one of its potentialities is transformed by change, it endures through the altering process, as the wood endures in one of its actualizations, e.g. a table. Change is thus a process of becoming, affected by a cause which acts determinately towards a goal to produce a result. Implicit in the Elizabethan world-view was the Aristotelian idea of causation as encompassing both potentiality and act, matter and mind. Rejecting as self-contradictory the Aristotelian notion of 'changeful potency' (*Troilus and Cressida* IV, iv, 96), Descartes, in contrast, considers process as a simple quality which things either have or do not have. Since it is merely extension, or passive geometrical space, he argues, the physical world cannot possess intrinsic possibilities for action. Implicit in a post-Cartesian world-view is thus the heritage presupposing a disjunction between mind and matter; a static and disparate, rather than interrelated idea of change; and a conception of motion as machine-like and activated by no final cause. In contrast, Elizabethan intellectual modes sustained the traditional notion of causation within a continuous and purposeful universe. Within that context, motion and action were engaged in a causal relationship extending throughout creation.

Shakespeare's pre-Cartesian universe, indeed, tended to retain a sense of the purposefulness of natural objects and their place in the divine scheme. While objects in the Aristotelian view of nature were distinguished by their own kind of movement – e.g. of fire, naturally upward; of earth, naturally downward – modern mechanics holds that laws of motion are the same for all material objects. For the Middle Ages and the Renaissance, objects, not as dead artifacts, influenced each other through mutual affinities and antipathies. Regarding nature ethically, for instance, Elizabethans could accept, medically, the correspondences of sympathies and antipathies in nature, including a homeopathic notion that 'like cures like'. Insufficiently evident to a post-Enlightenment spectator, moreover, the Elizabethan world was animistic and vitalistic, indeed, panpsychistic, magically-oriented, and, from our viewpoint, credulous. Well into the seventeenth century, alchemical, hermetical, astrological, and other pre-scientific beliefs continued to exert, even on the minds of distinguished scientists, a discernible influence.

In contrast to our belief through experimental verification, Elizabethans tended to a greater degree to believe by authority, by imaginative appeal, as in myth, and by disposition to entertain the marvellous, as in Othello's

> . . .Anthropophagi, and men whose heads
> Do grow beneath their shoulders.   (I, iii, 144-5)

Concerned with the need to believe, in an age of incipient doubt, Shakespeare's audiences witnessed in his central tragedies such struggles to sustain belief: Hamlet's need, in contrast to Horatio's, who at first 'will not let belief take hold of him' (I, i, 24), to trust the Ghost; Lear's wracked concern regarding the heavenly powers; and Othello's desperate necessity to preserve his belief in Desdemona – 'and when I love thee not / Chaos is come again' (III, iii, 92-3). For Othello and Lear, belief is sanity: their agon involves the striving to retain both. Although within Elizabethan belief of various kinds might be found numerous shades between total credence and heretical doubt, over all there lingered a credulity, or a need for belief, that permeated their cosmos and penetrated the nascent sciences themselves.

II   TRANSITIONS

While such inherited modes of thought provided some premises of Shakespeare's age, elements of his world as well as of his work often enough point towards the incipient disordering or breakdown of the analogical and pre-Cartesian tradition. In numerous spheres of Elizabethan thought occurred transitions and revaluations, if not actual crises and reversals.

Theologically, in the later sixteenth century, divine providence seemed increasingly to be questioned, or at least to be regarded as more bafflingly inscrutable. New orientations between man and the heavenly power, disintegrating the relative medieval sense of security, were in process of formation. Those changes coincided with such circumstances as the Renaissance revival of Epicureanism, which stressed the indifference of the powers above to man's concerns; the renewal of the ancient atomist and materialist traditions, along with other sceptical currents; and the reflection of the Reformation, especially of Calvinism, which argued, in effect, an incomprehensible and unappealable God, whose judgements of election and reprobation had already, beyond human intervention, been determined. In place of a special providence, capricious Fortune, with its counterpoise of *virtù*, or personal power, was re-emphasized in Machiavelli (1469–1527), and other Renaissance writers. Further, the Reformers, on the one hand, and such sceptics as Montaigne (1533–92), on the other, substituted for the earlier Deity a divine power who, beyond man's darkened reason, inscrutably hid himself. Like Calvin (1509–64), depreciating human reason and pride, Montaigne helped demolish man's own self-image which placed him above the animals, specially created and favoured by an analogical, anthropomorphic Deity. In sum, this new distancing of man from the now 'totally other' God had the effect of a Copernican revolution in man's pride in his privileged status. Despite his self-flattering conception, he might have discovered, like Lear, that he was not 'ague-proof' (IV, vi, 105). In claiming special providence, as a speaker in one of Galileo's dialogues observes, 'We arrogate too much to ourselves.'

Such changes in the relations of man and his Deity inevitably provided an altered climate for tragedy, within which both divine justice (as in *King Lear*) and meaningful action (as in *Hamlet*) seemed equally unattainable. In a decreasingly anthropocentric as well as geocentric universe, *King Lear* appears to question the forces above man's life, and *Hamlet* the powers beyond his death. For that northern European student, Hamlet, the quest for meaningful action, moreover, seems complicated by the irrelevance, from a Reformation viewpoint, of works towards salvation. The path to salvation – the major concern of most Elizabethans – depended, according to that view, not on personal merit or action, but upon impenetrable divine election. For Hamlet, in relation to the Ghost, the Reformation rejection of Purgatory appears further to complicate his task. Contrasting the Reformation and the Middle Ages, moreover, R. H. Tawney observes, 'Grace no longer completed nature: it was the antithesis of it.' The Reformers' radical split between the realm of grace and that of nature required, in a disorderly, brutal, and amoral world, a leap of faith. Alienated from the objective structure of the traditional Church, as well as from the release of the confessional, post-Reformation man, with burdened and isolated conscience, turned his guilt inward.

In contrast to *Hamlet* and *King Lear*, where evil appears more universally diffused, *Othello* and *Macbeth* evoke even more sharply a radical universe of evil, ever ready, seemingly, to work mankind harm. In Shakespearian tragedy generally, the extreme intensities of 'punishment' appear disproportionately incommensurate with 'guilt', or the instigating frailties of the human condition. Poetic justice and its twin, the 'tragic flaw', seem quantitatively as well as qualitatively less than adequate to account for the intense torments of Shakespeare's tragic explorations. Rather than the complacent satisfactions of poetic justice, many in Shakespearian tragic audiences may be said to have participated in a solemn celebration of the irreducible mystery of human suffering.

To turn from theological to philosophical contexts, the Renaissance epistemological crisis emphasized the notion of the relativity of perception, recalling the appearance-versus-reality motif recurrent through Renaissance drama. Present throughout dramatic history, it was a manifestation as well of theatrical illusion and the new theatre of the baroque. The confusion between appearance and reality and the exploration of their validity is a feature of such contemporary writing as Cervantes' *Don Quixote* (Pt. I, published in 1605). The separation of reality from illusion, truth from mere hallucination, is, in part, the task set Hamlet by the Ghost. Recognizing the contradictoriness of all truth, as well as the conflicts in his intellectual heritage, the influential Montaigne, doubting whether mankind would ever attain certainty, turned inward to explore his ambiguous and changing self. Perhaps, as Merleau-Ponty suggests, Montaigne ends with the awareness, related to the dialectic of drama, that contradiction is truth. As in Shakespearian drama, without dogmatic or reductive exclusions, he experiments, 'essays', and questions, in an open-ended and inconclusive manner, the world of experience. Of Shakespearian pertinence are numerous observations in Montaigne's essays: e.g. 'I engage myself with difficulty' (III, x); and 'In fine, we must live with the quick' (III, viii). In the plays of his English successor, Montaigne might have found that ideal work he had imagined, which not only expressed ideas, but also the very life in which they appear that qualifies their significance.

Although, for some Renaissance philosophers, words retained the magic power or essence of the thing named, late medieval and Renaissance nominalism, such as Montaigne's, questioned the relation of language and reality. As do the speeches of some Shakespearian villains, Hamlet's 'Words, words, words' (II, ii, 191) may, in the light of his other remarks, reflect a nominalistic tendency. Concerning 'honour', for instance, Falstaff's celebrated casuistry (*1 Henry IV* v, i, 131–40) suggests the tenuous state in that term's usage by 1598.

Analogously, upper-class social mobility had led, in the Elizabethan scramble for 'honour', to a confusion in social hierarchy. Such lack of discrimination is indicated, more generally, in Hamlet's observation that 'the toe of the peasant comes so near the heel of the courtier, he galls his kibe' (v, i, 136–8).

If the limits of language may be said to mark the limits of social life or civil existence, the abdication, for example, of Lear and his severance of the bonds of social duty help to isolate him from the orderly inter-course of dialogue. Reduced to communication outside the social order, he must resort to the discordant babble of madman, beggar, and Fool, sharing especially the Fool's disordered obliquity. Further, in *Coriolanus*, a profound exploration of the relation of language to civil life, of the word to the city itself, Coriolanus refuses the name, be-stowed on him as an honour by the citizens, when he rejects the city that has rejected him. For Macbeth, like Lear, language crumbles when he loses his sense of purpose in life: time is creepingly measured out 'to the last syllable' (v, v, 21); and life itself becomes an idiot's dis-ordered and furious account (v, v, 26–8), reduced, that is, to verbal nonsense.

Such questioning of language emerges in the relativism of Montaigne, to which, among other elements, the Renaissance problem of the noble savage contributed. A man playing with a cat, the essayist had sug-gested, might, depending on perspective, be regarded as a cat playing with a man. Depending on perspective, too, how was man to evaluate his place in the chain of being in relation to the New World's recently discovered natives? Without European civilization, yet lacking the conflicts and corruption of their cultivated discoverers, such creatures as the Brazilian Indian, for instance, might well be superior in manner of life. Thus, Montaigne's cultural relativism sounded a note which was, partly owing to new geographical discoveries that literally reshaped man's world, and partly to influences set in motion by the Renaissance and Reformation, more widely echoed by the sixteenth century's close. Furthermore, the new cosmography and the cultural relativism of explorers and missionaries stimulated self-consciously critical questions regarding European institutions and values. When, at times, the Renaissance attempted to substitute Arcadia for Eden, displacing Adam by the noble savage, it set an earthly paradise in the New Isles of America. Like *The Tempest*'s, Montaigne's idyllic account of the primitive isles employs a negative form to catalogue utopian aspects. His description thus helps provide an intellectual context for Shakespeare's play, rather than a demonstrable source, since there were a number of such Renaissance accounts. In that New World romance, the old counsellor Gonzalo, in an inset speech reflecting the play's political-utopian preoccupations, unfolds a soft-primitivistic Golden Age revery.

Relativism inhered, too, in the Renaissance's mingling of contradictory and disparate Christian and non-Christian currents. In its revival of Greek and Hebrew, and the introduction of radically different ways of regarding the cosmos, relativism as well as scepticism flourished. Moreover, a multiple and shifting hermeneutic, including the revival of ancient emblematic, metaphorical, and symbolic traditions, furthered the questioning of absolute and authoritative readings. In such fundamental doctrines as the Creation, for example, a counter-orthodoxy existed in the Renaissance, involving the cosmogony of chaos. In addition to creation out of nothing by divine design, Renaissance thought, through Near Eastern and hermetic influences, also affirmed creation from pre-existing chaos. Such views and their attendant amphibious-monster imagery appear not only in Spenser and other Renaissance writers, but in Shakespeare as well. In *Antony and Cleopatra*, for instance, contrasted with such orthodox order figures as Octavia and Octavius, is Cleopatra, 'serpent of old Nile' (I, v, 25).

Philosophic value attitudes were also in process of relativistic transition. Shakespearian drama reflects the conflict between traditional views, found in Aquinas, for whom value is present and bound up in the object, and the newer views of such figures as Bruno, with his aesthetic relativism, and Hobbes (b. 1588), with his notion of value as relative to a market-situation. Such later positions are implicit especially in the politic Ulysses' exchanges in *Troilus and Cressida*, where the wily counsellor is a manipulator both of men and of the market in honour. In Renaissance value theory, a turning point may also be reflected in Troilus' individualistic and wilful demand, 'What's aught but as 'tis valued?' (II, ii, 52). To this anarchic and subjective relativism, Hector's comprises a traditional restraining reply:

> But value dwells not in particular will:
> It holds his estimate and dignity
> As well wherein 'tis precious of itself
> As in the prizer.   (II, ii, 53–6)

In Edmund's libertine naturalism, similarly, is heard the dissolution of ethical absolutes and natural law, regarded as mere 'plague of custom' (*King Lear* I, ii, 1–4). Reaffirming the Sophists' distinction between 'natural right' and man-made law, and between nature (or *physis*) and convention (or *nomos*), Edmund's challenge shatters traditional absolutistic confidence in the universality of God's law. For Montaigne, as for Agrippa von Nettesheim a half century before him, what is in one place a virtue is elsewhere a vice; what was once a vice is regarded as a virtue. In the Shakespearian era, custom, previously linked with natural law, was regarded by some as a merely relative, or local rather than universal, hindrance to natural desire. Shakespeare's work, therefore, marks a transition between absolute natural *law* bestowed by God, and relativistic *natural* law, recognized by man. In this transformation, the new explorations of previously unfamiliar lands and customs led to a more tolerant perspective.

Apropos of such explorations, if it is true, as Lord Keynes has suggested, that England was 'just in a financial position to afford Shakespeare at the moment when he presented himself', the following may also be true: Shakespeare reflected in his works the financial condition which could afford him. To the typical acquisitive enterprise, for example, of such English explorers as Richard Hakluyt (1552?–1616), England was indebted in large part for her possession of the American colonies. Significantly, Shakespeare's age participated in the transition between the older 'use value', by which price was conceived according to a form of intrinsic utility, and 'market value', the price rising or falling according to scarcity or plenty of the commodity. Against the traditions of Aristotle and Aquinas, his age took part also in the conflict over forbidden usury, which, reflected in *The Merchant of Venice*, was being practically resolved in favour of the new Puritan class of lenders and investors. Often, though not always, handled negatively, mercantile imagery occurs in other Shakespearian plays, such as *Troilus and Cressida*, which, like Jonsonian comedy, is replete with buying and selling references. In *King Lear* notably, the Renaissance clash between love and quantity – *how much* love? – is most powerfully observed. Like *King Lear*, *Timon of Athens* condemningly explores, with more specific monetary allusion, the new acquisitive impulse.

If analogical relationships had, in the theological sphere, been questioned, the hierarchical correspondences supporting political order had also been challenged. While Shakespeare maintains the medieval image of the state as the body (e.g. in *Coriolanus*), the sense of unity sustaining the metaphor was, even in that play itself, in process of dissolution. Despite, moreover, a received notion of Shakespeare's subscription to the 'Tudor myth', the complexities both of his age and the plays should qualify that view. According to the 'Tudor myth', Shakespeare's histories were devoted to the glorification of Elizabeth's line, to propagandizing on behalf of the sanctity of the legitimate ruler, and to preaching against the sinfulness of rebellion. In short, Shakespeare's histories are held to be didactic dramatizations espousing the doctrines of the Establishment homilies (e.g. 'Against disobedience and wilfull Rebellion'), directed to be read in the obligatorily-attended Elizabethan church.

Against those who consider the plays orthodox 'mirrors of policy', it should be recalled that Elizabethan political views were themselves in process of change. For instance, the deposition scene of *Richard II*, which could be staged at one time, was omitted in the published quarto of 1597. Since the argument for divine right was bound up with Christian cosmology, alterations in the latter had begun to undermine the hierarchical argument by correspondence. If man and his specially-created earth were no longer at the centre of the great scheme, human frailty at the Fall would seem to have had less occasion to corrupt the enormous or limitless universe. In addition, the monarchic analogy with God, or the First Cause, was also weakened by the tendency of Renaissance empiricists to distance the First Cause as unknowable, in favour of the study of God's visible second cause, nature. Further, such analogical principles as plenitude and the even scale of creation suggested, without evidence, a kind of rigid determinism and pre-arranged perfection. Reformation thought, moreover, had tended to uphold a God of will, rather than one of visible reason, and a world whose supposed rational order was imperceptible to man's darkened faculties. Such human depravity argued against mankind's exemplary and unique state, a little lower than the angels. From the point of view of practical politics, on the other hand, the accelerated rise of the 'gentry' suggested less a fixed and immutable order than one that could be shaped by the human will.

Furthermore, the premises themselves of Elizabethan political thought were paradoxical, being based, as derived from Henry VIII, at once on the divinity and mortality of the king's two bodies. Divinely enthroned, he is also 'elected', his power being drawn from Parliament or people, and his tenure dependent on his beneficent behaviour. In the contradictory Henrician propaganda to which Elizabeth was heir, the monarch could not be usurped. But if he were, the usurper himself should not be replaced, for the orderliness of the commonwealth had priority. These contradictions led, on the one hand, to Samuel Daniel's urging of total submission to authority, to prevent the disorders of war; and, on the other, to Michael Drayton's insistence on the ill effects of unfit rulers. Such paradoxical attitudes were part of the intellectual heritage of Shakespeare, and helped provide the foundations of his ironical, dialectical art. Those positions support the dramatic ambivalences, for instance, of *Richard II* and *Henry IV*. In the former, an inadequate ruler is usurped; in the latter, the son of a usurper plays out his ambivalent role as man and king-to-be, a contradiction underlying his duality of relationships. In *Richard II*, the pathos of Richard as suffering monarch is evoked at the same time that his unsuitability for kingship is affirmed; while Bolingbroke's usurpation is shown as simultaneously dubious and inevitable. In addition, a related reductive view affirms that the deposition and killing of Richard II recurs in *Henry VI* and *Richard III* as a central theme of England's guilt, the whole tetralogy being structured on sin and atonement for Bolingbroke's crime. Yet Richard II seems curiously absent from the plays his ghost is supposed to haunt, while the moralizing implications of God's vengeance upon England for usurpation and regicide appear textually unsustained. While he affirms the primacy of the common welfare, further, Shakespeare complexly transcends the accepted view's simple didacticism and poetically-just formula of right and wrong and of the orderly sequence of sinfulness and atonement.

For Machiavelli and Machiavellianism, moreover, whose influence on Shakespeare's England has been demonstrated, worldly politics were shaped not by the City of God but by the will, desire, cunning, *virtù*, and energy of man. Machiavelli's anti-Aristotelian separation of politics from ethics proposes a behavioural study of 'policy', power, and reason of state. Among Elizabethan playwrights, it is Shakespeare who apparently provides the most numerous instances of 'policy' in the Machiavellian sense, e.g. in *Timon of Athens* where 'policy' is said to sit 'above conscience' (III, ii, 86). Machiavellian 'reason of state', the relativistic view that the interests of the state supersede principles of morality, was a recognized political notion of the later sixteenth century. In Ulysses' behaviour as well as in his celebration of the 'mystery of state' are discernible apologies for 'reason of state' and 'The providence that's in a watchful state' (*Troilus and Cressida* III, iii, 196–204).

Among the strongest testimonies to the new Renaissance relativism is the transformation of the traditional geocentric and well-enclosed Ptolemaic universe. While the Copernican revolution was only gradually accepted in England, its implications regarding man's conception of his status could not have been ignored in the Shakespearian climate. Indeed, Lear's shocked discovery of a universe apparently no longer specially concerned for his welfare, and ruled by apparently unbenevolent powers, suggests an analogue to the Renaissance questioning of scripturally-based anthropocentricity and geocentricity. In addition, implications of infinity and a plurality of worlds, proposed by the Copernican-influenced Bruno, were recognized, for instance, in Robert Burton's compendium of Renaissance thought, *The Anatomy of Melancholy* (1621). Suggesting discrepancies with religious orthodoxy, and Christ's unique incarnation in time, Burton asked, regarding a plurality of worlds and their possible inhabitants, '... are we or they lords of the world, and how are all things made for man?' Having broken the world's circle, how was man to reconstitute his own centuries-secured identity in the new vast and unfamiliar cosmos? To add to Copernicus' innovations, and modifications in them by Tycho Brahe, other disturbing developments included the recognition that corruption and mutability affected not only the sublunar, but also the supralunar, universe. In 1572, a bright new star, or *nova* – followed by others in 1600 and 1604 – suddenly appeared, and gradually disappeared, an event interpreted as demonstrating the impermanence even of the translunary cosmos. For the Renaissance, the terrifying effect of such phenomena was traceable not merely to their novelty. They reinforced, in addition, a contemporary pessimism which tended to anticipate signs of decay as apocalyptic portents of the approaching universal dissolution. 'O ruin'd piece of nature!' exclaims Gloucester at sight of his king. 'This great world / Shall so wear out to nought' (*King Lear* IV, vi, 134–5).

Between an innovating Renaissance empiricism and an obsolescent scholasticism, Shakespeare's plays move critically. From one point of view, it may be possible to approach *Othello* as a testing of that new empiricism. For, concerning Cassio and Desdemona, Iago has provided Othello with virtually all the evidence that a dehumanized and efficient empirical mind, devoid of the testimony of faith, love, and intuitive reason, might circumstantially collect. Indeed, the limitations of empiricism, albeit perversely distorted in the case of Iago, may suggest a critique of empirical data unmixed with human value. Yet, in its apparent scrutiny of empiricism, science, and what may be related to the inductive method, *Othello* seems to involve less an argument, as has been urged, on behalf of intuitive or angelic reason, than a negatively realistic, even Calvinist, commentary on the powers of human reason at all.

For Shakespeare's spectator, finally, this world no longer, as in the medieval metaphor, mirrored the reality of the next. As doubts and 'dread of something after death' increased concerning 'The undiscover'd country' (*Hamlet* III, i, 78), the beyond seemed more tantalizingly inaccessible. Instead of world-mirror, Shakespeare's era topically and repeatedly figured the world as stage, and man as actor in temporary and borrowed costume, strutting and fretting his meaningless hour. Continually, his theatrical self-reflexivity allows Shakespeare to resort to the temporary and illusory materials of the stage to depict man's worldly estate. Rather than acting out a meaningful role pointing towards the Last Judgement, Renaissance man might at times resemble a trivial plaything for the amusement of questionably benevolent higher powers. On such a stage he moved dialectically between the hopes and fears implicit in 'a special providence in the fall of a sparrow' (*Hamlet* V, ii, 212–13) and 'As flies to wanton boys are we to th' gods' (*King Lear* IV, i, 37).

III DIALECTIC

For the intellectual tensions of his analogical yet transitional age, Shakespeare's drama provided an appropriate conflict structure: a dialectic of ironies and ambivalences, avoiding in its complex movement and dialogue the simplifications of direct statement and reductive resolution. Further, the theatrical form itself permitted such internalizing of conflicts. For example, the questioning of identity inherent in drama, especially Renaissance drama, might be self-reflexively mirrored in the actor's assumed role as actor, and in his shifting of costumes; Renaissance ethical problems could be reflected in the necessity, within the dramatic action, of the actor's decision to take one direction rather than another, a movement tending to involve moral choice; and the Renaissance epistemological crisis might be evoked through the emphasis on illusion and appearance-versus-reality of the theatrical setting itself, as well as through the ambiguous juxtaposition of scenes, particularly in multiple plot structure. Embracing and juxtaposing the contradictions of his age, Shakespeare contrived an artistic virtue out of a contemporary necessity. Within his heterogeneous audience, playing off one antithetical preconception against another, he structured his works partly on numerous current issues of controversy. Manipulating such diverse attitudes, while engaging the attention of all, he achieved a unified, yet complex and multifaceted dramatic form.

Nothing if not critical, Shakespeare utilized such 'built-in' conceptual possibilities for his dramatic exploration of values. That exploring movement might be symbolized in a two-edged sword which, as it advances through the play, cuts with ironic sharpness in both directions. Recalling, for example, Augustine's view that, without justice, a kingdom is merely a band of robbers, Shakespeare shows us, in *1 Henry IV*, a kingdom as a band of robbers. In that piece, the thieves of the tavern are measured ironically against the greater thieves of the court, the prize being literally in both cases, the 'King's exchequer' (II, ii, 53). Contrapuntally, the dialectic of 'robber robbing the robber' (travellers – Falstaff – Hal at Gadshill; Henry IV – the rebels – Hal) is played out on several social levels. As usual in Shakespeare, while judgements of value are orchestrated, commentary, depending on the spectator's theatrical perceptions, is tacit.

When T. S. Eliot, finally, in reply to Coleridge, questions Shakespeare's philosophical mind, denying that 'Shakespeare did any thinking on his own', it is apparent that the issues have been confused. Since drama operates dialectically, the main care must be not to decontextualize lines and interpret them apart from their fluid and dynamic ironies. The great thing is to grasp Shakespeare's unparalleled profundities within, as Dryden called it, 'the living labour of a play'.

14

SHAKESPEARE'S PLAYS ON THE ENGLISH STAGE

A. C. SPRAGUE

I   FROM THE RESTORATION TO GARRICK

Not much is known about Shakespearian performances between 1616 and 1642. Such evidence as is afforded by literary allusions or the appearance of quarto editions is largely ambiguous. Even our scanty play-lists are of very limited use. The fact that *The Winter's Tale* was acted several times at court does not necessarily imply that the play was appreciated at the Globe. It is reassuring to come upon the clean-cut assertions of Leonard Digges. In commendatory verses to the 1640 collection of Shakespeare's *Poems*, Digges contrasts the lively appeal of *Julius Caesar* and *Othello* with the tedium of Ben Jonson's tragedies. Even *Volpone* and *The Alchemist*, great comedies admittedly, have sometimes had poor houses,

> When let but Falstaff come,
> Hal, Poins, the rest, you scarce shall have a room,
> All is so pester'd; let but Beatrice
> And Benedick be seen, loe in a trice
> The cockpit, galleries, boxes, all are full
> To hear Malvolio, that cross-garter'd gull.

In September 1642 the playhouses were closed by a Puritan-dominated Parliament. The excuse given, a good one so far as it went, was the outbreak of civil war. But Puritan hostility toward the theatre was deep seated, and it is significant that there was no move to re-open the playhouses when the fighting ceased. The actors got on as best they could. A number served with distinction in the King's army. Others had recourse to publishing their manuscript plays – it was a great play-reading time. There was a certain amount of surreptitious acting, but this was stamped out by new stringent measures, enforced by disastrous raids, in 1648. Inheritances from this desolate time are what were known as 'drolls' – excerpts, usually farcical in character, from earlier plays. Three are from Shakespeare: 'The Bouncing Knight' (Falstaff, of course), from *1 Henry IV*; 'The Grave Makers', from

Hamlet, and 'The Merry Conceited Humours of Bottom the Weaver', from *A Midsummer Night's Dream.*

With the re-opening of the theatres at the Restoration came changes of an enduring consequence. Women presently replaced boys as actresses, the earliest instance being, we are assured, in *Othello,* though where and just when this performance took place, and who the actress was, remain matters of conjecture and dispute. It is remarkable how early these actresses were taken seriously as artists (that no one of these was peculiarly associated with Shakespearian roles I find somewhat curious).

Another change had been anticipated in some productions before the wars. Although the action of the play usually took place well forward, in front of rather than within the proscenium arch, it was now regularly illustrated by painted scenes, which were supplemented for spectacular effects by descents, through traps, and devices for flying, exploited to the full by the Witches in *Macbeth.* Finally, in the patents granted to two courtier-dramatists, Davenant and Killigrew, in August 1660, we have the beginnings of a theatre monopoly which was to endure well into the nineteenth century. This last development, the limiting of authorized companies to two, encouraged tradition, so far as tradition existed after the suspension of playing for eighteen years.

Shakespeare's popularity in the new age was of slow growth. Even by 1710, when his plays were no longer outnumbered on the stage by those of Beaumont and Fletcher, some were still unrevived while others had been so modernized and 'improved' as to be scarcely themselves. Among the long neglected plays were several which were to be the favourites of a later time. Thomas Doggett played Shylock as a comic character in 1701, but the fact is of no great significance since *The Merchant of Venice* had been out of the acting repertory for years and its interpretation cannot have been traditional. *Hamlet,* on the other hand, and *Othello* were performed steadily and without serious mutilation. Indeed, when *Hamlet* was revived in 1663, we have the word of John Downes, the prompter, that Davenant coached Betterton, who was to play the Prince, and Davenant had seen 'Mr Taylor of the Blackfriars Company' act it, and this Mr Taylor (which is a little less likely) had been instructed in the part by Shakespeare himself. Any hint of how Betterton played Hamlet, as that he used miniatures in the Closet Scene with Gertrude, is thus of peculiar importance.

The identification of Betterton with his Shakespearian parts was remarked upon in his time. He was for those who saw him their only Brutus, Othello, Macbeth, and Hamlet; their Hotspur, till he grew old, and near the close of his career the best of Falstaffs. He was a student of the plays (we have Nicholas Rowe's word for this) and no one better understood Shakespeare's 'manner of expression'. The restraint of his acting was often praised. He neither ranted nor chanted. And if his voice left something to be desired, he could yet so tune it as to win the attention of the least responsive members of his audience, the very fops and orange-girls.

Some of the Restoration versions of Shakespeare's plays were mere modernizations, of critical interest only occasionally in their substitution of words or correction of images. Others are expressions of neo-classical thought, the practical applications of dramatic theory. The pseudo-Aristotelian unities of time and place were imposed, where possible, on works which continually violated them. Ideas of decorum led to the removal of such comic intrusions in tragedy as Macbeth's Porter and Lear's Fool. Poetic justice was served by ending *King Lear* happily, 'in a success to the innocent distressed persons'. On the other hand, the reducing of Shakespeare's long casts, effected in most of these versions, was desirable on theatrical grounds (it made for neatness too), and the frequent exploiting of the new scenic resources of the stage was only to be expected.

Into the merits of these strange plays it is unnecessary to enter. Enough, perhaps, to note a growth of tolerance towards them in recent years. What does concern us is the fact that several of the altered versions long supplanted the originals on the stage. Thus Dryden and Davenant in revising *The Tempest* gave Miranda a sister, Dorinda, and Ferdinand a rival, Hippolito, and these two added characters (Hippolito personated by an actress) figure in casts of the play well into the nineteenth century. Davenant's singing witches and the famous *Macbeth* music were other lasting inheritances. Nahum Tate's *King Lear* was the only form in which Lamb could have seen the play acted when he set forth his preference for merely reading Shakespeare's tragedies. It was with trepidation that Macready at last restored the Fool in 1838. Colley Cibber's *Richard III* (1700) flourished even longer. Both Phelps and Edwin Booth, after attempting Shakespeare's history, returned to what was felt to be the safer version, and this was acted in America by Fritz Leiber as recently as 1930. Sacrificing the larger reaches of the earlier play, Cibber concentrated upon Richard, his rise to power, his reign and death, treating these matters with much liveliness and an uncanny ability to imitate Richard's manner of speech. The famous claptraps,

Off with his head. – So much for Buckingham,

and 'Richard's himself again' are by no means isolated examples of this. Both have passed, on occasion, as Shakespeare's own.

The death of Betterton in 1710 marks the end of a theatrical era almost as convincingly as the advent of Garrick in 1741 marks the beginning of one. Between, lies a generation which saw a decline in the quality of tragic acting, not unfairly represented by the monotonous declamation of James Quin. Cibber (for whom this age has sometimes been named) must have been quite impossible in tragedy. Yet Shakespeare's popularity was advancing strongly all the while. The appearance of such readily accessible editions as Nicholas Rowe's in 1709, and those published subsequently by Tonson for a shilling or less a play, contributed to this. In the theatre it shows in the gradual enlargement of the Shakespearian repertory. Up to now this had included, among the tragedies: *Hamlet, Othello, Julius Caesar,* Tate's *King Lear,* and Davenant's *Macbeth. Timon of Athens* was given in Shadwell's adaptation, *Troilus and Cressida* in Dryden's, and *Romeo and Juliet* only in the distantly related *Caius Marius* of Otway. The tragedies came first with audiences, as indeed they had done since the re-opening of the theatres, but both the histories and the comedies were gaining in number. To the firmly established *1 Henry IV, Henry VIII,* and, as altered by Cibber, *Richard III,* were added *2 Henry IV* and, somewhat later, *King John* and *Henry V.* It was a flourishing period for the histories. As for the comedies, *The Merry Wives of Windsor,* not unknown earlier, began now to be much performed, thanks to Quin's Falstaff. In 1741 a revival of *The Merchant of Venice* (as Shakespeare wrote it) was made memorable by the passionate, evil Shylock of Charles Macklin. *Measure for Measure,* the original once more, was also played; and near the close of this transitional time, *Much Ado about Nothing, As You Like It* and *Twelfth Night,* favourite plays of the last years of the century.

II THE ACTOR'S THEATRE

The general esteem in which Betterton was held, remarkable as it was, fell short of the fame which was to attend Garrick. Reasons for this are not far to seek. Unlike Betterton, or any earlier English actor, Garrick was a public figure, one whose death in Dr Johnson's well-known phrase 'eclipsed the gaiety of nations'. He wrote and talked well; moved in literary and polite circles; was painted by Gainsborough and Sir Joshua Reynolds. His social gifts, his vivacity, amiability and *savoir faire,* were extraordinary. Acting, he made clear by demonstration, was an art to be taken as seriously, it might be, as painting. An age which delighted in connoisseurship welcomed the thought.

The range of parts in which Garrick excelled was extraordinary. It was questionable whether he was to be preferred as Archer, in *The Beaux' Stratagem*, Abel Drugger, in *The Alchemist*, or King Lear. In strong contrast to the pompous recitation of his predecessors, his characteristic effects were visual and arresting. He delighted in sudden starts: as in Richard III (pictured by Hogarth) starting from his couch in the Tent Scene; or Hamlet, upon sight of the Ghost. A famous passage in Cibber's *Apology* describes Betterton in the *Hamlet* scene and the comparison with Garrick is illuminating. The earlier actor is praised for rightness of conception; for restraint and propriety of speech. Garrick's start, the horror shown in his face, and a prolonged and elaborated exit, as he followed the Ghost out, are what impressed those who saw him.

But can it be said that this brilliant performer, who made fulsome protestations of loyalty to Shakespeare, really did much to serve his interests? It used to be questioned whether he did, and the fact that he altered a number of his plays, including *Hamlet*, was advanced as evidence. The work of an American scholar, George Winchester Stone, has largely succeeded in silencing the sceptics. Even the altered *Hamlet* proved upon examination somewhat less offensive than descriptions of it had suggested. Like Garrick's other adaptations, which include the long popular *Katharine and Petruchio*, it suffered mainly from cutting. The fashion of adding to the text, and improving Shakespeare's poetry, had passed.

There is no questioning Garrick's genius or, for that matter, the healthy state of the theatre in his time. That it was a theatre dominated by stars, an actor's theatre, is equally clear. The balanced strength of Garrick's company still permitted the adequate casting of as exacting a work as Ben Jonson's *Alchemist* but, with the emphasis where it now lay, deterioration was certain. Already one's chief purpose in attending the playhouse might be to see a particular actor as Romeo or Lear and then compare him with some rival – Garrick, say, with Spranger Barry. This habit of comparing one interpretation with another is closely related to a new and lively interest in the art of acting, which is reflected in the appearance of poems like Churchill's once famous *Rosciad*. Significantly, the provincial theatres, now flourishing at York, Norwich, and elsewhere, sent to London as their discoveries, not new plays but promising young players, like John Henderson, 'The Bath Roscius'. Texts were wanted, finally, for the numerous actors, amateur as well as professional, who were now appearing in the plays, and we have Bell's Shakespeare (in the 1770s), and a succession of acting editions, right down to that published by Samuel French in our time.

In judging a performance much importance came to be attached to

certain awaited moments and to what were known as 'new readings':
Hamlet's 'Did *you* not speak to it?' as he distinguished Horatio from
the other watchers, or Lady Macbeth's supremely confident 'Give *me*
the daggers'. Both these were points made by the Kembles. For the
style of acting introduced to London audiences in 1783 by John Philip
Kemble, and carried to heights beyond his reach by Sarah Siddons, was
at once heroic and meticulous. In him attention to detail might seem
pedantic. In his sister it was subordinate to passion and a strong sense
of character. Constance, Volumnia, Katharine (in *Henry VIII*), and
of course Lady Macbeth, were among her greatest performances – and
they were unsurpassed, in the memory of those who saw her. It is
absurd to dwell on her deficiencies in comedy or to judge her acting by
the performances of her later years.

Kemble's Shakespearian productions, his *Coriolanus*, for instance,
and *Henry VIII*, were heavy with pomp. Not much attention was
paid to historical verisimilitude (that was to come a little later) but
enthusiasm for detail appears in other ways. Kemble looked after the
proprieties and the observance of ceremonial form. He found names for
many of the little anonymous people in the plays and raised Servants
to the dignity of being 'Officers'. Typically the Messenger who brings
news of the Turkish fleet to the Duke and Senators in *Othello* gave
his letters to 'Marco', who in turn presented them to the Duke.

Garrick's last season came to an end in the spring of 1776. Edmund
Kean's first appearance as Shylock at Drury Lane was on 26 January
1814. There were persons who had seen both actors and declared that
Kean reminded them of Garrick. He was profoundly unlike Kemble.
The effects for which the new actor was lauded, his moments of illumination, 'flashes of lightning', depended on vivid pantomimic action or
some sudden, unexpected transition in speech. At times he seems
deliberately to have 'thrown away' lines. He achieved sustained beauty
in Othello's farewell (III, iii, 347), in which he was profoundly moving,
and Othello was certainly his greatest part. His desperate fighting and
death, in *Richard III*, are described unforgettably by Hazlitt, to whom
Kean owes much, as Hazlitt something, no doubt, to Kean. His spiritual
kinship with the romantic poets was early recognized and he was
their favourite actor.

During Kean's later years (he died in 1833) the condition of the two
patent theatres was going from bad to worse. Many causes contributed
to this, and when at last Macready took over the management of
Covent Garden (1837–9) and Drury Lane (1841–3) he was fighting
a losing battle. What he accomplished is the more remarkable. In
Shakespeare's case there were most obviously the restorations. That
of *King Lear* for Tate's *King Lear* took courage. Macready was worried

about the introduction of the Fool (would this not 'either weary and annoy or distract the spectator'). The choice of a young actress, Priscilla Horton, for the part relieved his mind, and the same Priscilla Horton as Ariel (an Ariel who flew as well as sang) delighted audiences in Macready's highly spectacular revival of *The Tempest*. His inclusion of the choruses in *Henry V* was unusual, and as if distrustful of their appeal to the imagination he 'illustrated' them by means of a diorama. In *As You Like It*, with greater subtlety, he used off-stage sounds, the tinkling of sheep bells especially, to create atmosphere.

In his own performances Macready concentrated upon the interpretation of characters as wholes rather than on the making of points. The definiteness of his conceptions was as unusual in his time as the seriousness with which he rehearsed. His name is associated with no single role, as Kean's was with Othello, but he was at his best in Macbeth and in another thoughtful study of moral deterioration, King John.

With the ending of the theatre monopoly, in 1843, the Shakespearian repertory, once the property of Covent Garden and Drury Lane, became available for production elsewhere, and good use was made of it at Sadler's Wells, first, and in the 1850s at the Princess's. Between 1844 and 1862 the strong company assembled by Samuel Phelps at Sadler's Wells gave all but six of Shakespeare's plays, omitting only the three parts of *Henry VI*, *Titus Andronicus*, *Troilus and Cressida*, and less predictably *Richard II*. They gave them well, too, and before popular audiences who, like those of the Old Vic at a later time, became genuinely appreciative of them. Phelps himself was an actor of fine ability. Indeed, the variety of parts which he assumed has rarely been matched. He passed with ease from the tragic heroes to Bully Bottom, and as a feat of virtuosity doubled Henry IV and Justice Shallow. His Shakespearian texts, though they were bowdlerized for Islington ears, contained a number of restorations. He even attempted a *Richard III* without recourse to Cibber.

It was said that Shakespeare's plays were always 'poems' at Sadler's Wells. At the Princess's under Charles Kean, they were more like educational pageants – but very magnificent. Archaeological enthusiasm had been finding expression in the theatre for some time, as in the remarkable production of *King John* at Covent Garden, on 24 November 1823, for which J. R. Planché, the antiquary, was engaged to devise the costumes and armour. But Kean went farther, even to distributing 'flyleaves', in which he indicated the learned authorities for what one was seeing on the stage. His carefully rehearsed crowds, as in an interpolated episode of the return of Henry V to London, and the effect of spaciousness which he sometimes gained on a comparatively small stage, are to be remembered to his credit. *Punch* ridiculed him destructively as the 'upholsterer' of Shakespeare.

Henry Irving's great productions of *Romeo and Juliet* and *Much Ado about Nothing* at the Lyceum in 1882 were different from those of Kean, but the difference lay chiefly in the artistic refinement of the later master. Kean would have accepted Irving's statement of purpose: that of showing his audience a hovel, if the scene was a hovel, and if it was the palace of Cleopatra, then as gorgeous a palace as 'the possibilities of art would allow'. If, however, at one point his accomplishment is perceptibly within a tradition, at another it was amazingly original. To Charles Fechter, a continental player who brought to performances of *Hamlet* and *Othello* at the Princess's the methods, comparatively realistic, of melodrama, Irving may have owed something. As an actor he had few other debts. His apprenticeship in the provinces was in a repertory which no longer contained much Shakespeare. His first successes in London were in modern plays. Then, too, his mannerisms of speech and movement were limiting and set him apart. Was he not always himself?

Yet even very critical playgoers yielded to their enthusiasm. For them there was no other actor, as there was no theatre except Irving's Lyceum. He had intellect and an almost hypnotic power of attraction. He used for his purposes as an actor the resources of a stage which he controlled. Romeo's macabre descent into the tomb, Hamlet's seizing of the throne at the close of the Play Scene, above all, Shylock's lonely homecoming, these were wonderful moments most skilfully stage-managed, or as we would say today directed, by the actor himself.

III   THE RISE OF THE DIRECTOR

That there was an alternative to Irving's manner of presenting Shakespeare would have seemed incredible to most playgoers. Yet as early as the spring of 1881 when an obscure actor named William Poel directed his now celebrated matinée of the First Quarto *Hamlet*, there were persons who advocated a return to the stage for which the plays were designed. Poel had no theatre of his own and only amateur actors. The demonstration of his ideas remained incomplete. What his productions did make clear was that Shakespeare played before plain curtains was still perfectly intelligible, and that the time saved in shifting heavy scenery could be spent to great advantage in restoring some of the many lines omitted in contemporary performances. That Shakespeare was a craftsman of amazing skill, who in any given instance pretty certainly 'knew what he was about', was not a truism to Poel's generation.

Even the generally hostile William Archer gave Poel credit for the care which he bestowed on rehearsing plays and the 'perfect smoothness' with which as a rule they went in performance. His responsibility for a production was complete. His interest extended even to such matters as the speaking of the verse. Yet he did not always appear in the cast himself and was not a star actor. This fact instantly differentiates his connection with a performance from that of Irving or Macready, who whatever concern they might show for the play as a whole could not be expected to forget the central importance of one character in it.

Poel's ideas gained wide currency through the productions of Ben Greet, given sometimes on the 'draped stage', more frequently out-of-doors, and those of Nugent Monck at the excellent Maddermarket Theatre, Norwich. How far the same ideas influenced Harley Granville-Barker is difficult to determine, because of the latter's eclecticism. Granville-Barker had appeared under Poel's direction as Richard II. Both men departed wholly from the heavily cut, constantly interrupted texts then current in the theatre. But it is only with effort that one thinks of Granville-Barker's productions at the Savoy as belonging to an Elizabethan revival. There *The Winter's Tale* and *Twelfth Night*, in 1912, and *A Midsummer Night's Dream*, in 1914, were given in startling, fantastic dresses. Those for *The Winter's Tale*, designed by Albert Rothenstein, were sophisticated in colour and quite forsook any single period. In *A Midsummer Night's Dream* the fairies had gilded faces, an idea much ridiculed by the conservative. There were important innovations in lighting, as well, and the sets were rather decorative than realistic and could be shifted in a moment. Granville-Barker planned also to give *Antony and Cleopatra* and *Macbeth*, but hope of these was destroyed by the outbreak of the First World War.

Before its close there were other losses as well, though none quite so serious. The famous Benson Company paid its final visit to Stratford-upon-Avon. Sir Herbert Beerbohm Tree gave the last of his many Shakespearian revivals at His Majesty's Theatre. The success of these last, grandiose productions is a little hard to account for, as we read of them today, since they were enough like Irving's to make comparison inevitable. And Tree, for all his flamboyance and inventiveness, was very far from being Irving's equal, whether as actor or producer. Frank Benson had brought his company to Stratford-upon-Avon for the first time in 1886. By 1914 they had performed almost, but not quite all of Shakespeare's works, with an unusual bent for the histories. Benson himself is associated particularly with Richard II (memorably reviewed by C. E. Montague) and Henry V. Many actors of subsequent fame served their apprenticeship with this happy, healthy company who gave the people of a great many provincial towns their only chance to see Shakespeare's plays.

Two new men came into prominence in the years immediately after the war. At Stratford, W. Bridges-Adams as director of a recently established company there used simple sets of great beauty and texts of notable completeness. What he accomplished, with the means at his disposal, was extraordinary. At the Old Vic, where Shakespeare (under Greet and others) had begun to be played during the war years, Robert Atkins, a follower of Poel's, became manager in 1920. Of Mr Atkins it has been well remarked that he might have 'entered and taken charge of an Elizabethan playhouse'. In the five years of his stay at the Vic he produced all of the Folio plays (except *Cymbeline*), and *Pericles* as well. The Old Vic was to be identified with Shakespeare's plays for a full generation to come.

I shall not attempt to describe the events of this busy time (1920–51). Characteristic of it was the great increase in the number of Shakespearian productions: some three hundred in London alone, not counting those at the Old Vic. Long neglected works now became familiar. In *The Theatrical World of 1895* William Archer lists those he had not yet seen after years of industrious playgoing. They included: *Richard II*, *The Tempest*, *Coriolanus*, and *2 Henry IV*. *1 Henry IV*, *Love's Labour's Lost*, and *Measure for Measure*, he had seen only in performances by amateurs; *Julius Caesar* had been acted in London, 'within the memory of man', but only by a German company. Archer's ambition (he confessed) stopped short of *Troilus and Cressida*, 'which was not intended for the stage'. He would be able to see many of the others before long. What is remarkable is that he had not yet seen them. *Richard II* was to be particularly successful in the new time of Gielgud and Maurice Evans, when there would be audiences to whom the idea that *Troilus and Cressida* was not an acting play, and a very effective one, would be strange indeed.

Not only were there more productions, a much larger number of Shakespeare's lines were now spoken. Bowdlerization, where it existed, had become an amusing anachronism and cuts were not made for reasons of propriety. The speech of actors, those of Bridges-Adams, for instance (as earlier those of Granville-Barker), was far more rapid than it had once been. Such scenery as was still used no longer demanded frequent and lengthy pauses for its manipulation. Tree's intervals between acts and scenes might take up something like a third of one's evening; the new way was to have only one or two breaks in all.

With the restoration of Shakespeare's text, and the greater swiftness and continuity of many performances, it became possible to appreciate aspects of his technique which had long been obscured. Episodes once thought irrelevant assumed meaning. The opposing of consecutive scenes – as Marc Antony's oration and the murder of the harmless poet Cinna – seemed deliberately ironic. Any sweeping restoration of Elizabeth stage conditions was impossible in the theatres available. But the actor, as if on intimate terms with his audience, now tended to address them in soliloquy, abandoning any attempt at abstraction. Only low comedians had done this, earlier in the century, when the practice was considered destructive of illusion.

As for the directors, with their newly gained, despotic power, they used it with varying degrees of wisdom but on the whole benevolently. The idea that so far as Shakespeare was concerned the director's function was to bring out qualities in the work itself, rather than impose novel interpretations upon it, was pretty generally accepted as an idea, though it was sometimes forgotten in practice. From the early 1920s there were lively experiments with modern dress. This did well for certain scenes, for the Gravediggers and Christopher Sly, the banquet in *Macbeth* and three whole acts of *Julius Caesar*, and very badly for others. There were experiments also with costumes belonging to some serviceable period, more recent than that of the play, but not quite our own, and ingenuity was displayed in substituting characters of this period for their Elizabethan counterparts. With romance as such, that delight in strangeness and wonder which Shakespeare shared with many of his contemporaries, there was little sympathy; but most directors stopped short of deliberate travesty.

The year 1951 does well as a terminal date. In that Festival of Britain year the characteristics which I have been describing showed to particular advantage. At Stratford the production of *Richard II*, the two parts of *Henry IV*, and *Henry V* brought out the closeness of their relationships, the larger unity which they possessed as a group. It was a purpose of immediate appeal to scholars. In London the two great actors of our time were both to be seen in Shakespearian roles; and if Laurence Olivier was disappointing as Antony, in *Antony and Cleopatra*, John Gielgud was near his best as Leontes in a finely sensitive production of *The Winter's Tale* by Peter Brook. More exciting still, for some playgoers, was *2 Henry VI*, directed by Douglas Seale at the Birmingham Repertory Theatre. This was to be followed, next year, by the Third Part, and all three histories were finally given in sequence with a degree of success which few readers would have prophesied for them.

Since 1951 there have been signs of reaction against the popularity of Shakespearian drama on the stage. When the plays were given, and there was no want of productions during these years, it was with less obvious liking and respect on the part of the director. For him what mattered most was to be creative, to have ideas of his own. Critics, too, grown tired of a familiar work, were ready to welcome almost any sort of originality in its production. Fault has been found with the plays on ideological grounds. They were not what their author should have written, not what is wanted here and now. The temptation to alter and improve them became irresistible. At Stratford itself, where simple persons might have expected to see Shakespeare's plays acted as Shakespeare wrote them, Mr John Barton added some hundreds of lines to the three parts of *Henry VI*, given as two plays in 1963. His adaptations were repeated in 1964 as items in a long succession of histories. That the original versions had been successfully revived only a few years before, when they proved to be quite intelligible as they stood, and exciting 'theatre', mattered not at all.

The danger of over-emphasizing what may have been no more than a passing mood is obvious. The English stage between 1951 and 1970 has not been without Shakespearian productions comparable to the best of the generation before. It is enough to recall Peter Brook's *Titus Andronicus*, and, as given in Edinburgh in 1962, Peter Hall's *Troilus and Cressida*. In both these there was an unusual and strangely effective mingling of symbol and savage realism. In the tragedy, ritual was frequently introduced as well. In *Troilus and Cressida*, a play of impermanence, dominated by the presence of Time, the stage itself was deeply covered with sand.

15

SHAKESPEARE AND THE
DRAMA OF HIS TIME

PETER URE

I INTRODUCTORY

Shakespeare sometimes drew upon plays (or other works) by fellow-dramatists for his own plays and poems. He often remembered bits of what they had written. Occasionally, he chose a play as his main source: an old two-part play by George Whetstone (1578) was the basis of *Measure for Measure*. This chapter is not about sources in that sense, although they cannot be completely excluded; it is about Shakespeare's contacts with the work of other Elizabethan playwrights, with special reference to those who might have shaped his own art in important ways. He borrowed a whole play from Whetstone, a thing which he never did to Marlowe; but it is Marlowe who is discussed here, and not Whetstone. We are concerned with those playwrights who may have induced Shakespeare to attend to them enough to accept (or reject) them as artists, in the fullest sense. Absolute proofs of the 'contacts' themselves are often missing; when discussing this topic, modern literary criticism has sometimes built bricks without straw. It is easy to imagine the distorted face of a contemporary in Shakespeare's vast mirror – one can dream up a Marlovian Shakespeare even more easily than a Brechtian one. Ingenuities of this sort have had to be overlooked here, together with much other work and detail of greater value.

II MARLOWE

Shakespeare alludes to or echoes Marlowe's writings every now and then, but it is likely that there was also a complex artistic encounter between the two dramatists; the matter works itself out in elaborate topics such as the Machiavel in *The Jew of Malta* and *Richard III*, king and kingdom in *Edward II* and *Richard II*, or even more speculatively: humanism and orthodoxy are examined, or a contrast is proposed between Marlowe's 'restless scepticism' and Shakespeare's 'optimistic view of life'. Shakespeare was the same age as Marlowe (about thirty when Marlowe was murdered in 1593) but there is no good evidence that they ever collaborated or that they thought of themselves as rivals, friendly or unfriendly.

Shakespeare may or may not have invented the popular English history play, but there can be little doubt that in his three plays on Henry VI (?December 1589–June 1592), he and he alone gave life to the form and made it thematically and poetically coherent. In *Henry VI* the supposed influence of *Tamburlaine* on the blank verse, the rhetoric and the construction proves fairly hard to pin down; and certainly Shakespeare does not seem to endorse and involve himself, in Marlowe's way, with the over-reaching tone and imperative rhythms which he derives from Marlowe's huf-cap hero (heard, for example, in the speeches of the aspiring Duke of York and of his son Richard). With this son, the future Richard III, Shakespeare's response to Marlowe crystallizes. Richard, in *3 Henry VI* and its sequel *Richard III*, is his first full-scale study of the Marlovian superman in his Machiavel role. During the years it was being fashioned (?1591–3), Shakespeare had not only Tamburlaine but probably also the Guise (in *The Massacre at Paris*) and Barabas (in *The Jew of Malta*) to think about. In these characters Marlowe had established the murderous Machiavel of the playhouse, ruthless and magnetic, self-delighting and self-destructive. Their author is himself implicated in the disturbing union of intensity and (apparently) cynical indifference found in these plays. Shakespeare, on the other hand, is able to embody all the energies of Machiavellism in his Richard and yet to interrelate them with the positives that elsewhere in the play spring from conscience, providence or pity (as, for example, pity for Clarence, one of Richard's victims, a figure outside Marlowe's range). It is not – or not wholly – a case of Shakespeare's being more orthodox and complacent, but of his being willing to take a more penetrating look at Machiavellism itself than Marlowe did. Shakespeare may have arrived at this by way of *Titus Andronicus* (?1589–90): Aaron, in that play, is a creation of Marlovian exuberance, almost a 'villain as hero', like Richard and Barabas.

An even more famous case of interaction concerns Marlowe's *Edward II* (*c.* 1590–2), which was influenced by at least the last two parts of the *Henry VI* trilogy. The general resemblances between *Henry VI* and Marlowe's play include a weak king murdered after a rebellion, varying fortunes in a civil war, and characters towards whom our sympathies fluctuate accordingly. Though Marlowe was learning from Shakespeare, his attitude to history is so different that he has been accused of writing it 'without morality', detached from ordinary human sympathies and in rejection of life. Others have found the verse arid: Edward's inlaid, ranting apostrophes seem too often to proceed only from the author's pen, while Richard III has already internalized his speech.

In his turn Shakespeare must have had *Edward II* well in mind when he wrote *Richard II* about 1594–5. His close knowledge of the piece, though it left its marks, sometimes decisive ones such as the deposition scene (IV, i), would have been perfectly compatible with what C. H. Herford termed a 'decisive reaction' *against* Marlowe. For me, the shared ingredient is the helpless king, the personal tragedy of the 'king who must', ruled by those who have wrested from his own power to rule. Marlowe's handling of Edward brought the tragic impropriety into focus for Shakespeare, but it is already hinted at in much that befalls Henry VI. The characteristically Shakespearian device of gradually re-ordering our feelings about individuals (from detachment or reproof to sympathy, or *vice versa*) is found in Marlowe, too; but Shakespeare (in *Henry VI*) seems to have been first to try it. This makes it less likely that he needed an impulsion from Marlowe to build it into the great thing that it is in *Julius Caesar* and *The Merchant of Venice*.

These are the other two Shakespeare plays for which a major Marlovian influence has been invoked. Although it must be easier for those who can see Caesar as a 'Roman Tamburlaine' (in Dover Wilson's phrase), it is much more difficult to detect Marlowe in *Julius Caesar* than in *The Merchant of Venice*. They were the only dramatists of their era to make a Jew a central figure in a play; there are verbal parallels which include the deliberate assignment of Tamburlaine–and Guise-like rhodomontade to the solemn princes of Morocco and Arragon. As for Shylock and Jessica, editors mostly agree that *The Jew of Malta* must be regarded as a major source – though, again, as is the case with *Richard II*, Shakespeare's use of Marlowe is by no means incompatible with a 'decisive reaction' against his limited, if incandescent, vision. A recent editor says sensibly that Marlowe's Jewish father and daughter are the 'complements rather than the parallels' to Shakespeare's.

Marlowe's work seems, in Yeats's phrase, to finish in a flare. The mind that made it so blaze up must have been very unlike Shakespeare's; but there are signs that it invited his admiring compassion, and that he had to come to terms with it before he could go on.

III LYLY AND OTHER WITS

The idea that Lyly's *Euphues* (1578) was an aberration has given place to the view that euphuism – or the movement of which it was the climax – was a big step in the development of sixteenth-century prose away from invertebrate muddle towards dealing with complex material in an adequately ordered and logical way (productive, in drama, of poised elegance, bite and sparkle). If this is true, Shakespeare, like many of his contemporaries, stayed Lyly's beneficiary to the end; it has been said that *all* Shakespeare's prose has some resemblances to euphuism. A debt of a more particular kind has been observed in the influence of Lyly's court-comedies (mostly performed in the 1580s) on Shakespeare's five earlier comedies, *The Comedy of Errors*, *The Taming of the Shrew*, *The Two Gentlemen of Verona*, *Love's Labour's Lost* and *A Midsummer Night's Dream*.

One of the obscurities of this topic is that specific source-type links are disputable, because the two dramatists may have been drawing independently on the traditions of Roman or Italian comedy; and, when the debt seems necessarily more generalized (as in the treatment of love and lovers), Shakespeare's reliable gift for seeing further and more finely has persuaded commentators to study his improvements upon Lyly, rather than his resemblances to him. Lyly, however, was the first writer to produce a substantial collection of English prose comedies; they display wit-combats between courtiers and ladies; and offer us engaging servants and their encounters with their lords, malapert little boys and shining nymphs, girls disguised as boys, songs, fairies, and a fine-grained and deferential cultivation of the audience's 'delight', its 'soft smiling'. Lyly makes a little world of harmonies, which is linked with Ovidian poetry through its mythology and metamorphoses, and with dance, tapestry, masque and pastoral. English comedy before Lyly had been vigorous enough; now it was elegant. The great symbolic activity of this comedy is courtship, and a search, half-humorous and half-serious, for a definition of love; and its maiden-meditations extend to nature and society as well.

The *general* resemblances between that kind of comedy and Shakespeare's up to *Twelfth Night* are obvious. Indeed, it is broadly true that Lyly and Shakespeare are the *only* Elizabethan playwrights whose comedies enact a manifest concern with the definition of love, its meaning, value and order in the life of the individual and society. 'Being in love' is often the central experience of their comedy; it is not, as in most comedy, a mere datum from which interest is displaced onto the bustle of intrigue against the detested rival or tyrannical parent. Like Lyly, Shakespeare constructed his comic societies by placing different groups in apposition to one another (courtiers, ladies; masters, servants; fairies, humans; schoolboys, pedants; and so on); but he not only deepened the reality of individuals (Lyly has no 'stock types' so rammed with life as Launce, Armado or Bottom), he also bound the groups to one another in an elaborate, critical and relativistic way, often under-cutting Lyly's courtly values with subtle analogies and parody. As G. K. Hunter puts it, Shakespeare *interlaces* his episodes (as he does his servants and masters), but Lyly's are kept separate.

Love's Labour's Lost and *A Midsummer Night's Dream*, especially the former, are the plays that (as wholes) approach nearest to Lylian court-entertainment. Shakespeare has adopted many Lylian conventions, and the parallels are generally (though not universally) admitted. The stylish wit, the love-debates, the complementarily arranged groups are all like Lyly's. But Shakespeare is much more concerned with the emotional history of his lovers and with their struggle to understand their own experience. (Valentine and Proteus in *The Two Gentleman of Verona*, Hermia and Lysander in *A Midsummer Night's Dream*, Berowne and his company in *Love's Labour's Lost* are all alike in this). The result is that we become involved with that experience, too, especially when we are helped by the exquisitely penetrating verisimilitude of Shakespeare's verse and prose. But Lyly's less individuated courtiers are shielded from us inside the crystal cabinet of their courtly professionalism: by it alone, by nothing more universal, can they submit to be judged.

Participation in the heart-mysteries of comedy Shakespeare brought about for the first time in English. Lyly's example seems to have marked an important phase in a movement from intrigue-comedy of a chiefly Plautine sort (*The Comedy of Errors*) to the mature love-comedies which are so uniquely Shakespearian. It is a fair guess that the poise and radiance and other unnameable qualities of even Shakespeare's most triumphant heroines – Beatrice or Rosalind or Viola – owe something to him. Shakespeare just intensified the 'delight' – almost, but not entirely, beyond recognition.

A conceivable exception to the rule that only Lyly and Shakespeare are profoundly concerned with 'being in love' might be sought in the work of another university wit, Robert Greene. From time to time good cases have been made out for his kinship with Shakespeare. This appears in their common interest in romantic love and romantic heroines (sometimes dressed up as boys), in their multiple plots, in their use of play-framing devices (like Christopher Sly in *The Taming of the Shrew* and Bohan in Greene's *James IV*) and playlets-within-the-play (compare the eavesdropping scenes in *Much Ado about Nothing* with the 'prospective glass' scenes in Greene's *Friar Bacon and Friar Bungay*). Kinship is a hard thing to be sure about, and both playwrights were using their inheritance of improbable old fictions, the Hellenistic romances and Italian *novelle*; but the hypothesis, accepted or rejected, does help to define features not only of Shakespeare's earlier comedies

but of his late romances as well. In Greene's best plays there is a spirit –
it has been called magnanimity and loving insight – which resembles
Shakespeare's.[1]

Thomas Kyd did not go to a university, but he learnt his wit and his
Latin at a famous school in company with Spenser, so perhaps he may
be considered here. He was apparently the first man to write plays
about revenge for murder, thereby founding a tradition which includes
Titus Andronicus and *Hamlet*. He may have written the old Hamlet
play (the model for Shakespeare's *Hamlet*) which had – for we know
what its sources must have been, though we have lost the play itself –
a ghost, a son's (delayed) revenge for a father, a hero who goes crazy,
and a play within a play. His *The Spanish Tragedy* (?1587), the first
extant full-blown revenge-play, has a number of similar episodes.

Kyd was, in the strictest sense, a very great dramatist – greater, as
T. S. Eliot declared, than Marlowe. He used his theatre brilliantly, and
knew of many different ways in which to show it off. His savage ironies
have a more personal thrust than Marlowe's. He used soliloquy,
dialogue and gesture for actualizing inner confusion, grief, solitary
brooding, tragic foolery. All this can be underrated if we do not
recognize how subtly he animates the modes which he derived largely
from medieval metrical tragedies (there is very little 'Senecanism' in
him). When all is said, a scene such as Hieronimo's discovery of the
dead body of his son hanging in the garden (*The Spanish Tragedy* II, v)
is one of the most tremendous in English drama. He was amongst the
first to contrive that intensification of tragic by comic modes that
everybody knows about in *Hamlet* and *King Lear* and *Macbeth*. He
created personages of unusual awareness and located the motives for the
action in them and not in the gods or their innumerable surrogates. It is
easy to believe that Shakespeare was deeply impressed; and that he may
have owed much more to Kyd than just the *schema* of revenge-tragedy.

All the major Wits fell on evil days; nearly all died before their time.
It is Shakespeare himself and his work as actor and playwright, which
most obviously bridges the gap between their plays and the new
writers whom we begin to hear about in the late 1590s. Embodying
that continuity must have been a salient part of his life-experience.

IV   JONSON AND THE SATIRISTS

Shakespeare acted in Jonson's *Every Man in his Humour* (1598). This
play, or its immediate forerunner Chapman's *An Humorous Day's
Mirth* (1597), started the vogue for humour-comedy, shifting into
its cognate modes, comical (and tragical) satires, black comedy, malcontent plays. Culminating in Jonson's *Sejanus* (1603) or Marston's

The Malcontent (1604), the movement left its mark on much subsequent writing, on Webster's tragedies and Chapman's comedies, on Middleton, on Tourneur, and on Jonson's own comic masterpieces from *Volpone* (1606) onwards. Satire (increasingly agile and provocative in the late 1590s) had got a lodgement in the drama and proved its kinship by sprouting out into all kinds of daring devices. The 'comical satires' of Jonson and Marston offer combinations which are new to the theatre, though much indebted to both Roman and medieval satirical ideas: first, affected (= 'humorous') or vicious or criminal persons, commonly subjugated by *one* affectation, vice, or crime, in the same way that a diseased humour was believed to surcharge the human body and discompose its elements. Secondly, there takes his place inside the play the necessary counterpoise to these satirized persons – the satirist himself: he may be the virtuous, temperate, foursquare Poet (like Horace in Jonson's *Poetaster*), or (more frequently) he is the flailing commentator, the scourge who is not immune from the 'strange surquedries' that he castigates; a darker version of the same figure is the malcontent-revenger, like Malevole in *The Malcontent* or Vindice in *The Revenger's Tragedy*, who, in inhibiting vices, especially sexual ones, enjoys a prurient complicity with a world which to him appears a graveyard, muck-heap, and pestilential congregation of vapours. Thirdly, comical satires are built up from the development of these characters through their own internal logic, especially during their submission to some ramifying court or city intrigue. The humour-character needs, because of his obsessions, continually to exhibit his viciousness or folly. This is where satire approaches close to allegory. It is the business of the penal agent in satire whether revenger, homilist, righteous victim, or cynic dog, to induce the humour-character to act out his humour fully, to wind up the clock of his mania until it strikes; it is also the business of the play as a whole to move steadily towards the place and moment when the affectations and vices are finally stripped bare, punished, and ejected with contempt from the society of the play. The process is mythic enough – the scapegoat purifies his community of burdens otherwise pernicious to it. But the commonest metaphors in the plays are of scourging and purging; these were mirrored in the penal code, and literally enacted on the stage in Dekker's *Satiromastix* and Jonson's *Poetaster*.

Shakespeare's mature art of the middle period, from *Henry V* (1599) onwards, was undoubtedly affected by all this. His artistic acknowledgement of it is perhaps the clearest demonstration we have, once the formative years are over, of his being always wide awake to what other playwrights were doing. This seems clear enough even though Shakespeare, like them, was also responding to something in the 'spirit of the age', a new restlessness and sardonic intellectuality, which would have affected his art anyway. But he never went in whole-heartedly for these paradigms of punishment. The satirical elements are scattered here and there, but they do not take control. Even his early humour-characters, Pistol and Nym in *Henry V*, have got an extra un-Jonsonian dimension. His unequalled genius for seeing the man beneath the mask unfitted him for the wall-eyed stare of the humour-satirist.

The wariness of Shakespeare's response is clearly seen in *Troilus and Cressida*. Thersites in that play is an uncompromising version of the immoderate, contemptible railer. *Troilus and Cressida* is unique, and hard to construe, but the claim that it is an example of comical (or tragical) satire, with everybody in it held up to ridicule (as though Thersites had *written* the play) must, I believe, be denied. Jacques and *As You Like It* make up, *mutatis mutandis*, a parallel case. Malvolio in *Twelfth Night* has many affinities with satirical and humour-comedy and is temperately subjected to its purgative and dismissive routines; but no one has claimed *Twelfth Night* as a whole for the Jonsonian mode (though Sir Toby is a more squalid figure than is usually recognized). *Measure for Measure* can only be allocated a 'basic satiric anatomy' on the hypothesis that Isabella and her cause upset an original design; the play that we have, though things in it may have been derived from Marston or Middleton, achieves a final effect unlike either's work. Hamlet takes malcontentism in his stride, and is not encompassed by it. He has some affinity (as indeed has Lear) with Timon, but the view that *Timon of Athens* is a 'tragical satire' (like *Sejanus*) depends upon a reading which ignores too much in the play to be plausible. In short, we can justifiably talk of Shakespeare's satire, and all the plays and characters I have just mentioned, and others beside, can be illuminated by some knowledge of what was going on in the theatre from 1598 to 1604 or later; but we cannot talk of Shakespeare's *satires*.[2]

V FLETCHER AND THE LAST PLAYS

The four last plays or romances, beginning with *Pericles* (?1607–8), make up a constellation rather different from any other in Shakespeare. Each of the four has its own character, nor ought we to exaggerate the apartness of their group: in earlier plays, such as *All's Well that Ends Well* and *Troilus and Cressida*, there are the same qualities – discontinuous characterization, 'baroque' or 'old comedy' forms, satire mixed with far-fetched story, an analytic approach to ideas – that are to be more richly and magniloquently deployed in *The Tempest* and its immediate predecessors.

It is, therefore, extraordinarily difficult to say how much of the new strain grows out of earlier achievements and how much may be due to new dramatists and a changing theatrical climate. Early in 1609 the King's men started playing in the Blackfriars theatre and were launched on their great experiment of being the first adult company to run two London theatres simultaneously. Although a recent habit of referring to it as a 'coterie' theatre is perfectly misleading, the Blackfriars was smaller, dearer and more exclusive than the Globe; this must have made the company think a bit more about fashion and refinement, as well as about music and masques. John Fletcher started working for them in 1609 – Shakespeare's junior by fifteen years, he had been writing (for other companies) for about two. His career overlapped with Shakespeare's for four or five years (1609–13), and it was he who, in the theatrical and professional sense, was to be Shakespeare's successor as chief poet. In the artistic sense Fletcher (and his partner during the vital period, Beaumont) were so far below Shakespeare as to be virtually invisible; but the fact that their work was to be highly esteemed during the rest of the era indicates the sort of changes in taste, just then beginning, to which Shakespeare may have wished to respond.

Did Fletcher influence the last plays? Behind this puzzle stands the common belief that Shakespeare actually collaborated with Fletcher in *Henry VIII* and *The Two Noble Kinsmen* (current theories that Shakespeare wrote them unaided are exceptionally improbable). But both these collaborative exercises, as well as that involving the lost *Cardenio*, are very late (1612–13), probably done during the semi-retirement at Stratford; they cast only a retrospective light on the main problem. This problem cannot be solved in terms of contact between play and play in the *Edward II/Richard II* manner. Efforts to prove the specific indebtedness of *Cymbeline* to *Philaster* (or *vice versa*), or of *The Tempest* to *The Faithful Shepherdess*, have not succeeded. We are driven to compare the art of the two playwrights at a higher level of generalization, to talk about patterns. A pattern may be defined simply as an aggregate of various characteristic features, or, more obscurely, as a critically abstracted principle of design or development. Either way, there is a certain liberty of interpreting.

It is wrong to feel that Shakespeare would have refused to learn – about, for example, the modish Italian-style pastoral – from younger men, especially in the new Blackfriars situation (perhaps it was Shakespeare himself who spotted Fletcher's timeliness). But, before Fletcher's advent, he had written or rewritten the last three acts of *Pericles*, the prototype of the romances – and for the Globe, too. The taste for romance was old as well as new, as is shown by the King's men revival of *Mucedorus*, an old tragical-comical-pastoral thriller, which left its traces in *The Winter's Tale* and *The Tempest*; similarly another old (1582) play of the same kind, *The Rare Triumphs of Love and Fortune*, may have affected *Cymbeline*. When we *can* specify, what come first to mind are 'old plays', Spenser, *Arcadia*, *Pandosto*, the archaic fictions that we hear about in *The Winter's Tale* and the Hellenistic romances which had long supplied material for popular writers such as Greene or Peele.

And yet these borrowings underline the kinship between the old romantic thrillers and the new sumptuous tragicomedy that, like *Philaster* and *Cymbeline*, 'wants deaths...yet brings some near it'. The basic patterns of Fletcherian tragicomedy resemble the patterns of generations lost-and-found explored in the last plays, though tragicomedy itself is not new to Shakespeare and has a long history on the English stage before Fletcher: one thinks of Richard Edwardes's *Damon and Pithias* (1565) or of the romance elements in *The Comedy of Errors* or of the 'deaths' of Claudio or Hero; likewise, the conjunction of *satyr* and *pastor*, complicated in Fletcher, had been clearly established by Jaques and Touchstone. Even the conscious theatrical artifice, the play's exposure of its own machinery, the virtuoso daring of much of the plotting in the romances, the declamatory and passionate arias – these are things Shakespeare has in common with Fletcher; yet there is no phase of his earlier work that does not forecast their magnification in the final plays. The Fletcherian stigma – a peculiar, mawkish intensity of tone and language – did not afflict Shakespeare: even *Cymbeline*, the most Fletcher-like of the plays, keeps a toughly obscure late-Shakespearian style; and all of them contain writing that, for solemnity and splendour of imagination, outpaces Fletcher beyond any reckoning. What we are dealing with is a confluence rather than an influence; Fletcher's art was one of a number of tributaries running in the same direction, its waters now drowned in the great river. Indeed, the really incalculable gulf between the insight of genius, more penetrating than ever in the last plays, and Fletcher's rather vapid talent, makes any comparison between them, however much it is stated in terms of *underlying* patterns, seem inescapably of the surface.

VI CONCLUSION

With the possible exception of two or three of the great tragedies – more distinctly *sui generis* than any other group – a less summary treatment of the subject of this chapter would need to give some consideration to every one of Shakespeare's plays: for none is without some kind of contextual relationship to other plays of the time. 'Shakespeare,' G. E. Bentley says, 'was more completely and continuously involved with theatres and acting companies than any other Elizabethan dramatist whose life we know.' The inescapable corollary of this is Hazlitt's '...distinguished from his immediate contemporaries, not in kind, but in degree and greater variety of excellence...He did not form a class or species by himself, but belonged to a class or species.' On the other hand, classification, though it may help or hinder them, has no necessary overlap with literary criticism or theatre-performance. This may explain why we have had tolerable productions and suggestive criticism neither of which has appeared to be much damaged by a stupendous indifference to the rest of the species.

16

SHAKESPEARE'S TEXT: APPROACHES AND PROBLEMS

G. BLAKEMORE EVANS

Interest, even a passionate interest, in the challenging problems raised by the text of Shakespeare's plays and poems is scarcely a modern phenomenon. From the beginning of the eighteenth century many scholars and amateurs have devoted themselves, in the light of current textual approaches, to establishing what they firmly believed represented the 'best' or 'true' text. The seventeenth century, on the other hand, had adopted a much less idolatrous view of the sanctity of Shakespeare's every word, and a progressive and unauthorized tendency to modernize grammar, syntax, and language may be traced from the early quartos to the First Folio (1623) and then on through the Second (1632), Third (1664) and Fourth (1685) Folios.

This accumulation of compounded error and thoughtless if well-intentioned meddling was the inheritance of Shakespeare's early editors, and nearly a hundred years passed before these surface blemishes were finally sloughed off and the primacy of the earliest printed editions vindicated. This done, the basic problems were, as we shall see, only partially understood and it was not until the present century that their full implications were squarely faced. Even today, after two hundred and fifty years devoted to the study of Shakespeare's text, there is much that remains to be learned, much that is only hypothetically explained, much that we can probably never know with any certainty. What we do know, what we guess, and, by implication, what we would still like to know is the subject of the present essay.

The extant materials for an examination of Shakespeare's text may be quickly listed. Thirty-nine plays, in whole or in part by Shakespeare, the poems *Venus and Adonis* and *Lucrece*, the sonnets, and a few other short poems form the body of the Shakespeare canon. Thirty-six of these plays were gathered together in the earliest collected edition of Shakespeare's works (1623), now generally known as the First Folio (F1).[1] Eighteen plays appeared there for the first time in any printed form and for these F1 furnishes the sole authority for the text, any changes that were made in the later folios being entirely without

Addition (D) to Sir Thomas More, *lines 126–140*

what Country by the nature of yor error
fhoold gyve you harber go yo^u to ffraunc or flanders
to any Jarman pvince, ~~to~~ fpane or portigall
nay any where ~~why yo^u~~ that not adheres to Ingland
why yo^u muft neede be ftraingers, woold yo^u be pleafd
to find a nation of fuch barbarous temper
that breaking out in hiddious violence
woold not afoord yo^u, an abode on earth
whett their detefted knyves againft yor throtes
fpurne yo^u lyke dogge, and lyke as yf that god
owed not nor made not yo^u, nor that the elamente
                          yor
wer not all appropriat to ~~their~~ Comforte.
but Charterd vnto them, what woold yo^u thinck
to be thus vfd, this is the ftraingers cafe
and this your momtanifh inhumanyty

Our deereſt *Regan*, wife to *Cornwell*, ſpeake?

Reg. Sir I am made of the ſelfe ſame mettall that my ſiſter is,
And prize me at her worth in my true heart,
I find ſhe names my very deed of loue, onely ſhe came ſhort,
That I profeſſe my ſelfe an enemie to all other ioyes,
Which the moſt precious ſquare of ſence poſſeſſes,
And find I am alone felicitate, in your deere highnes loue.

Cord. Then poore *Cord.* & yet not ſo, ſince I am ſure
My loues more richer then my tongue.

Lear. To thee and thine hereditarie euer
Remaine this ample third of our faire kingdome,
No leſſe in ſpace, validity, and pleaſure,
Then that confirm'd on *Gonorill*, but now our ioy,
Although the laſt, not leaſt in our deere loue,
What can you ſay to win a third, more opulent
Then your ſiſters.

Cord. Nothing my Lord.   (againe.

Lear. How, nothing can come of nothing, ſpeake

Cord. Vnhappie that I am, I cannot heaue my heart into my
mouth, I loue your Maieſtie according to my bond, nor more nor
leſſe.

Lear. Goe to, goe to, mend your ſpeech a little,
Leaſt it may mar your fortunes.

Cord. Good my Lord,
You haue begot me, bred me, loued me,
I returne thoſe duties backe as are right fit,
Obey you, loue you, and moſt honour you,
Why haue my ſiſters huſbands if they ſay they loue you all,
Happely when I ſhall wed, that Lord whoſe hand
Muſt take my plight, ſhall cary halfe my loue with him,
Halfe my care and duty, ſure I ſhall neuer
Mary like my ſiſters, to loue my father all,

Lear. But goes this with thy heart?

Cord. I good my Lord.

Lear. So yong and ſo vntender.

Cord. So yong my Lord and true.

Lear. Well let it be ſo, thy truth then be thy dower,
For by the ſacred radience of the Sunne,

B 2   The

Our deereſt *Regan*, wife of *Cornwall?*

Reg. I am made of that ſelfe-mettle as my Siſter,
And prize me at her worth. In my true heart,
I finde ſhe names my very deede of loue :
Onely ſhe comes too ſhort, that I profeſſe
My ſelfe an enemy to all other ioyes,
Which the moſt precious ſquare of ſenſe profeſſes,
And finde I am alone felicitate
In your deere Highneſſe loue.

Cor. Then poore *Cordelia*,
And yet not ſo, ſince I am ſure my Ioue's
More ponderous then my tongue.

Lear. To thee, and thine hereditarie euer,
Remaine this ample third of our faire Kingdome,
No leſſe in ſpace, validitie, and pleaſure
Then that conferr'd on *Gonerill.* Now our Ioy,
Although our laſt and leaſt ; to whoſe yong loue,
The Vines of France, and Milke of Burgundie,
Striue to be intereſt. What can you ſay, to draw
A third, more opilent then your Siſters? ſpeake.

Cor. Nothing my Lord.

Lear. Nothing ?

Cor. Nothing.

Lear. Nothing will come of nothing, ſpeake againe.

Cor. Vnhappie that I am, I cannot heaue
My heart into my mouth: I loue your Maieſty
According to my bond, no more nor leſſe.

Lear. How, how *Cordelia*? mend your ſpeec ah little,
Leaſt you may marre your Fortunes.

Cor. Good my Lord,
You haue begot me, bred me, lou'd me.
I returne thoſe duties backe as are right fit,
Obey you, Loue you, and moſt Honour you.
Why haue my Siſters Husbands, if they ſay
They loue you all ? Happily when I ſhall wed,
That Lord, whoſe hand muſt take my plight, ſhall carry
Halfe my loue with him, halfe my Care, and Dutie,
Sure I ſhall neuer marry like my Siſters.

Lear. But goes thy heart with this ?

Cor. I my good Lord.

Lear. So young, and ſo vntender ?

Cor. So young my Lord, and true.

Lear. Let it be ſo, thy truth then be thy dowre:
For by the ſacred radience of the Sunne,

independent manuscript authority. The remaining eighteen plays in
F I had been published earlier in separate quarto editions[2] and for all
but seven these quartos furnish the most authoritative texts. Three
other plays, now generally admitted as at least in part by Shakespeare,
were not included in F I: *Pericles*, published in quarto in 1608, was
added to the F I collection in the Third Folio (1664);[3] *The Two Noble
Kinsmen*, probably by Fletcher and Shakespeare, appeared in quarto
in 1632; and *Sir Thomas More*, a play in which Shakespeare is usually
accorded a single scene of 147 lines and (in the opinion of some) one
other speech, was printed from a manuscript, now in the British
Museum, for the first time in 1844. This so-called *More* fragment,
since the single scene is believed to be in Shakespeare's autograph, is
of special interest and will be referred to in later discussions. These,
then, simply listed, are the primary materials with which the student
of Shakespeare has to work, but the many-faceted problems raised by
this body of materials are far from simple.

Two basic questions at once present themselves, questions which,
curiously enough, were never seriously or systematically considered
until about sixty years ago. First, what kind or kinds of manuscripts
can be postulated as lying behind the earliest printed texts? Second,
what sort of treatment, both editorial and mechanical, did these
manuscripts undergo in the Elizabethan–Jacobean printing house? Or,
to reduce the two questions to one: how close do the printed texts
bring us to what Shakespeare actually wrote? The answers to these
questions, fundamental as they are, are extremely complex and not
infrequently still hypothetical.

Let us consider, first, the matter of the manuscripts from which the
earliest printed texts were necessarily derived. The modern reader will
naturally tend to assume that Shakespeare's plays were printed from
carefully prepared author's final copy, 'absolute in their numbers, as he
conceived them'. Such, indeed, was the claim Heminges and Condell,
Shakespeare's fellow actors and the 'editors' of F I, made in their
preface, 'To the Great Variety of Readers', for the texts in that volume.
But recent investigations, begun under the leadership of R. B.
McKerrow, A. W. Pollard, W. W. Greg, and J. Dover Wilson, have
painted a sadly different picture. Except, possibly, in the case of *2 Henry
VI* and *3 Henry VI*, *Troilus and Cressida*, *Antony and Cleopatra*, and
Coriolanus, it has been demonstrated that, even when it is possible to
postulate Shakespearian autograph as the source of a printed text, the
manuscript involved must be recognized as Shakespeare's 'foul papers'
(i.e. the original, or an early draft of the play) and not his final (or
'fair') copy. The reasons for this state of affairs are not difficult to
guess. Once an author had sold his play to a company of actors (in

Shakespeare's case the Chamberlain's men, later known as the King's men), he ceased, except in special circumstances, to have any personal rights in the play, and, when a company decided to make a little extra money by selling the printing rights to a publisher, the manuscript they turned over, since they probably possessed only one official copy (the prompt-book), was most likely to be some state of the author's original draft ('foul papers'), something presumably of no further value to them. Such a manuscript would inevitably tend to be untidy and carelessly written, containing unclearly marked deletions, additions, revisions, interlineations, inconsistent speech-prefixes, incomplete and sporadic stage directions. Enough examples of this kind of manuscript have survived (including parts of the *Sir Thomas More* manuscript) to support such a generalization. It is scarcely surprising, therefore, that compositors when faced with 'foul papers' for printer's copy frequently produced a confused and inaccurate text. Certainly, the hypothetically difficult and potentially confusing condition of Shakespeare's 'foul papers' will go far to explain the compositorial misreadings and mis-understandings found in such basic texts as the second quartos of *Romeo and Juliet* and *Hamlet*. In addition to these two plays, *The Comedy of Errors, Titus Andronicus, The Taming of the Shrew, Love's Labour's Lost, Richard II, A Midsummer Night's Dream, King John, The Merchant of Venice, 1 Henry IV* and *2 Henry IV, Much Ado about Nothing, Henry V, All's Well that Ends Well*, and *Timon of Athens* have been widely thought to have been printed more or less directly from some stage of Shakespeare's 'foul papers'. Such, at least, is W. W. Greg's final judgement (1955). But there is disagreement, and some recent opinion prefers to postulate an intermediate scribal transcript from the 'foul papers' as the manuscript copy for certain of these plays.

But, even if we accept Greg's view, author's copy, fair or foul, will account for only about half of the plays. At least four other kinds of what may be termed secondary copy have to be allowed for: scribal copy (either from author's foul or fair copy or from another scribal copy); theatre prompt copy (a manuscript possibly authorial, but more often scribal, which has served as the prompt-book for stage produc-tion); memorially reconstructed copy (the hypothetical source of the so-called 'bad' quartos); and what may be called combination-copy, partly printed (the quartos), partly manuscript (the manuscript in question again being of several possible kinds).

The first two categories, scribal and theatre copy, clearly overlap, since theatre copy seems usually to have been a scribal transcript, not infrequently, one suspects, made from a late stage of an author's 'foul papers'. There is, however, a class of scribal copy prepared for such a non-theatrical occasion as a manuscript gift (perhaps such a Shake-spearian fair copy lies behind the quarto edition of *Troilus and Cressida*) or publication. This kind of scribal copy is believed to be the basis of the F I texts of *The Tempest, The Two Gentlemen of Verona, The Merry Wives of Windsor, Measure for Measure,* and *The Winter's Tale,* the manuscript copy for which is now generally accepted as the work of Ralph Crane, who is sometimes loosely described as scrivener to the King's men. These transcripts are thought to have been specially pre-pared for publication in F I, and Crane's characteristics as a scribe, strongly marked and well documented from other non-Shakespearian Crane transcripts, are still recognizable even after being filtered through the F I compositors. The texts of these plays in F I are comparatively clean and present few serious textual problems, but two nagging and essentially unanswerable questions must always remain. How much editorial tinkering and tidying up did Crane (or any other scribe) undertake in the process of transcription? And, from what kinds of manuscripts, authorial, scribal, or theatrical, were the transcripts made?

Theatre copy is thought to lie behind such plays as *Julius Caesar, As You Like It, Twelfth Night, Macbeth, Cymbeline,* and to some extent the F I texts of *Hamlet, Othello* and *King Lear.* Again these folio texts are relatively clean and tidy, but the problems noticed in con-nection with scribal copy are in most cases again present, aggravated by the additional interference of theatrical provenience. *Macbeth,* an extreme case, satisfactory as it may appear in some respects, almost certainly represents a shortened and somewhat telescoped stage version, which, short as it is compared with any of the other tragedies except *Timon of Athens* (probably never completed by Shakespeare), ironically preserves some fifty additional lines (the Hecate appearances) com-monly attributed to Thomas Middleton. *The Taming of the Shrew,* although probably printed from Shakespeare's 'foul papers', illustrates the danger of theatre influence even on manuscripts which did not serve as the official prompt-book. The F I text lacks the conclusion to the inimitable Christopher Sly framework and all but one of the interscene commentaries by Sly, a sad state of affairs that can best be explained by supposing that the 'foul papers' had been marked for cutting (fortunately not always very clearly) preparatory to the tran-scription of a prompt-book that would limit the play to the central taming plots. In this instance, however, we are fortunate enough to possess an earlier play (considered indeed by some critics to be a 'bad' quarto version of Shakespeare's play) called *The Taming of a Shrew* from which Shakespeare's treatment of the missing Sly material can in part be reconstructed.

The third kind of secondary manuscript copy, one based on some form of memorial reporting, introduces the question of the so-called 'bad' quartos. In the early years of this century, A. W. Pollard suggested the distinction, now regularly accepted, between what he termed 'good' and 'bad' quartos. Heminges and Condell in their preface to F1 talked disparagingly about certain earlier editions of the plays as 'stolen, and surreptitious copies'. Before Pollard's important distinction, although certain quartos were recognized as offering good texts, Heminges and Condell's remark was interpreted as a blanket attack on all the pre-Folio quartos, inspired by their desire to puff the authenticity of the texts in F1. Pollard, however, proposed that they were referring only to a special group of quartos, which he thereupon dubbed 'bad' quartos, the texts of which had been in some way piratically obtained, hence 'stolen, and surreptitious'. In this category are now included the first quartos of *Romeo and Juliet* (1597) and *Hamlet* (1603) and the quartos of *The Merry Wives of Windsor* (1602), *Henry V* (1600), *The Contention* (1594) and *True Tragedy of Richard Duke of York* (1595) (i.e. *2 Henry VI* and *3 Henry VI*), *Richard III* (1597), *King Lear* (1608), and *Pericles* (1609).[4] The quartos of *Richard III* and *King Lear* present special problems that make their inclusion here open to some question. The textual difficulties in *Richard III* will be discussed in some detail later. The 1608 quarto of *King Lear*, although it suffers seriously from some kind of memorial contamination, also gives evidence in parts of being printed from a transcription (perhaps through dictation) from Shakespeare's 'foul papers'.

At about this same time, an older theory, first suggested in the eighteenth century, was revived to account for the kinds of texts that, in varying degrees of 'badness', comprise this group of nine quartos. In his introduction to an edition (1910) of the quarto of *The Merry Wives of Windsor*, W. W. Greg offered the first detailed exploration of what is now called the memorial theory. Prior to this, these texts had been usually viewed either as early drafts by Shakespeare or others of plays which he later revised, or as shorthand reports of the plays taken down during performance. The memorial reconstruction theory is now commonly accepted, though with various qualifications and emphases, depending upon the particular play under consideration. In a later classic monograph, Greg extended the memorial theory in his discussion of Greene's *Orlando Furioso* and illustrated another kind of maimed text in an examination of Peele's *Battle of Alcaʒar*, an officially cut and simplified version prepared for provincial touring. Although none of the Shakespearian 'bad' quartos seems exactly to fit into this second category, a provincial tour probably explains the genesis of some of the unofficially perpetrated 'bad' quarto texts.

Briefly put, a memorially reconstructed text is one based primarily on what an actor (or actors) could recall from having played one or more roles, usually of a comparatively minor sort, in an authorized production of a play. The resulting version would thus produce, more or less accurately, the basic action of the original play, although not always in correct sequence, but its verbal text would, in greater or lesser degree, evidence the various tricks which memory can play: anticipation (placing phrases, lines, even scenes too early in the play), recollection (the reverse of anticipation), unconscious borrowing (using lines and phrases from other plays which are suggested by the immediate context), and, above all, simple forgetfulness, which forced the 'author' to ad-lib in an effort to give some semblance of logic and connection to his half-remembered bits and pieces. It has been observed that these texts tend to be more reliable when certain characters are present in a scene and this phenomenon, not without disagreement, has been used to suggest the actor (or actors) most likely to be responsible for the report (e.g. the Host in the quarto of *The Merry Wives of Windsor* or Marcellus and Lucianus, probably played by one actor, in Q1 of *Hamlet*). One other characteristic of many 'bad' quarto texts should be noticed – their employment of the visual memory. Again and again these texts give us visually recollected reports on stage business or costume of a sort not commonly found in texts printed from authorial or even theatrical copy. It is from the 'bad' quarto of *Hamlet*, for example, that we learn that the Ghost enters in his nightgown in the famous bedroom scene and that Hamlet leaps into Ophelia's grave after Laertes. The 'bad' quartos of *Romeo and Juliet*, *2 Henry VI* and *3 Henry VI*, and *The Merry Wives of Windsor* are also rewarding in affording this sort of sudden insight into a contemporary production.

The fourth kind of secondary printer's copy, combination-copy – part manuscript, part printed – appears largely in connection with F1 texts. Several (*Richard III*, *2 Henry VI* and *3 Henry VI*, *Henry V*, *King Lear*, *Troilus and Cressida*, and probably *Hamlet* and *Othello*) can be shown to have been printed from an earlier quarto edition (or editions) that had been collated and corrected against an independent manuscript, in most cases probably the official prompt-book. Words, phrases and lines from the manuscript were added to the printed copy, or substituted for readings already there, and longer passages, copied on slips, attached for insertion. Ideally, this method should produce something like a substantive facsimile of the manuscript, but given human carelessness, abetted by probable haste, the resulting printer's copy was in fact far from ideal.

For the eighteen plays which were printed for the first time in any form in F1 no problem can arise for an editor in his choice of basic copy-text, since, whatever kind of manuscript we may decide underlies these F1 texts, no other choice is possible. But the problem is potentially more complicated for the remaining eighteen plays in F1 where there are earlier quarto editions and a question may be posed as to the relative authority of quarto versus folio. For thirteen of these plays, however, no serious conflict exists. For four of them (*2 Henry VI* and *3 Henry VI, Henry V, The Merry Wives of Windsor*), the F1 texts are unchallenged because the only earlier quarto editions fall into the category of 'bad' quartos. For another nine (*Titus Andronicus, Romeo and Juliet, Love's Labour's Lost, A Midsummer Night's Dream, The Merchant of Venice, Richard II, 1 Henry IV and 2 Henry IV, Much Ado about Nothing*), a quarto edition is now generally accepted as the basic copy-text because the F1 texts, though they may contain additional lines from an independent source, are essentially only slightly sophisticated and edited reprints of the earlier quartos. But with such plays as *Richard III, Hamlet, Troilus and Cressida, Othello*, and *King Lear* various difficulties arise that tend to confuse the choice of copy-text and present an editor with many problems, some of them beyond any entirely satisfactory solution. Two case-histories (*Richard III* and *Hamlet*) may serve to clarify some of these difficulties and uncertainties and, at the same time, illustrate more concretely certain of the generalities treated in earlier parts of the discussion.

There are two important early texts of *Richard III*: Q1 printed in 1597 and the F1 text. Between Q1 and F1 five more quarto editions were published. Recent scholarship is now generally agreed that F1 should be taken as the basis for any modern edition and that Q1 is some kind of memorially reported version and must be classified as a 'bad' quarto, though what may be called a good 'bad' quarto, similar in this respect to the quarto of *King Lear*. Although F1 is thus accorded a primary place, the resulting textual situation is far from satisfactory. The greater part of the F1 text was printed from a copy of Q6 that had been corrected and amplified (by about 190 lines) from an authoritative manuscript, probably Shakespeare's 'foul papers'. For some reason, however, at which we can do no more than guess, about five hundred lines of the play (a short stretch, III, i, 1–158, and all of the play after v, iii, 48) were printed from an uncorrected copy of Q3 (1602). For these five hundred lines, then, we are thrown back to the authority – or lack of it – of Q1. Since, moreover, the F1 text was, in great part, set up from a corrected late quarto, one that had amassed in a mounting spiral of error all the mistakes added along the way as each new quarto edition was printed from the one immediately preceding it, we are able to check the accuracy of the person making the collation between Q6 and the manuscript. Where, for example, F1 retains a reading first introduced in Q 2–6 (readings which were without any authority, mere printing-house guesses or errors), we can be relatively certain that the collator has failed to make the necessary correction in his copy of Q 6. Forty-one such readings were overlooked by the collator out of a possible 340, that is, he failed to correct one out of every eight readings. In these instances we are able to check his accuracy, but in the thousands of readings common to Q 1 and F 1 (remembering that Q 1 is a memorially reported text and its readings consequently of doubtful authority), we have no means of checking the collator's accuracy. Alice Walker, for example, calculates that at least 110 corrections from the manuscript were missed and others would put the figure even higher. Baldly stated, the only substantial parts of *Richard III* that we can be relatively sure represent what Shakespeare wrote are the 190 lines that appear for the first time in F 1 and that must have been derived directly from the manuscript.

The some thirty-seven hundred lines which we read today as *Hamlet* were never read by an Elizabethan and almost certainly at no single reading even by Shakespeare himself. Our modern *Hamlet* is in fact an eclectic text combining materials from three sources: Q 2 (1604), F 1 (1623), and Q 1 (1603), a 'bad' quarto. Of these, however, only Q 2 and F 1 figure in the choice of a copy-text. Q 2 is now, since the important work of Dover Wilson in 1934, recognized as the more authoritative, being for the most part demonstrably set from Shakespeare's 'foul papers', and it contains roughly 200 lines found neither in F 1 nor Q 1. F 1, which contains some 85 lines not in Q 1 or Q 2, shows obvious connections with an official theatre prompt-book, though whether it was printed directly from that prompt-book manuscript or from a copy of Q 2 collated against and augmented from such a manuscript remains a debatable question that affects the relative independent authority of the F 1 text. Recent research has shown, moreover, that the F 1 text evidences considerable indications of contamination by long use in the theatre (an important factor in the gradual corruption of a text), and its readings are becoming increasingly suspect – except, of course, for the more substantial additional passages, which we must suppose to be genuine Shakespearian additions made at some point between the writing of the play around 1600 and Shakespeare's death in 1616.

Q 1 is a typical example of a 'bad' quarto. It is about half as long as Q 2 and offers a text that suffers markedly from all the characteristic weaknesses of a memorial reconstruction – misplaced scenes and groups of lines, garbled and farced-out speeches, sophomoric and unmetrical verse, commonplace word substitutions and flat prosaic paraphrases, bits and pieces from other plays – even, perhaps, a scene (between

Gertrude and Horatio, which will be found in no modern critical text) from the original *Hamlet* play on which Shakespeare based his own version. But even this miserable excuse for *Hamlet* makes its comparatively small contribution to a modern edition: first, through its stage directions that reflect visually reported Elizabethan stage business (see the examples noted earlier, p. 230); and second, through the number of single readings (usually corroborated by F 1) through which it corrects the authoritative Q 2 text. This second debt to a 'bad' quarto (the textual situation in *Romeo and Juliet* offers an exactly parallel case) is one of the ironies that confront an editor. Given an edition like *Hamlet* Q 2, printed from Shakespeare's own manuscript, one might suppose that the text would be relatively free from error. But it is apparent in this case (and in *Romeo and Juliet*) that Shakespeare's 'foul papers' were just exactly that – foul, and that the two compositors who set Q 2 had a difficult time deciphering Shakespeare's handwriting, frequently botching the job badly. Finally, to confound confusion another step, it is highly probable that the whole of the first act of Q 2 was printed, where possible, from a copy of Q 1 corrected by collation with Shakespeare's manuscript. The uncertainty of this sort of copy was illustrated in the discussion of *Richard III* and throws doubt on all readings for Act I shared by Q 2 and Q 1, while it increases the potential authority of F 1 variants for this act.

What then are the implications of the complicated textual picture just sketched? Perhaps the simplest answer is to record the distressing fact that a modern critical edition of *Hamlet* contains roughly 190 emended substantive readings, that is, readings which do not follow the basic Q 2 copy-text but have been adopted either from F 1 and Q 1 or from a long line of later editorial conjectures.

We must turn now from the manuscript sources of Shakespeare's text and the various influences that shaped those sources to some consideration of what happened to the manuscript of a play in the printing house and how printing-house practices may have influenced the reliability of the printed text. Concentrated interest in this matter is comparatively recent and was given its first significant statement in E. E. Willoughby's *The Printing of the First Folio of Shakespeare* (1932). Later studies, particularly Charlton Hinman's magisterial two volumes, *The Printing and Proof-Reading of the First Folio of Shakespeare* (1963), and Alice Walker's *Textual Problems of the First Folio* (1953), have greatly extended and corrected Willoughby's pioneer work.

The various and intricate techniques of printing-house practice in the sixteenth and seventeenth centuries cannot be dealt with here. For this sort of information the student should consult R. B. McKerrow's

Introduction to Bibliography for Literary Students (1927) and the new edition (edited by Herbert Davis and Harry Carter, 1958) of Moxon's *Mechanick Exercises* (1683). Nevertheless, certain aspects of the printing process that may have affected the accuracy and completeness of the text may be briefly discussed.

(1) *The compositor.* Being human, compositors were liable to error, some more liable than others. Such seems to have been the case, for example, with Compositors A (less) and B (more), the two principal compositors for F1. Moreover, a compositor might be an inexperienced apprentice and hence tend to multiply mistakes (as Compositor E in F1). Since dramatic manuscripts were generally very sporadically and lightly punctuated (the 147 lines of the *More* scene attributed to Shakespeare contain only two or three examples of line-end punctuation and some 35 of internal punctuation), the task of 'pointing' the text seems in great part to have been the responsibility of the compositor. This was a large responsibility and, again varying with the expertness and literary sense of the compositor, often led to misunderstandings of an author's meaning. Despite the dangers, however, it should always be remembered that the pointing in the early printed editions was done by men who had a contemporary feeling for the spoken relation of words and the rhythm and emphasis of Elizabethan English, and editors who, like those of the eighteenth and nineteenth centuries, tamper with it unnecessarily do so at their peril and with unfortunate strait-jacketing of the idiomatic turn and run of the dialogue.

Spelling was also in the hands of the compositor. Unlike modern prescriptive spelling, Elizabethan spelling was a highly idiosyncratic affair and Shakespeare's was no exception. The *More* scene evidences a handful of unusual spellings, a number of which appear in other plays believed to have been set from Shakespeare's autograph. It also shows how inconsistent a writer could be: *sheriff* (in the form *shrieve*) is spelled five different ways within five lines and *More* three within a single line. Generally, compositors (and scribes) tended to 'normalize' an author's spelling by imposing on it their own spelling habits or the general forms favoured by the establishment for which they worked, but, even so, many authorial spellings escaped into print and can be a helpful guide in determining what kind of manuscript underlies a printed text.

In recent years, work has been done on what is called compositor determination with a view to establishing, so far as possible, the special characteristics and relative reliability of certain compositors, notably those concerned with the printing of F1. A compositor's characteristic spelling preferences have formed the basis for much of this investigation, an approach first suggested by Thomas Satchell in 1929, when he distinguished what he called the work of Compositors A and B in the F1 text of *Macbeth*. Since that time, the investigation has been greatly extended by Alice Walker and Charlton Hinman, the latter refining the technique by proving for F1 that, through the identification of 'distinctive types' (i.e. pieces of type characteristically enough damaged to be individually identified), a particular case of type could regularly be associated with a particular compositor. Further, where a control exists, an earlier printed text, for example, from which it can be shown a compositor is working – as in those plays in F1 printed from quarto copy – it is possible to gain a general impression of the probable accuracy, faithfulness to copy, and dependability of the compositor. Theoretically, the knowledge gained from this kind of study places an editor in the position of being able to say that certain portions of a text were set by a compositor liable to eyeskip, carelessness, etc., and that therefore one may expect to find such weaknesses in his work and feel freer to emend what appear to be unsatisfactory passages. In practice, however, the whole approach is fraught with evident dangers and even in expert hands tends to produce editions which seriously threaten whatever stability Shakespeare's text may lay claim to.

(2) *Press correction.* It is often said, with probable truth, that no two extant copies of F1 are textually exactly alike. Behind this statement lies the fact of what is called press correction. In printing off either side of a sheet (outer or inner forme), it was the general practice to send the first sheet printed off to the press-corrector (or an equivalent functionary), who marked whatever errors in the typesetting caught his eye. While he was thus engaged, printing continued and a number of sides of the sheet (inner or outer) were printed off in what is called the uncorrected state. When the corrected proof was returned to the press worker, the type was removed from the press, corrected, returned to the press, and printing resumed. Sometimes such an interruption might happen two, or even more, times in the printing off of either side of the sheet, further errors being spotted in the course of the run. The sheets printed from the uncorrected type were not discarded. In this way, an Elizabethan book is usually made up of a mixture of corrected and uncorrected sheets, and until as many copies as is reasonably possible have been minutely compared – a process now made quicker and more accurate by the Hinman collator – an editor cannot be sure that he has not missed significant corrected states of the text. It is equally important to be able to examine the uncorrected states, since, first, the press corrector seems usually to have 'corrected'

without consulting the printer's copy and his 'corrections' are often little better than guesses, which can themselves be corrected by an examination of the uncorrected state, and second, the compositor making the indicated changes was liable to fresh error in the process of supposed correction.

(3) *Cancels*. A cancel leaf (or leaves) is called for when textual changes are necessary in a part of a book already printed off. Since the type will in most cases have been redistributed, both sides of the leaf (recto and verso) will have to be completely reset, the resulting leaf (or leaves) being substituted for the original setting when the sheets are assembled to form the book. Occasionally copies of the volume can be discovered that preserve either the original setting or both the original and the reset leaves. The detection of a cancel (the *cancellans*) and where possible the retrieval of the original setting of the leaf (the *cancellandum*) are obviously matters of importance for the establishment of a text, particularly where the textual changes involved may have been authorial or dictated by political or religious censorship.

(4) *Casting-off copy*. The potential importance to the completeness and accuracy of a text of what is called the process of casting- (counting-) off copy has only recently begun to be realized. Simply put, to cast-off copy means to estimate how much of a manuscript text may be fitted into a page of the chosen printed format and then to divide up the copy into clearly marked sections. Charlton Hinman has shown, for example, that casting-off was used extensively throughout F 1, and it is becoming clear that the process was employed also in the setting of some of the quartos. A saving in time (i.e. the possibility of simultaneous composition by two, or more, compositors and the concurrent use of more than one press) and in type (i.e. the freeing of type for earlier redistribution and re-use, particularly in the printing of folios) is the rationale behind the use of this technique, but it had its special dangers. If the casting-off process had been carelessly performed, a compositor might well find himself with either too much or too little copy and nowhere to go, since the following (or preceding) page had already been printed off. He may thus have to stretch his material by heavier 'leading' – and here no great harm results except aesthetically – or he may have to compress by crowding or printing verse as prose. Worse, he may be forced to omit words or lines. In instances where the use of cast-off copy can be supported by bibliographical evidence, an editor can now at least sometimes explain why there seems to be some dislocation in the text, even though he can rarely do anything to remedy the fault.

Our discussion so far has mainly concerned itself with approaches to Shakespeare's text developed during the last sixty years. But much work by generations of textual scholars lies behind these approaches and, in fact, made them possible. The eighteenth century brought the beginning of a significant split between what may be termed 'the theatre' and 'the study'. Shakespeare became increasingly a 'classic' and was accorded all the learned attention formerly lavished only on Greek and Latin authors. Editor after editor, beginning with Nicholas Rowe, in 1709, on through Alexander Pope (1723–4), Lewis Theobald (1733), Thomas Hanmer (1744), William Warburton (1747), Samuel Johnson (1765), Edward Capell (1768), George Steevens (1778) and Edmond Malone (1790), expended endless hours and untold pains in seeking to establish what they believed was the 'true text'. Each in his way made his contribution, particularly Theobald, Capell, and Malone, but they were relatively hampered by the lack of any clear conception of the kinds of problems outlined earlier in this study and depended largely on ingenuity in emendation and the exercise of contemporary 'taste' in grammar and language to solve what seemed to them the problems of the text. Among them Capell stands apart, and has, with good cause, been called the first 'modern'. In his crabbed way (his contemporaries insisted, not without reason, that he could not write English), he sorted out the relative authority of the early texts, particularly the quartos, and laid the foundation of the principle of copy-text. He also published the first extensive textual apparatus, recording the readings of all the early editions and his editorial predecessors. By such fundamental work he struck a blow against the widely eclectic approach of earlier editors and pointed the way towards the textual approaches of the twentieth century. Unfortunately, his edition was derided by his two principal successors, Steevens and Malone, who silently pillaged his text and notes, and largely ignored the significant implications of his textual approach.

The nineteenth century, though it produced a large number of new editions by men of distinguished reputations as Shakespearian scholars (Charles Knight, J. Payne Collier, Grant White, Halliwell-Phillipps, Alexander Dyce), did little to advance any understanding of basic textual problems and continued the tradition of eclecticism little changed from pre-Capell times. The culmination of the tradition was the impressive and vastly influential Cambridge *Shakespeare*, edited by W. G. Clark and W. A. Wright (1863–6) and revised by Wright in 1892–3, a text on which the famous 'Globe' (1864) one-volume edition was based. Here, for the first time since Capell, the student was afforded a full textual apparatus. It was a remarkable work and crystallized the editorial labours of a hundred and fifty years. Out of it grew the monumental American *New Variorum*, begun under the tire-less hand of H. H. Furness in 1871 (with *Romeo and Juliet*) and still, with ten plays to go, in the process of completion.

The present century has seen the advent of what is called the 'new bibliography'. Under the aegis of pioneers like R. B. McKerrow, W. W. Greg, A. W. Pollard, and J. Dover Wilson the approaches out-lined in the first part of this essay were laid down and their work has been carried on and refined by many later textual critics, notably Peter Alexander, Fredson Bowers, Charlton Hinman, Charles Sisson, and Alice Walker. Out of this ferment has come the most challenging edition of Shakespeare yet published – the New Cambridge Shake-speare (1921–66) under the editorship primarily of Dover Wilson. Full of energy and new ideas (many later jettisoned by Wilson himself) it aroused a new and lively interest in Shakespeare, even when the interest was generated by healthy and productive disagreement, and has inspired other important new attacks on the problems of the text: the editions by G. L. Kittredge (1936), Peter Alexander (1952), C. J. Sisson (1954), and John Munro (1958), as well as the individually edited volumes of the New Arden (1951–), and the collected Pelican *Shakespeare* (1969, general editor, Alfred Harbage). Each of these editions not only has contributed to a better critical understanding of Shakespeare but has served to bring us one step nearer to what we wistfully dream of as his 'true text'.

17

SHAKESPEARE CRITICISM: DRYDEN TO BRADLEY

M. A. SHAABER

The first critic of Shakespeare is Dryden. Earlier comment on the plays and their author, abundant enough, is as a rule simply admiring or anecdotal. It is true that Jonson, in differentiating Shakespeare's natural gifts from his art, and Milton, in making by implication the same distinction, defined an issue over which critical battle was to be joined by future generations. In the poem he wrote for the First Folio Jonson praised both the natural gifts and the art; in his gossip with Drummond and in his note-book, however, he found that Shakespeare 'wanted art'. 'But he redeemed his vices, with his virtues. There was ever more in him to be praised than to be pardoned.' The latter opinion is also Dryden's and that of many of his successors.

The vices that Dryden found in Shakespeare were chiefly faults of expression. 'He is many times flat, insipid; his Comick Wit degenerating into Clenches, his serious Swelling into Bombast' (*Of Dramatic Poesy*). Dryden's aversion to Shakespeare's comic wit remained insuperable: the wit of the Elizabethan age 'was not that of Gentlemen, there was ever somewhat that was ill-bred and Clownish in it' (*An Essay on the Dramatic Poetry of the Last Age*), distasteful to the more refined times in which he lived. His attitude towards Shakespeare's bombast is somewhat ambivalent. 'I will not say of so great a Poet, that he distinguish'd not the blown puffy stile, from true sublimity; but I may venture to maintain that the fury of his fancy often transported him, beyond the bounds of Judgment, either in coyning of new words and phrases, or racking words which were in use, into the violence of a Catachresis: ... to say nothing without a Metaphor, a Simile, an Image, or description, is I doubt to smell a little too strongly of the Buskin' (preface to *Troilus and Cressida*). Yet in *The Author's Apology* to *The State of Innocence* (1677), without specific reference to Shakespeare, he denies that 'the flights of Heroick Poetry ... [are] bombast, unnatural, and meer madness', and affirms that 'the boldest strokes of Poetry, when they are manag'd Artfully, are those which most delight the Reader'. Two other shortcomings upon

239

which Dryden insists much less frequently also became parts of the usual eighteenth-century view of Shakespeare. One of them is 'lameness' of plot, a fault which he imputes to all the Elizabethan playwrights, and by which he perhaps means chiefly plots violating the unities, for he stigmatizes such a plot as 'some ridiculous, incoherent story, which, in one Play many times took up the business of an Age' (*An Essay on the Dramatic Poetry of the Last Age*). The other is violations of 'the decorum of the stage'. It is possible partly to discount these strictures since they all occur in essays and prefaces whose overriding purpose was to justify Dryden's own plays and those of his contemporaries to (among others) *laudatores temporis acti*. Moreover Dryden himself discounted them by putting some of the blame for Shakespeare's defects on the barbarity of the age in which he lived. On balance, however, he always comes down on the side of Shakespeare, as in *Of Dramatic Poesy*:

he was the Man who of all Modern, and perhaps Ancient Poets, had the largest and most comprehensive soul. All the Images of Nature were still present to him, and he drew them not laboriously, but luckily: when he describes any thing, you more than see it, you feel it too. Those who accuse him to have wanted learning, give him the greater commendation: he was naturally learn'd; he needed not the Spectacles of Books to read Nature; he look'd inwards, and found her there... But he is always great, when some great occasion is presented to him; no Man can say he ever had a fit subject for his wit, and did not then raise himself as high above the rest of Poets,

Quantum lenta solent inter Viburna Cupressi.

The eighteenth century adopted and cherished this picture of Shakespeare as an untutored genius who lived in a rude society and wrote for mean and undiscriminating audiences, who, though he committed many faults through ignorance of what Pope called 'the rules of writing', by his extraordinary natural gifts excelled all other poets or equalled the best of them. 'The Poetry of *Shakespear* was Inspiration indeed,' said Pope: 'he is not so much an Imitator, as an Instrument, of Nature; and 'tis not so just to say that he speaks from her, as that she speaks thro' him.' Pope enumerates Shakespeare's excellences as follows:

His *Characters* are so much Nature her self, that 'tis a sort of injury to call them by so distant a name as Copies of her...
The *Power* over our *Passions* was never possess'd in a more eminent degree, or display'd in so different instances...
Nor does he only excell in the Passions: In the coolness of Reflection and Reasoning he is full as admirable.

The palinode duly follows:

It must be own'd that with all these great excellencies, he has almost as great defects; and that as he has certainly written better, so he has perhaps written worse than any other.

But the disparity between the pleasure which the plays gave readers and theatregoers and the displeasure expressed by critics of the rigid sect sometimes led admirers of Shakespeare to question the fundamental assumptions of the latter. Dryden, Addison, Pope, and Johnson all depreciated the importance of observing the unities. The strict notions of decorum applied to the plays by Rymer and Voltaire were often shrugged off. Rymer (*A Short View of Tragedy*, 1693) objected to the character given Iago because it does not conform to the type of soldier fixed by Horace; to Voltaire 'Not a mouse stirring' was too mean for tragedy. Few English critics felt that Shakespeare must be held to such strict standards. Even Shakespeare's learning was upgraded as close readers discovered evidence or presumed evidence of some acquaintance with the classics. Sometimes the critics' bark is worse than their bite. In *The Adventurer* of 25 September 1753 Joseph Warton begins the first of two essays on *The Tempest* with an echo of Pope: 'he exhibits more numerous examples of excellencies and faults, of every kind, than are, perhaps, to be discovered in any other author'; then he summarizes briefly both the faults and the excellencies. But in his discussion of the play it is only the excellencies that he expatiates on. In a subsequent series on *King Lear* (4, 15 December 1753, 5 January 1754) the faults appear only in the final paragraph.

If Shakespeare's plays were blemished by faults of expression, the faulty passages might be expunged and what was left read with greater pleasure. In his edition Pope excised lines and passages so displeasing to him that he thought Shakespeare could never have written them and he also put inverted commas at the beginning of lines and series of lines that he found specially admirable. The plays came to be admired for their beauties rather than as wholes. Charles Gildon's *Remarks on the Plays of Shakespeare* (added to the seventh volume of Rowe's 1709 edition) consist largely of lists of the most praiseworthy episodes and passages. Regarding the plays as puddings from which plums may be pulled colours much subsequent criticism, even as late as that of Hazlitt. A little later, in *The Complete Art of Poetry* (1718), Gildon published the first anthology of 'Shakespeare's Beauties'. Many more followed. The most durable, William Dodd's *Beauties of Shakespear* (1752), was still in print one hundred and fifty years later.

The prevailing attitude is summed up most memorably – and very nearly for the last time – in Dr Johnson's preface to his edition of the plays (1765). Its comprehensive scope, its magisterial style, and its judicial temper make it not only the most considerable criticism so far written but also the best. Johnson praises Shakespeare as 'the poet of nature',

the poet that holds up to his readers a faithful mirror of manners and of life. His characters are not modified by the customs of particular places, unpractised by the rest of the world; by the peculiarities of studies or professions, which can operate but upon small numbers; or by the accidents of transient fashions or temporary opinions; they are the genuine progeny of common humanity, such as the world will always supply, and observation will always find...In the writings of other poets a character is too often an individual; in those of Shakespeare it is commonly a species.

He also praises Shakespeare as the founder of English drama and commends his differentiation of his characters, his power of expressing the passions, his mastery of a style 'above grossness and below refinement' which is 'more agreeable to the ears of the present age than any other author equally remote'. He defends Shakespeare against some of the charges usually lodged against him. He finds that 'the unities of time and place are not essential to a just drama'. He justifies the mixture of the serious and the comic: '*Shakespeare*'s plays are not in the rigorous and critical sense either tragedies or comedies, but compositions of a distinct kind; exhibiting the real state of sublunary nature, which partakes of good and evil, joy and sorrow, mingled with endless variety of proportion and innumerable modes of combination.' The indecorum imputed to Shakespeare's characters he brushes aside. He even relents so far as to admit that 'The mind, which has feasted on the luxurious wonders of fiction, has no taste of the insipidity of truth' and thus to ascribe the extravagance he finds in the plays to the immaturity of Shakespeare's audiences.

At the same time he specifies a number of faults. Shakespeare's plots are often 'loosely formed' and his fifth acts carelessly huddled up. Anachronisms abound. He is deplorably prone to quibbling and playing on words. His comic wit is too often gross and licentious, his tragic speeches strained, his narrative passages inflated. He is too often content with something less than his best: when his plays 'would satisfy the audience, they satisfied the writer'. Johnson is uncomfortable about Shakespeare's failures to satisfy poetic justice: the destruction of Claudius, a usurper and a murderer, affords him 'gratification', but the death of innocents like Ophelia and Cordelia pains him. His chief charge against Shakespeare is his lack of moral purpose: 'He sacrifices virtue to convenience, and is so much more careful to please than to instruct, that he seems to write without any moral purpose.'

Johnson's judicial posture may seem at times to give the preface a too-lofty tone, but his praise is always splendid.

This therefore is the praise of *Shakespeare*, that his drama is the mirror of life; that he who has mazed his imagination, in following the phantoms which other writers raise up before him, may here be cured of his delirious extasies, by reading human sentiments in human language; by scenes from which a hermit may estimate the transactions of the world, and a confessor predict the progress of the passions.

But when Johnson wrote his preface the winds of romanticism had already begun to stir. It was only a few years later that Lessing rejected French classical tragedy and exalted Shakespeare above Corneille and Voltaire (*Hamburgische Dramaturgie*, 1769). The continental revolters against neo-classical rigidity often held up Shakespeare as its antithesis. In 1796 Goethe, in *Wilhelm Meister*, gave the world the delicate and impotent Hamlet. In a letter of 14 April 1818 Stendhal wrote: 'I am a mad romantic, that is to say I am for Shakespeare against Racine.'

In England, while the full-blown romantic idea of Shakespeare hardly appears before Coleridge, there are signs of altered emphases in the latter part of the eighteenth century. It has even been argued that Dr Johnson's 'sense of the inseparability of a man and his work makes him the first of our Romantic critics' (H. V. D. Dyson and John Butt, *Augustans and Romantics*, 1940, p. 67). In 1774 William Richardson published *A Philosophical Analysis of some of Shakespeare's Remarkable Characters*, an early example of the growing interest in Shakespeare's characters as the aspect of his plays in which his excellence is most evident. Richardson was a moral philosopher rather than a literary critic and he deduces from the characters 'the principles of human conduct'. In his *Essay on the Dramatic Character of Sir John Falstaff* (1777) Maurice Morgann anticipates the romantic attitude towards Shakespeare at several points. His ostensible purpose is to vindicate Falstaff's courage. He enjoyed Falstaff, and therefore admired him, and therefore disliked hearing him derided as a coward. To prove that Falstaff is not a constitutional coward he transcends the evidence of the text of the play and appeals to 'secret Impressions' which Shakespeare contrives to make upon us and which endow Falstaff with a real character different from his apparent one – the courageous, dignified, honoured character of Morgann's imagination. His reasoning is of course specious and the impressions upon which he builds up a more respectable character for Falstaff sometimes naive (e.g. because he invites Master Gower to dinner and to supper, Falstaff must have kept a regular table). But Morgann also describes Shakespeare's art as 'exquisite', not irregular or defective; he thinks that 'True Poesy is *magic*, not *nature*; an effect from causes hidden or unknown', and that all dramatic truth consists in the impressions made on the feelings of readers rather than in what the understanding derives from the external action. Shakespeare, he finds, infuses 'his own spirit' into his characters and must 'have spoken thro' the organ he had formed'. Clearly Morgann is breaking away from the attitude of his predecessors. When he says, 'If the characters of *Shakespeare* are thus *whole*, and as it were original,...it may be fit to consider them rather as Historic than Dramatic beings; and, when occasion requires, to account for their conduct from the *whole* of character, from general principles, from latent motives, and from policies not avowed', he opens a Pandora's box. In 1794 Walter Whiter published a pioneering study of Shakespeare's imagery (*A Specimen of a Commentary on Shakspeare*), an aspect of the plays to which criticism had paid little attention and, in spite of Whiter's example, was to continue paying little attention until the twentieth century.

Whether August Wilhelm Schlegel in Vienna or Samuel Taylor Coleridge in London created the Shakespeare of the romantics is matter for dispute, of unimportant dispute despite the fact that Coleridge resented the charge that he derived his ideas from Schlegel. Schlegel's celebrated course of lectures *Über dramatische Kunst und Literatur* and Coleridge's first course of lectures were delivered in the same year, 1808. Schlegel, however, had anticipated some of his ideas about Shakespeare in essays published twelve years earlier; of Coleridge's first series there is little record, though it is unlikely that he then expressed ideas different from those expounded in later series. For the most part Schlegel and Coleridge agree. Schlegel's lectures on Shakespeare form part of a much broader discussion of dramatic art in which he tosses the debate over neo-classical and romantic standards out of the window by assuming essential differences between ancient and modern poetry which make comparisons idle. Shakespeare is 'a profound artist, and not a blind and wildly luxuriant genius'. Shakespeare's plays are romantic works of art: 'In all Art and Poetry, but most especially in the romantic, the Fancy lays claim to be considered as an independent mental power governed according to its own laws'; from the great plays 'nothing could be taken away, nothing added, nothing otherwise arranged, without mutilating and disfiguring the perfect work'. 'Never perhaps was there so comprehensive a talent for characterization as Shakespeare.' He has 'the capability of transporting himself so completely into every situation...that he is enabled ...to act and speak in the name of every individual'. Shakespeare 'gives us the history of minds'. 'In strength a demigod, in profundity of view a prophet, in all-seeing wisdom a guardian spirit of a higher order, he lowers himself to mortals as if unconscious of his superiority, and is as open and unassuming as a child.'

Coleridge's writings on Shakespeare are mostly desultory and unsystematic: a chapter of the *Biographia Literaria* (1817), scraps of lecture notes, reports, of various degrees of completeness and accuracy, of eight courses of lectures (as a rule not wholly devoted to Shakespeare), marginalia, and *obiter dicta* written down by friends. They are nevertheless seminal and most subsequent criticism derives from them. Coleridge demands reverence for Shakespeare: criticism 'will be genial in proportion as the criticism is reverential' (ed. Raysor, 1960, i, 113). He scorns the idea of the untutored genius: 'does God choose idiots to convey divine truths by?' (i, 202). 'The judgement of Shakespeare is commensurate with his genius' (i, 114); his was 'a most profound, energetic, and philosophical mind' (i, 189). The form of his plays is not determined by mechanical rules; each one has organic form determined by its own nature. Shakespeare's greatest excellence is his portrayal of character; 'The plot interests us on account of the characters, not *vice versa*' (i, 199). 'Shakespeare's characters are like those in life, to be *inferred* by the reader, not *told to him*' (i, 201). Shakespeare projects himself into his characters: 'he had only to imitate certain parts of his own character, or to exaggerate such as existed in possibility, and they were at once true to nature, and fragments of the divine mind that drew them' (ii, 85); he 'darts himself forth, and passes into all the forms of human character and passion' (*Biographia Literaria* xv). As the products of Shakespeare's meditation, the characters are ideal (ii, 123), as is poetry itself, which results from 'the effort of perfecting ourselves' (ii, 53). At the same time Shakespeare keeps 'at all times the high road of life' (ii, 216). Since Coleridge believed in 'the close and reciprocal connections of just taste with pure morality' (i, 226), he vindicates Shakespeare's moral purity along with his taste. Coleridge's discussions of particular plays are, with a few notable exceptions, too fragmentary to carry much weight; his achievement was to define new canons of criticism, a new perspective which his successors enthusiastically adopted. He deployed and passed on a new critical vocabulary with key words such as 'divine', 'sublime', 'philosophical', 'intellectual'.

Many of the contemporaries of Coleridge engaged themselves with Shakespeare. Hazlitt's *Characters of Shakespear's Plays* (1817) is, as Francis Jeffrey said of it, an encomium rather than a critique. Hazlitt preferred Schlegel's version of Shakespeare to Dr Johnson's, which he found wanting in sensibility and ardour of response. But, except when he disputes some of Johnson's pronouncements, he is little given to generalization; he deals with particulars – plays, scenes, characters, speeches – without much attempt to erect his responses into critical principles. The responses are as a rule warmly sympathetic. That inveterate theatregoer Charles Lamb wrote a few descriptions of favourite actors in Shakespearian roles which interpret the roles. De Quincey wrote a fine criticism *On the Knocking at the Gate in Macbeth*. Shakespeare is the topic in a number of the *Imaginary Conversations* of Landor, who thought that 'a rib of Shakspeare would have made a Milton: the same portion of Milton, all poets born ever since' ('Southey and Landor'). Keats records a few shrewd insights in his letters, including his imputation to Shakespeare of 'negative capability' – 'when man is capable of being in uncertainties, Mysteries, doubts, without any irritable reaching after fact and reason...with a great poet the sense of Beauty overcomes every other consideration, or rather obliterates all consideration' (21 December 1817) – a phrase which has become a shibboleth of recent criticism.

The romantic critics usually divorce Shakespeare from the theatre or ignore the fact that he wrote plays. Charles Lamb (*On the Tragedies of Shakespeare*, 1811) pronounced the tragedies impossible to realize at their full potential on the stage; to be sure, the performances he saw and was dissatisfied with were not of Shakespeare's plays but of Tate's, Cibber's, and Garrick's denatured versions. Goethe thought that 'Shakespeare's whole method finds in the stage itself something unwieldy and hostile' (*Schäkspear und kein Ende*, 1815). Carlyle laments: 'Alas, Shakspeare had to write for the Globe Playhouse: his great soul had to crush itself, as it could, into that and no other mould' (*On Heroes, Hero-worship, and the Heroic in History*, 1841).

On one point the romantic critics divided – the presence of Shakespeare himself in his works. To Coleridge 'Shakespeare's poetry is characterless; that is, it does not reflect the individual Shakespeare' (*Table Talk*, 12 May 1830). To Schlegel it does. On the whole, Schlegel's opinion has prevailed over Coleridge's; at any rate, the subsequent attempts to infer Shakespeare's interests and opinions, to align him with this or that cause or philosophy, are countless. Edward Dowden, whose *Shakspere: a Critical Study of his Mind and Art* (1875) exerted a pervasive influence for a quarter century or more, saw the plays as explorations of moral problems that oppressed Shakespeare in his private life. To 'have built up his own moral nature, and have fortified himself for the conduct of life, was...to Shakspere the chief outcome of his toil'. Shakespeare was subject to two temptations to excess – 'the Romeo form and the Hamlet form – abandonment to passion, abandonment to brooding thought' – and his plays record his gradual attainment of equilibrium. In a 'primer' published in 1877 Dowden divided Shakespeare's career into four periods which he labelled, a little apologetically, 'In the workshop', 'In the world', 'Out of the depths', 'On the heights'.

Thus the nineteenth century invented the oracular Shakespeare, a demiurge who created characters embodying the deepest insights into human nature and speaking lines impregnated with sublime wisdom. For the most part, his artistry is taken for granted or examined only when it can be used to support the picture of him as a seer; whatever does not easily fit this view, like his bawdry, is ignored. Shakespeare is the Poet (the capital letter is almost invariable) rather than the playwright, and the Poet includes the Philosopher. The weakness of nineteenth-century criticism, if it is agreed that Shakespeare *is* a supreme oracle, is its tendency to turn its back on the text in order to write philosophical and moralistic speculation in the margins.

The writings of A. C. Bradley are among the last and the best of the romantic school of critics. They are of limited scope: a book on *Shakespearean Tragedy* (1904), which discusses *Hamlet*, *Othello*, *Macbeth*, and *King Lear*, essays on 'The Rejection of Falstaff' (1902) and *Antony and Cleopatra* (1906), and a lecture on *Coriolanus* (1912). Bradley's prestige nevertheless has been very great and is deserved. The book is highly intelligent, conscientious, and suavely written. After an opening chapter on Shakespearian tragedy in which Bradley pursues that will o' the wisp, a concept of tragedy that will fit all of Shakespeare's tragedies, and a chapter on the structure of the plays, he proceeds to an examination of his four tragedies, or rather of their leading characters. He assumes that everything in a play is explicable, that Shakespeare knew all the answers, and that we can discover them too if we apply our minds with sufficient discernment and sympathy. He assumes that Shakespeare would allow no part to inconsistency or chance or unreason in the scheme of a play and labours to eliminate them wherever he finds them. When Shakespeare offers insufficient explanation Bradley supplies what is wanting. The result is a psychological analysis of each character which fully accounts for his behaviour and vindicates the consistency and completeness of the presentation. In doing so, Bradley often comes perilously close to treating the characters as real people. In doing so, he sometimes, like Morgann, trusts his own impressions rather than the statements of the text (e.g. though Kent says he is forty-eight years old, 'we get the impression' that he is over sixty). In doing so, he often ignores aspects of the plays that other schools of critics make great play with. Of its kind there is nothing better than Bradley's criticism, but like all his predecessors and all his successors, he is prone to picturing Shakespeare in his own image.

The triumph of nineteenth-century criticism was the canonization of Shakespeare. Earlier objections to his violation of the rules of writing were nullified by explaining away the violations or cancelling the rules. The improbability and looseness of some of his plays and scenes were reconciled with romantic taste. Even the most stubborn objection of all, the exuberance of his style, his propensity for torturing the language out of 'an irritability of fancy', as Matthew Arnold, a firm objector, put it, was submerged in the concentration on Shakespeare's philosophy and morality. The nineteenth century passed on to the twentieth a Shakespeare securely placed on his towering pinnacle.

18

SHAKESPEARE CRITICISM
SINCE BRADLEY

STANLEY WELLS

A. C. Bradley's *Shakespearean Tragedy*, published in 1904, serves as
a convenient landmark by virtue of its date as well as its stature. It
comes almost at the beginning of a century that has seen an astonishing
growth of professionalism in Shakespeare studies. Bradley is characteristic of an earlier period in that his training was not primarily in
English literature. But he anticipates the shape of things to come in
that his great book was published when he was a Professor of English,
and is a development of lectures he gave in that capacity. In some ways
he was himself anticipated by Edward Dowden, whose *Shakspere:
His Mind and Art* appeared in 1875 and is still in print. But before
Dowden the great names in Shakespeare criticism are not those of
professional teachers of literature. Dryden, Pope, Johnson, Morgann,
Hazlitt, Coleridge: most of them are primarily men of letters, only
secondarily teachers and lecturers. They are in the highest sense
amateurs, writing on Shakespeare because his plays are at the forefront
of their minds and there is something they feel impelled to say about
him. Such an attitude is not extinct, nor can it be wholly isolated from
that of the professional academic. Robert Bridges, John Masefield,
T. S. Eliot, P. Wyndham Lewis, Harley Granville-Barker, and
W. H. Auden are among the creative writers of this century who have
written stimulatingly about Shakespeare; and of some academics
(G. Wilson Knight is only one example) we feel that this is what they
would have been doing even had it not been part of their professional
duty.

Nevertheless, by far the larger part of the mass of Shakespeare
criticism produced since Bradley's time has been academic, some of it
obviously originating in the lecture room, and some of it still more
restricted in appeal, being published in learned journals that are read
only by a limited number of specialists. This situation is partly the
result of a great swing in the bias of literary education which occurred
during Bradley's lifetime, and of which his own career is a result. The
literature on which he was educated was classical literature. When he

went to Liverpool, where he was the first Professor of English, he thought seriously of applying for the Chair of Philosophy and Political Economy. G. K. Hunter has written of the image of *Shakespearean Tragedy* 'as an Establishment synthesis, making possible the absorption of Shakespeare into the higher educational system, long dominated by the Greats syllabus of Classics and Philosophy'. The absorption has been complete; Shakespeare's plays are now regarded as the foundation of a literary education.

When Bradley's book appeared, only one periodical devoted itself to Shakespeare. It was, significantly, the *Shakespeare-Jahrbuch*, published by the Deutsche Shakespeare Gesellschaft. The systematic study of Shakespeare appeared earlier in Germany than anywhere else, and there it was closely linked with the structure of the higher-educational system. Now the *Jahrbuch* has doubled itself (partly, it is true, for political rather than academic reasons), *Shakespeare Survey* has appeared annually since 1948, the American *Shakespeare Quarterly* has flourished for almost as long, and *Shakespeare Studies* made the first of its annual appearances in 1965. Many other periodicals concern themselves at least partly with Shakespeare. Some of the criticism that appears in the periodicals represents work in progress and later appears as part of more substantial studies in book-form. Other essays receive a wider circulation in the critical anthologies that help non-specialist readers with their problem of choice. If the remainder of this chapter shows little concern with articles in the journals, it is not from any feeling that important work appears only in book-form. More respect may be felt for the man who writes economically to a given point than for one who inflates a comparatively minor insight into excessive proportions. A critic may have something to say on *As You Like It* without wanting to write a book on all Shakespeare's comedies. Thus, to give only one example, Harold Jenkins's essay on that play, which first appeared in *Shakespeare Survey 8*, is acknowledged as one of the best to have been written; and there are other outstanding essays by critics who have not attempted longer studies.

Bradley has been important both as a critic to be agreed with and as one to be reacted against. It is because of influence provoked by disagreement that he may be held responsible for part of the emphasis given in scholarly journals and elsewhere to writing that attempts to interpret a Shakespeare play by reference to historical factors. Two critics who were early to express disagreement with Bradley's method were E. E. Stoll and L. L. Schücking, both of whom insisted on the need to see Shakespeare in the context of the life and literature of his age, and opposed themselves against what they regarded as the subjectivism of their colleagues. Schücking's *Character Problems in Shake-*

speare's Plays was first published in German in 1917, and was translated into English in 1922. He does not hesitate to find fault with Shakespeare's art, and in this respect he was reacting against a bardolatrous attitude not uncommon in Romantic and Victorian times. Two famous authors, one English and one Russian, had already given notable vent to adverse criticism. Robert Bridges, in his brief but trenchant essay 'On the Influence of the Audience', published in the tenth volume (1907) of the Shakespeare Head Press edition, had been concerned almost entirely to define in Shakespeare's works 'the matters that most offended my simple feelings', and he alighted especially on what he regarded as bad jokes and obscenities, as brutalities, and as the too easy forgiveness of 'offences of the first rank' such as Angelo's in *Measure for Measure*. He anticipates Stoll and Schücking especially in his accusation that Shakespeare produced his effects by deliberately pandering to the supposed stupidity and 'moral bluntness' of Elizabethan audiences, in the process deliberately blurring motives and sacrificing logic and consistency in order merely to surprise. Tolstoy's extraordinary diatribe, *Shakespeare and the Drama*, which appeared in 1906, is so extreme in expression, and so indicative of a failure to comprehend the nature of any kind of poetic drama, that it is more likely to have had an emotional appeal to those who shared his prejudices (it first appeared along with an article called 'Shakespeare and the Working Classes', to which it had been intended as a Preface, and was published by the Free Age Press) than a rational one to those who were seeking the truth. But salvoes such as these, coming from creative writers, must have done something to breach a gap for more academic studies that also took a somewhat sceptical view.

Schücking, in the book referred to, develops the thesis that Shakespeare's 'art-form is in fact a mixture of the most highly developed with quite primitive elements'. Like Bridges, he finds that Shakespeare neglects consistency and logic, and seeks the immediate effect at the expense of the overall design. Also like Bridges, he regards such characteristics as flaws in Shakespeare's art, and does not, as some later critics have done, attempt to justify them in terms of a higher appropriateness. He agrees in fact with Ben Jonson, that Shakespeare 'wanted art'. Adopting commonsense explanations where they are available, he tends to reduce everything to its lowest terms; but his book is a good corrective to over-subjective attitudes.

Schücking has much in common with E. E. Stoll, who began before him and went on to publish a much larger body of writing on Shakespeare over a period of many years. *'Othello': An Historical and Comparative Study* appeared in 1915, *'Hamlet': An Historical and Comparative Study* in 1919, *Shakespeare Studies* in 1927, *Art and Artifice in*

Shakespeare in 1933, *Shakespeare's Young Lovers* in 1935, and *Shake-speare and Other Masters* in 1940. Like Schücking's, Stoll's is a hard-headed, down-to-earth approach. He asserts the primacy of plot over characterization, and the importance of poetry: 'one's ear, not one's reason, is the best judge of Shakespeare's characters' he wrote in *Art and Artifice in Shakespeare*, reminding us of George Bernard Shaw's similar remarks in connection with *Othello*. In spite of this, he does not offer detailed examination of the verse. Also like Shaw, Stoll makes frequent analogies with music, discussing the ways in which the playwright, like the composer, plays upon and manipu-lates his audience's responses. He is much concerned with dramatic convention, and fails sometimes to consider that a convention may also express truth. Like Schücking he reacts against that kind of criti-cism that lays great emphasis on the dramatist's 'creation of character', as if the principal value of a play lay in the sense it gives us of individual character. Such a view has often been attributed to Bradley, and much subsequent criticism takes as its starting point the debate about character in which Bradley stands as spokesman for one side, Stoll and Schücking for the other. For a while, indeed, Bradley was in danger of becoming a whipping boy, just as Dowden's unfortunate simplification in his *Shakespeare Primer* of Shakespeare's development into periods to which he gave such labels as 'Out of the Depths' and 'On the Heights' has been too easily taken as representative of his critical achievement. Lytton Strachey, in his well-known essay, 'Shakespeare's Final Period' (1906), uttered a counterblast to Dowden, suggesting that boredom rather than a hard-earned serenity was responsible for the special characteristics of the late plays. Inevitably the 'realists' have themselves been reacted against, and later critics have even drawn on the evidence and techniques of Freudian and post-Freudian psychological research in their Shakespearian investigations, and in the process have rendered themselves as liable to the charge of importing private preoccupations into their reading of the plays as did earlier critics who employed less sophisticated methods. Freud himself wrote several papers on Shake-speare, but more influential has been *Hamlet and Oedipus* by Ernest Jones (the book of 1949 is the final development of ideas first published in 1910), who is more convincing on *Hamlet* itself than in his attempts to investigate Shakespeare's personality on the basis of the play.

Attention to Shakespeare's portrayal of character became unfashion-able with the increasing emphasis in the 1930s on verbal criticism, so that in 1938 H. B. Charlton, taking a reactionary stand-point, wrote in *Shakespearian Comedy*: 'the present trend of fashionable criticism appears to have little use even for drama. To our most modern coteries, drama is poetry or it is nothing; and by poetry they mean some sort of allegorical arabesque in which the images of Shakespeare's plays are far more important than their men and women.' In his attitude to character Charlton proclaimed himself a disciple of Bradley, and J. I. M. Stewart, in *Character and Motive in Shakespeare* (1949), attempted to reassert the view that 'Shakespeare understood the passions and described, or conveyed, their several and conjoined operations with certainty, subtlety and power'. Bridges, Schücking, and Stoll are the principal critics whose views he examines. He is more aware than they are of Shakespeare's complexity – partly perhaps because of some of the criticism that intervenes between the date of his book and the time when their views were first formulated – but goes too far the other way in some of his own interpretative comments. Later writers, too, have been willing to discuss certain characters, at least, in language resembling that used by Bradley. Actors, especially, need to think in terms of individual character, so it is understandable that Granville-Barker's *Prefaces* include sections on the principal characters in the play under discussion. John Palmer's writings on the comic and political characters have been popular, and John Bayley's chapter on *Othello* in *The Characters of Love* (1960) is a sophisticated example of the kind.

The tendency to study Shakespeare's plays in the context of the literature and thought of their time has had a considerable influence both on critics whose main concern is with Shakespeare, and on others who have concentrated rather on the background. The direct sources of the plays have been fruitfully studied in the introductory chapters of Geoffrey Bullough's *Narrative and Dramatic Sources of Shakespeare* (from 1957) and in Kenneth Muir's *Shakespeare's Sources* (vol. 1, 1957), and many critics have brought investigations of analogous material to bear on their explorations of Shakespeare's creative processes. W. W. Lawrence in *Shakespeare's Problem Comedies* (1931) approaches a particular group of plays by way of a study of the conventions of narrative writing, and to a lesser extent of social behaviour, that lie behind them. Even so valuable a specimen of this kind of study occasionally reveals some of the dangers of the method, perhaps the most serious being the assumption that Shakespeare can properly be judged by the supposed standards of his age.

Some writers have studied dramatic conventions, often making comparisons with Shakespeare's forebears and contemporaries. This has been one of the approaches employed by M. C. Bradbrook in a series of books more or less directly concerned with Shakespeare, of which two of the most influential have been *Themes and Conventions of Elizabethan Tragedy* (1935) and *Shakespeare and Elizabethan Poetry* (1951). Her work is valuable especially for the way in which it places

Shakespeare in the full intellectual, dramatic, and theatrical context of his time, showing an unusual awareness of the possible significance of such matters as the social environment, the physical conditions of the theatres, and the overall literary milieu. S. L. Bethell in *Shakespeare and the Popular Dramatic Tradition* (1949) suggestively examines Shakespeare's capacity to manipulate responses, showing how features of the plays that 'realist' critics regard as primitivist can just as well be seen as a sophisticated exploitation of various levels of the spectator's awareness. Alfred Harbage, in books such as *Shakespeare's Audience* (1941), *As They Liked It* (1947), and *Shakespeare and the Rival Traditions* (1952), has been specially concerned with Shakespeare's relationship with his audience and the artistry with which he responded to their demands. In *Theatre for Shakespeare* (1955) he stimulatingly examines the problems of presenting the plays in modern conditions. His books are among the most attractively written of modern contributions. Bernard Spivack's *Shakespeare and the Allegory of Evil* (1958) is an impressive study of Shakespeare's portrayal of certain types of character (particularly Iago and his antecedents) in relation to earlier English drama.

Many studies of theatrical conventions are inextricably bound up with researches into the structure of Elizabethan theatres and the social composition of the audiences, and so fit more easily into the history of scholarship than that of criticism. The dividing line is exceedingly difficult to draw, since much work that reveals detailed scholarly investigation has a critical aim, and few even of the most subjective among critics rely entirely on their own unaided response to a work of art. Some studies of Elizabethan life and literature which are not centred on Shakespeare, and even some which hardly refer to him, probably would not have been written except in the hope of casting light, directly or indirectly, on his plays. Enid Welsford's *The Fool: His Social and Literary History* (1935) ranges from classical literature to Charlie Chaplin, but begins with a quotation from *Twelfth Night* and includes a valuable section on *King Lear*. Books wholly or partly concerned with Elizabethan thought, such as A. O. Lovejoy's *The Great Chain of Being* (1936), Hardin Craig's *The Enchanted Glass* (1936), and E. M. W. Tillyard's *The Elizabethan World Picture* (1943), have done much to activate response both to large patterns and to poetic details of Shakespeare's plays, and even the most determined advocate of the examination of verbal techniques could not deny the relevance of such studies, as also of far starker tools of scholarship, such as above all the *New English Dictionary*. Editors too have contributed to the critical as well as the more evidently 'scholarly' scene. In many respects the editor's task may be regarded as mainly 'scholarly'.

He is establishing his text, glossing and annotating it, providing information rather than interpretation. Yet even in the choice of information to provide he is exercising critical judgement, and in most editions he is given the opportunity to expound his own views. The editorial discipline at its fullest demands close familiarity with all aspects of the text, and some of the soundest critical writing on Shakespeare comes in introductions written no doubt at the end of the editorial agony, such as some of those in the New Cambridge, new Arden, and New Penguin series. Some editors, too, have found their thoughts on the plays overflowing into independent critical writings such as John Dover Wilson's *What Happens in Hamlet* (1935) and *The Fortunes of Falstaff* (1943).

Although, contrary to common belief, there is evidence even in the pages of *Shakespearean Tragedy* that Bradley sometimes attended the theatre, he is not noted for having considered the plays in close relation to their theatrical effect. Schücking and especially Stoll are more aware of the need to give this its due, but undoubtedly the most theatrically concerned of the major Shakespeare critics since Bradley has been Harley Granville-Barker, himself an actor, playwright, and producer. His *Prefaces*, which began to appear in full-dress form in 1927, are valuable above all because they appeal on two important fronts. Academics with little interest in the practical theatre can read Granville-Barker, and theatre people to whom academic criticism is a closed library can find practical help in him too. His awareness of the theatrical potential of Shakespeare's plays when thought of in relation to the conditions for which they were written has been immensely influential and valuable, encouraging the performance of previously neglected plays, such as *Love's Labour's Lost*, the reinstatement of passages that had been generally omitted in the theatre from others, and the rethinking of the staging of Shakespeare in modern conditions.

This influence on the practical theatre has indirectly affected literary criticism too. Some critics have written directly on Shakespeare in relation to the stage of both his own and later times. G. C. D. Odell's *Shakespeare – from Betterton to Irving* (1920) is critically naive, and valuable rather for the information it conveys than the attitudes lying behind it, but Arthur Colby Sprague's writings on stage history such as *Shakespeare and the Actors* (1944) are informed by a wise critical judgement and, in a book such as his *Shakespeare's Histories: Plays for the Stage* (1964), are applied to critical ends. Shakespeare critics have become increasingly aware of the theatre, and this trend seems likely to continue. The critical terminology associated with plays in performance is limited, and even those professionally concerned with the theatre are apt to talk and write in surprisingly academic language, but some critics seem to be making an attempt to write about the plays with their effect in performance at the forefront of their minds. Marvin Rosenberg in *The Masks of Othello* (1961) draws together the history of the play on the stage and in the study in the effort to investigate our response to it, John Russell Brown in *Shakespeare's Plays in Performance* (1965) interestingly explores the unwritten theatrical dimension in the texts of plays, and Maynard Mack makes good critical use of stage-history in *'King Lear' in Our Time* (1965). This kind of study reflects awareness that our response to Shakespeare is inevitably coloured by what has happened to the plays between his time and ours. We have inherited prejudices and attitudes of which we may be hardly aware. As T. J. B. Spencer has written, 'The great task of criticism is, no doubt, to see the object as it really is. But in order to do this we need to disentangle ourselves from the past as well as, to some extent, the present.' This is true in relation to areas other than stage history, but its truth is a justification of the use in critical work of scholarly investigations into the history of Shakespeare's plays on the stage.

Shakespeare criticism inevitably reflects changes in general critical method and fashion. It would scarcely be unfair to say that the most powerful literary critics of the century so far have not been the major Shakespeare critics. Many of them have nevertheless exerted considerable influence, direct and indirect. T. S. Eliot's essay on *Hamlet*, especially his pronouncement that it is 'an artistic failure', has teased later writers on the play more perhaps than he would ever have thought likely; and his view of *Othello*, especially that in his final speech the hero is 'cheering himself up', has influenced actors as well as critics. Eliot's essays on Elizabethan dramatists other than Shakespeare have cast light on Shakespeare's technique, and his writings on poetic drama in general have stimulated those concerned mainly with Shakespeare. F. R. Leavis's influence has been even less direct, working largely through the dissemination of attitudes and critical techniques, and not infrequently through a reaction against them. Many of the pieces on Shakespeare first published in *Scrutiny* were written under his powerful influence. Northrop Frye's essay 'The Argument of Comedy' (1948, incorporated in *Anatomy of Criticism*, 1957) has had a seminal influence, but his more extended Shakespeare studies, in *A Natural Perspective: The Development of Shakespearean Comedy and Romance* (1965) and *Fools of Time: Studies in Shakespearean Tragedy* (1967), are remarkable rather for the sparks that are thrown off than for the illumination of a sustained argument.

The emergence round about 1930 of a school of criticism much concerned with close verbal analysis had a major effect on Shakespeare criticism. The work of I. A. Richards looms behind the movement, though he has contributed little to the Shakespearian side of it. In

1933 appeared L. C. Knights's clever 'How Many Children had Lady Macbeth?'. The title parodies those of Bradley's less happy appendices (it is said to have been suggested by Leavis), and in attacking the study of the plays as if they were novels, and especially the Bradleian approach through character, Knights propounds the view that 'a Shakespeare play is a dramatic poem'. The emphasis is on the poem, not the drama, and in this respect Knights's trenchant essay seems now to belong to its time as much as Bradley's book does to his. Bradley has some interesting remarks on style, but Stoll and Schücking had been little concerned with details of language. Now within a few years there appeared Caroline Spurgeon's essays on imagery (1930, 1931) and her book *Shakespeare's Imagery and What it Tells Us* (1935), G. Wilson Knight's *Myth and Miracle* (1929), *The Wheel of Fire* (1930), *The Imperial Theme* (1931), and *The Shakespearian Tempest* (1932), William Empson's *Seven Types of Ambiguity* (1930) and *Some Versions of Pastoral* (1935), the essay by L. C. Knights already referred to, and, in German, W. H. Clemen's book (1936) later translated as *The Development of Shakespeare's Imagery* (1951). These were all by critics with a highly developed interest in language. Critically, Caroline Spurgeon's book is the least sophisticated. Often referred to as a 'pioneering' study, it suffers from a limited definition of imagery, an excessively statistical approach, and too strong an emphasis on imagery as biographical evidence. But it remains a book that has to be consulted, and its influence has been widespread. Clemen's study is more rigorous in approach and more consistently rewarding in its results. L. C. Knights's later writings on Shakespeare, while preserving a perceptive concern with the texture of language, have increasingly adopted the moralistic tone associated with *Scrutiny*. Similar pre-occupations characterize the work of D. A. Traversi, another contributor to *Scrutiny* who has gone on to write extensively about Shakespeare. His is a judicial approach, much concerned to relate details of poetic language to overall moral attitudes. He displays little interest in historical considerations, in this resembling Wilson Knight, who followed up his early spate of books with many others, including *The Crown of Life* (1947), *The Mutual Flame* (1955), and *The Sovereign Flower* (1958). Together they form a complex, highly interrelated body of work. *Shakespearian Production* (1964), a revision of *Principles of Shakespearian Production* (1936 and 1949), most obviously reflects his concern with the practical theatre – he has performed some of the great tragic roles. Knight ought, one feels, to be the major Shakespeare critic after Bradley. He is a verbal critic of great subtlety. Stressing 'interpretation' as distinguished from 'criticism' he tends to work from an assumption of 'organic unity', of the play as an 'expanded metaphor', and to proceed to expound underlying themes and symbols. The critic's attempt to submit himself totally to the work can be immensely valuable. Knight has been partly responsible for a broadening of our view of the possibilities of Shakespeare's art of which only a minor result is the rehabilitation into the Shakespeare canon of parts of the plays, such as the vision in *Cymbeline* and Antigonus's dream speech in *The Winter's Tale*, that previously had often seemed unrelatable to the overall design. He is especially interesting too on the relationships between the plays, on for instance the symbolical significance of storms and music. He has been justly described as 'one of the great seminal critics'. Yet his potential seems not to have been fully realized, and some readers are understandably deterred by his obscurities of style, a feeling that he tends to lose hold on reality, and an excessively personal approach that causes us sometimes to suspect that he is concerned to interpret himself through Shakespeare rather than the reverse.

Later critics, too, have pursued studies in which an interest in the devices of linguistic style is paramount. E. A. Armstrong's *Shakespeare's Imagination* (1946) is a fascinating exploration of Shakespeare's creative processes as revealed by a study of a number of 'image clusters'. In *Shakespeare and the Arts of Language* (1947), Sister Miriam Joseph is concerned especially with rhetorical devices. R. B. Heilman writes thorough and perceptive studies of individual plays in *This Great Stage: Image and Structure in 'King Lear'* (1948), and *Magic in the Web: Action and Language in 'Othello'* (1956). M. M. Mahood's *Shakespeare's Wordplay* (1957), which concentrates on five plays and the Sonnets, is a clever assault on some of Shakespeare's verbal complexities. Those who have written usefully on the poems include Edward Hubler in *The Sense of Shakespeare's Sonnets* (1952), Patrick Cruttwell in *The Shakespearean Moment* (1956), and J. B. Leishman in *Themes and Variations in Shakespeare's Sonnets* (1961). On the whole, writers on Shakespeare's verbal techniques have shown more interest in the verse than the prose, but Brian Vickers's *The Artistry of Shakespeare's Prose* (1968) does something to redress the balance. Still, no one has yet written with sufficient passion on the fact that Shakespeare is our greatest prose-writer as well as our greatest poet.

Bradley is known above all for *Shakespearean Tragedy*, and many critics have followed him in writing on particular groups of plays, sometimes in the effort to arrive at a definition of Shakespeare's concept of the genre in which he was working, sometimes (perhaps more usefully) trying to define the characteristic effects of the genre. Lily B. Campbell, in *Shakespeare's Tragic Heroes: Slaves of Passion* (1930), follows Bradley in concentrating on the four 'great' tragedies. Studying them against the background of contemporary medicine and philosophy, with which she believes Shakespeare to have been familiar, she sees the hero of each play as a study in the influence of one dominating passion. She is not a disciple of Bradley, and has two appendices criticizing his criticism. H. B. Charlton, on the other hand, proclaimed himself 'a devout Bradleyite', and, in *Shakespearian Tragedy* (1948), attempts to reaffirm Bradley's approach to character. In *The Story of the Night* (1961) John Holloway attempts an anthropologically based study of the tragedies with results that are sometimes brilliant, though uneven.

M. W. MacCallum's *Shakespeare's Roman Plays and their Background* (1910) remains the standard, most comprehensive study of this group of plays. It makes extensive use of source study, and also attempts lengthy character studies of the main figures. Maurice Charney's *Shakespeare's Roman Plays: the Function of Imagery in the Drama* (1961) is more specialized. The two principal studies of the plays that take English history as their subject matter both consider the political implications of the plays as well as their historical background. E. M. W. Tillyard in *Shakespeare's History Plays* (1944) is the more historiographical in his approach, whereas Lily B. Campbell, in *Shakespeare's 'Histories': Mirrors of Elizabethan Policy* (1947), offers more thorough consideration of the contemporary political background, which she finds specially relevant. M. M. Reese's *The Cease of Majesty* (1961) is a useful corrective to some of the more extreme features of Tillyard's approach.

Although the comedies form the largest single group of Shakespeare's plays, criticism of them lagged behind that of the tragedies and histories except in relation to a few dominating characters, such as Shylock. As a character of potentially tragic status Shylock received attention from Stoll, yet the same critic wrote that 'the essential thing for comedy, the critical spirit...is not abundant in Shakespeare'. Stoll thus associates himself with the satirical tradition of comedy which, as Nevill Coghill shows in his essay 'The Basis of Shakespearian Comedy' (1950), flourished in Renaissance England, and which has perhaps been more amenable to analysis than the romantic tradition which Shakespeare found more congenial. The twentieth century is to be credited with a realization on the part of at least some commentators that the greatness of Shakespearian comedy is not necessarily in proportion to its critical intent, and various writers have tried to define its characteristic modes and effects. The concept of Shakespearian comedy has proved even more difficult to pin down than that of Shakespearian tragedy, and the plays have yielded more to individual analysis than to the application of single-minded theories or rigorously defined critical techniques. H. B. Charlton's *Shakespearian Comedy* (1938) employs a scholarly approach through literary analogues, related to that used by Lawrence in *Shakespeare's Problem Comedies*. Charlton's is a substantial study, dated by a ponderous style. C. L. Barber in *Shakespeare's Festive Comedy* (1959) succeeds more than most critics in finding a rewarding framework of discussion. His approach is anthropological. His subtitle is *A Study of Dramatic Form and its Relation to Social Custom*, and he finds in the comedies up to *Twelfth Night* a 'saturnalian pattern' derived from both social and artistic traditions. Bertrand Evans in *Shakespeare's Comedies* (1960) closely examines the artistry by which Shakespeare manipulates the reactions of his audience, creating 'exploitable gaps or discrepancies among the awarenesses of participants and between the awarenesses of participants and audience'. The method is not equally illuminating for all plays.

Shakespeare's works remain (more or less) constant, but those who read and see them are always changing. In this lies the justification for the continuous stream of writing about them. As T. S. Eliot wrote in the previous *Companion*, 'Shakespeare criticism will always change as the world changes.' As the plays become more remote in time they stand more in need of explanation and interpretation. Not all who write about them are, or should be, trying hard to say something new. Moreover, even the most original critics often need their mediators, whether in print or in the lecture hall. For this reason, much good writing on Shakespeare is not specially exciting. The truest, most balanced criticism is that which takes account of many different points of view, which synthesizes a variety of approaches. Inevitably it is likely to seem judicious rather than brilliant, sound rather than revelatory. Conversely, extremist approaches are liable to be one-sided. John Holloway, in the Introduction to *The Story of the Night*, which is an independent and stimulating discussion of fundamental critical issues, speaks of the need 'to restore traditional clarity by removing modernistic over-ingenuity'. But even over-ingenious critics can perform useful functions. Theirs are likely to be more readable, because more surprising, than middle-of-the-road interpretations. This is sad, because the obvious is often true, and a generally accepted view of a play is liable to be just. But the older the truth, the better it needs to be put. It takes a writer of real skill to present forcefully an established point of view. The critic who writes with the excitement that comes from a knowledge that he is being shocking, that he is challenging received opinion, may attract attention; and even if he does not convince he may usefully disturb. This is a valid function of criticism. Readers, especially those for whom familiarity is in danger of dulling their responses, need to be shaken up. Even so extreme a piece as Jan Kott's chapter on *A Midsummer Night's Dream* in *Shakespeare Our Contemporary* (1965, revised 1967), may vivify our response to aspects of the play, however violently we reject his total argument. But the best criticism, and that which stands the best chance of survival, is that which combines a balanced approach with the ability to engage and sustain the attention of the reader without excessive concern with local and temporal matters. It is too early yet to sort out with any confidence the post-Bradleian sheep from the goats. Certain names would be likely to figure in any account, however brief, but many which might have been included have been omitted here, and to others a different degree of prominence might easily have been accorded. And those who are working now may well develop in different and surprising ways. Criticism based on a strong sense of the play as something that is incomplete until it is performed seems likely to grow in importance, but it is a difficult area of discussion. The study of linguistics is likely to be applied to Shakespeare, but will not have much immediate effect unless its practitioners can devise a more readily comprehensible terminology than that in which they communicate with one another. But it is useless to speculate, for what happens in the future is not conditioned by what we may feel to be desirable, but by the future itself: the needs of readers, and the capacities of the individuals who write for them.

NOTES AND READING LISTS

1. THE LIFE OF SHAKESPEARE

Note

1 Much confusion has arisen from the entry of licence, made the previous day in the Bishop of Worcester's *Register*, which names Anne Whateley of Temple Grafton as the bride. Presumably the entry clerk made a careless mistake. That Shakespeare's wife was a Hathaway is confirmed by the independent tradition reported in Rowe's *Account* (1709).

Reading List

Baldwin, T. W., *William Shakspere's Small Latine & Lesse Greeke*, 2 vols. (Urbana, Ill., 1944)

Bentley, G. E., *Shakespeare: A Biographical Handbook* (New Haven, 1961)

Chambers, E. K., *William Shakespeare: A Study of Facts and Problems*, 2 vols. (Oxford, 1930)

Eccles, Mark, *Shakespeare in Warwickshire* (Madison, Wis., 1961)

Fripp, Edgar I., *Shakespeare, Man and Artist*, 2 vols. (1938)

Hotson, Leslie, *I, William Shakespeare, Do Appoint Thomas Russell, Esq.* (1937)

Shakespeare versus Shallow (1931)

Reese, M. M., *Shakespeare: His World and His Work* (1953)

Rowse, A. L., *William Shakespeare: A Biography* (1963)

Schoenbaum, S., *Shakespeare's Lives* (1970)

Smart, J. S., *Shakespeare: Truth and Tradition* (1928)

2. THE PLAYHOUSES AND THE STAGE

Notes

1 Herbert Berry, 'The Playhouse in the Boar's Head Inn, Whitechapel', in *The Elizabethan Theatre*, ed. David Galloway (Toronto, 1969).

2 Alfred Harbage, *Shakespeare and the Rival Traditions* (New York, 1952).

3 William A. Armstrong, *The Elizabethan Private Theatres* (1958).

4 'Reconstitution du théâtre du Swan', in *Le Lieu théâtral à la Renaissance*, ed. Jean Jacquot (Paris, 1964), pp. 295–316.

5 Texts of the two contracts and reproductions of most of the pictorial sources cited in this chapter may be found in *The Globe Restored* (1953) by C. Walter Hodges.

6 Irwin Smith, 'Theatre into Globe', *Shakespeare Quarterly*, III (1952), pp. 113–200.

7 'A Reconstruction of the Second Blackfriars', in *The Elizabethan Theatre*, ed. David Galloway.

8 See the article by D. F. Rowan in *The New Theatre Magazine* (1969).

See 'The Staging of the Monument Scenes in *Antony and Cleopatra*', *The Library Chronicle*, XXX (University of Pennsylvania), (1964), pp. 62–71.
'The Discovery-space in Shakespeare's Globe', *Shakespeare Survey 12* (Cambridge, 1959), pp. 35–46.
'The Staging of Desdemona's Bed', *Shakespeare Quarterly*, XIV (1963), pp. 57–65.
'The Gallery over the Stage in the Public Playhouse of Shakespeare's Time', *Shakespeare Quarterly*, VIII (1957), pp. 15–31; 'Shakespeare's Use of a Gallery over the Stage', *Shakespeare Survey 10* (Cambridge, 1957), pp. 77–89.
'Was There a Music-room in Shakespeare's Globe?', *Shakespeare Survey 13* (Cambridge, 1960), pp. 113–23.
See 'The Origins of the So-called Elizabethan Multiple Stage', *The Drama Review*, XII, 2 (1967–8), pp. 28–50.
It is a pleasure to record my indebtedness to Dr Richard Southern for making the drawings that illustrate this chapter.

Reading List

Adams, Joseph Quincy, *Shakespearean Playhouses* (Boston, 1917)
Armstrong, William A., *The Elizabethan Private Theatres: Facts and Problems* (1958)
Beckerman, Bernard, *Shakespeare at the Globe* (New York, 1962)
Bentley, Gerald Eades, *The Jacobean and Caroline Stage*, 7 vols. (Oxford, 1941–68), vol. 6: *Theatres*, 1968.
Chambers, E. K., *The Elizabethan Stage*, 4 vols. (Oxford, 1923), vols. 2 and 3
Harbage, Alfred, *Shakespeare's Audience* (New York, 1941)
  Theatre for Shakespeare (Toronto, 1955)
Hodges, C. Walter, *The Globe Restored* (1953; rev. ed., 1968)
  Shakespeare's Theatre (1964)
Nicoll, Allardyce, *Stuart Masques and the Renaissance Stage* (1937)
Reynolds, George F., *The Staging of Elizabethan Plays at the Red Bull Theater, 1605–1625* (New York, 1940)
Southern, Richard, *Changeable Scenery* (1952)
  The Medieval Theatre in the Round (1957)
  The Open Stage (1953)
Wickham, Glynne H., *Early English Stages, 1300 to 1660*, vol. 1 (1959); vol. 2, pt. 1 (1963)

3. THE ACTORS AND STAGING

Notes

1 E. H. Gombrich, *Art and Illusion* (1960), p. 394.
2 See Reading List.
3 *Cf.* Bernard Beckerman, *Shakespeare at the Globe, 1599–1609* (New York, 1962), pp. 183–6.
4 Although such computation as this is naturally limited by a factor of

individual interpretation, I have tried to include for consideration only those lines in which evidence is definite; i.e. for which there is an explicit stage direction of theatrical provenance, for which another character is explicit in descriptive terms of business being acted, or for which certain business would have to be conducted simultaneously to make sense of the lines. Two relevant facts should be noted about this evidence: first, that so far as can be determined from the texts considered for this study, the figures pertain as much to performance in private theatres as in public ones; and, second, that commonsense leads one to assume that any category of action for which documentation exists would also take place less apparently in other parts of a text. For what it is worth, categories of stage business such as those being investigated here cover, ordinarily, at least half of the words of most modern plays; and even if one acknowledges that our theatre may be more physically and psychologically 'busy' than the Elizabethan, we may assume with some confidence that the percentage figures noted above must be minimal, and that much more stage business of all kinds took place than we will ever be able to detect and document.

5 Prologue, *Summer's Last Will and Testament*.

6 Cited by Alfred Harbage, *Theatre for Shakespeare* (Toronto, 1955), Appendix B, p. 109.

7 In computing these averages, I have omitted consideration of 'massed' scenes, such as those taking place in a monarch's court, before a battle, trials, etc.

8 Beckerman, *op. cit.*, p. 184.

9 John Russell Brown, 'On the Acting of Shakespeare's Plays', *Quarterly Journal of Speech*, XXXIX (1953), 479.

Reading List

Beckerman, Bernard, see 2, above

Bradbrook, M. C., *Themes and Conventions of Elizabethan Tragedy* (Cambridge, 1935), ch. I and III.

Brown, John Russell, *Shakespeare's Plays in Performance* (1966)

Chambers, E. K., see 2, above

Coghill, Nevill, *Shakespeare's Professional Skills* (Cambridge, 1964)

Foakes, R. A., 'The Player's Passion', *Essays and Studies* (1954)

Harbage, Alfred. see 2, above

Joseph, Bertram, *Acting Shakespeare* (1960)
  Elizabethan Acting (1951; rev. 1964)
  The Tragic Actor (1959)

Rosenberg, Marvin, 'Elizabethan Actors: Men or Marionettes?', *PMLA*, LXIX (1954), 915–27

Seltzer, Daniel, 'Elizabethan Acting in *Othello*', *Shakespeare Quarterly*, X (1959), 201–10
  'The Staging of the Last Plays', *Stratford-upon-Avon Studies*, vol. 8 (1966)

Styan, J. L., *Shakespeare's Stagecraft* (Cambridge, 1967)

SHAKESPEARE'S READING

Reading List

The books in this list are arranged in the order in which the topics they cover are dealt with in this chapter.

Anders, H. R. D., *Shakespeare's Books* (Berlin, 1904)

Muir, Kenneth, *Shakespeare's Sources I* (1957)

Wilson, F. P., 'Shakespeare's Reading', *Shakespeare Survey 3* (1950)

Bullough, Geoffrey, *Narrative and Dramatic Sources of Shakespeare*, 7 vols. (1957–72)

Whiter, Walter, *A Specimen of a Commentary on Shakespeare* (1794), ed. Over and Bell (1967)

Armstrong, Edward A., *Shakespeare's Imagination* (1946)

Isaacs, J., 'Shakespeare's earliest years in the theatre', *Proc. Brit. Acad.* XXXIX (1953), 119–38

Weiss, Roberto, *Humanism in England in the Fifteenth Century* (1941)

Walker, Alice, 'The reading of an Elizabethan', *R.E.S.*, VIII (1932), 264–81

Thomson, J. A. K., *Shakespeare and the Classics* (1952)

Farmer, Richard, 'An Essay on the Learning of Shakespeare' (1767) in *Eighteenth Century Essays on Shakespeare*, ed. D. Nichol Smith (Oxford, 1903)

Baldwin, T. W., see 1, above

Baldwin, T. W., *William Shakespeare's Five Act Structure* (Urbana, 1947)

Salingar, L. G., 'The design of *Twelfth Night*', *Shakespeare Quarterly*, IX (1958), 117–39

Jenkins, Harold, 'Shakespeare's *Twelfth Night*', *Rice Institute Pamphlets*, XLV (1959), 19–42

Prouty, C. T., *The Sources of 'Much Ado About Nothing'* (New Haven, 1950)

Noble, Richmond, *Shakespeare's Biblical Knowledge* (1935)

Hart, Alfred, *Shakespeare and the Homilies* (Melbourne, 1934)

Wilson, F. P., *Marlowe and the Early Shakespeare* (Oxford, 1953)

Honigmann, E. A. J., 'Shakespeare's lost source-plays', *Modern Language Review*, XLIX (1954), 293–307

Lascelles, Mary, *Shakespeare's 'Measure for Measure'* (1953)

Spencer, Theodore, *Shakespeare and the Nature of Man* (Cambridge, Mass., 1942)

Whitaker, Virgil K., *Shakespeare's Use of Learning* (San Marino, 1953)

Taylor, G. Coffin, *Shakespeare's Debt to Montaigne* (Cambridge, Mass., 1925)

Hogden, Margaret, 'Montaigne and Shakespeare', *Huntington Library Quarterly*, XVI (1952), 23–42

Wilson, J. Dover, *What Happens in 'Hamlet'* (Cambridge, 1935)

Bald, R. C., 'Edmund and Renaissance Free thought', *Joseph Quincy Adams Memorial Studies*, ed. J. G. McManaway *et al.* (Washington, D.C., 1948), pp. 337–49.

5. SHAKESPEARE AND THE ENGLISH LANGUAGE

Reading List

Abbott, E. A., *A Shakespearian Grammar* (3rd ed., 1872)

Byrne, M. St. Clare, 'The Foundations of Elizabethan Language', *Shakespeare Survey 17* (1964), pp. 223–39

Clemen, W. H., *The Development of Shakespeare's Imagery* (1951)

Dobson, E. J., *English pronunciation 1500–1700* (Oxford, 2nd ed., 1968)

Evans, B. Ifor, *The Language of Shakespeare's Plays* (2nd ed., 1959)

Franz, W., *Die Sprache Shakespeares in Vers und Prosa* (Halle, 4th ed., 1939)

Hulme, Hilda M., *Explorations in Shakespeare's Language* (1962)

Kökeritz, H., *Shakespeare's Pronunciation* (New Haven, 1953)

McIntosh, A., '*As You Like It*: A Grammatical Clue to Character', *R.E.L.*, IV (1963)

Mahood, M. M., *Shakespeare's Wordplay* (1957)

Millward, C., 'Pronominal Case in Shakespearian Imperatives', *Lg*, XLII (1966)

Mulholland, J., ' "Thou" and "You" in Shakespeare', *E.S.*, XLVIII (1967)

Onions, C. T., *A Shakespeare Glossary* (Oxford, 2nd ed., 1919)

Salmon, V., 'Elizabethan Colloquial English in the Falstaff Plays', *Leeds Studies in English*, n.s. I (1967)

'Sentence Structures in Colloquial Shakespearian English', *TPS* (1965)

Schmidt, A., *Shakespeare-Lexicon*, rev. G. Sarrazin (Berlin and Leipzig, 4th ed., 1923)

Willcock, G. D., 'Shakespeare and Elizabethan English', *Shakespeare Survey 7* (1954)

'Language and Poetry in Shakespeare's Early Plays', *Proc. Brit. Acad.*, XL (1954)

6. SHAKESPEARE'S USE OF RHETORIC

Reading List

Abrams, M. H., *The Mirror and the Lamp: Romantic Theory and the Critical Tradition* (New York, 1953)

Baldwin, C. S., *Medieval Rhetoric and Poetic* (New York, 1928)

Baldwin, T. W., see I, above

Bolgar, R. R., *The Classical Heritage and its Beneficiaries* (Cambridge, 1954)

Barish, J. A., 'The Antitheatrical Prejudice', *Critical Quarterly*, VIII (1966), 329–48

Curtius, E. R., *European Literature and the Latin Middle Ages*, tr. W. R. Trask (New York, 1953)

Faral, E., *Les Arts Poétiques du XIIe et du XIIIe Siècle* (Paris, 1924)

Hoskins, J., *Directions for Speech and Style*, ed. H. Hudson (Princeton, 1935)

Howell, W. S., *Logic and Rhetoric in England 1500–1700* (Princeton, 1956)
Joseph, Sister Miriam, *Shakespeare's Use of the Arts of Language* (New York, 1947)
Kennedy, G. A., *The Art of Persuasion in Greece* (London 1963)
Marrou, H. I., *A History of Education in Antiquity*, trans. G. Lamb (London, 1956)
Peacham, H., *The Garden of Eloquence*, ed. W. G. Crane (Florida, 1954)
Puttenham, G., *The Arte of Englishe Poesie*, ed. G. Willcock and A. Walker (Cambridge, 1936, 1970)
Sonnino, L. A., *A Handbook to Sixteenth-Century Rhetoric* (1968)
Stone, P. W. K., *The Art of Poetry 1750–1820*. (London, 1967)
Tuve, Rosemond, *Elizabethan and Metaphysical Imagery* (Chicago, 1947)
Vickers, Brian, *The Artistry of Shakespeare's Prose* (1968)
Classical Rhetoric in English Poetry (1970)

7. SHAKESPEARE'S POETRY

Reading List

Clemen, W. H., *The Development of Shakespeare's Imagery* (1951)
Hubler, Edward, *The Sense of Shakespeare's Sonnets* (Princeton, 1952)
Knight, G. Wilson, *The Wheel of Fire* (1930)
The Imperial Theme (1931)
The Crown of Life (1947)
Lever, J. W., *The Elizabethan Love Sonnet* (1956)
Nicoll, Allardyce (ed.), *Shakespeare Survey 15* (1962)
Nowottny, Winifred, *The Language Poets Use* (1962)
Spurgeon, Caroline F. E., *Shakespeare's Imagery and What It Tells Us* (Cambridge, 1935)

8. SHAKESPEARE'S NARRATIVE POEMS

Notes

1 George Wyndham, *The Poems of Shakespeare* (1898), Introduction, p. cxxii.
2 Bion, *Idyl* I, trans. Andrew Lang.
3 Adrian Junius, *Nomenclator*, trans. John Higgins, 1585. Cited in Madeleine Doran, *Endeavors of Art* (1954), p. 382.
4 The 'Argument' differs in many respects from the version of events in the poem. Shakespeare's authorship has been questioned; alternatively it has been thought of as an early outline for the later work.

Reading List

Allen, D. C., *Image and Meaning*, 2nd ed. (Maryland, 1968)
Baldwin, T. W., *On the Literary Genetics of Shakespeare's Poems and Sonnets* (Urbana, 1950)

Bradbrook, M. C., *Shakespeare and Elizabethan Poetry* (1951)

Coleridge, S. T., *Biographia Literaria* (1817), ch. xv

Hamilton, A. C., 'Venus and Adonis', *Studies in English Literature, 1500–1900*, I (1961)

   The Early Shakespeare (San Marino, 1967)

Maxwell, J. C. (ed.), *The Poems* (Cambridge, 1966)

Muir, Kenneth, '*A Lover's Complaint*: A Reconsideration' in *Shakespeare 1564–1964*, ed. E. A. Bloom (Providence, R. I., 1964)

Nicoll, Allardyce, *Shakespeare Survey 15* (1962)

Price, Hereward T., 'The Function of Imagery in *Venus and Adonis*' (*Papers of the Michigan Academy*, 1945), pp. 275–97

Prince, F. T. (ed.), The Arden Shakespeare: *The Poems* (1960)

Rollins, H. E. (ed.), New Variorum Shakespeare: *The Poems* (Philadelphia, 1938)

Smith, Hallett, *Elizabethan Poetry* (Cambridge, Mass., 1952)

Wyndham, George, *The Poems of Shakespeare* (1898)

9. SHAKESPEARE THE ELIZABETHAN DRAMATIST

Reading List

Barber, C. L., *Shakespeare's Festive Comedy* (Princeton, 1959)

Frye, Northrop, 'The Argument of Comedy', *English Institute Essays* (New York, 1949)

   'Characterization in Shakespearean Comedy', *Shakespeare Quarterly*, IV (1953), 271–7

Granville-Barker, H., *Prefaces to Shakespeare* (1927, 1930)

Hunter, G. K., 'Shakespeare's Politics and the Rejection of Falstaff', *Critical Quarterly*, I (1959), 229–36

Hunter, R. G., *Shakespeare and the Comedy of Forgiveness* (New York, 1965)

Reese, M. M., *The Cease of Majesty* (1961)

Rossiter, A. P., 'Much Ado about Nothing', *Angel with Horns* (1961), pp. 67–81

Tillyard, E. M. W., *Shakespeare's History Plays* (1944)

Wilson, J. Dover, *The Fortunes of Falstaff* (Cambridge, 1944)

Young, David, *Something of Great Constancy; The Art of 'A Midsummer Night's Dream'* (New Haven, 1966)

10. SHAKESPEARE THE JACOBEAN DRAMATIST

Notes

1 F. P. Wilson, *Elizabethan and Jacobean* (1945), p. 26.

2 Clifford Leech, *The John Fletcher Plays* (1962), p. 32.

3 See Irving Ribner, *The English History Play in the Age of Shakespeare* (New York, 1965), ch. 9.

4 George Kernodle, 'Open stage; Elizabethan or Existentialist?', *Shakespeare Survey 12* (1959), 2–3.

5 *A Century of Revolution* (1961), p. 96.
6 Nicholas Brooke, *Shakespeare's Early Tragedies* (1968), p. 143.
7 By David Frost, *The School of Shakespeare* (1968).
8 See Glynne Wickham, *Early English Stages*, vol. II (1963), 242.
9 In 'Shakespeare's Primitive Art', *British Academy Annual Shakespeare Lecture* (1965)
10 With such titles as *The Raging Turk*. See the introduction to *Mulleasses the Turk* in Bang's *Materialien*.
11 Bernard Spivack, *Shakespeare and the Allegory of Evil* (New York and London, 1958), pp. 424, 426.
12 Fulke Greville, *Life of Sir Philip Sidney* (ed. Nowell Smith, 1907), p. 15.
13 Thomas Heywood, *A Woman Killed with Kindness*, V, vi.
14 T. S. Eliot, 'Shakespeare and the Stoicism of Seneca', *Selected Essays* (1951), pp. 130–1.
15 J. I. M. Stewart, *Character and Motive in Shakespeare* (1949), pp. 108–9.
16 W. H. Auden, 'The Joker in the Pack', *The Dyer's Hand* (1963), pp. 246–72.
17 See M. C. Bradbrook, *Shakespeare the Craftsman* (1969), ch. 3.
18 John Donne, *Devotions upon Emergent Occasions* (1624), No. XVII.
19 *The Shakespeare Allusion Book*, II, p. 23.
20 Anne Righter, Introduction to *The Tempest*, New Penguin Shakespeare (1968), p. 17.
21 See *Shakespeare the Craftsman*, ch. 1, pp. 22–6.

Reading List

Elton, W. R., *King Lear and the Gods* (San Marino, 1966)
Empson, William, *The Structure of Complex Words* (1951)
Farnham, Willard, *Shakespeare's Tragic Frontier* (Berkeley, 1950)
Jacquot, Jean (ed.), *Les Fêtes de la Renaissance*, 2 vols. (Paris, 1956–60)
  Le Lieu Théâtral à la Renaissance (Paris, 1964)
Leech, Clifford, *Shakespeare's Tragedies and other studies in Seventeenth Century Drama* (1950)
Mack, Maynard, 'The Jacobean Shakespeare' in *Jacobean Theatre*, ed. J. R. Brown and B. Harris (1960)
Muir, Kenneth (ed.), *Shakespeare Survey 21* (1968) (on *Othello*)
Nicoll, Allardyce (ed.), *Shakespeare Survey 10* (1957) (on Roman Plays)
  Shakespeare Survey 11 (1958) (on Last Plays)
Raab, Felix, *The English Face of Machiavelli* (1964)

11. SHAKESPEARE AND MUSIC

Notes

1 This half-line is supplied from Q 1, as in K. Muir's Arden edn., 1952.
2 Q 1 has 'rough'. The emendation 'still' is based on Wilkins's *Pericles*: 'that they should command some still music to sound'; cf. E. Schanzer's Signet edn., 1965.
3 Q 1 reads 'viole', Q 4 has 'viall'; cf. Schanzer's edn.

Reading List

Bowden, W. R., *English Dramatic Lyric, 1603–1642* (New Haven, 1951)
Cutts, John P., *Musique de la troupe de Shakespeare* (Paris, 1959)
Fellowes, E. H. (ed.), *English Madrigal Verse* (3rd ed. rev. F. W. Sternfeld and D. Greer, Oxford, 1967)
  English School of Lutenist Song Writers, 32 vols., (1920–32)
Hartnoll, P. (ed.) *Shakespeare in Music* (1964)
Long, John H. (ed.), *Music in English Renaissance Drama* (Lexington, 1968)
  Shakespeare's Use of Music – Comedies, 2 vols. (Gainesville, 1955, 1961)
Naylor, Edward W. (ed.), *Shakespeare Music*, 2nd ed. (1928)
  Shakespeare and Music, 2nd ed. (1931)
Noble, Richmond, *Shakespeare's Use of Song* (1923)
Seng, Peter J., *Vocal Songs in the Plays of Shakespeare* (Cambridge, Mass., 1967)
Sternfeld, F. W., *Music in Shakespearean Tragedy*, 2nd impr. (1967)
  (ed.) *Songs from Shakespeare's Tragedies* (1964)

12. THE HISTORICAL AND SOCIAL BACKGROUND

Notes

1 J. E. Neale, *Elizabeth I and her Parliaments* (1957), II, 391.
2 J. E. Neale, *Elizabeth I* (1934), p. 381.
3 Thomas Smith, *De Republica Anglorum*, ed. L. Alston (Cambridge, 1906), p. 106.
4 *Ibid.*, p. 46.
5 *Ibid.*, p. 41.
6 *Ibid.*, p. 39.
7 *Ibid.*, p. 40. Cf. W. Harrison, *Description of England* (1577), upon which Smith almost certainly drew.
8 Thomas Wilson, *The State of England Anno Domini 1600*, ed. F. J. Fisher, *Camden Miscellany*, 1936, XVI, 24.
9 *Ibid.*, p. 19.
10 *Ibid.*, p. 24–5.
11 D. H. Willson, *King James VI and I* (1956), p. 243.
12 *Ibid.*, p. 350.
13 Cited in P. Collinson, 'The Beginnings of English Sabbatarianism', *Studies in Church History*, I, 221.
14 Thomas More, *Utopia*, ed. J. R. Lumby (Cambridge, 1885), p. 162. I am using the Tudor translation not the modern one.

Reading List

Bindoff, S. T., *Tudor England* (Harmondsworth, 1950)
Morris, C., *Political Thought from Tyndale to Hooker* (London, 1953)
Neale, J. E., *Elizabeth I* (1934)

Ramsey, P., *Tudor Economic Problems* (1963)
Rowse, A. L., *The England of Elizabeth* (1951)
Smith, A. G. R., *The Government of Elizabethan England* (1967)
Smith, Sir Thomas, *De Republica Anglorum*, ed. L. Alston (Cambridge, 1906)
Willson, D. H., *King James VI and I* (1956)
Wilson, Thomas, 'The State of England Anno Domini 1600', ed. F. J. Fisher, *Camden Miscellany*, XVI (1936)

13. SHAKESPEARE AND THE THOUGHT OF HIS AGE

Reading List

Anderson, Ruth L., *Elizabethan Psychology and Shakespeare's Plays* (New York, 2nd ed., 1966)
Baker, Herschel, *The Image of Man* (New York, 1961)
  The Wars of Truth (Cambridge, Mass., 1952)
Bamborough, J. B., *The Little World of Man* (1952)
Cassirer, Ernst, *The Individual and the Cosmos in Renaissance Philosophy* (New York, 1964)
Craig, Hardin, *The Enchanted Glass: The Elizabethan Mind in Literature* (New York, 1936)
Curry, Walter C., *Shakespeare's Philosophical Patterns* (Baton Rouge, La., 2nd ed. 1959)
Greenleaf, W. H., *Order, Empiricism, and Politics: Two Traditions of English Political Thought, 1500–1700* (1964)
Haydn, Hiram, *The Counter-Renaissance* (New York, 1950)
Johnson, Francis R., *Astronomical Thought in Renaissance England: A Study of the English Scientific Writings from 1500 to 1645* (Baltimore, 1937)
Kantorowicz, Ernst H., *The King's Two Bodies: A Study in Mediaeval Political Theology* (Princeton, 1957)
Kocher, Paul H., *Science and Religion in Elizabethan England* (San Marino, Calif., 1953)
Kristeller, P. O., *Renaissance Thought: the Classic, Scholastic, and Humanist Strains* (New York, 1961)
Lewis, C. S., *The Discarded Image* (1967)
Lovejoy, A. O., *The Great Chain of Being: A Study of the History of an Idea* (Cambridge, Mass., 1936)
Nicoll, Allardyce (ed.), 'Shakespeare in his own Age', *Shakespeare Survey 17* (1964)
Popkin, Richard H., *The History of Scepticism: from Erasmus to Descartes* (New York, 1968)
Tillyard, E. M. W., *The Elizabethan World Picture* (1943)
Walker, D. P., *Spiritual and Demonic Magic from Ficino to Campanella* (1958)

Winny, James, ed., *The Frame of Order: An Outline of Elizabethan Belief...* (1957)

Yates, Frances A., *Giordano Bruno and the Hermetic Tradition* (1964)

14. SHAKESPEARE'S PLAYS ON THE ENGLISH STAGE

Reading List

Crosse, Gordon, *Shakespearean Playgoing 1890–1952* (1953)

Dickins, Richard, *Forty Years of Shakespeare on the English Stage: August, 1867 to August, 1907* (1907)

Hogan, C. B., *Shakespeare in the Theatre*, 2 vols. (Oxford, 1952–7)

Odell, G. C. D., *Shakespeare from Betterton to Irving*, 2 vols. (New York, 1920)

Spencer, Christopher (ed.), *Five Restoration Adaptations of Shakespeare* (Urbana, 1965)

Spencer, Hazelton, *Shakespeare Improved* (Cambridge, Mass., 1927)

Sprague, A. C., *Shakespeare and the Actors: The Stage Business in his Plays* (New York, 1963) [First published in 1944]
  Shakespearian Players and Performances (1954)
  Shakespeare's Histories: Plays for the Stage (1964)

Sprague, A. C. and Trewin, J. C., *Shakespeare's Plays Today: Some Customs and Conventions of the Stage* (1970)

Trewin, J. C., *Shakespeare on the English Stage 1900–1964* (1964)

Trewin, J. C. and Kemp, T. C., *The Stratford Festival* (Birmingham, 1953)

Winter, William, *Shakespeare on the Stage*, 3 vols. (New York, 1911–16)

There are good brief stage histories of the separate plays by Harold Child, continued by C. B. Young, in the New Cambridge Shakespeare. Marvin Rosenberg, *The Masks of Othello* (Berkeley, 1961), and Joseph Price, *The Unfortunate Comedy* [*All's Well That Ends Well*] (Liverpool, 1968), are excellent recent books.

15. SHAKESPEARE AND THE DRAMA OF HIS TIME

Notes

1 Apart from his debt to Greene's romance *Pandosto* (the source for *The Winter's Tale*), there is plenty of evidence that Shakespeare had read some of Greene's other novels and pamphlets, as also that he knew work by other playwriting Wits of the 1580s and 1590s – Nashe, Lodge, Mundy, Peele, Chettle. The question of his kinship with any or all of them is an open one. As an established actor and playwright by or before 1592, he should have had by that date unusually good opportunities for getting to know their work for the stage.

2 What was going on included the 'War of the Theatres' (1599–1602), an intensification of the satirical spirit and a quarrel of personality and principle which involved Jonson, Marston, Dekker, Heywood and perhaps Shakespeare himself. Its development is obscure. If it is true

(as has been argued) that the War was simply a phase during which a conscious and enduring opposition of literary ideals between the 'popular' and 'coterie' theatres temporarily broke surface, it is plain from his work that Shakespeare ordinarily inclined to the former. One may agree that there were differences between two sorts of theatre, public and private, without adopting an attitude of moralistic-sentimental approval for Shakespeare's side and of reproof for the other. Shakespeare does not on the whole go in for urbanities about homosexuality, faithless wives and longing heirs, but it is overzealous to regard them as, in Alfred Harbage's phrase, conducting us straight towards a 'perversion and defeat of the human spirit'. It was zeal of that kind that so ingloriously shut down the theatres in 1642.

Reading List

A *Marlowe*

Bakeless, John, *The Tragicall Historie of Christopher Marlowe* (Cambridge, Mass., 1942)

Brooke, Nicholas, 'Marlowe as a Provocative Agent in Shakespeare's Early Plays', *Shakespeare Survey 14* (1961)

Wilson, F. P., *Marlowe and the Early Shakespeare* (Oxford, 1953)

B *Lyly and other Wits*

Bradbrook, M. C., *The Growth and Structure of Elizabethan Comedy* (1955)

Freeman, Arthur, *Thomas Kyd: Facts and Problems* (Oxford, 1965)

Hunter, G. K., *John Lyly: The Humanist as Courtier* (1962)

Mincoff, Marco, 'Shakespeare and Lyly', *Shakespeare Survey 14* (1961)

Sanders, Norman, 'The Comedy of Greene and Shakespeare', *Early Shakespeare*, ed. J. R. Brown and B. Harris (1961)

C *Jonson and the Satirists*

Campbell, Oscar J., *Shakespeare's Satire* (New York, 1943)

Harbage, Alfred, *Shakespeare and the Rival Traditions* (New York, 1952)

D *Fletcher and the Last Plays*

Bentley, G. E., 'Shakespeare and the Blackfriars Theatre', *Shakespeare Survey 1* (1948)

Edwards, Philip, 'Shakespeare's Romances, 1900–1957', *Shakespeare Survey 11* (1958)

Leech, Clifford, *The John Fletcher Plays* (1962)

Pettet, E. C., *Shakespeare and the Romance Tradition* (1949)

16. SHAKESPEARE'S TEXT

Notes

1 *Folio* is a printer's term describing a book in which the sheet, the basic unit of any book, has been folded once to produce two leaves (four pages). In the Shakespeare First Folio three sheets were placed together

and then folded once to form a single gathering of six leaves (twelve pages). Abbreviated as F.

2 *Quarto*, also a printer's term, is used to describe a book, roughly half the size of a folio, in which the sheet has been folded twice to produce four leaves (eight pages) to a gathering. Abbreviated as Q.

3 In addition to *Pericles*, six other plays, attributed to Shakespeare, were included in F3 (and F4): *The London Prodigal, The Life and Death of Thomas Lord Cromwell, The History of Sir John Oldcastle, The Puritan, A Yorkshire Tragedy*, and *The Tragedy of Locrine*. None of these plays is now accepted as even in part by Shakespeare. *The Reign of King Edward the Third* (1596) was claimed for Shakespeare by Edward Capell in the eighteenth century and is still considered by a few critics to be partly his work. Finally, two 'lost' plays (*Love's Labour's Won* and *Cardenio*) have been associated with Shakespeare. *Love's Labour's Won* was included by Francis Meres in a list of twelve of Shakespeare's plays in his *Palladis Tamia* in 1598. It is now known that a play so titled was actually published, since the volume formed part of a bookseller's stock in 1603 (see T. W. Baldwin, *Shakspere's 'Love's Labor's Won'*, 1957), but no copy of the quarto has survived. It is possible, though less likely since Baldwin's discovery, that the play was included in F1 under another title. *The History of Cardenio* was first assigned to John Fletcher and Shakespeare by the publisher Humphrey Moseley in an entry on the Stationers' Register in 1653, but never published. In 1728 Lewis Theobald published his *Double Falsehood*, claiming that he had adapted it from three manuscript copies (since lost) of the hitherto missing *Cardenio* and attributing the original play wholly to Shakespeare. Recent scholarship now generally admits that some vestiges of Shakespeare's and Fletcher's hands, both rather dolefully disguised, may indeed be detected in Theobald's play.

4 There is growing support for the view that *The Taming of a Shrew* (1594) is a 'bad' quarto of *The Taming of the Shrew*; some scholars would also include *The Troublesome Reign of John, King of England* (1591 two parts) as a 'bad' quarto version of *King John*.

Reading List

Bowers, Fredson, *Bibliography and Textual Criticism* (Oxford, 1964)
  On Editing Shakespeare (Charlottesville, Virginia, 1966)
Chambers, E. K., *William Shakespeare: A Study of Facts and Problems*, 2 vols. (Oxford, 1930)
Greg, W. W., *The Variants in the First Quarto of 'King Lear'*, Bibliographical Society (1940)
  The Editorial Problem in Shakespeare: A Survey of the Foundations of the Text, 3rd. ed. (Oxford, 1954)
  The Shakespeare First Folio: Its Bibliographical and Textual History (Oxford, 1955)
Hinman, Charlton, *The Printing and Proof-Reading of the First Folio of Shakespeare*, 2 vols. (Oxford, 1963)

Honigmann, E. A. J., *The Stability of Shakespeare's Text* (1965)
McKerrow, R. B., *An Introduction to Bibliography for Literary Students*, rev. ed. (Oxford, 1928)
Prolegomena for the Oxford Shakespeare (Oxford, 1939)
Pollard, A. W., *Shakespeare Folios and Quartos, 1594–1685* (1909)
    Shakespeare's Hand in the Play of Sir Thomas More (Cambridge, 1923)
    [A collection of essays by Pollard, W. W. Greg, E. M. Thompson, J. D. Wilson, R. W. Chambers; Wilson's essay on Shakespeare's spellings is important for general study of the text.]
Walker, Alice, *Textual Problems of the First Folio* (Cambridge, 1953)
Wilson, John Dover, *The Manuscript of Shakespeare's 'Hamlet'*, 2 vols. (Cambridge, 1934)
    Important textual studies of individual plays: *2 Henry VI* and *3 Henry VI* (Madeleine Doran, Peter Alexander); *Richard III* (Peter Alexander, D. L. Patrick, Kristian Smidt); *Romeo and Juliet* (H. R. Hoppe, G. W. Williams); *Hamlet* (G. I. Duthie); *King Lear* (G. I. Duthie). See also the textual discussions in the more recent volumes of the *New Variorum Shakespeare* (*1 Henry IV* and *2 Henry IV*, *Richard II*, *Troilus and Cressida*, the Poems, and the Sonnets) and in the separate introductions to the New Cambridge and New Arden editions. Articles dealing with various aspects of Shakespeare's text may be found in *The Library*, *Studies in Bibliography*, *Shakespeare Survey*, and *Shakespeare Quarterly*.

17. SHAKESPEARE CRITICISM: DRYDEN TO BRADLEY

Reading List

Anthologies of criticism
Halliday, F. E., *Shakespeare and his Critics* (1949; 2nd ed., 1958)
Kermode, Frank, *Four Centuries of Shakespearian Criticism* (New York, 1965)
Siegel, Paul N., *His Infinite Variety: Major Shakespeare Criticism since Johnson* (Philadelphia, 1964)
Smith, D. Nichol, *Eighteenth Century Essays on Shakespeare*, 2nd ed. (Oxford, 1963)
    Shakespeare Criticism, a Selection (1916)
The writings of particular critics
Samuel Johnson. Ed. Walter Raleigh (1908); ed. W. K. Wimsatt, Jr. (New York, 1960); ed. Arthur Sherbo (New Haven, 1968)
Walter Whiter. See 4, above
S. T. Coleridge. Ed. Thomas M. Raysor (Cambridge, Mass., 1930; 2nd ed. 1960); ed. Terence Hawkes (New York, 1959)
William Hazlitt, *Characters of Shakespeare's Plays* (numerous editions)
Histories of the criticism of Shakespeare
Babcock, R. W., *The Genesis of Shakespeare Idolatry 1766–1799* (Chapel Hill, 1931)

Eastman, A. M., *A Short History of Shakespearean Criticism* (New York, 1968)

Lounsbury, Thomas R., *Shakespeare as a Dramatic Artist, with an Account of his Reputation at Various Periods* (New York, 1901)

Ralli, Augustus, *A History of Shakespeare Criticism*, 2 vols. (Oxford, 1932)

Smith, D. Nichol, *Shakespeare in the Eighteenth Century* (Oxford, 1928)

Westfall, A. V. R., *American Shakespearian Criticism, 1607–1865* (New York, 1939)

18. SHAKESPEARE CRITICISM SINCE BRADLEY

Reading List

Eastman, A. M., See 17, above

Holloway, John, 'Criticism – 20th Century' in *The Reader's Encyclopedia of Shakespeare*, ed. Oscar J. Campbell (New York, 1966)

Muir, Kenneth, 'Fifty Years of Shakespearian Criticism: 1900–1950', *Shakespeare Survey 4* (1951), pp. 1–25

Murray, Patrick, *The Shakespearian Scene* (1969)

Ralli, Augustus. See 17, above

CHRONOLOGICAL TABLE

The following chronological table covering Shakespeare's working years shows (*a*) some important national and theatrical events; (*b*) the date of publication of some important books; (*c*) approximate date of the first production of the most important plays during Shakespeare's career; (*d*) the dates of their first publication. The evidence for (*c*) and (*d*) will be found principally in Sir E. K. Chambers's *Elizabethan Stage* and *William Shakespeare: a study of facts and problems*. It is seldom possible to date the first appearance of a play exactly: before 1595 and after 1605 the margin of error may be as much as five years. Nor is there general agreement on the dates of Shakespeare's earliest and latest plays: some scholars would date the first as early as 1587. Plays which may be dated with some precision are marked ‡.

	EVENTS	BOOKS PUBLISHED
1587	Execution of Mary Queen of Scots Funeral of Sir Philip Sidney	
1588	Defeat of the Spanish Armada Robert, Earl of Leicester, died	Greene's *Perimedes* and *Pandosto* Marprelate controversy
1589	A Parliament held The Portugal Voyage Duke of Guise and Henri III murdered Civil war in France	Hakluyt's *Voyages* Greene's *Menaphon*
1590	Sir Francis Walsingham died	Lodge's *Rosalynde* Spenser's *Faerie Queene*, Bks 1–3
1591	Hacket's treason The loss of the 'Revenge' Proclamation against Jesuits and seminaries	Harington's *Orlando Furioso* Sidney's *Astrophel and Stella* Spenser's *Complaints*

1592	Scottish Witchcraft trials
	Greene died
	The Great Carrack captured
	Edward Alleyn marries
	  Henslowe's step-daughter
		Greene's *The Conny-catching*
		  pamphlets. Groatsworth of Wit
		Nashe's *Piers Penniless*
		Constable's *Diana*
		Daniel's *Delia*
		Chettle's *Kind Heart's Dream*

1593	Parliament held Marlowe killed Plague stops playing	VENUS AND ADONIS Chapman's *Shadow of Night* *The Phoenix Nest* Hooker's *Laws of Ecclesiastical* *Polity*

1594	Plague till summer
	Playing reorganized: the
	  Admiral's men at Rose;
	  Chamberlain's at Theatre
	Kyd died
		LUCRECE
		Willobie his Avisa
		Nashe's *Jack Wilton*
		Drayton's *Idea's Mirror*

PLAYS FIRST PRODUCED	PLAYS PUBLISHED
I Tamburlaine	
Alphonsus of Aragon	
Dido, Queen of Carthage	
Endimion	
II Tamburlaine	
Spanish Tragedy	*Rare Triumphs of Love and Fortune*
Jew of Malta	
Friar Bacon	
Midas	
Mother Bombie	
Looking Glass for London and England	*Three Lords and three Ladies of London*
Love's Metamorphosis	*I and II Tamburlaine*
I HENRY VI	
Orlando Furioso	*Endimion*
James IV	*I and II Troublesome Reign of King John*
The Woman in the Moon	
II, III HENRY VI	
Dr Faustus	*Arden of Feversham*
Edward II	*Spanish Tragedy*
RICHARD III	*Galathea*
	Midas
Massacre at Paris	*Edward II*
TAMING OF THE SHREW	*Edward I*
COMEDY OF ERRORS	
TWO GENTLEMEN OF VERONA	
TITUS ANDRONICUS	
John a Kent and John a Cumber	*Orlando Furioso**
LOVE'S LABOUR'S LOST	*Knack to Know a Knave*
	TITUS ANDRONICUS
	Looking Glass for London and England
	I Contention York and Lancaster
	Taming of a Shrew
	Pedlar's Prophecy

* The probable explanation of the sudden increase in printed plays in 1594 is that the companies were so disorganized by the plague that they raised money by selling their MSS.

EVENTS	BOOKS PUBLISHED
1594 *(cont.)*	
1595 Riots in London Ralegh's Guiana Voyage Last expedition of Drake and Hawkins (both died)	Spenser's *Amoretti* Sidney's *Defence of Poesy* Southwell's *St Peter's Complaint*
1596 Calais captured by Spaniards The Cadiz expedition	Harington's *Metamorphosis of Ajax* Lodge's *Wit's Misery* Spenser's *Faerie Queene*, Bks 4–6; *Four Hymns* Drayton's *Mortimeriados* Davies's *Orchestra*
1597 The Islands Voyage A Spanish armada wrecked A Parliament held	Bacon's *Essays* (1st version) Hall's *Virgidemiarum* Deloney's *Jack of Newbury* and *Gentle Craft*
1598 Rebellion and disaster in Ireland The Queen boxes Essex's ears Lord Burghley died Philip II of Spain died The 'Theatre' demolished	Marlowe's *Hero and Leander* Chapman's Trans. of *Iliad* (7 books) Meres's *Palladis Tamia* Marston's *Scourge of Villainy*
1599 Spenser died Essex in Ireland Satires burnt	Hayward's *Henry IV* THE PASSIONATE PILGRIM Davies's *Nosce teipsum*

PLAYS FIRST PRODUCED	PLAYS PUBLISHED
	Famous Victories of Henry V
	James IV
	Friar Bacon and Friar Bungay
	King Leir
	David and Bethsabe
	Jew of Malta
	Wounds of Civil War
	Cobbler's Prophecy
	Four Prentices of London
	True Tragedy of Richard III
	Locrine
	Fair Em
	Battle of Alcaʒar
	Selimus
	Dido, Queen of Carthage
MIDSUMMER NIGHT'S DREAM	*George a Greene*
RICHARD II	*Old Wives' Tale*
ROMEO AND JULIET	*Woman in the Moon*
	Knack to Know an Honest Man
	Edward III
	True Tragedy of Richard Duke of York
Blind Beggar of Alexandria‡	
KING JOHN	
MERCHANT OF VENICE	
Humorous Day's Mirth‡	RICHARD II
Isle of Dogs (lost)‡	RICHARD III
The Case is Altered	ROMEO AND JULIET
I HENRY IV	
I and II Robert, Earl of Huntingdon	I HENRY IV
Englishmen for my Money	MERCHANT OF VENICE
Every Man in his Humour‡	*Blind Beggar of Alexandria*
Two Angry Women of Abingdon	LOVE'S LABOUR'S LOST
Pilgrimage to Parnassus‡	*Mucedorus*
II HENRY IV	
MUCH ADO ABOUT NOTHING	
Shoemakers' Holiday‡	*I and II Edward IV*
Every Man out of his Humour	*Warning for Fair Women*
I Sir John Oldcastle‡	*Humorous Day's Mirth*

EVENTS	BOOKS PUBLISHED
1599 Chamberlain's men occupy new (*cont.*) 'Globe' Invasion scare Essex fails in Ireland and returns in disgrace Children of Paul's begin playing	
1600 Mountjoy in Ireland Kempe's dance to Norwich Alleyn builds 'Fortune' theatre The Gowry conspiracy Children of Chapel begin playing at Blackfriars East India Company formed	*England's Helicon* Exorcism controversy
1601 Essex's rebellion and execution The 'War of the Theatres' Siege of Ostend begun Spanish expedition lands in Ireland A Parliament held: the agitation concerning monopolies	Catholic controversy Holland's Translation of Pliny
1602 Tyrone defeated in Ireland Spaniards surrender Biron's conspiracy	Campion's *Observations in the Art of English Poesy* Deloney's *Thomas of Reading*
1603 Tyrone submits QUEEN ELIZABETH DIED ACCESSION OF JAMES I Chamberlain's men become King's men Plague stops playing Ralegh and others tried and condemned	Davies's *Microcosmos* Dekker's *Wonderful Year* Daniel's *Defence of Rhyme* Florio Translation of Montaigne's *Essays* James I's *Dæmonology* (London ed.)

PLAYS FIRST PRODUCED	PLAYS PUBLISHED
Histriomastix	*Two Angry Women of Abingdon*
Antonio and Mellida	*Alphonsus of Aragon*
Antonio's Revenge	
Old Fortunatus‡	
I Return from Parnassus‡	
HENRY V‡	
AS YOU LIKE IT	
JULIUS CAESAR‡	
Blind Beggar of Bethnal Green‡	*Old Fortunatus*
Patient Grissell‡	*Patient Grissell*
MERRY WIVES OF WINDSOR	*Every Man out of his Humour*
TROILUS AND CRESSIDA	*A Larum for London*
	Maid's Metamorphosis
	HENRY V
	MUCH ADO ABOUT NOTHING
	I and II Sir John Oldcastle
	II HENRY IV
	Jack Drum's Entertainment
	MIDSUMMER NIGHT'S DREAM
	Shoemakers' Holiday
Cynthia's Revels	*Love's Metamorphosis*
Poetaster	*I and II Robert, Earl of Huntingdon*
Satiromastix	*Dr Faustus*
Blurt Master Constable	*Cynthia's Revels*
What You Will	*Every Man in his Humour*
II Return from Parnassus	(1st version)
HAMLET	
Gentleman Usher	*Antonio and Mellida*
Family of Love	*Antonio's Revenge*
Sir Thomas Wyatt‡	*Satiromastix*
TWELFTH NIGHT‡	*Poetaster*
	MERRY WIVES OF WINDSOR
	Blurt Master Constable
	Thomas Lord Cromwell
Woman Killed with Kindness‡	HAMLET (Q1)
Hoffman	
Sejanus	
The Phœnix	

EVENTS	BOOKS PUBLISHED
1603 Renewed vogue of Court (*cont.*) masques	
1604 Hampton Court Conference End of Siege of Ostend James's first Parliament Peace with Spain	
1605 Act to expel Jesuits and seminary priests Gunpowder plot	Bacon's *Advancement of Learning*
1606 Gunpowder plotters executed State visit of King of Denmark	Dekker's *Seven Deadly Sins of London*
1607 Renewed troubles in Ireland Virginia colonized Riots over enclosures A great frost	

PLAYS FIRST PRODUCED	PLAYS PUBLISHED
Dutch Courtesan	*The Malcontent*
All Fools	*I Honest Whore*
The Malcontent	HAMLET (Q2)
Wise Woman of Hogsdon	
Monsieur D'Olive	
Law Tricks	
Bussy D'Ambois	
I and II Honest Whore	
Westward Hoe	
ALL'S WELL THAT ENDS WELL	
MEASURE FOR MEASURE	
OTHELLO	
The Fawn	*Sejanus*
Eastward Hoe‡	*Fair Maid of Bristow*
Northward Hoe	*When you See me, you Know Me*
I and II If you Know Not me	*Dutch Courtesan*
Trick to Catch the Old One	*I If you Know Not me*
KING LEAR	*Eastward Hoe*
	All Fools
	London Prodigal
	I Jeronimo
Whore of Babylon	*II If you Know me Not*
Sophonisba	*II Return from Parnassus*
Woman Hater	*Gentleman Usher*
Volpone	*Sir Giles Goosecap*
Isle of Gulls‡	*The Fawn*
Rape of Lucrece	*Sophonisba*
MACBETH	*Wily Beguiled*
	Monsieur D'Olive
	Isle of Gulls
Knight of the Burning Pestle	*Westward Hoe*
Travels of the Three English	*Whore of Babylon*
Brothers	*Fair Maid of the Exchange*
Humour out of Breath	*The Phœnix*
Atheist's Tragedy	*Michaelmas Term*
ANTONY AND CLEOPATRA	*Woman Hater*
CORIOLANUS	*Bussy D'Ambois*
TIMON OF ATHENS	*Cupid's Whirligig*
	Travels of the Three English
	Brothers

	EVENTS	BOOKS PUBLISHED
1607 (cont.)		
1608	Children at Blackfriars disbanded King's men take over the private playhouse Notorious pirates executed	
1609	Jonson's *Masque of Queens* at Court Truce in the Netherlands The Oath of Allegiance administered	Dekker's *Belman of London* Dekker's *Gull's Hornbook* Shakespeare's SONNETS
1610	The plantation of Ulster Henri IV murdered A great drought	
1611	Carr made Viscount Rochester James quarrels with Parliament	A.V. Translation of Bible Chapman's Translation of *Iliad* completed Donne's *Anatomy of the World*
1612	Sir Thomas Overbury poisoned in the Tower	Shelton's Translation of *Don Quixote*

PLAYS FIRST PRODUCED	PLAYS PUBLISHED
	Miseries of Enforced Marriage
	The Puritan
	Northward Hoe
	What You Will
	Revenger's Tragedy
	Devil's Charter
	Volpone
	Woman Killed with Kindness
	Sir Thomas Wyatt
Faithful Shepherdess	*Trick to Catch the Old One*
Philaster	*Family of Love*
Maid's Tragedy	*Merry Devil of Edmonton*
Charles, Duke of Biron‡	KING LEAR
Appius and Virginia	*Law Tricks*
PERICLES	*Humour out of Breath*
	Yorkshire Tragedy
	Rape of Lucrece
	Tragedy of Biron
	Mad World, my Masters
	Dumb Knight
	PERICLES
Epicœne	*The Case is Altered*
Bonduca	*Every Woman in her Humour*
Woman is a Weathercock	*Two Maids of Moreclack*
	Faithful Shepherdess
The Alchemist	*Histriomastix*
Revenge of Bussy D'Ambois	
Roaring Girl	
If it be not Good, the Devil is in It	
CYMBELINE	
King and no King	*Ram Alley*
Catiline	*Atheist's Tragedy*
Amends for Ladies	*Golden Age*
Golden Age	*Catiline*
Silver Age	*May Day*
THE WINTER'S TALE	*Roaring Girl*
THE TEMPEST	
Brazen Age	*The Alchemist*
White Devil	*Woman is a Weathercock*
	Christian Turned Turk

EVENTS	BOOKS PUBLISHED
1612 Robert Cecil, Earl of Salisbury, (cont.) died Prince Henry died	
1613 Marriage of Princess Elizabeth The Essex divorce suit The Globe Theatre burnt	Drayton's *Polyolbion* Browne's *Britannia's Pastorals*
1616 Death of William Shakespeare	
1619 Jaggard's 'False folio' published	
1623 The First Folio published	

PLAYS FIRST PRODUCED	PLAYS PUBLISHED
	Widow's Tears
	White Devil
	If it be not Good the Devil is in It
Chaste maid in Cheapside	*Revenge of Bussy D' Ambois*
Duchess of Malfi	*Silver Age*
Honest Man's Fortune	*Brazen Age*
Iron Age	*Insatiate Countess*
TWO NOBLE KINSMEN	*Knight of the Burning Pestle*
HENRY VIII	

INDEX

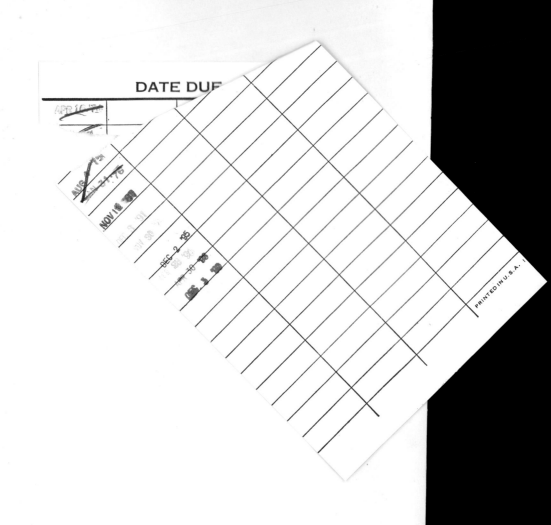

DATE DUE